■ The Puerto Rico Constitution

The Oxford Commentaries on the State Constitutions of the United States
Lawrence Friedman, Series Editor.

Lawrence Friedman, Professor of Law at New England Law | Boston, serves as General Editor for this series. Each volume of The Oxford Commentaries on the State Constitutions of the United States contains a historical overview of the state's constitutional development and a section-by-section analysis of the state's current constitution. In addition to the complete text of every state's current constitution, each volume features a bibliographical essay and comprehensive index. The series aims to provide a ready guide to each state constitution for lawyers, judges and anyone seeking to understand the basic development and structure of the nation's other fifty constitutions.

The Puerto Rico Constitution

Rafael Cox Alomar

THE OXFORD COMMENTARIES ON THE STATE
CONSTITUTIONS OF THE UNITED STATES
Lawrence Friedman, Series Editor

Oxford University Press is a department of the University of Oxford. It furthers the University's objective of excellence in research, scholarship, and education by publishing worldwide. Oxford is a registered trade mark of Oxford University Press in the UK and certain other countries.

Published in the United States of America by Oxford University Press
198 Madison Avenue, New York, NY 10016, United States of America.

© Oxford University Press 2022

All rights reserved. No part of this publication may be reproduced, stored in a retrieval system, or transmitted, in any form or by any means, without the prior permission in writing of Oxford University Press, or as expressly permitted by law, by license, or under terms agreed with the appropriate reproduction rights organization. Inquiries concerning reproduction outside the scope of the above should be sent to the Rights Department, Oxford University Press, at the address above.

You must not circulate this work in any other form
and you must impose this same condition on any acquirer.

CIP data is on file at the Library of Congress

ISBN 978-0-19-046126-3

DOI: 10.1093/law/9780190461263.001.0001

Note to Readers
This publication is designed to provide accurate and authoritative information in regard to the subject matter covered. It is based upon sources believed to be accurate and reliable and is intended to be current as of the time it was written. It is sold with the understanding that the publisher is not engaged in rendering legal, accounting, or other professional services. If legal advice or other expert assistance is required, the services of a competent professional person should be sought. Also, to confirm that the information has not been affected or changed by recent developments, traditional legal research techniques should be used, including checking primary sources where appropriate.

(Based on the Declaration of Principles jointly adopted by a Committee of the American Bar Association and a Committee of Publishers and Associations.)

> You may order this or any other Oxford University Press publication by visiting the Oxford University Press website at www.oup.com.

To my father and son, infinite sources of love and strength for committing to the higher values of dignity, honesty, and service.

■ CONTENTS

Series Foreword by Lawrence Friedman	*xiii*
Prefatory Note	*xvii*
Foreword by Chief Justice Federico Hernández Denton	*xix*
Acknowledgments	*xxi*

PART ONE ■ The Constitutional History of Puerto Rico

The Council of Indies 1493–1812	3
The Cádiz Constitution 1812–1814	6
Constitutional Developments 1814–1834	9
The Royal Statute of 1834	11
The Constitution of 1837	13
The Constitution of 1845	14
The Constitution of 1869	17
The Constitution of 1876	19
Constitutional Developments 1877–1897	20
The Autonomic Charter of 1897	23
The 1898 Spanish American War and the Treaty of Paris	25
U.S. Military Rule 1898–1900	27
The 1900 Foraker Act	28
The U.S. Supreme Court and the Insular Cases 1901	30
The 1917 Jones Act	33
The 1947 Elective Governor Act	34
The 1950 Public Law 600, the Constitutional Convention, and the 1952 Constitution	35
Politico-Constitutional Developments Post-1952	37
Sánchez Valle and *Franklin Trust*	40
PROMESA, *Aurelius* and *Vaello Madero*	42
Epilogue: Between Scylla and Charybdis	46

PART TWO ■ The Puerto Rico Constitution and Commentary

Preamble	**51**
Article I: The Commonwealth	**55**
Section 1. The Commonwealth of Puerto Rico	55
Section 2. Form of Government	56

VIII ■ CONTENTS

Section 3. Geographic Area 57
Section 4. Seat of Government 57

Article II: The Bill of Rights 59

Section 1. Human Dignity and Equality; Discrimination Prohibited 59
Section 2. Suffrage; Electoral Franchise 65
Section 3. Freedom of Religion; Complete Separation of Church and State 67
Section 4. Freedom of Speech and Press; Peaceful Assembly; Petition for a Redress of Grievances 69
Section 5. Public Education 72
Section 6. Freedom of Association 75
Section 7. Right to Life, Liberty, and Enjoyment of Property; No Death Penalty; Due Process; Equal Protection of Laws; Impairment of Contracts; Exemption of Property from Attachment 76
Section 8. Protection against Attacks on Honor, Reputation, and Private Life 80
Section 9. Just Compensation for Private Property 82
Section 10. Searches and Seizures; Wiretapping; Warrants 84
Section 11. Criminal Prosecutions; Jury Trial; Self Incrimination; Double Jeopardy; Bail; Imprisonment 88
Section 12. Slavery; Involuntary Servitude; Cruel and Unusual Punishments; Suspension of Civil Rights for Prisoners; Ex Post Facto Laws; Bills of Attainder 97
Section 13. Habeas Corpus; Military Authority Subordinate 100
Section 14. Titles of Nobility; Gifts from Foreign Countries 100
Section 15. Employment and Imprisonment of Children 101
Section 16. Rights of Employees 102
Section 17. Right to Organize and Bargain Collectively 104
Section 18. Right to Strike, Picket, and Other Legal Concerted Activities 104
Section 19. Liberal Construction of Rights of People and Powers of Legislative Assembly 106

Article III: The Legislature 109

Section 1. Legislative Assembly 109
Section 2. Number of Members 110
Section 3. Senatorial and Representative Districts; Senators and Representatives at Large 110
Section 4. Board to Revise Senatorial and Representative Districts 111
Section 5. Qualifications of Members of Legislative Assembly 113
Section 6. Residence in District 113

Section 7. Representation of Minority Parties; Additional Members 114
Section 8. Terms of Office; Vacancies 116
Section 9. Powers of Each House 118
Section 10. Regular and Special Sessions 119
Section 11. Open Sessions 121
Section 12. Quorum 121
Section 13. Place of Meeting; Adjournment 122
Section 14. Privileges and Immunities of Members 122
Section 15. Membership Incompatible with Other Offices 123
Section 16. Power to Change Executive Departments 125
Section 17. Legislative Proceedings 126
Section 18. Joint Resolutions 128
Section 19. Passage of Bills; Approval by Governor 128
Section 20. Line-item Veto 130
Section 21. Impeachment Proceedings 131
Section 22. Comptroller 132

Article IV: The Executive 135

Section 1. Governor 135
Section 2. Terms of Office; Residence and Office 137
Section 3. Qualifications of Governor 138
Section 4. Powers and Duties of Governor 138
Section 5. Appointment of Secretaries; Council of Secretaries 143
Section 6. Executive Departments 143
Section 7. Succession to Office of Governor—Permanent Vacancy 145
Section 8. Temporary Vacancy 145
Section 9. Election by Legislative Assembly in Advance of Qualified
    Successor 145
Section 10. Removal of Governor 147

Article V: The Judiciary 149

Section 1. Judicial Power; Supreme Court; Other Courts 149
Section 2. Unified Judicial System; Creation, Venue, and Organization
    of Courts 151
Section 3. Supreme Court as Court of Last Resort; Composition 152
Section 4. Sessions and Decisions of Supreme Court; Judicial Review 154
Section 5. Original Jurisdiction of Supreme Court 155
Section 6. Rules of Evidence and of Civil and Criminal Procedure 157
Section 7. Rules of Administration; Chief Justice to Direct
    Administration and Appoint Administrative Director 159
Section 8. Appointment of Judges, Officers, and Employees 160
Section 9. Qualifications of Justices of Supreme Court 161

X ■ CONTENTS

Section 10. Retirement of Judges 162
Section 11. Removal of Judges 163
Section 12. Political Activity by Judges 164
Section 13. Tenure of Judge of Changed or Abolished Court 165

Article VI: General Provisions 167

Section 1. Municipalities 167
Section 2. Power of Taxation; Power to Contract Debts 168
Section 3. Rule of Taxation to be Uniformed 170
Section 4. Elections 171
Section 5. Promulgation of Laws; Effective Date 172
Section 6. Failure to Make Appropriations 172
Section 7. Appropriations not to Exceed Revenues 174
Section 8. Priority of Disbursements if Revenues Insufficient 175
Section 9. Use of Public Property and Funds 176
Section 10. Extra Compensation for Services; Extension of Term or
Decrease of Salary of Public Officer; Salary for More than
One Office 178
Section 11. Salaries of Officials; Increase or Decrease 178
Section 12. Residence of Governor 180
Section 13. Franchises, Rights, Privileges, and Concessions 180
Section 14. Land Holding by Corporations 181
Section 15. Flag, Seal, and Anthem 182
Section 16. Oath of Public Officials and Employees 183
Section 17. Removal of Seat of Government in Emergency 184
Section 18. Criminal Actions Conducted in Name of People
of Puerto Rico 185
Section 19. Natural Resources; Historic or Artistic Sites; Penal
Institutions; Delinquents 186

Article VII: Amendments to the Constitution 189

Section 1. Proposal of Amendments 189
Section 2. Revision of Constitution by Constitutional Convention 192
Section 3. Limitation of Amendments 193

Article VIII: Senatorial and Representative Districts 195

Section 1. Boundaries of Senatorial and Representative Districts 195
Section 2. Electoral Zones in San Juan 199

Article IX: Transitory Provisions 201

Section 1. Laws, Rights, and Liabilities 201
Section 2. Existing Officers Continued in Office 201

Section 3. Existing Judges Continued in Office	202
Section 4. Commonwealth of Puerto Rico as Successor of People of Puerto Rico	202
Section 5. Citizen of the Commonwealth of Puerto Rico to Replace Term Citizen of Puerto Rico	203
Section 6. Political Parties	203
Section 7. Laws Supplementing Transitory Provisions	203
Section 8. Division of Department of Agriculture and Commerce	204
Section 9. First and Second General Elections	204
Section 10. Effective Date of Constitution	204

Table 1 Puerto Rico's Political Parties circa 1951–1952	207
Table 2 Election of the Constitutional Convention August 27, 1951	208
Table 3 Constitutional Convention Delegates per Political Party	208
Table 4 Delegates to 1951–1952 Constitutional Convention Mentioned in Commentary	208
Table 5 Puerto Rico Supreme Court Justices Mentioned in Commentary	212
Table 6 Insular Cases Involving Puerto Rico	214
Bibliographical Essay	217
List of Cases	251
List of U.S. Treaties and Statutes	261
Index	263
About the Author	279

■ SERIES FOREWORD

It is difficult today to escape the focus in American political discourse on the United States Constitution and the Supreme Court's interpretations of it. But it is worth remembering that the U.S. Constitution did not emerge fully formed from the head of James Madison in 1787. Before the United States, there were the states—and state constitutions. As noted by G. Alan Tarr, the first Series Editor of the *Oxford Commentaries on the State Constitutions of the United States*, in his Series Foreword, the original state constitutions reflected a variety of approaches to democratic self-rule, experiments in governance that inspired audiences both across the Atlantic and closer to home.

Indeed, despite the misgivings about the state of the states entertained by some of the delegates gathered at the Constitutional Convention, they found in the existing state constitutions much to admire, from the Virginia Constitution's Declaration of Rights to the bicameral legislative scheme embraced by John Adams's Massachusetts Constitution of 1780. Which is not to slight the audacity of the U.S. Constitution, with its grant of limited powers of national scope to the federal government and preservation of state rule in virtually all other aspects of the lives of citizens. The framers, as Supreme Court Justice Anthony Kennedy observed in *U.S. Term Limits v. Thornton* (1995), had in effect "split the atom of sovereignty."

And the U.S. Constitution, as interpreted by Chief Justice John Marshall's Supreme Court, provided the young republic the national governmental structure it needed to thrive. The outcome of the Civil War validated the preeminence of the federal government in our constitutional scheme and the subsequent ratification of the Fourteenth Amendment anticipated the U.S. Constitution's eclipse of its state counterparts. For the Fourteenth Amendment's commitments to due process and equal protection in the face of state action became, in the middle decades of the twentieth century, the vessels by which the judiciary federalized the protection of individual rights and liberties as against the states.

The Supreme Court's extension of the Fourteenth Amendment's reach followed a period of change in the nature of state constitutions themselves, as popular movements succeeded in revising state charters to allow for varying opportunities for direct democratic lawmaking. One result was an increase in state constitutional provisions that resembled more closely legislative enactments than the core, foundational principles typically associated with constitutions. And so, as the decades passed, the utility of state constitutions as

xiii

constitutions increasingly suffered by comparison to the U.S. Constitution—if not in terms of authority, for these documents still controlled the organization of state governments and served as the primary means by which those governments regulated their citizens, at least in terms of respect.

Just as changes to the federal judiciary's approach to the Fourteenth Amendment ushered in a new era of restrictions on the police power of states, with *Brown v. Board of Education* (1954) perhaps the most famous example, lawyerly and judicial interest in state constitutions was awakened when, in the 1970s, the U.S. Supreme Court signaled the beginning of its retreat from federal rights enforcement, a development playing out to this day. From this retreat was born the phenomenon called the "new judicial federalism," as individual rights advocates began to look to the protections contained in state constitutions as the basis for challenging state action. In state constitutions, moreover, lay what Alan Tarr referred to as "an unsuspected richness"—not just provisions that parallel those in the Bill of Rights, but constitutional guarantees regarding such matters as privacy and equality that have no federal counterpart. And rather than the exclusively negative orientation of federal constitutional protections, which forbid state action exceeding certain limits, state constitutions contain positive protections which appear to demand such action in respect to a range of interests, from the adequacy of educational standards to environmental protection.

And so, notwithstanding the predominance of the U.S. Constitution in American public discourse, state constitutions continue to play a vital and important role in the daily lives of citizens. The federal judicial retreat from rights-enforcement through the Fourteenth Amendment has led not just to the revitalization of state constitutional individual rights protections, but to fewer federal constitutional restraints on the ability of state governments to be the laboratories of American democracy to which Supreme Court Justice Louis Brandeis famously referred in *New State Ice Co. v. Liebmann* (1932). And the content of state constitutions continues to be a source of energetic debate among citizens, whether through efforts to codify in the state's charter a symbolic resistance to federal encroachment or to constitutionalize, through the initiative process, policy positions that legislatures would otherwise reject.

Operating in the shadow cast by the U.S. Constitution, state constitutions and the state court decisions interpreting them remain critical sources of governmental authority and restraint. It has been the goal of the *Oxford Commentaries on the State Constitutions of the United States* to illuminate these constitutions for a wide audience—to explain the unique history of each state constitution and explore, in an accessible way, what the various provisions of the American state constitutions in their great variety mean and how they have been interpreted and applied over time. Each book in the series—many now in their second or third editions—provides, in addition to a history of and commentaries on the provisions of each state's constitution, a bibliography of materials related to the constitution as well as a table of notable cases and a topical index. The series aims, in short, to present to lawyers, scholars and students the most relevant and comprehensive guides to all the other United States constitutions.

Lawrence Friedman
Series Editor

■ PREFATORY NOTE

As noted in the Series Foreword, the aim of the *Oxford Commentaries on the State Constitutions of the United States* is "to present to lawyers, scholars and students the most relevant and comprehensive guides to all the other United States constitutions." Like my predecessor, G. Alan Tarr, I believe that this aim is sufficiently capacious to include within it a volume on a U.S. territory, Puerto Rico. Though its constitutional history may distinguish Puerto Rico from the states, its modern constitutional development—in particular, the disputes about individual rights and separation of powers that its courts regularly address—reflects many of the same concerns that arise under the constitutions of the states. Professor Rafael Cox Alomar's comprehensive work accordingly serves to ensure that, while Puerto Rico may not be a state, all of the "other United States constitutions" are truly represented in this series.

Lawrence Friedman

xvii

■ FOREWORD

Professor Rafael Cox Alomar's volume is an extraordinary scholarly contribution to the study of Puerto Rico's sui generis constitutional architecture as well as its historical development.

His work is both timely and unique, coming at a transformative moment in the history of our democratic institutions. Not only is this the first volume on the Puerto Rico Constitution published in the *Oxford Commentaries on the State Constitutions of the United States* series, but this is the only comprehensive work in the English language tracing with meticulous attention to detail the uneven trajectory of Puerto Rico's constitutionalism from the early days of Spanish colonial rule to the third decade of the twenty-first century. In an impressive tour de force, Professor Cox Alomar's volume begins in the early sixteenth century with the rise of the ancient Council of Indies and from then on carefully takes the reader, in chronological order, through the rough and tumble of Puerto Rico's colonial life under the multitude of Spanish Constitutions that in quick succession Madrid inaugurated and dissolved during the tumultuous nineteenth century.

A legal scholar who is also an academic historian by training, Professor Cox Alomar furthermore brings to the surface the catalysts triggering the American invasion of 1898 while throwing light on the geostrategic and constitutional considerations leading the political branches in Washington, D.C., to gradually reform Puerto Rico's territorial superstructure, through the piecemeal enactment of the 1900 Foraker Act, 1917 Jones Act, 1947 Elective Governor Act, and Public Law 600 in 1950—which opened the door to the 1951–1952 constitution-making exercise that is the focus of this volume.

Professor Cox Alomar's work, moreover, provides a detailed analysis of each section of Puerto Rico's 1952 Constitution with reference to the Puerto Rico Supreme Court's constitutional jurisprudence, covering the three decades in which I was a member of the court as associate justice (1985–2004) and as chief justice (2004–2014) until my retirement.

Professor Cox Alomar's commentary on the Puerto Rico Constitution pays significant attention to the intent of the framers, evidenced in his references to the archival record and Constitutional Convention Diary, and more specifically to the framers' reading of American constitutionalism and the international human rights ideology enveloping Europe in the aftermath of Nuremburg. His scholarship brings to the fore the foundational values of a hybrid legal tradition that sits at the crossroads of the European civil law and the Anglo-American common law.

xix

Puerto Rico's legal syncretism comes to light in the depth and breadth of the 1952 Constitution, which in seminal respects parts ways with its federal counterpart. The outer perimeters of the Puerto Rico Bill of Rights are far broader than those of its federal counterpart's, offering protections that go beyond those required under the U.S. Constitution: explicitly establishing inter alia a right to privacy and human dignity unencumbered by state action which is applicable to governmental and private actors alike; constitutionalizing gender and illegitimacy as suspect classes subject to strict scrutiny under the equal protection clause; prohibiting the death penalty; providing for a constitutional right to bail. Those protections were incorporated by our framers taking into consideration the 1948 Universal Declaration of Human Rights. Unlike the federal Constitution, the Puerto Rican constitutional text also imposes obligations on the local authorities: explicitly requiring that the government provides primary education while safeguarding the rights of workers to inter alia equal pay for equal work, to reasonable minimum wages, to a workday that cannot exceed eight hours, to organize, collective bargain, strike, and picket.

In its perusal of Puerto Rico's constitutional topography, Professor Cox Alomar's work pays heed to how Congress's enactment, at the height of the island's insolvency crisis, of the 2016 Puerto Rico Oversight, Management and Economic Stability Act (PROMESA) has disrupted some of the more critical aspects of Puerto Rico's constitutional design. In his epilogue, Professor Cox Alomar concludes that the time may be ripe for Puerto Rico to embark on a process of constitutional restructuring.

His book offers the intellectual roadmap for engaging in that debate—a debate that could effectively lead to the island's constitutional transformation during these challenging times, when Puerto Rico is facing a financial crisis that has changed the role of government as well as its political landscape and when the Supreme Court of the United States has also been re-examining its jurisprudence regarding the scope of Congress's power over Puerto Rico in the aftermath of PROMESA.

Federico Hernández Denton
Former Chief Justice of Puerto Rico

◼ ACKNOWLEDGMENTS

The unique opportunity to write this treatise on Puerto Rico's constitutionalism at one of the more decisive, yet complex, periods in Puerto Rico's constitutional life has been an invaluable privilege.

The completion of this volume would have been impossible without the support, intellectual engagement and friendship of former Attorney General and former Judge Carmen Rita Vélez Borrás, Ambassador Mari Carmen Aponte, former Chief Justice of the Puerto Rico Supreme Court Federico Hernández Denton, the late Judge Juan R. Torruella of the U.S. Court of Appeals for the First Circuit, Associate Justice of the Puerto Rico Supreme Court Ángel Colón Pérez, former Appellate Judge Hiram Sánchez Martínez, former Secretary of State and former Mayor of San Juan Héctor Luis Acevedo, Professor José Julián Álvarez González, Professor Efrén Rivera Ramos, Professor Ernesto Chiesa, Professor Carlos Gorrín Peralta, Professor Hiram Meléndez Juarbe, and my colleagues at the David A. Clarke School of Law, Dean Renée McDonald Hutchins, Professor John Brittain, Professor Susan Waysdorf, and Professor Phil Lee. To Evelyn Ortiz Hernández and her team at the Puerto Rico Supreme Court Library, as well as to my research assistants Juan José Jiménez Lizardi at Yale Law School and Javier Sevillano Vicéns my most sincere gratitude for their commitment. A special word of appreciation must also go to the editor of this series, Professor Lawrence Friedman, as well as to Tony Lim and his colleagues at the Oxford University Press, for believing in the pertinence and timeliness of this project.

My views, moreover, do not reflect the opinions of any of the above-referenced friends and collaborators. All opinions, viewpoints, mistakes, and omissions are clearly mine alone.

PART ONE

The Constitutional History of Puerto Rico

■ THE COUNCIL OF INDIES 1493–1812

Puerto Rico's legal tradition traces its origins back to medieval Spain. Discovered (figuratively) by Christopher Columbus on his second voyage to the Americas, on November 19, 1493, Puerto Rico soon became an overseas colony of the Spanish Crown.[1] The stage was thus set for a colonial entanglement that lasted over four hundred years, making Puerto Rico one of Spain's oldest possessions in the Americas.[2]

---

[1] For further reading on the initial stages of Spain's colonization of Puerto Rico, *see, e.g.,* Fray Íñigo Abbad y Lasierra, *Historia geográfica, civil y natural de la isla de San Juan Bautista de Puerto Rico* (annotated by José Julián Acosta y Calbo) (Madrid: Ediciones Doce Calles, 2002); Arturo Morales Carrión, *Puerto Rico: A Political and Cultural History* (New York: W.W. Norton & Company, Inc., 1983); Francisco A. Scarano, *Puerto Rico: Cinco siglos de historia,* 4 ed. (México: McGraw Hill, 2015); Eugenio Fernández Méndez, *Crónicas de Puerto Rico* (Río Piedras: Editorial de la Universidad de Puerto Rico, 1969); and Salvador Brau, *La colonización de Puerto Rico* (San Juan: Heraldo Español, 1907). For an overview of Spain's colonization of the Americas, *see* Juan Bosch, *De Cristóbal Colón a Fidel Castro: El Caribe, frontera imperial* 12ma edición (Santo Domingo: Alfa & Omega, 2005).

[2] As shall be discussed in further detail below, following the signing of the Treaty of Paris, on December 10, 1898, the Spanish Kingdom relinquished in favor of the United States "all claim of sovereignty over and title to Cuba," while also ceding Puerto Rico (then a Spanish overseas province by virtue of the 1897 Autonomic Charter), Guam and the Philippines to the victor of the so-called Spanish-American War. For a detailed account of the situation in the Philippines, *see* Alicia Castellanos Escudier, *Filipinas: De la insurrección a la intervención de Estados Unidos. 1896–1898* (Madrid: Silex, 1998). For an

4 ■ THE CONSTITUTIONAL HISTORY OF PUERTO RICO

Puerto Rico's legal culture belongs to the civil law system, deriving its defining features from legal institutions as ancient as Justinian's *Corpus Iuris Civilis*[3] and Alfonso X's *Siete Partidas*.[4] It would be impossible to grasp the historical evolution of Puerto Rican law without paying heed to the discontinuous, and rather arbitrary, ways in which the Spanish Crown extrapolated to its far-flung colony in the Caribbean its own endogenous legal institutions. It is essential to note, moreover, that for the first three hundred years of Spanish colonial rule, initially under the Catholic Kings,[5] and subsequently under their Hapsburg and Bourbon heirs, the crown ruled over Puerto Rico through a complex web of laws, decrees, and *cédulas*, highly steeped in the Castilian legal tradition, under the exclusive jurisdiction of *el Real y Supremo Consejo de las Indias* (Council of Indies).[6]

Originally established in 1519 by order of Emperor Charles V as a subdivision of the Council of Castile (*el Real y Supremo Consejo de Castilla*),[7] the Council of

---

in-depth analysis of the initial stages of the 1898–1899 Filipino-American War, *see* Benito J. Legarda, *The Hills of Sampaloc* (Makati City: The Bookmark, 2001). For the Puerto Rican narrative, consult Fernando Picó, *1898: La guerra después de la guerra* 2da edición (Río Piedras: Ediciones Huracán, 1998).

[3] The *Corpus Iuris Civilis*, commonly known as Justinian's Code, was enacted in two separate installments, in 527 AD and 534 AD, respectively. Perhaps the most ambitious attempt at codification engineered during the very early Middle Ages, the *Corpus Iuris Civilis* was heavily influenced by, inter alia, Caracalla's legislation, the *Codex Gregorianus* (294 AD), the *Codex Hermogenianus* (314–324 AD), and the *Codex Theodosianus* (438 AD). It is essential to note that Justinian's codification effort was at the heart of his geopolitical strategy for the recolonization of the Mediterranean, which resulted in Byzantium's re-annexation of the southern tip of the Iberian Peninsula. *See, e.g.*, Manuel Torres Aguilar, *Manual de historia del Derecho* (Madrid: Tecnos, 2015), 62–65.

[4] *Las Siete Partidas*, published under the auspices of King Alfonso X (1252–1284) and perhaps the single most influential legal text produced in Castile during the Middle Ages, was an attempt at harmonizing Castile's complex legal repertoire, marred by internal inconsistencies due to an untrammeled degree of discontinuous syncretism. *Las Siete Partidas* compiled and synthesized legal principles found in Roman and Visigoth law, as well as in medieval canonical law and even in so-called Castilian customary law. It was officially sanctioned under the 1348 *Ordenamiento de Alcalá*, available to Spanish courts and litigants until the late nineteenth century. Torres Aguiar, *Manual de historia del Derecho*, 142. Refer to John Thomas Vance, *The Background of Hispanic-American Law* (New York: Central Book Co., 1943), 93–107. For a highly illuminating biography of King Alfonso X, which ably touches upon the geopolitical intricacies of the Spanish thirteenth century, *see* H. Salvador Martínez, *Alfonso X, El Sabio: Una biografía* (Madrid: Ediciones Polifemo, 2003).

[5] For a basic understanding of the geopolitical environment facing Catholic Kings, and the transformations undergone by Spain under their reign, *see* William H. Prescott, *History of the Reign of Ferdinand and Isabella* (New York: Heritage Press, 1962).

[6] For a complete analysis of the administrative structure of the Council of Indies and its interactions with the Spanish Crown, *see* Feliciano Barrios, *La gobernación de la monarquía española: consejos, juntas y secretarios de la administración de corte (1556–1700)* (Madrid: Centro de Estudios Políticos y Constitucionales, 2015), 545–556.

[7] For an authoritative text on the origins of the Council of Castile and its subsequent role during the early days of Charles V's reign, *see* Salustiano De Dios, *El Consejo Real de Castilla (1385–1522)* (Madrid: Centro de Estudios Constitucionales, 1982).

Indies outgrew the monarch's initial and rather limited design.[8] The sheer magnitude of Spain's vast colonial project in the Americas, particularly after Hernán Cortés's and Francisco Pizarro's exploits in Mexico and Peru, respectively, led the crown in 1524 to decree the complete independence of the Council of Indies from the Castilian Council.[9] From then on, until its definitive suppression in 1834,[10] the Council of Indies controlled every aspect of Puerto Rico's colonial life.[11] It exercised unencumbered legal authority over the island's executive, legislative, judicial, commercial, military, and even ecclesiastical affairs.[12] The council drafted all colonial legislation, appointed the colonial bureaucracy while retaining impeachment authority, designed all colonial budgets, and similarly to the British Privy Council also acted as the final court of appeals for all Spanish colonies, including Puerto Rico.[13] The avalanche of legislation, decrees, and *cédulas* rendered by the Council of Indies soon evolved into an intricate corpus

---

[8] Under the 1519 design, all colonial issues pertaining to Spain's trade with its newly acquired possessions were directed to the *Casa de Contratación de Sevilla*—an institution under the aegis of the Council of Castile. Having nullified the Santa Fe Capitulations (*Capitulaciones de Santa Fe*) entered into with Christopher Columbus in 1492, the Spanish Crown now exercised absolute control over the new territories. *See* John Thomas Vance, *The Background of Hispanic-American Law*, 129–130. Note, moreover, that by then Seville was squarely under the control of the Castilian Crown—which in 1248, under the reign of King Ferdinand III, had taken over the city from the Moors.

[9] Under the royal decree of August 1, 1524, the Council of Indies was put under the control of Cardinal García de Loaisa, Charles V's confessor. *See* José María Ots y Capdequi, *Historia del Derecho español en América y del Derecho indiano* (Madrid: Aguilar, 1969), 116.

[10] While definitively disbanded in 1834, the Council of Indies had been initially abolished under the 1808 and 1812 Bayonne and Cádiz Constitutions, only to be reinstituted during Ferdinand VII's absolutist restoration in 1814.

[11] For a detailed analysis of the Council of Indies's internal structure and operation, *see* Ernst Schäfer, *El Consejo Real y Supremo de Indias* 2 vols. (Sevilla: Carmona, 1935–1947).

[12] The degree of centralization endured by Puerto Rico, throughout the life of the Council of Indies, was a far cry from the more autonomous condition of Spain's provinces. The definitive political unification of Spain at the hands of the Catholic Kings, following the fall of Granada in 1492, did not do away with the peninsula's legal heterogeneity—particularly in the realm of private law. Each region held on to its endogenous legal repertoire, while pledging allegiance to the Spanish Crown. Thus, while Spain denied Puerto Rico any flexibility as to the articulation of autochthonous legal institutions, Catalonia, Aragon, Navarre, Galicia, Valencia, Biscay, and the Balearic Islands enjoyed ample autonomy to keep their own legal repertoire. Note that the superimposition of a more centralized governmental model, in the French mold, following the accession to the Spanish throne of Philip V of Anjou in 1700 did erode the ascendancy of the regional legal systems. For a relevant rendition on Spain's so-called *derecho foral, see* Federico Barrachina y Pastor, *Derecho foral español* (Castellón: J. Armengot e Hijos, 1911). *See also* Jorge de Esteban, *Las constituciones de España*, 2nd ed. (Madrid: Centro de Estudios Políticos y Constitucionales, 2000), 24–26.

[13] The size of the Council of Indies increased through the centuries. Initially made up of one president and up to four or five councilors, by the end of the seventeenth century its membership had expanded to over nineteen councilors. José Trías Monge, *Historia Constitucional de Puerto Rico*, vol. 1 (Río Piedras: Editorial de la Universidad de Puerto Rico, 1980), 13–14.

of public law, commonly known as *derecho indiano*,[14] which formed the basis of Puerto Rico's early legal order up to the first decades of the nineteenth century.[15] Together with the *derecho indiano*, which for the most part was public in nature, Castilian law was also an important source of Puerto Rico's incipient private law.

The disbandment of the Council of Indies in 1834 left Puerto Rico's colonial condition intact. Spain's firm grip on the island remained undisturbed. Emboldened by the dictatorial powers granted to them under the royal decree signed by King Ferdinand VII on May 28, 1825, the Spanish colonial governors continued to rule the island as a military camp even after the abolition of the Council of Indies.[16]

Meanwhile, on the ground, the first three hundred years of Spanish colonial rule had proven rather calamitous. Following the early stages of the colonization period led by Juan Ponce de León, Juan Cerón, and Cristobal de Sotomayor, the island remained isolated, scarcely populated, and beholden to an underperforming slave economy heavily dependent on the so-called *Situado Mexicano*.[17]

The application to Puerto Rico of Spain's decadent mercantilist system not only shut the door to free trade but also opened the island to inflation, contraband, corruption, and foreign invasions.[18]

■ THE CÁDIZ CONSTITUTION 1812–1814

Due to the vastness of the Atlantic Ocean, news from Madrid always made its way to Puerto Rico at an exceedingly slow pace. While the Cádiz Constitution was promulgated on March 19, 1812, it only entered into full force and effect in Puerto Rico on July 14, 1812.

---

[14] The Spanish Crown published various compilations of the laws and regulations issued by the Council of Indies. The first compilation, commissioned by Charles V, was published on November 20, 1542 (*Las leyes nuevas*). Charles V's son, Philip II, ordered a second compilation, which came to light in 1571 (*Las ordenanzas*). The most definitive work on *Derecho indiano* finally made its appearance in 1680 with the publication of *La Recopilación de las Leyes de Indias* during the reign of Charles II. Feliciano Barrios, *La gobernación de la monarquía española: consejos, juntas y secretarios de la administración de corte (1556–1700)*, 548.

[15] Ots y Capdequi, *Historia del Derecho español en América y del Derecho indiano*, 205.

[16] Juan Gualberto Gómez and Antonio Sendras y Burín, *La isla de Puerto Rico: Bosquejo histórico* (Madrid: Imprenta de José Gil y Navarro, 1891), 69.

[17] Lidio Cruz Monclova, *Historia de Puerto Rico (Siglo XIX)*, 2nd ed., vol. 1 (Río Piedras: Editorial de la Universidad de Puerto Rico, 1958), 19. Note that the Mexican *Situado* or subsidy came to an abrupt end in 1810, following Mexico's declaration of independence from Spain.

[18] For an illuminating study on the dynamics of contraband and the looming threat of foreign invasions (mostly from the British and the Dutch), *see, e.g.*, Arturo Morales Carrión, *Puerto Rico and the Non-Hispanic Caribbean: A Study in the Decline of Spanish Exclusivism* (Río Piedras: University of Puerto Rico Press, 1952).

By then, Napoleon's 1808 invasion of the Iberian Peninsula had opened the floodgates of revolution across the Spanish Kingdom. His brutal coercion of Charles IV and his son Ferdinand into resigning the throne and dynastic rights, together with his highhanded imposition of his elder brother Joseph on the Spanish throne, had been met with unyielding resistance both in the peninsula and throughout the colonies.[19]

Besieged by a relentless invader and devoid of any semblance of institutional coherence, the Spanish *Consejo de Regencia* called for the election of delegates from across the empire to draft a non-absolutist legal instrument premised on the constitutional monarchy model.

Structurally, the 1812 experiment inaugurated in Spain a governmental system based on the triangular separation of constitutional powers. While Article 15 of the Cádiz Constitution endowed the *cortes* (then a unicameral legislature) with the sole authority to enact the kingdom's laws, Article 16 left in the hands of the Spanish Crown exclusive authority to execute those laws. Article 17, furthermore, vested in the courts of the kingdom the power to apply the law to all civil and criminal actions before them.[20]

The 1812 Cádiz Constitution was, effectively, Spain's first autochthonous modern constitution. It explicitly subordinated the crown to the popular will. Sovereignty, under the Cádiz design, would reside not within the crown but within the nation.[21]

At Cádiz, the idea of colonial assimilation won the day, namely, that the colonies ought to be incorporated as constituent elements of the Spanish Kingdom, on equal footing with the provinces in the peninsula. For the colonies this meant meaningful participation in the governance of the kingdom, guaranteed representation in the *cortes*, and full access to the bundle of fundamental rights available under the new Cádiz Constitution.[22]

---

[19] Interestingly, amid this chaotic period, *l'empereur* promulgated the short-lived Bayonne Constitution on May 25, 1808. Although never in full force and effect in Puerto Rico, the Bayonne Constitution established, at least in theory, a rather advanced institutional framework for the overseas colonies. Articles 88 and 89 of the Bayonne Constitution opened free trade within the Spanish colonies in the Americas, while Article 92 granted the colonies twenty-two seats in the Spanish *Cortes* (of which one belonged to Puerto Rico). For the text of the Bayonne Constitution visit https://www.congreso.es/docu/constituciones/1812/Bayona.pdf (last visited May 8, 2022).

[20] For the original version in Spanish of these provisions visit https://www.congreso.es/cem/const1812 (last visited May 8, 2022).

[21] Article 3 of the Cádiz Constitution left no room for equivocation: "*La soberanía reside esencialmente en la Nación, y por lo mismo pertenece a ésta exclusivamente el derecho de establecer sus leyes fundamentales.*" Visit https://www.congreso.es/cem/const1812 (last visited May 8, 2022).

[22] *See* Articles 4 and 131(24), guaranteeing individual civil liberties, as well as property and printing press rights. Visit https://www.congreso.es/cem/const1812 (last visited May 8, 2022).

8 ■ THE CONSTITUTIONAL HISTORY OF PUERTO RICO

The Cádiz Constitution, moreover, did away with the Council of Indies. There would no longer be a *lex specialis* for the colonies.[23] Spanish nationality would no longer be restricted on account of geography. Article 5 made it clear that all free men born and domiciled in the Spanish dominions would be considered Spanish nationals.[24] Article 10, for its part, included all of Spain's American and Asian colonies in the definition of Spanish dominions.[25] Interestingly, under Article 28 of the Cádiz Constitution, both colonial and peninsular deputies to the *cortes* would be apportioned on the basis of the same population formula.[26]

For Puerto Rico, one of the most significant consequences of Spain's fleeting constitutional experiment was the selection of Naval Lieutenant Ramón Power y Giralt (1775–1813) as the island's sole delegate to the *Cortes Constituyentes*.[27] Together with Catholic Bishop Juan Alejo Arizmendi (1757–1814),[28] Power y Giralt has been widely considered as one of the first exponents of a Puerto Rican national consciousness.

Power y Giralt, who by the time the *cortes* were inaugurated on September 24, 1810, had been elected first vice president of the assembly,[29] was responsible for introducing legislation that had far-reaching economic and even ideological impact on the island. The Power y Giralt bill, enacted into law in Cádiz on November 28, 1811, opened up new trade routes through the ports of Aguadilla, Mayagüez, Cabo Rojo, Ponce, and Fajardo;[30] did away with an excessive entanglement of discriminatory taxes;[31] and led to the establishment of an engine for entrepreneurial promotion (*La Sociedad Económica de Amigos del País*)[32] and, equally importantly, to the appointment of Alejandro Ramírez as the island's *intendente*.[33] While ushering a short-lived economic boom, this period set the stage for the belated rise of the island's liberal movement.

---

[23] Cádiz, however, did not put an end to this debate. Finding the proper place for the overseas colonies within Spain's wider constitutional tapestry would haunt the peninsular political leadership for the remainder of the century, spelling doom for Spain's imperial project in the Americas and Southeast Asia.

[24] For the text of Article 5 access https://www.congreso.es/cem/const1812 (last visited May 8, 2022).

[25] Ibid.

[26] Article 31 required one deputy for every seventy thousand persons. Ibid.

[27] For a detailed narrative of Ramón Power y Giralt's election as Puerto Rico's delegate, *see, e.g.*, Aída R. Caro Costas (edited by María de los Ángeles Castro), *Ramón Power y Giralt: Diputado puertorriqueño a las Cortes Generales y Extraordinarias de España* (Río Piedras: Publicaciones Gaviota, 2012), 50–60.

[28] For a biography of Juan Alejo Arizmendi, the first Puerto Rican appointed bishop of the Catholic Church, *see* Cayetano Coll y Toste, *Puertorriqueños ilustres* (Río Piedras: Editorial Cultural, 1978), 33–36.

[29] Lidio Cruz Monclova, *Historia de Puerto Rico (Siglo XIX)*, 2nd ed., vol. 1, at 38. For the role of the colonial delegates at the Cádiz Constittutional Convention, *see, e.g.*, Rafael María de Labra, *Los Presidentes Americanos de las Cortes de Cádiz* (Cádiz: Manuel Álvarez, 1912).

[30] Lidio Cruz Monclova, *Historia de Puerto Rico (Siglo XIX)*, 2nd ed., vol. 1, at 66.

[31] Ibid.

[32] Ibid.

[33] For a complete analysis of the measures implemented by Alejandro Ramírez during the 1811–1814 period, *see, e.g.*, Luis González Vales, *Alejandro Ramírez y su tiempo* (Río Piedras: Editorial de la

THE CONSTITUTIONAL HISTORY OF PUERTO RICO ■ 9

The Cádiz experiment, however, soon came to an abrupt end.

■ CONSTITUTIONAL DEVELOPMENTS 1814–1834

1814–1820

The restoration of Ferdinand VII on March 22, 1814, put an end to the Cádiz constitutional experiment.[34] Monarchical absolutism took hold again, not only across the Iberian Peninsula but also in Puerto Rico.[35]

The dissolution of the *cortes* led to the reinstatement of the colonial *anciene régime*. Puerto Rico would no longer enjoy representation in the constitutive institutions of the Spanish Kingdom. Moreover, the proposition that the overseas colonies could be "assimilated" to the kingdom on an equal footing with the peninsular provinces was quickly put to rest.

This period also witnessed the end of the *intendencia*. The reins of the island's fiscal, monetary, and commercial policies were placed, once more, under the tight control of the Spanish military governor, with deleterious consequences for the island's zigzagging economy.

1820–1823

Lieutenant Colonel Rafael del Riego's 1820 *pronunciamiento* stands as the opening salvo of a long continuum of military upheavals that swung Spain's politico-constitutional pendulum all throughout the nineteenth century.[36] The del Riego rebellion led to the short-lived reinstatement of the Cádiz Constitution and, thus, to the reconstitution of the *cortes* in Madrid. Puerto Rico, like Cuba, soon sent a delegate in the person of Demetrio O'Daly to the newly inaugurated *cortes*.[37]

Both O'Daly and his successor, José María Quiñones, together with the Cuban priest, Félix Varela y Morales,[38] far from embracing the assimilation

---

Universidad de Puerto Rico, 1978). Note that the *intendencia* was a French administrative construct imported to the Spanish colonies under the reign of Charles III. The idea behind the *intendencia* was entrusting the finances of the colonies to seasoned technocrats.

[34] Ferdinand VII abrogated the 1812 Cádiz Constitution on May 4, 1814.

[35] By the time news of Ferdinand VII's triumphant return to Madrid reached Puerto Rico, the restored monarch had already abrogated the 1812 Cádiz Constitution. The archival record shows that the island's Spanish governor, Brigadier General Salvador Meléndez Bruna, received official notice of these events on June 30, 1814. *See, e.g.,* Lidio Cruz Monclova, *Historia de Puerto Rico*, 101.

[36] Interestingly, the news of del Riego's uprising only reached Puerto Rico on May 12, 1820—almost five months after the *pronunciamiento* and two months after Ferdinand VII was forced to reinstate the late Cádiz Constitution. Lidio Cruz Monclova, *Historia de Puerto Rico*, 141.

[37] The record suggests O'Daly was born in San Juan in 1780. Like Power y Giralt, O'Daly enjoyed military prestige—having participated alongside del Riego in the peninsular rebellion. *See, e.g.,* Lidio Cruz Monclova, *Historia de Puerto Rico*, 145.

[38] Félix Varela y Morales (1788–1853) was born in Havana, where he was ordained as a Catholic priest in 1811. Varela was one of Cuba's foremost nineteenth-century intellectuals.

10 ■ THE CONSTITUTIONAL HISTORY OF PUERTO RICO

project ingrained in the Cádiz constitutional experiment, took the mantle from the late Ramón Power y Giralt proposing the enactment of a sui generis colonial statute for Puerto Rico and Cuba.

The 1823 Quiñones-Varela bill, similar to the 1811 Power y Giralt legislation, called, on the one hand, for the devolution of a significant degree of administrative authority to Puerto Rico and, on the other, recommended the establishment of representative institutions at the colonial level.[39] By granting far-reaching autonomy to endogenous institutions such as *la Diputación Provincial* (island-wide legislative body) and the *ayuntamientos* (municipalities), with respect to budgets, taxes, tariffs, and other local issues, the Quiñones-Varela bill intended to dilute the Spanish governor's asphyxiating grip on all aspects of colonial life.

Needless to say, the implosion of the so-called liberal triennium, due in no small measure to Ferdinand VII's strategic alliance with France's Louis XVIII,[40] put a rather abrupt end to this most recent attempt at infusing oxygen to the Puerto Rican landscape. The appointment, moreover, of the infamous Miguel de la Torre y Pando as captain general and governor in 1823,[41] together with the enactment of the abominable royal decree of May 28, 1825, bestowing on de la Torre y Pando, and all his successors at *La Fortaleza*, full plenary military and civil powers (*poderes omnímodos*) sealed the island's fate for the remainder of Ferdinand VII's tumultuous reign.[42]

1823–1833

The so-called "ominous" decade, which ran from the demise of the Cádiz re-enactment in 1823 to Ferdinand VII's death in 1833, not only eviscerated the possibility of regenerating Puerto Rico's politico-constitutional jigsaw puzzle but, more importantly, set the stage for the explosion of the bloody (and lengthy) Carlist Wars, with unforeseen consequences for Spain's overseas colonies in the Caribbean.

The king's secret execution of his pragmatic sanction not only abrogated the medieval Salic law,[43] paving the way for the proclamation of Isabel (his three-year-old daughter) as his only legitimate and rightful heir, it opened the door to

---

[39] Lidio Cruz Monclova, *Historia de Puerto Rico*, 194–199.

[40] *See, e.g.,* Raymond Carr, *Spain 1808–1939* (Oxford: Clarendon Press, 1975), 141.

[41] Miguel de la Torre y Pando (1786–1853) arrived in Puerto Rico shortly after his defeat at the hands of Simón Bolívar in the decisive battle of Carabobo, which sealed the independence of Venezuela. He was Spain's longest serving governor of Puerto Rico during the nineteenth century; his despotic rule extended from 1822 to 1837.

[42] Lidio Cruz Monclova, *Historia de Puerto Rico*, 312.

[43] Pursuant to the medieval Salic law, women could only inherit the throne in the complete absence of male heirs; namely, younger brothers, uncles, or nephews. Thus, Ferdinand VII's abolition of this legislation on June 30, 1833 (only three months before his death) shut the door to his brother's dynastic pretensions.

a strikingly weak regency led by María Cristina de Borbón y Dos Sicilias—the dowager queen.[44]

The untimely death of Ferdinand VII opened up the floodgates of civil war in Spain for the foreseeable future.[45] For the next four decades, Ferdinand's younger brother, Carlos María Isidro de Borbón, his heirs, and his allies, would challenge Isabel II's legitimate claim to the Spanish throne.[46] Faced with the ever-present Carlist threat, which effectively hung like Damocles' sword over her head, the queen mother was soon caught up in a dangerous crossfire among the various warring factions within the peninsula's military and political establishments. It was precisely this background, together with an overriding imperative of dynastic survival, which led to the proclamation in less than three years of two very different constitutional instruments for Spain—none of which provided a discernible colonial policy with respect to Puerto Rico.

■ THE ROYAL STATUTE OF 1834

The Royal Statute of 1834, arguably modeled against *la Charte* of Louis XVIII,[47] was the first legal document of constitutional pedigree enacted under María Cristina's regency.[48] Contrary to the 1812 Cádiz Constitution, the Royal Statute brought to the fore a completely different theory of the state: sovereignty resides, not in the hands of the nation but rather in the hands of the crown.[49]

The intellectual offspring of Francisco Martínez de la Rosa and a cadre of conservative legal theorists, the enactment of the Royal Statue was but a misguided strategic maneuver by the queen's coterie to win the allegiance of the more conservative elements of Spanish society—those more susceptible to defect to the Carlist pretender's camp.

---

[44] María Cristina de Borbón y Dos Sicilias (1806–1878), the king's niece and fourth wife, had become Spain's queen consort in 1829 following her marriage to Ferdinand VII.

[45] For a detailed analysis of the catalysts behind the Carlist wars, consult the dispatches drafted by the U.S. embassy in Madrid and addressed to then U.S. Secretary of State Hamilton Fish. *Papers relating to the foreign relations of the United States, transmitted to congress, with the annual message of the president, December 4, 1876* (Washington: U.S. Government Printing Office, 1876), 442–445. For a detailed analysis of the events leading to the Carlist conflict, *see, e.g.,* Raymond Carr, *Spain 1808–1939*, at 150–155.

[46] The end of the Carlist Wars, which coincided with the restoration of Bourbon rule in the person of Alfonso XII, would come in 1876 with the definitive military defeat of the insurgents at the hands of General Arsenio Martínez Campos.

[47] For a comparative analysis of the above-referenced Spanish and French constitutional texts, *see* Raymond Carr, *Spain 1808–1939*, at 157.

[48] The Royal Statute of 1834, which entered into full force and effect on April 10, 1834, was published in Puerto Rico by Captain General Miguel de la Torre y Pando on June 19 of the same year.

[49] Although the 1834 Royal Statute made no explicit reference to the concept of "national sovereignty," a close perusal of its provisions suggests that its framers embraced an absolutist reading of sovereignty; namely, they believed it resided in the crown alone.

12 ■ THE CONSTITUTIONAL HISTORY OF PUERTO RICO

Unlike the Cádiz Constitution, the Royal Statute was not made extensive to Puerto Rico. Thus, the assimilation policy did not find echo during María Cristina's regency.

Under the Royal Statute, Puerto Rico's status remained unchanged: an overseas colony at the mercy of a military dictator appointed by the Spanish Crown. Ironically, not even the definitive disbandment of the Council of Indies, which coincided with the enactment of the Royal Statute in 1834, alleviated Puerto Rico's perils. The island's woes became even more desperate when Madrid flatly refused to renew the 1815 *Real Cédula de Gracias*, which had expired by 1836.[50]

In attempting to strike a balance between the traditional Spanish aristocracy and the emergent merchant classes, Article 2 of the Royal Statute established an unprecedented bicameral system in the peninsula: *el estamento de los próceres* and *el estamento de los procuradores*. Interestingly, Puerto Rico was granted two seats in *el estamento de los procuradores*.[51] The island's representation in the lower house, however, was not required under the Royal Statute but was mandated by ordinary legislation (*decreto complementario*).[52]

This discrete concession led the more liberal elements of Puerto Rico's incipient political leadership to press for the nomination of progressive figures to *el estamento de los procuradores*, who could conclude the unfinished agenda of Power y Giralt, O'Daly, and Quiñones. It was in this vein that José San Just and Esteban de Ayala were selected by the *ayuntamiento de San Juan* on July 20, 1834, as the island's representatives before the *estamento de los procuradores*. And while San Just and de Ayala would be subsequently replaced by Juan Francisco Pérez and José Francisco Díaz in April 1836, their collective agenda focused on the same set of neglected petitions; namely, the liberalization of trade and immigration, tax reform, and the strengthening of the island's emaciated infrastructure, agriculture, and industry within a framework of administrative decentralization.[53]

Unbeknown to the insular *procuradores* and to the colonial authorities on the island, the Royal Statute was soon to die a violent death at the hands of the Spanish military officers who revolted at the royal palace of *La Granja de San Ildefonso* (Segovia) on August 13, 1836, requesting the restitution of the old Cádiz Constitution. This most recent military *pronunciamiento*, similar to del Riego's sixteen years earlier, was but another attempt by the more progressive elements of the Spanish military, political, and merchant classes to swing the

---

[50] José Trías Monge, *Historia Constitucional de Puerto Rico*, vol. 1, at 48.

[51] For the structural design of *el estamento de los procuradores*, see Articles 13–18 of the Royal Statute, available in Jorge de Esteban, *Las constituciones de España*, 179–180.

[52] Lidio Cruz Monclova, *Historia de Puerto Rico*, 278.

[53] Ibid., 282.

ideological pendulum of the realm away from those absolutist values ingrained in the Royal Statute.

Hence, the path to crafting yet another constitutional instrument that could somehow accommodate the centrifugal and centripetal forces tearing Spain to shreds was wide open.

■ THE CONSTITUTION OF 1837

Faced with the impending unraveling of her political base among the liberal progressives, both within and without the military, the queen regent sanctioned the opening of yet another constitutional convention in the wake of the upheaval at *La Granja*.[54]

In this light, the proclamation of the 1837 Constitution should be viewed as a last-ditch attempt at saving María Cristina's uniquely weak regency.[55] In their blatant effort to win the support of a wide multitude of audiences espousing contrarian ideological views and interests,[56] the drafters of the 1837 instrument produced a hybrid that did little to dissipate the progressives-moderates divide, let alone dissolve the ever-looming Carlist threat.

The 1837 Constitution fell considerably short of the Cádiz benchmark. Although its preamble,[57] similarly to Article 3 of the 1812 Constitution,[58] established that sovereignty would now reside in the nation, it endowed the crown with broad authority. Article 26 of the 1837 constitutional text made it plain clear that the monarch alone enjoyed unencumbered authority to convene, suspend, or dissolve the annual sessions of the newly created congress of deputies.[59] The monarch, moreover, would now share with the legislative bodies the power to initiate legislation without losing her veto prerogative.[60] Contrary to the Royal Statute, which had no semblance of separation of powers or recognition of individual fundamental rights, the 1837 Constitution did address this latter point, albeit discreetly.

---

[54] The constituent *cortes* were first convened on October 24, 1836.

[55] Raymond Carr, *Spain 1808–1939*, at 178.

[56] Note that the anti-clerical movement, buoyed by the regency's policy of confiscation (*desamortización*) of Catholic Church property, supported the queen mother.

[57] For the preamble's text, access https://www.congreso.es/cem/const1837 (last visited May 8, 2022).

[58] Visit https://www.congreso.es/constitucion/ficheros/historicas/cons_1812.pdf (last visited May 8, 2022).

[59] Successor to *el estamento de los procuradores* established under the Royal Statute of 1834. For the specific wording of Article 26, see https://www.congreso.es/cem/const1837 (last visited May 8, 2022).

[60] *See* Articles 36 and 39, at https://www.congreso.es/cem/const1837 (last visited May 8, 2022).

While extrajudicial arrests and prosecutions, together with illegal expropriations, were now proscribed by constitutional mandate, the execution of these rights was made contingent on the enactment of enabling legislation.[61]

Interestingly, the right to publish freely without governmental censorship figured prominently in Article 2 of the 1837 Constitution,[62] and yet it was of no consequence to Puerto Rico—where, pursuant to a royal decree of April 22, 1837, the island's colonial governor was granted further authority to arbitrarily exercise prior restraint of the press.[63]

Contrary to its Cádiz counterpart, the 1837 Constitution was not made extensive to Puerto Rico; nor did it provide for colonial representation at the newly minted chamber of deputies. Additional Article 2 purposefully left the issue of colonial governance unresolved: "the overseas provinces shall be governed by *special laws*."[64]

Thus, the 1837 Constitution did not follow the Spanish flag to the Caribbean. Puerto Rico was, essentially, left at the mercy of despotic colonial governors enjoying extraconstitutional powers. Structurally, the island remained bound to the kingdom, not as a Spanish province[65] but as a colonial possession under the strictures of an antiquated corpus of medieval legislation.[66]

Under the new constitution, moreover, Spanish nationality was not explicitly extended to Puerto Ricans. Thus, the limited catalogue of individual rights enumerated therein remained inaccessible to them. The absence of an institutional framework for assuring a semblance of colonial representation in Madrid marked the parting of the ways with Cádiz. More tragically, the waiting period for the so-called special legislation turned out to be eternal. The elusive *leyes especiales* never came.

■ THE CONSTITUTION OF 1845

Of all the constitutional texts enacted in Spain throughout the nineteenth century, the 1845 Constitution survived the longest: twenty-four years.[67] Because

---

[61] *See* Articles 7, 9, and 10, at https://www.congreso.es/cem/const1837 (last visited May 8, 2022).

[62] For Article 2's exact wording, *see* Ibid.

[63] Lidio Cruz Monclova, *Historia de Puerto Rico*, 300.

[64] For the original text, access https://www.congreso.es/cem/const1837 (last visited May 8, 2022).

[65] *See* Article 10 of the 1812 Cádiz Constitution.

[66] Refer to Book Three of the Laws of Indies (dating to the times of Philip II), the *Siete Partidas* and various other ancient legal texts incorporated into the *Novísima Recopilación* of 1795. *See* Juan Gualberto Gómez and Antonio Sendrás y Burín, *La isla de Puerto Rico: Bosquejo histórico* (Madrid: Imprenta de José Gil y Navarro, 1891), 69–70.

[67] The Constitution of 1845 was only suspended during the so-called progressive biennium (1854–1856) led by General Baldomero Espartero. The proposal put forward by Espartero in 1856 for a new constitution to replace the 1845 Constitution never prospered. Espartero's proposed constitution would have restored many of the more liberal provisions of the 1837 Constitution: sovereignty in the hands of

it was the constitutional instrument in full force and effect in Spain at the time of some of the more tumultuous episodes in Puerto Rico's and Cuba's colonial history,[68] the Constitution of 1845 deserves particular attention. The implosion of María Cristina's regency in October 1840,[69] together with General Ramón María Narváez's coup d'état against General Baldomero Espartero's interim government in July 1843,[70] set the stage for yet another constitution-making exercise.

Narváez swung the ideological pendulum to the right. And, not surprisingly, the Constitution of 1845 mirrored this. Sovereignty no longer resided in the nation alone. It now coexisted within the nation and the crown.[71]

Under the new constitutional arrangement, appointments to the senate were the exclusive province of the monarch.[72] Thus, the 1845 Constitution effectively transformed this chamber into a purely aristocratic institution, which now also enjoyed an unlimited membership.[73]

Jury trials for printing press offenses were no longer constitutionally required.[74] The national militias spread across the peninsula were also suppressed.[75] With respect to the overseas colonies, the drafters of the 1845 Constitution superimposed on the new document the same language used in Additional Article 2 of the 1837 Constitution. Thus, Article 80 of the 1845 Constitution

---

the nation alone, freedom of the press without prior restraint, an elective senate, national militias, and administrative decentralization in favor of the municipalities (*ayuntamientos*). Under Espartero's design, the constitution was not to be extended to Puerto Rico or Cuba, nor would these colonies have representation in the *cortes*. They would both be required to wait for the enactment of special legislation. *See* Article 86 of the draft 1856 Constitution in Arnold Verduin, *Manual of Spanish Constitutions 1808–1931* (Michigan: University Lithoprinters, 1941), 57.

[68] Puerto Rico's most emblematic separatist uprising took place on September 23, 1868 (immortalized as *el Grito de Lares*), while Cuba's first war of independence against Spain (which lasted ten grueling years) began on October 10, 1868, with the uprising known as *el Grito de Yara*, which took place in the *Demajagua* plantation of Carlos Manuel de Céspedes in the Oriente Region.

[69] Outmaneuvered both politically and militarily, the queen mother resigned her status as regent of the realm on October 12, 1840, and went into exile in France, leaving her daughter under General Espartero's protection.

[70] Espartero's spectacular fall brought about by a heterogeneous constituency (anti free traders, textile workers, industry magnates, Catalonian nationalists, radicals, and conservatives alike), put an end to the regency and led to Isabel II's coronation in November 1843.

[71] Compare the language of the 1837 and 1845 Preambles, at https://app.congreso.es/consti/otras/historicas/index.htm (last visited May 12, 2022).

[72] *See* Article 14, at https://www.congreso.es/constitucion/ficheros/historicas/cons_1845.pdf (last visited May 8, 2022).

[73] Ibid.

[74] Compare Article 2 of the 1845 Constitution with Article 2 of the 1837 Constitution, at https://app.congreso.es/consti/otras/historicas/index.htm (last visited May 12, 2022).

[75] Note that the 1845 Constitution did away with Article 77 of the 1837 Constitution.

16 ■ THE CONSTITUTIONAL HISTORY OF PUERTO RICO

read as follows: "[T]he overseas provinces shall be governed by *special laws*."[76] And, as before, the *cortes* in Madrid never promulgated the *leyes especiales*.

Meanwhile, across the Atlantic, after centuries of repression and neglect, colonial discontent was moving to a tipping point, especially in Cuba.[77] In Puerto Rico, colonial governors came and went in quick succession (their length of stay pegged to the ups and downs of peninsular politics), but the deteriorating condition of the island remained unchanged.

During this period, physical infrastructure: namely, roads, ports, bridges, schools, and hospitals, was mostly nonexistent. The rural peasantry was now the victim of harsh vagrancy laws.[78] Cruel black codes made the miserable existence of slaves and even of free persons of color a living hell.[79] Abolition was not in the cards. Political repression was pervasive. There was no freedom of the press. Censure was the rule and, consequently, hundreds of abolitionists, separatists and autonomists were forced into exile.[80] Not surprisingly, at no point during the reign of Isabel II did Puerto Rico witness the emergence of endogenous political parties.

The insular economy, moreover, devoid of *el Situado Mexicano* and without recourse to the incentives available under the expired 1815 *Real Cédula de Gracias*, was unable to spur the necessary levels of growth for reinvesting in the island's agricultural industries.

It was against this background, that in the waning years of Isabel II's reign, the Spanish Council of Ministers called for the election of Puerto Rican delegates to a *Junta de Información* to discuss the particulars of the elusive *leyes especiales*.[81]

The newly elected Delegates Segundo Ruiz Belvis, José Julián Acosta y Calbo, and Francisco Mariano Quiñones demanded the abolition of slavery,[82] the extension to Puerto Rico of the limited catalogue of rights available under the

---

[76] Access https://www.congreso.es/constitucion/ficheros/historicas/cons_1845.pdf (last visited May 8, 2022).

[77] For an indispensable study of Cuba's Ten Year War and its antecedents, *see, e.g.,* Ramiro Guerra, *Guerra de los 10 Años* (La Habana: Editorial de Ciencias Sociales, 1972).

[78] Refer to the *régimen de la libreta* established by the Spanish colonial governor, General Juan de la Pezuela in June 1849. Lidio Cruz Monclova, *Historia de Puerto Rico*, 377.

[79] Special attention should be paid to the infamous *Bando Contra la Raza Africana* enacted by General Juan Prim y Prats in 1848, following the abolition of slavery in the French Caribbean.

[80] Two of the more prominent exiles during Isabel II's reign were Ramón Emeterio Betances (considered the father of the Puerto Rican nation) and Segundo Ruiz Belvis.

[81] The Puerto Rican and Cuban *Juntas de Información* were convened pursuant to a royal decree signed on November 25, 1865. Interestingly, then Colonial Minister Antonio Cánovas del Castillo drafted the royal decree. For its text, *see, e.g.,* Juan Gualberto Gómez and Antonio Sendrás y Burín, *La isla de Puerto Rico: Bosquejo histórico*, 51–57. *See also* Lidio Cruz Monclova, *Historia de Puerto Rico*, 486–490.

[82] For the abolition proposal put forward by the Puerto Rican delegates, *see* Segundo Ruiz Belvis, José Julián Acosta y Calbo, and Francisco Mariano Quiñones, *Proyecto para la abolición de la esclavitud en Puerto Rico* (San Juan: Instituto de Cultura Puertorriqueña, 1969).

1845 Constitution, and the devolution to the island of administrative authority with respect to trade, commerce, and internal governance.[83]

The *Juntas de Información* (for both Puerto Rico and Cuba) were unceremoniously disbanded soon after their inauguration.[84] The disappointing failure of the *Juntas de Información*, furthermore, coincided with the military coup d'état of September 1868 that brought to a close both Isabel II's twenty-five year reign and the Constitution of 1845. Spain's political implosion came at a time when the insurrections of Lares and Yara exploded in Puerto Rico and Cuba, respectively.[85]

The expulsion of the Spanish queen put an end to the 1845 Constitution.

■ THE CONSTITUTION OF 1869

The 1869 Constitution emerged from the ashes of the 1868 debacle. It remained in full force and effect during most of the next six years, a period in Spanish history often referred as the *sexenio revolucionario*. The 1869 Constitution was yet another attempt at instituting in Spain a stable constitutional monarchy. Promulgated in June 1869, the new constitutional instrument survived the interim government of General Francisco Serrano (1869–1870), the short reign of Amadeo I (1871–1873),[86] the unstable republican period (1873),[87] and Serrano's last provisional government (1874).

Similar to the 1837 and 1845 Constitutions, the 1869 charter was not extended to Puerto Rico. Nor was its ample repertoire of fundamental rights, such as universal male suffrage,[88] religious freedoms,[89] free speech and association,[90] as well as free press,[91] made available to the inhabitants of Puerto Rico.

---

[83] Lidio Cruz Monclova, *Historia de Puerto Rico*, 506–557.

[84] Ibid.

[85] The military *pronunciamientos* of Spanish Generals Francisco Serrano and Juan Prim y Prats in September 1868 drew to a close a particularly weak reign, headed by a rather immature and ineffective queen who by then had lost all legitimacy as a neutral power broker among the various military and political factions vying for power in Madrid. Unable to fend off an acute financial crisis, incapable of eradicating corruption, and bereft of a military champion that could defend her reign and dynastic rights (particularly after the successive deaths of Generals Leopoldo O'Donnell and Ramón María Narváez in November 1867 and April 1868, respectively), Isabel II's days on the throne were numbered.

[86] King Amadeo I's reign began on January 2, 1871 (having been elected by the *cortes* on November 16, 1870) and finished on February 11, 1873, with his abdication to the throne and return to Italy.

[87] During the republican period, the only part of the 1869 Constitution that remained in full force and effect was Title I (Articles 1 through 31), which contained a detailed enumeration of the individual rights available to Spanish nationals.

[88] *See* Article 16, at https://www.congreso.es/constitucion/ficheros/historicas/cons_1869.pdf (last visited May 8, 2022).

[89] *See* Article 21, at https://www.congreso.es/constitucion/ficheros/historicas/cons_1869.pdf (last visited May 8, 2022).

[90] *See* Article 17, at https://www.congreso.es/constitucion/ficheros/historicas/cons_1869.pdf (last visited May 8, 2022).

[91] Ibid.

18 ■ THE CONSTITUTIONAL HISTORY OF PUERTO RICO

While on the surface Article 108 of the 1869 Constitution did not reproduce the language of Additional Article 2 of the 1837 Constitution or of Article 80 of the 1845 Constitution, in essence it stood for a more elaborate version of the same: "The Constituent *cortes* shall reform the present system of government of the overseas provinces when the deputies of Cuba and Puerto Rico have taken seats in the *cortes*, in order to extend to those provinces those rights designated in the Constitution, with the modifications considered necessary."[92]

For the duration of the 1869 Constitution, rather than articulating a comprehensive solution to the colonial problem the *cortes* in Madrid chose to address colonial issues on an ad hoc basis, due in no small measure to the outbreak of Cuba's fierce war of independence a year earlier. Hence, the few institutional reforms finding their way to Puerto Rico during this period came through special legislation on a case-by-case basis: the royal decree of December 14, 1869, granting Puerto Rico representation in the *cortes*;[93] the abolition statute of March 22, 1873, ending slavery in the island;[94] and the enabling statute of August 6, 1873, extending to Puerto Rico the application of Title I of the 1869 Constitution.[95] As a result of these reforms, new conditions on the ground led to the organization in November 1870 of the island's first political parties, namely, the *Partido Liberal Reformista* and the *Partido Liberal Conservador*.[96]

Yet the severe restrictions placed on colonial suffrage, together with the nefarious effects of the colonial government's espionage and ideological repression, meant these incipient political parties amounted to nothing but debating societies with no real influence on issues of local governance.

In the end, the chaotic implosion of Spain's politico-constitutional ecosystem, particularly after the collapse of the republican experiment in January 1874,[97] led to the dynastic restoration of the Bourbons in the person of Alfonso XII, plunging Puerto Rico back to the middle ages. In less than eight weeks after the coup that put an end to the republic,[98] Spain's new military governor in the island José Laureano Sanz with a stroke of his pen suspended the application to Puerto Rico of the freedoms available under Title I of the now defunct 1869 Constitution.[99]

---

[92] For the English translation of the text of Article 108 of the 1869 Constitution see Arnold Verduin, *Manual of Spanish Constitutions 1808–1931*, at 66.

[93] Lidio Cruz Monclova, *Historia de Puerto Rico*, vol. 2 (part 1), 5–6.

[94] Lidio Cruz Monclova, *Historia de Puerto Rico*, vol. 2 (part 1), 268.

[95] Lidio Cruz Monclova, *Historia de Puerto Rico*, vol. 2 (part 1), 330.

[96] Lidio Cruz Monclova, *Historia de Puerto Rico*, vol. 2 (part 1), 68. Trías Monge, *Historia Constitucional de Puerto Rico*, vol. 1, at 57–65.

[97] In less than eleven months, the chaotic republic was led by four different presidents: Estanislao Figueras, Francisco Pi y Margall, Nicolás Salmerón, and Emilio Castelar.

[98] This coup was led by General Manuel Pavía, Castile's captain general, on January 3, 1874.

[99] Lidio Cruz Monclova, *Historia de Puerto Rico*, vol. 2 (part 1), 381.

■ THE CONSTITUTION OF 1876

The Bourbon restoration, and the resulting coronation of Alfonso XII, was part of a well-choreographed maneuver led by politicians Antonio Cánovas del Castillo and Práxedes Mateo Sagasta to institute in Spain the basic trappings of the British Westminster model: a constitutional monarchy premised on a strong bipartisan political system with a stable power-sharing arrangement, with the military subordinated to civilian control. The 1876 Constitution was thus the legal embodiment of the political compromise binding Spain's two most powerful monarchical parties. Structurally, it reproduced the design of the 1845 Constitution, while incorporating almost all of the civil liberties included in the 1869 Constitution.

Similar to the 1845 Constitution, the 1876 text reproduced the cohabitation formula under which the nation's sovereignty resided both in the crown and in the *cortes*.[100] The senate, furthermore, would no longer remain a fully elective body. The king was, once again, endowed with authority to nominate a considerable number of senators.[101] Interestingly, Article 16 of the 1869 Constitution (guaranteeing universal male suffrage) was left out of the 1876 Constitution.[102]

Equally important, and contrary to the 1869 Constitution, the corpus of fundamental rights enumerated under Title I of the 1876 Constitution were not self-executing; their enforcement would now require the enactment of appropriate enabling legislation.[103] The 1876 Constitution's colonial approach, however, mirrored the policy of neglectful indifference adopted by its predecessors. Article 89 reiterated the unkept promise of the *leyes especiales*: "The overseas provinces shall be governed by special laws; but the government is authorized to apply to them, with modifications that it deems suitable, and giving account thereof to the *cortes*, the laws promulgated for the peninsula. Cuba and Puerto Rico shall be represented in the *cortes* of the kingdom in the manner prescribed by a special law, which may be different for each of the two provinces."[104]

Similar to the Royal Statute of 1834 and the Constitutions of 1837, 1845, and 1869, the Constitution of 1876 did not apply to Puerto Rico *ex proprio vigore*. Even the belated extension to Puerto Rico in 1880 of the individual rights found in Title I of the 1876 Constitution came by way of special legislation.[105] This was

---

[100] Compare the language of the 1876 and 1869 Preambles, at https://app.congreso.es/consti/otras/historicas/index.htm (last visited May 12, 2022).

[101] *See* Article 20 at https://www.congreso.es/constitucion/ficheros/historicas/cons_1876.pdf (last visited May 8, 2022).

[102] Universal male suffrage in Spain would be re-established in 1890 through special legislation.

[103] *See* Article 14, at https://www.congreso.es/constitucion/ficheros/historicas/cons_1876.pdf (last visited May 8, 2022).

[104] For the English translation of Article 89, *see* Arnold Verduin, *Manual of Spanish Constitutions 1808–1931*, at 84.

[105] The Spanish Council of Ministers declared the extension to Puerto Rico of Title I of the 1876 Constitution on January 16, 1880. Lidio Cruz Monclova, *Historia de Puerto Rico*, vol. 2 (part 2), 553.

20 ■ THE CONSTITUTIONAL HISTORY OF PUERTO RICO

mostly a symbolic gesture because, in the absence of specific enabling legislation, none of these rights was fully enforceable in the island. The period beginning in 1876 witnessed the piecemeal extension to Puerto Rico of the Spanish Civil Code of 1888,[106] the Spanish Code of Commerce of 1885,[107] the Spanish Criminal Code of 1870,[108] the Spanish Law of Civil Procedure of 1855,[109] and the Spanish Law of Criminal Procedure of 1872.[110] At the same time, the essence of Spain's colonial project in Puerto Rico and Cuba was left intact, setting the stage for a rather anticlimactic denouement.

■ CONSTITUTIONAL DEVELOPMENTS 1877–1897

The next two decades turned out to be decisive for Puerto Rico's constitutional development. Not only had the political situation on the island evolved, a series of new global imperatives soon began to have an impact on the insular landscape, setting the stage for a debate that would consume Puerto Rico's emerging political class for the remainder of the nineteenth century.

The 1880s, more specifically, saw the emergence of a politically vibrant autonomist movement under the charismatic leadership of Román Baldorioty de Castro.[111] Before this period, open and vigorous political debate was virtually nonexistent due, in no small measure, to the systemic repression of the Spanish colonial apparatus. Interestingly, the eruption of the autonomist debate on the island did not come through special legislation but rather as a result of an obscure decision rendered in December 1883 by the Spanish Supreme Court.[112] In construing more

---

[106] See Royal Decree of July 31, 1889.

[107] See Royal Decree of January 28, 1886.

[108] See Royal Decree of May 23, 1879.

[109] See Royal Decree of September 25, 1885. Note that Spain's Law of Civil Procedure had been amended in 1881, prior to its extension to Puerto Rico.

[110] See Royal Decree of October 19, 1888. Note that Spain's Law of Criminal Procedure had been amended in 1879, 1882, and 1888 prior to its extension to Puerto Rico.

[111] Note that Román Baldorioty de Castro represented Puerto Rico in the Spanish Cortes in 1870–1871. His tenure coincided with the provisional government of General Francisco Serrano y Domínguez and, more importantly, with the transition leading to the coronation of King Amadeo I. While in Madrid, Baldorioty pressed for the unconditional abolition of slavery in Puerto Rico and the devolution to the island of administrative authority. Of significance is the fact that Baldorioty was among the nineteen deputies who on November 16, 1870, abstained from voting in favor of the election of Amadeo de Saboya as king of Spain. See, e.g., Lidio Cruz Monclova, Historia de Puerto Rico, vol. 2 (part 1), 151. Following the reappointment of the despotic José Laureano Sanz as governor in January 1874, in the aftermath of the Spanish Republic's implosion, Baldorioty (in an act of self-preservation) chose to exile himself to the Dominican Republic. Shortly after his return to Puerto Rico in 1878, Baldorioty resumed his political activities, this time from the southern city of Ponce, as publisher of La crónica from where he infused intellectual vigor to the then erratic autonomist movement.

[112] This case originated in Cuba in February 1882 and revolved around the criminal conviction of Pablo Yustiz Luzardo under Articles 169 and 170 of the Spanish Criminal Code for shouting "viva la

expansively the scope of Articles 169 and 170 of the Spanish Criminal Code, as applied to Cuba and Puerto Rico, the Spanish high court found that the mere mention or discussion of autonomist ideas, in the absence of a clear intent to overthrow the king, the regency, or the *cortes* by the use of force, was not illegal and consequently could not be censured.[113]

It was precisely against this background that Baldorioty de Castro in 1886 published the island's first autonomist manifesto, entitled *El Plan de Ponce*,[114] and, subsequently, in 1887 founded Puerto Rico's first authentic political party, namely, the *Partido Autonomista Puertorriqueño*.[115] The ideological underpinnings of Baldorioty's autonomist project are found in the dominion status relationship that the British Crown inaugurated with Canada in 1867 pursuant to the British North America Act,[116] and the Irish Home Rule Bill introduced in 1886 by British Prime Minister William Gladstone in the House of Commons.[117]

Baldorioty, contrary to some of the island's more prominent liberal voices,[118] believed Madrid should endow Puerto Rico with far-reaching political (as opposed to mere administrative) autonomy, which meant full legislative authority

---

autonomía!" at a public event presided by Cuba's Spanish military governor. The *Audiencia* in Puerto Príncipe (Cuba) sustained the defendant's conviction. The Spanish Supreme Court annulled the lower court's conviction on December 24, 1883. *See Colección Legislativa de España Sentencias del Tribunal Supremo en materia criminal: Salas segunda y tercera (segundo semestre de 1883)* (Madrid: Imprenta del Ministerio de Gracia y Justicia, 1884), 977–980.

[113] Ibid., 978–979.

[114] Published on November 14, 1886, *el Plan de Ponce* argued for the devolution to Puerto Rico of administrative autonomy in areas of seminal significance, particularly in the realm of tax, commercial, fiscal, agricultural, and educational policies, but always within a relationship of union with Spain. The Ponce Manifesto, moreover, forcefully advocated for the incorporation to the Puerto Rican landscape, on a self-executing basis, of the whole panoply of fundamental rights enumerated under Title I of the 1876 Constitution. Curiously, *el Plan de Ponce* favored the republic over the monarchy, with respect to Spain's constitutional predicaments. *See, e.g.*, Lidio Cruz Monclova, *Historia de Puerto Rico*, vol. 3 (part 1), 33–36. *See also* José Gautier Dapena, *Baldorioty, Apóstol* (San Juan: Instituto de Cultura Puertorriqueña, 1970), 135–144.

[115] Puerto Rico's Autonomist Party was founded during the proceedings of a historic assembly held in Ponce under the presidency of Román Baldorioty de Castro on March 7–9, 1887. For the proceedings of the Ponce assembly, *see, e.g.*, Lidio Cruz Monclova, *Historia de Puerto Rico*, vol. 3 (part 1), 49–59; and Pilar Barbosa, *De Baldorioty a Barbosa: Historia del Autonomismo Puertorriqueño 1887–1896* (San Juan: Instituto de Cultura Puertorriqueña, 1957), 107–121.

[116] Constitution Act, 1867, 30 & 31 Vict., c.3, §3 (U.K.), *reprinted in* R.S.C. 1985, app. II, no. 5 (Can.).

[117] For the text of Prime Minister Gladstone's Irish Home Rule Bill, *see What Home Rule Means Now* (Dublin: The Liberal Union of Ireland, 1893), 59–80, *available at* https://archive.org/stream/wha thomerulemean00dubliala#page/60/mode/1up (last visited May 8, 2022).

[118] Manuel Corchado Juarbe, Julián Blanco Sosa, José Julián Acosta, José de Celis Aguilera, and Pedro Gerónimo Goyco, among others.

22 ■ THE CONSTITUTIONAL HISTORY OF PUERTO RICO

over the island's internal governance together with the power to negotiate and ratify treaties with foreign sovereigns.[119] Seduced by the Gladstonian model, Baldorioty advocated for the superimposition to the island of the Anglo-Canadian autonomic construct.[120] Although the British design ran counter to Spain's post-restoration project and was at odds with the centralizing spirit of the 1876 Constitution, a new catalogue of geopolitical imperatives would soon force Spain to plod along the autonomic route.[121]

The roaring explosion of Cuba's second and definitive war of independence on February 24, 1895, under the intellectual and political leadership of José Martí,[122] together with the United States' growing impatience with Spain's failed policies in Cuba,[123] forced Madrid's hand.

On November 25, 1897, less than three months prior to the fateful explosion of the *USS Maine* in Havana's harbor,[124] Queen Regent María Cristina de Habsburgo y Lorena proclaimed an autonomic regime for Cuba and Puerto Rico at the urging of her council of ministers.[125] The belated concession of the 1897 Autonomic Charter should be seen as Spain's last-ditch effort to save what was left of her ancient colonial empire in the Americas.

For Spain, however, the die was cast.

---

[119] Refer, for instance, to Section 132 of the Canadian Constitution.

[120] For some of Baldorioty's writings on the desirability of adopting in Puerto Rico the Canadian model, *see, e.g.*, José Gautier Dapena, *Baldorioty, Apóstol*, 128–129.

[121] The historical record clearly suggests that during the 1890s the Spanish Council of Ministers considered extending to Puerto Rico and Cuba a rather limited version of autonomy only with respect to administrative matters. The 1893 bill authored by then Colonial Minister Antonio Maura stands as the most progressive of such attempts. It died a quiet death at the *cortes*, precipitating Maura's own resignation in 1894. Subsequently, on March 15, 1895, special legislation was enacted granting Cuba and Puerto Rico only a limited catalogue of reforms. By then, with Cuba's Second War of Independence in full throttle, the so-called *ley de bases* and its accompanying enabling legislation became moot. For a detailed account of the meetings held during this period in Madrid between Puerto Rico's autonomist leadership and Spain's most prominent political actors, *see, e.g.*, Pilar Barbosa de Rosario, *Historia del Pacto Sagastino a través de un epistolario inédito* (Río Piedras: Editorial de la Universidad de Puerto Rico, 1981).

[122] For an in-depth look at José Martí's political project, *see* his *Manifiesto de Montecristi* dated March 25, 1895, which he co-signed with General Máximo Gómez, available in Raimundo Lazo (ed.), *José Martí: Sus Mejores Páginas* (México: Editorial Porrúa, S.A., 1992), 67–72.

[123] The archival record shows that the recently inaugurated McKinley administration was exerting pressure by diplomatic channels on Madrid to ease its grip on Cuba. *See, e.g.*, the dispatch authored by U.S. Secretary of State John Sherman and addressed to Stewart Woodford (U.S. Ambassador in Madrid), dated July 16, 1897, in the Foreign Relations of the United States (hereafter FRUS), *available at* https://history.state.gov/historicaldocuments/frus1898/d490 (last visited May 8, 2022).

[124] February 15, 1898.

[125] Note that following the untimely death of King Alfonso XII on November 25, 1885, the dowager queen became queen regent, acting on behalf of her infant son Alfonso XIII (posthumous son of Alfonso XII) from 1886 until 1902.

THE AUTONOMIC CHARTER OF 1897

Undoubtedly the most advanced politico-constitutional instrument ever promulgated in Puerto Rico, the Autonomic Charter of 1897, enacted by royal decree on November 25 of the same year, was the offspring of a very unusual set of geopolitical catalysts. Pinned against the wall by a costly and unwinnable war of liberation in Cuba and besieged by the pressing demands of the hemisphere's rising superpower,[126] the Spanish Council of Ministers (behind the back of the *cortes*)[127] extrapolated to its two remaining colonies in the Americas a modality of autonomy premised on the British dominion status.[128]

Structurally, the 1897 Autonomic Charter mirrored not only the autonomy model then in full force and effect in Canada but, equally important, bore an evident resemblance to the conceptions of autonomy subsequently embraced by the Netherlands, Denmark, and Finland with respect to their far-flung colonial possessions in the Caribbean, the North Atlantic, and the Baltic Sea.[129]

Substantively, the 1897 Charter signaled a complete break from the previous four hundred years of Spanish domination. Feudal colonial rule, buttressed by an ancient corpus of legal norms dating back to the Middle Ages, gave way to a system of full internal self-government.

While remaining a constitutive unit of the Spanish Kingdom,[130] Puerto Rico was soon granted an unprecedented radius of political authority. The island, more specifically, was now endowed with far-reaching legislative powers over all internal matters not explicitly and specifically reserved to the *cortes* in Madrid.

---

[126] Of special interest is President William McKinley's State of the Union Address, dated December 6, 1897, where he devoted considerable attention to Spain's concession of the Autonomic Charter to Cuba and Puerto Rico. Available at https://millercenter.org/the-presidency/presidential-speeches/december-6-1897-first-annual-message (last visited May 8, 2022).

[127] The historical record shows the 1897 Charter was hastily approved by the Spanish Council of Ministers, and signed by Queen María Cristina, while the *cortes* were not in session. By the time the *cortes* reconvened in May 1898, they passed an indemnity bill retroactively ratifying the actions undertaken by the council—not without considerable opposition. See the debates taking place in the Congress of the Deputies on May 11, 1898. *Diario de las Sesiones de Cortes*, Congreso de los Diputados, vol. II, at 458 *et seq.*

[128] For Britain's use of the dominion model in the Anglophone Caribbean, refer to Rafael Cox Alomar, *Revisiting the Transatlantic Triangle: The Constitutional Decolonization of the Eastern Caribbean* (Miami: Ian Randle Press, 2009), 184–208.

[129] For a comparative analysis of the various European modalities of autonomy, *see* Rafael Cox Alomar, *The Ideological Decolonization of Puerto Rico's Autonomist Movement*, in *Reconsidering the Insular Cases: The Past and Future of the American Empire* (Gerald L. Neuman and Tomiko Brown-Nagin eds.) (Cambridge: Harvard University Press, 2015), 129–166.

[130] Refer to the Autonomic Charter's Preamble, available in the *Gaceta de Madrid*, dated November 27, 1897, available at https://www.boe.es/datos/pdfs/BOE//1897/331/A00639-00643.pdf (last visited May 8, 2022).

24 ■ THE CONSTITUTIONAL HISTORY OF PUERTO RICO

Article 32 of the charter vested in a local bicameral legislature power to regulate all internal matters not explicitly delegated to the Spanish authorities in the peninsula.[131] Rather than leaving an inordinate quantum of residual legislative power in the hands of the Spanish Council of Ministers and the *cortes* in Madrid, the charter specifically enumerated those areas where Spain would still exercise jurisdiction. Contrary to the wording of the U.S. Constitution's Tenth Amendment and Section 9 of the 1950 Puerto Rican Federal Relations Act (henceforth 1950 Federal Relations Act),[132] those policy areas under the aegis of the Puerto Rican legislative chambers were now identified with precision. Pursuant to Article 32 of the charter, the members of the newly minted house of representatives and council of administration would now be in control of the island's fiscal, monetary, and commercial policies.

Perhaps the most significant aspect of the charter was its bilateral nature. The 1897 text, contrary to the pathological compact allegedly found in U.S. Public Law 600 of 1950 and U.S. Public Law 447 of 1952,[133] provided for a mutual consent arrangement. Additional Article 2, at least theoretically, leaves little room for equivocation: "*Una vez aprobada por las cortes del Reino la presente Constitución para las Islas de Cuba y Puerto Rico, no podrá modificarse sino en virtud de una ley y a petición del Parlamento insular.*"[134]

Nonetheless, the charter's mutual consent clause left uncovered a plethora of highly significant matters. Control over the judiciary was explicitly left in the hands of Madrid,[135] and thus outside the scope of the charter's mutual consent requirement. Moreover, determining the scope of those civil rights found in Title I of the 1876 Spanish Constitution, now applicable to the island by virtue of special legislation, was also left to the unilateral control of Madrid; this included issues of nationality and citizenship. Interestingly, all matters pertaining to the applicable electoral law and, equally important, all determinations regarding Puerto Rico's representation in the chamber of deputies and the senate, would lie in the hands of Spain.[136]

---

[131] The island's legislative power would now be vested in a fully elected house of representatives and a council of administration made up of fifteen members, eight elected by the Puerto Rican electorate and seven appointed by the queen regent. *See* Articles 4 and 5 of the 1897 Charter.

[132] *See* 48 U.S.C. § 731. For a comparative analysis of the language found in Article 32 of the 1897 Charter vis-à-vis the textual structure of the Tenth Amendment and Section 9 of the 1950 Federal Relations Act, *see, e.g.*, José Julián Álvarez González, "El viejo pacto: El elemento de bilateralidad en la Carta Autonómica de 1897," *Revista Jurídica de la Universidad de Puerto Rico* 67 (1998): 985, 986.

[133] 48 U.S.C. § 731 et seq.

[134] "Once approved by the *cortes* of the Spanish Kingdom the present constitution for Cuba and Puerto Rico shall not be amended except pursuant to a law by petition of the insular parliament." (Author's translation).

[135] *See* Article 34 of the 1897 Charter.

[136] During this period, Puerto Rico possessed sixteen seats in the Spanish Chamber of Deputies and three seats in the Spanish Senate. *See* José Trías Monge, *Historia Constitucional de Puerto Rico*, vol. 1, at 129–130.

However, Article 37 of the charter, contrary to all succeeding politico-constitutional arrangements under the sovereignty of the United States, empowered Puerto Rico's insular authorities to actively participate (together with the Spanish Council of Ministers) in the negotiation of the commercial treaties entered into by Spain with other sovereigns that could somehow affect the interests of the island. In so doing, Article 38 also provided that, if absent from those negotiations, Puerto Rico could very well choose to leave any such commercial treaty without effect if detrimental to its interests.[137] Similarly, Article 39 of the 1897 Charter granted Puerto Rico authority to set its own tariff system, while establishing a dispute resolution mechanism to settle with Madrid disagreements arising out of Puerto Rico's exercise of its tariff authority.[138]

The 1897 Charter, however, left significant power in the hands of the now-styled governor general, the remaining embodiment of the Spanish Crown in the island. Under Article 15 of the charter, the governor general was granted authority to open, suspend, or dissolve the local legislative chambers. Under Articles 30, 42, and 43 the governor general enjoyed wide discretion to leave without effect legislation enacted by the insular legislature that could somehow be incompatible with the best interests of the Spanish Kingdom. In the event of an insurmountable jurisdictional impasse between the governor general and the autonomic parliament, Article 31 of the charter opened the door to the Spanish judiciary for the resolution of any such interjurisdictional dispute.

The United States' invasion of Puerto Rico on July 25, 1898, a week after the inaugural session of the autonomic house of representatives held on July 17, 1898,[139] put an untimely end to the most significant (yet untried) experiment in self-government ever enjoyed by Puerto Rico.

■ THE 1898 SPANISH AMERICAN WAR AND THE TREATY OF PARIS

The so-called Spanish American War, dubbed a "splendid little war" by U.S. Secretary of State John Hay,[140] marked the coming of age of the United States as an imperial power in its own right. Imbued in the expansionist ideas of Alfred T. Mahan and William Randolph Hearst at a time when London, Paris, Berlin, Brussels, Lisbon, Moscow, and Tokyo were scrambling for Africa and Asia, the McKinley administration brought Manifest Destiny full circle.

---

[137] Note that Articles 25, 26, and 28 of the Charter for the Kingdom of the Netherlands contained similar provisions.

[138] *See* Article 40 of the Charter.

[139] Carmelo Delgado Cintrón, *Imperialismo jurídico norteamericano en Puerto Rico (1898–2015)* (San Juan: Publicaciones Gaviota, 2015), 91.

[140] Letter from John Hay to Theodore Roosevelt, dated July 27, 1898. *See* William R. Thayer, *The Life and Letters of John Hay* (Boston and New York: Houghton Mifflin Co., 1915).

26 ■ THE CONSTITUTIONAL HISTORY OF PUERTO RICO

The purported rationale behind Congress's declaration of war against Madrid was liberating Cuba from the oppressive yoke of Spanish colonialism. Yet Washington's geopolitical objectives transcended the cry for a *Cuba libre*. Driving the Spaniards from neighboring Havana,[141] while placing the unborn Cuban Republic under its suzerainty was but the tip of the iceberg. Seizing by military force the remaining colonial outposts of Spain's obsolescent empire in the Caribbean and the Pacific was at the heart of the McKinley administration's geopolitical calculus. Upon the ratification of the Treaty of Paris on April 11, 1899,[142] not only did Spain relinquish "all claim of sovereignty" over Cuba,[143] it ceded Puerto Rico,[144] Guam,[145] and the Philippines[146] to the United States.

The 1898 Treaty of Paris departed from U.S. treaty practice in significant ways.[147] Unlike the 1787 Northwest Ordinance,[148] the 1803 Louisiana Purchase Treaty,[149] the 1819 Adams Onís Treaty,[150] the 1846 Oregon Treaty,[151] the 1848 Guadalupe Hidalgo Treaty,[152] and the 1867 Alaska Cession Treaty,[153] the 1898 Treaty of Paris did not make a promise of statehood to Puerto Rico, or extend American citizenship to its people. Instead, Article 9 of the Treaty of Paris vested in Congress plenary power to unilaterally determine the civil rights and political status of the people of Puerto Rico.

A tortuous uncharted path, full of turns and twists, now lay ahead for Puerto Rico.

---

[141] The idea of seizing Cuba was not foreign to the founding generation. Refer, for instance, to Benjamin Franklin's letter to his son William Franklin, dated August 28, 1767. William T. Franklin, *Memoirs of the Life and Writings of Benjamin Franklin* (Quarto Edition: London, 1817), 143–144.

[142] 30 Stat. 1754 (1898). Signed on December 10, 1898, in Paris, the treaty's ratification in the federal Senate faced intense opposition. But for Vice President Hobart's casting his tie-breaker vote, the treaty would have been rejected.

[143] Article I of the Paris Treaty.

[144] Article II of the Paris Treaty.

[145] Article II of the Paris Treaty.

[146] Article III of the Paris Treaty.

[147] For the diplomatic correspondence between the McKinley administration and the Spanish Council of Ministers led by the Práxedes Mateo Sagasta, *see* Alfonso García Martínez (ed.), *El libro rojo: Tratado de París Documentos presentados a las cortes en la legislatura de 1898 por el Ministro de Estado* (Río Piedras: Editorial de la Universidad de Puerto Rico, 1988).

[148] An Act to Provide for the Government of the Territory of the United States North-West of the River Ohio, ch. 8, 1 Stat. 50 (1789).

[149] Louisiana Purchase Agreement, U.S.-Fr., Apr. 30, 1803, 8 Stat. 200.

[150] Treaty of Amity, Settlement, and Limits between the United States of America and His Catholic Majesty, U.S.-Spain, Feb. 22, 1819, 8 Stat. 252.

[151] Treaty Establishing the Boundary in the Territory on the Northwest Coast of America Lying Westward of the Rocky Mountains, U.S.-Gr. Brit., June 15, 1846, 9 Stat. 869.

[152] 120 Treaty of Peace, Friendship, Limits, and Settlement with the Republic of Mexico, U.S.-Mex., Feb. 2, 1848, 9 Stat. 922.

[153] Convention Ceding Alaska, U.S.-Russ., Mar. 30, 1867, 15 Stat. 539.

■ U.S. MILITARY RULE 1898–1900

From the time the Massachusetts and Illinois 6th Regiments disembarked in Guánica on July 25, 1898,[154] until the entry into full force and effect of the Foraker Act on May 1, 1900, the U.S. War Department placed Puerto Rico under military rule.[155] Besides witnessing the swift succession of three different military governors,[156] this brief, yet tumultuous,[157] period forever changed Puerto Rico's political and legal topography, establishing the basis of the island's institutional repertoire well into the twentieth century.

The legal foundations of the military government did not go unchallenged.[158] The archival record shows that President William McKinley, in his role as commander in chief, did not issue explicit military directives to the commanders on the ground. At no point did the president establish the proper legal scope of the military's authority over the island's civil affairs.[159] In the absence of a discernible legal framework, General Nelson Miles and his lieutenants extrapolated to the island the general orders the U.S. War Department had made applicable to Cuba through the auspices of General Leonard Wood.[160]

Congress's silence, moreover, compounded even further the legal uncertainty surrounding some of the more arbitrary commands issued by the island's military governors who, more often than not, acted ultra vires. Not only did the U.S. military command in Puerto Rico abrogate, on a whim, the 1897

---

[154] Fernando Picó, *1898: La guerra después de la guerra*, 57.

[155] For a detailed narrative of the military period from the vantage point of the metropolis, *see, e.g.*, Report of the Military Governor of Porto Rico on Civil Affairs (Washington, D.C.: Government Printing Office, 1902), 18–30.

[156] General John Brooke (August 14 through December 9, 1898), General Guy Henry (December 9, 1898 through May 9, 1899), and General George Davis (May 9, 1899 through May 1, 1900). Note that General Brooke changed the official name of the island to Porto Rico. It was not until May 17, 1932, that Congress reversed course, reinstating the island's name to Puerto Rico. See 47 Stat. 158 (1932).

[157] For a penetrating account on U.S. military justice in the island *circa* 1899, *see* Arcadio Díaz Quiñones, *Once tesis sobre un crimen de 1899* (San Juan: Luscinia, 2019).

[158] Refer, for instance, to *Santiago v. Nogueras*, 214 U.S. 260 (1909) (finding that the military governor enjoyed authority to establish the U.S. provisional court).

[159] Note that pursuant to the precedent set by the Act of Congress of October 31, 1803, conferring on President Thomas Jefferson carte blanche in administering the Louisiana Territory, President McKinley's authority in the Spanish former colonies appeared absolute in the absence of congressional action. Simeon E. Baldwin, "Constitutional Questions Incident to the Acquisition and Government by the United States of Island Territory," *Harvard Law Review* 12 (1898–1899): 393; Abbott Lawrence Lowell, "Status of Our New Possessions a Third View," *Harvard Law Review* 13 (1899–1900): 155.

[160] José Trías Monge, *El choque de dos culturas jurídicas en Puerto Rico* (Orford NH: Equity Publishing Company, 1991), 68. For a well-documented analysis, *see also* Carmelo Delgado Cintrón, *Imperialismo jurídico norteamericano en Puerto Rico (1898–2015)*, 127–130. For the examination of the Cuban context, *see* Rafael Cox Alomar, "Cuba's Constitutional Moment," *Texas Hispanic Journal of Law & Policy* 23 (Spring 2017): 1.

28 ■ THE CONSTITUTIONAL HISTORY OF PUERTO RICO

Autonomic Charter along with the island's high court and local parliament before the signing of the peace treaty in Paris,[161] it also unilaterally eviscerated the island's fiscal infrastructure, imposing an onerous tariff and currency exchange regimes.[162] Along similar lines, the incipient corpus of fundamental rights, then belatedly flourishing in the island, was severely restricted. Universal male suffrage was once again abolished,[163] while the expressive freedoms of the people of Puerto Rico were abruptly put on hold.

Puerto Rico had returned to the dark ages. The Hapsburgs and the Bourbons were gone, but the ghost of military absolutism lived on.

■ THE 1900 FORAKER ACT

Modeled on the crown colony construct found in Britain's 1865 Colonial Laws Validity Act,[164] the Foraker Act, signed by President McKinley on April 12, 1900,[165] was the antithesis of the Spanish Autonomic Charter. While this first organic act bound the erstwhile Spanish colony to the federal Union through a common market, a common customs area,[166] and a common currency, it nonetheless exempted Puerto Rico from the heavy burdens flowing from the federal Constitution's Tax Uniformity Clause,[167] thus granting the island fiscal autonomy.

The Foraker Act set the foundations of Puerto Rico's fiscal architecture— an architecture that survives to this day. A close perusal of Puerto Rico's first organic act reveals that Congress merely replaced military absolutism with civilian authoritarianism—keeping the island bound by the asphyxiating grip of the U.S. War Department in Washington, D.C. A civilian governor, appointed by the president with the advice and consent of the U.S. Senate, now controlled the executive branch.[168] Like the governor, the principal officers of the territorial government—the secretary, attorney general, treasurer, auditor, and commissioners of interior and education—were also presidential appointees subject to the advice and consent of the U.S. Senate.[169]

---

[161] U.S. War Department, *General Orders and Circulars* 1898–1900 (Washington, D.C.: Government Printing Office, 1900).

[162] The new customs tariff became fully effective on August 15, 1898. Report of the Military Governor of Porto Rico on Civil Affairs (Washington, D.C.: Government Printing Office, 1902), 22.

[163] Refer to General Order 160, U.S. War Department, *General Orders and Circulars* 1898–1900 (Washington, D.C.: Government Printing Office, 1900).

[164] British Colonial Laws Validity Act 1865, 28 & 29 Vict. c 63.

[165] Note that the Foraker Act, while signed on April 12, 1900, became fully effective on May 1, 1900.

[166] Pursuant to Section 3 of the Foraker Act, the customs union did not become immediately effective. It only became operative after the island's new civil authorities put in place a local tax regime.

[167] U.S. Const., Art. I, § 8, Cl. 1.

[168] *See* Section 17.

[169] *See* Section 18.

Mimicking the legislative council then found in most British crown colonies in the Caribbean, the Foraker Act established an executive council made up of the heads of the six executive departments and five "native inhabitants" of Puerto Rico.[170] The executive council, together with a thirty-five member fully elected house of delegates, made up the island's legislature.[171] Neutralized by an executive council controlled by the federal bureaucracy, the radius of action of the house of delegates was severely limited. The Foraker Act further exacerbated the house of delegates' structural weakness by explicitly reserving to Congress the power to annul all laws enacted by the territorial legislature.[172] The election of a resident commissioner,[173] as required by the Foraker Act, did not cure the organic act's fatal flaws.

The Foraker Act, furthermore, left intact the judicial infrastructure put in place by the military governors.[174] The act reauthorized both the Puerto Rico Supreme Court and the U.S. Provisional Court (now styled U.S. District Court),[175] originally established by military general orders. At the same time, the first organic act did not provide for a local bill of rights; nor did it extend to the people of Puerto Rico the constitutional protections available under the federal Bill of Rights.[176]

Unlike the 1900 Hawaiian Organic Act,[177] moreover, the Foraker Act did not confer on Puerto Ricans American citizenship. On the contrary, Puerto Rico's first organic act established that the inhabitants of the island were now citizens of Puerto Rico, "entitled to the protection of the United States."[178] With the Foraker Act, Congress made no promise of statehood to Puerto Rico; nor did it declare the island an organized territory to be groomed for statehood.

In silencing the plight of the people of Puerto Rico for "home rule,"[179] the Foraker Act sowed the seeds of discord and distrust between the island's political leadership and Congress.

---

[170] *See* Section 18.

[171] *See* Section 27.

[172] *See* Section 31.

[173] *See* Section 39.

[174] *See* Section 33.

[175] *See* Section 34.

[176] For the extension to Puerto Rico of the federal due process and equal protection rights, *see* discussion under Article II's Section 7.

[177] 31 Stat. 141 (1900).

[178] *See* Section 7. Also *see González v. Williams*, 192 U.S. 1 (1904) (holding that Puerto Ricans were not aliens for purposes of the applicable federal immigration legislation and, thus, enjoyed free access to the mainland).

[179] Refer to letter from Luis Muñoz Rivera to José de Diego, July 25, 1913, in Muñoz Rivera, *Campañas Políticas*, vol. 3 (Madrid: Editorial Puerto Rico, 1925), 155.

THE U.S. SUPREME COURT AND THE INSULAR CASES 1901

The annexation of Puerto Rico, the Philippines, and Guam, along with the temporary military occupation of Cuba, raised complex constitutional questions of first impression that had remained unanswered since the founding of the American Republic. By the time General Nelson Miles landed in Guánica on July 25, 1898, it was well settled that Congress, in the words of Chief Justice John Marshall, "possessed the power of acquiring territory either by conquest or by treaty."[180] Yet President McKinley's amputation, and subsequent absorption, of Spain's dwindling Caribbean and Southeast Asian empires brought to the fore a host of hitherto unexplored constitutional issues.[181] Could Congress hold Puerto Rico, the Philippines, and Guam in a permanent state of "colonial dependence"?[182] Did the U.S. Constitution place any limits to Congress's power over the territories? Did the federal constitutional text require that the territories acquired in the aftermath of the Spanish-American War stand on an equal footing with those territories annexed prior to 1898? Which constitutional provisions, if any, were now applicable to Spain's former possessions? Did the U.S. Constitution *always* follow the American flag?

The momentous task of solving this constitutional conundrum fell to the Fuller Court.

An erratic and reactionary court[183] made up (for the most part) of justices appointed by Presidents Rutherford Hays, Chester Alan Arthur, Grover Cleveland, Benjamin Harrison, and William McKinley, the Fuller Court (over the lone

---

[180] *American Insurance Co. v. Canter*, 26 U.S. 511, 542 (1828). For a fuller understanding of Chief Justice Marshall's thinking, *see Loughborough v. Blake*, 18 U.S. 317, 319 (1820) ("[. . .] United States [. . .] is the name given to our great republic, which is composed of States and territories."). *See also Serè v. Pitot*, 6 Cranch 332, 336 (1810) ("The power of governing and of legislating for a territory is the inevitable consequence of the right to acquire and to hold territory.") Chief Justice Roger Taney, however, embraced the contrarian view in the infamous *Dred Scott Case*, 60 U.S. 393, 446 (1856) ("There is certainly no power given by the Constitution to the Federal Government to establish or maintain colonies bordering on the United States or at a distance, to be ruled and governed at its own pleasure; nor to enlarge its territorial limits in any way, except by the admission of new States.").

[181] For the fierce debate that soon raged in the pages of the *Harvard Law Review, see, e.g.,* Carman F. Randolph, "Constitutional Aspects of Annexation," *Harvard Law Review* 12 (1898–1899): 291; Christopher Columbus Langdell, "Status of Our New Territories," *Harvard Law Review* 12 (1898-1899): 365; Simeon E. Baldwin, "Constitutional Questions Incident to the Acquisition and Government by the United States of Island Territory," *Harvard Law Review* 12 (1898–1899): 393; Abbott Lawrence Lowell, "Status of Our New Possessions a Third View," *Harvard Law Review* 13 (1899–1900): 155.

[182] Baldwin, *supra*, at 412.

[183] Not only did the Fuller Court open the door to Lochnerism in *Allgeyer v. Louisiana*, 165 U.S. 578 (1897), but it also eviscerated Congress's power under the Commerce Clause to regulate trusts in *United States v. E.C. Knight*, 156 U.S. 1 (1895). One of its most senior members, Justice Horace Grey, had concurred with the majority in the *Civil Rights Cases*, 109 U.S. 3 (1883), and, a year later, had authored

dissent of Justice John Harlan) had by then concocted the "separate but equal" doctrine announced in *Plessy v. Ferguson*.[184] It is not at all unreasonable to suggest that the outcome of the Insular Cases was shaped by the Fuller Court's ethnocentric and racist proclivities.[185] The Insular Cases, more often than not excluded by the American legal academy from the canon of U.S. constitutional law, stand on a par with *Dred Scott*, the *Civil Rights Cases*, *Plessy*, and *Korematsu*.[186]

The Insular Cases rubric, at its most expansive, refers to twenty-three decisions handed down by the U.S. Supreme Court between 1901 and 1922.[187] By far, the most influential of the Insular Cases was *Downes v. Bidwell*,[188] in which the court held, in a 5–4 decision,[189] that Puerto Rico even after the enactment of the 1900 Foraker was still not "part" of the United States for purposes of the federal Constitution's Tax Uniformity Clause. Because, in the words of the same Justice Henry Brown who had written *Plessy*, Puerto Rico was "a territory appurtenant and belonging to the United States, but not a part of the United States within the revenue clauses of the Constitution,"[190] Congress was free from the encumbrances of the Tax Uniformity Clause in levying tariffs on Puerto Rican imports.

Writing for a balkanized court,[191] Justice Brown argued that the "United States," as a political concept, only comprised the states and not the territories.[192] According to Brown, the Constitution only placed limitations on the power

---

the court's opinion in *Elk v. Wilkins*, 112 U.S. 94 (1884), finding that Native Americans were not natural born citizens under the Fourteenth Amendment.

[184] 163 U.S. 537 (1896).

[185] Refer to Justice Brown's references to the inhabitants of Puerto Rico and the Philippines as "alien races" in *Downes v. Bidwell*, 182 U.S. 244, 282, 287 (1901). There is wide consensus among legal historians that the Fuller Court left "an unmatched record of reactionary, bigoted, and rejected precedents [...]." "By all accounts, Fuller's Court 'ranks among the worst' in Supreme Court history." *See* Herbert Hovenkamp, "Owen M. Fiss' Troubled Beginnings of the Modern State, 1888–1910," *Yale Law Journal* 104 (1995): 2309–2310.

[186] 323 U.S. 214 (1944).

[187] *See* Christina Duffy Burnett, *A Note on the* Insular Cases, in *Foreign in a Domestic Sense: Puerto Rico, American Expansion, and the Constitution* (Christina Duffy Burnett & Burke Marshall eds., 2001) (Durham: Duke University Press, 2001), 389, 389–390 (noting "near[] universal consensus that the series" begins with cases decided in 1901 and "culminates with *Balzac v. Porto Rico*" in 1922). For a detailed enumeration of the Insular Cases involving Puerto Rico, *see* Table 6.

[188] 182 U.S. 244 (1901).

[189] Note that Justices Brown, White, McKenna, Shiras, and Grey stood in the majority, whereas Chief Justice Fuller along with Justices Harlan, Peckham, and Brewer were in the minority.

[190] *Downes*, 182 U.S. at 287.

[191] Note that out of the four justices concurring with Justice Brown's conclusion, not one joined his opinion. Justice White's concurrence was joined by Justices Shiras and McKenna, while Justice Grey wrote a separate concurrent opinion.

[192] *Downes*, 182 U.S. at 285–286.

32 ■ THE CONSTITUTIONAL HISTORY OF PUERTO RICO

Congress exercised "within the United States,"[193] and not on Congress's power over the territories. In Brown's view, both with respect to the pre-1898 territories and to their post-1898 counterparts, Congress was not constitutionally required to extend to their inhabitants any of the rights or structural safeguards available under the federal constitutional text.[194] In his opinion for the court, Brown argued that the extension of the federal Bill of Rights to the pre-1898 territories was a mere "liberality"[195] on the part of Congress. Nothing in the Constitution required it. Interestingly, in his opinion Brown also drew, albeit vaguely, the inexact limits of Congress's territorial power: in "legislating for the territories,"[196] Congress was nonetheless "subject to those fundamental limitations in favor of personal rights which are formulated in the Constitution."[197]

In his concurring opinion, Justice Edward White noted that "restrictions of so fundamental a nature that they cannot be transgressed"[198] did limit Congress's plenary power under the Constitution's Territorial Clause. The significance of White's opinion, however, resides in his articulation of the doctrine of territorial incorporation, which is still alive today. In White's view, which soon thereafter became the court's "unquestioned position"[199] on the territorial issue, the pre-1898 territories did not stand on an equal footing with those annexed in 1898. The pre-1898 territories, in light of their respective treaties of annexation,[200] had been "incorporated" into the Union and, hence, were "part" of it. The ratification, for instance, of the 1803 Louisiana Purchase Treaty, the 1819 Adams Onís Treaty, the 1846 Oregon Treaty, the 1848 Guadalupe Hidalgo Treaty, and the 1867 Alaska Cession Treaty had required their "incorporation" into the Union, along with the extension of most constitutional protections, the conferral of American citizenship on their inhabitants, and the chartering of a path to statehood. Thus, in the pre-1898 territories the Constitution had indeed followed the flag. Because the Paris Treaty, different from all previous treaties of annexation, "did not stipulate for incorporation,"[201] leaving the civil and political rights of the people of Puerto Rico, the Philippines, and Guam in the hands of Congress, these were in White's view "unincorporated" territories at the mercy of the political branches in Washington, D.C. As Chief Justice William Taft, two decades later, expounded in *Balzac v. Puerto Rico*,[202] transforming Puerto

---

[193] *Downes*, 182 U.S. at 285.

[194] *Downes*, 182 U.S. at 286.

[195] *Downes*, 182 U.S. at 286.

[196] *Downes*, 182 U.S. at 268.

[197] *Downes*, 182 U.S. at 268.

[198] *Downes*, 182 U.S. at 291.

[199] Efrén Rivera Ramos, *The Legal Construction of Identity: The Judicial and Social Legacy of American Colonialism in Puerto Rico* (Washington, D.C.: American Psychological Association, 2001), 80.

[200] *Downes*, 182 U.S. at 338–339.

[201] *Downes*, 182 U.S. 244, 340 (1901).

[202] 258 U.S. 298 (1922),

Rico from an "unincorporated" to an "incorporated" territory would require "a clear declaration of purpose"[203] of Congress.

Thus, Puerto Rico was to remain indefinitely in purgatory. Colonialism under the American flag had now been fully constitutionalized, "hovering like a dark cloud"[204] over Puerto Rico.

■ THE 1917 JONES ACT

Puerto Rico's second organic statute, sponsored by Democratic Congressman William Jones and signed by President Woodrow Wilson on March 2, 1917,[205] was the byproduct of a circuitous and winding legislative journey that began in the Taft years.[206] The birth of the so-called Jones Act was heavily influenced by Congress's enactment of the second Philippines Organic Act a year earlier.[207] Moreover, President Wilson's new geopolitical concerns in the Caribbean Basin, following the United States' successive military interventions in Mexico (1914), Haiti (1915), the Dominican Republic (1916), and Cuba (1917), together with the impending entry into World War I, cannot be divorced from the calculus leading to the enactment of the Jones Act.

Far from generous, the Jones Act was a reactionary statute only effecting minor administrative modifications to the island's political topography. Under the Jones Act, Puerto Rico remained shackled to the U.S. War Department. By far the most significant aspect of the Jones Act was its conferral of American citizenship on the people of Puerto Rico.[208] American citizenship was now required for voting and for holding any office of public trust.[209]

Contrary to the Foraker Act, and following the blueprint of the 1916 Philippines Organic Act,[210] the Jones Act included a bill of rights,[211] providing for religious and expressive freedoms, due process, equal protection, right to counsel, right to public and speedy trials, protections against unreasonable searches and seizures, double jeopardy, illegal takings and the impairment of contracts, among other safeguards.

Structurally, the Jones Act introduced a series of cosmetic alterations to the island's governmental superstructure. The establishment of a fully elective senate

---

[203] *Balzac v. Puerto Rico*, 258 U.S. 298, 311 (1922).

[204] *Aurelius Investment, LLC v. Commonwealth of Puerto Rico*, 915 F.3d 838, 855 (1st Cir. 2019) (Torruella J.).

[205] 39 Stat. 951 (1917).

[206] For a detailed study of the legislative history leading to the Jones Act, *see* José Cabranes, *Citizenship and the American Empire* (New Haven: Yale University Press, 1979).

[207] 39 Stat. 545 (1916).

[208] *See* Section 5. For a comprehensive discussion on the legal nature of Puerto Ricans' American citizenship, *see* José Julián Álvarez González, "The Empire Strikes Out: Congressional Ruminations on the Citizenship Status of Puerto Ricans," *Harvard Journal on Legislation* 27 (1990): 309.

[209] *See* Sections 10 and 35.

[210] Refer to Section 3 of the 1916 Philippines Organic Act.

[211] *See* Section 2.

made up of fourteen district and five at-large senators[212] was the most innovative feature of the act's governmental redesign. Together with the newly styled house of representatives, successor to the old house of delegates and composed of thirty-five district and four at large representatives, the senate made up Puerto Rico's first fully elective legislature under the American flag.[213] This concession, however, came at a high price.

The Jones Act put an end to the legislature's power to override the governor's vetoes, which had been available under the Foraker Act. Overriding the governor's veto would now require the approval of the president of the United States.[214] Further, the appointed governor would now wield additional powers to offset the elected legislature's newly gained ascendancy. The line-item veto,[215] together with the prohibition of legislative riders[216] and the replacement of annual ordinary sessions with biannual ones,[217] were all measures designed to keep the insular legislature—and, more specifically, the island's political leadership—in check.

The Jones Act left the island's judicial branch, for the most part designed by the military governors, untouched.[218] Similarly, the Foraker Act's fiscal framework was left undisturbed.[219] The island's fiscal autonomy, the debt ceiling formula, the common market, and the customs area, all of which were established under the Foraker Act, remained in full force and effect.

Contrary to what the Puerto Rico Supreme Court intimated in *Muratti v. Foote*,[220] the Jones Act left Puerto Rico in the same constitutional limbo it had inhabited since the invasion led by General Nelson Miles in 1898. The Jones Act did not transform the island into an "incorporated" territory. To the contrary, as Chief Justice Taft found in *Balzac*,[221] Puerto Rico under the Jones Act remained an "unincorporated" territory of the federal Union.

■ THE 1947 ELECTIVE GOVERNOR ACT

After three long decades of empty rhetoric, unmet promises, and congressional paralysis, the constellation of new geopolitical imperatives enveloping

---

[212] *See* Section 26.

[213] *See* Sections 25 and 27.

[214] *See* Section 34.

[215] *See* Section 34.

[216] *See* Section 34.

[217] *See* Section 33. This provision was amended in 1927 to provide for annual ordinary sessions. *See* discussion under Article III's Section 10.

[218] *See* Section 40.

[219] *See* Section 3.

[220] 25 D.P.R. 568, 582–583 (1917).

[221] See discussion on the Insular Cases, in section entitled "The U.S. Supreme Court and the Insular Cases 1901" supra.

the postwar period led the political branches in Washington, D.C., to revisit the Puerto Rican labyrinth. It is no coincidence that President Harry Truman's signing of the Elective Governor Act in 1947[222] came at a time when the British were finally withdrawing from India, Pakistan, and Sri Lanka, as well as preparing to decolonize their Caribbean, African, Middle Eastern, and Asian colonies. By then, the Dutch were also demobilizing their colonial empire in Indonesia, while grooming their Caribbean colonies for greater self-government. It was precisely during this same period, in 1946, that the newly born Fourth French Republic made Martinique and Guadeloupe overseas departments of France. As the Iron Curtain was descending on Eastern Europe, in the Churchillian allegory, the Truman administration (along with a Republican Congress) was in search of a new policy with respect to Puerto Rico.

Rather than replacing in toto the Jones Act, both the U.S. Department of the Interior[223] and the Puerto Rican leadership agreed on the gradual transformation of the Jones Act.[224] Providing for an elective governor, an aspiration that Puerto Rico's leadership had pursued without any success since the Roosevelt years, soon became the first item in the island's transformative agenda.

Unlike the Foraker and Jones Acts, the Elective Governor Act moved through Congress relatively swiftly. Introduced in the U.S. House of Representatives in May 1947, President Truman signed the Elective Governor Act on August 5, 1947. The subsequent election of Luis Muñoz Marín on November 2, 1948, as Puerto Rico's first elected governor, opened the door to the island's next installment of self-government.

■ THE 1950 PUBLIC LAW 600, THE CONSTITUTIONAL CONVENTION, AND THE 1952 CONSTITUTION

On July 3, 1950, President Truman signed U.S. Public Law 600, providing "for the organization of a constitutional government by the people of Puerto Rico."[225] Congress adopted this statute "in the nature of a compact so that the people of Puerto Rico may organize a government pursuant to a constitution of their own adoption."[226] U.S. Public Law 600 was ratified by the people of Puerto Rico in

---

[222] 61 Stat. 770 (1947).

[223] President Franklin D. Roosevelt transferred responsibility over Puerto Rico from the U.S. War Department to the Interior Department in 1934.

[224] Of significance is the fact that the Elective Governor Act established in no uncertain terms that the privileges and immunities enjoyed by the citizens of the United States under Article IV Section 2 of the federal Constitution "shall be respected in Puerto Rico to the same extent as though Puerto Rico were a State of the Union." Both the Foraker and Jones Acts had remained silent with respect to this subject.

[225] Act of July 3, 1950, Pub. L. No. 81-600, 64 Stat. 319 (codified at 48 U.S.C. §§ 731 et seq.).

[226] Act of July 3, 1950, Pub. L. No. 81-600, 64 Stat. 319 (codified at 48 U.S.C. §§ 731 et seq.).

36 ■ THE CONSTITUTIONAL HISTORY OF PUERTO RICO

a referendum held on June 4, 1951, after which delegates to the constitutional convention were selected by the local electorate on August 27, 1951, to draft the constitution.[227] The people of Puerto Rico approved the new constitution in a referendum held on March 3, 1952, and it was subsequently transmitted to Congress for definitive approval.[228] On July 1, 1952, Congress sanctioned the new constitution, but not without first modifying several of its provisions.[229] President Truman's signature of U.S. Public Law 447,[230] on July 3, 1952, cleared the way for Governor Muñoz Marín's inauguration of the constitution on July 25, 1952.

The new internal constitutional framework came to life under the name "Commonwealth," intentionally translated to Spanish as *Estado Libre Asociado*, on July 25, 1952.[231] Meanwhile, the provisions of the Foraker and Jones Acts perpetuating the island's political and economic subordination to the United States continued in full force and effect under a new statutory instrument known as the 1950 Federal Relations Act.[232] Nevertheless, Puerto Rico's governmental authorities, emboldened by the island's removal from the United Nations' list of non-self-governing territories in 1953,[233] characterized the overall political relationship between the people of Puerto Rico and Congress as one premised on a bilateral compact, unalterable unless by mutual consent, following "the precedent established by the Northwest Ordinance."[234]

---

[227] *See* Tables 1, 2, 3, and 4.

[228] The Constitution of Puerto Rico was approved by 80 percent of the voters participating in the referendum. *See* Constitutional Convention, Res. No. 34 of July 10, 1952 (1952) (P.R.) (codified in P.R. Laws Ann. tit. 1, at 144–146).

[229] For the congressional act approving the 1952 Constitution, *see* Pub. L. No. 82-447, 66 Stat. 327 (1952). Congress eliminated Article II's Section 20, which, modeled after the Universal Declaration of Human Rights, elevated free education, work, and adequate living standards, among others, to the rank of constitutional rights. *See* José Trías Monge, *Historia Constitucional de Puerto Rico*, vol. 3, at 270–312. Refer to discussion under Article VII's Section 1.

[230] Refer to discussion under Article IX's Section 10.

[231] *See* Constitutional Convention, Resolution No. 22 of February 4, 1952 (1952) (P.R.). Refer to discussion under Article IX's Section 4.

[232] *See* 48 U.S.C. § 731(b) (2013).

[233] *See* G.A. Res. 748 (VIII), U.N. GAOR, 8th Sess., Supp. No. 17, at 25, U.N. Doc. A/2630 (Nov. 27, 1953). The representations made by the U.S. delegation with respect to Puerto Rico's new constitutional arrangement at the United Nations must be seen in light of the acute imperatives of the Cold War. These geopolitical considerations were not lost on the Puerto Rican leadership. In a letter to Henry Cabot Lodge, Jr., U.S. ambassador to the United Nations, Governor Muñoz Marín made it abundantly clear that "Puerto Rico can be a weapon of some significance in the psychological warfare in which the free world under American leadership is engaged in the defense of human freedom." Luis Muñoz Marín, letter to Henry Cabot Lodge, Jr., May 25, 1953. For a historical account of the process leading to U.N. Resolution 748, *see* Rafael Cox Alomar, *Fernós Isern y la jornada puertorriqueña ante la ONU de 1953*, in *Dr. Antonio Fernós Isern: De médico a constituyente* (Héctor Luis Acevedo (ed.) (San Juan: Editorial de la Universidad Interamericana, 2014), 493–531.

[234] Statement of Resident Commissioner Antonio Fernós Isern, dated May 17, 1950. Hearing before a Subcommittee of the Committee on Interior and Insular Affairs, United States Senate 81st Congress,

In this way, the compact mythology was born,[235] notwithstanding that U.S. Public Law 600 neither modified "the status of the island of Puerto Rico relative to the United States,"[236] nor altered "the powers of sovereignty acquired by the United States over Puerto Rico under the terms of the Treaty of Paris,"[237] as Resident Commissioner Antonio Fernós Isern had clearly forewarned during the congressional hearings that preceded the passing of U.S. Public Law 600.[238] Congress's unilateral authority over Puerto Rico, even after the inauguration of the 1952 Constitution, remained plenary.

■ POLITICO-CONSTITUTIONAL DEVELOPMENTS POST-1952

The compact mythology, however, raised more questions than answers. Had Congress permanently divested itself of its plenary authority over Puerto

---

2nd Session, on S. 3336, A Bill to Provide for the Organization of a Constitutional Government by the People of Puerto Rico, 81st Cong. 4 (1950).

[235] Under the intellectual leadership of Chief Judge Calvert Magruder, the U.S. Court of Appeals for the First Circuit infused the compact mythology with life. In *Mora v. Mejías*, 206 F.2d 377, 387 (1st Cir. 1953), Chief Judge Magruder suggested that the Commonwealth or *Estado Libre Asociado* was now "a political entity created by the act and with the consent of the people of Puerto Rico and joined in union with the United States of America under the terms of the compact." Three years later, in *Figueroa v. People of Puerto Rico*, 232 F.2d 615, 620 (1st Cir. 1956), Magruder concluded that "the constitution of the Commonwealth is not just another Organic Act of the Congress. We find no reason to impute to the Congress the perpetration of such a monumental hoax. U.S. Public Law 600 offered to the people of Puerto Rico a 'compact' [...]." In *First Federal Savings and Loan Association v. Ruiz de Jesús*, 644 F.2d 910, 911 (1st Cir. 1981), Judge Levin Campbell followed Chief Judge Magruder's thesis declaring, in no uncertain terms, that "Puerto Rico's territorial status ended, of course, in 1952." Judge Stephen Breyer arrived at the same conclusion in *Ezratty v. Commonwealth of Puerto Rico*, 648 F.2d 770, 776, n.7 (1st Cir. 1981) ("The principles of the Eleventh Amendment ... are fully applicable to the Commonwealth of Puerto Rico."). Similarly, in *Córdova & Simonpietri Insurance Agency v. Chase Manhattan Bank*, 649 F. 2d 36, 41 (1st Cir. 1981), Breyer found that "Puerto Rico's status changed from that of a mere territory to the unique status of Commonwealth." In *U.S. v. López Andino*, 831 F.2d 1164, 1168 (1st Cir. 1987), Judge Hugh Bownes held that "Puerto Rico is to be treated as a state for purposes of the Double Jeopardy Clause." Despite this history, the First Circuit's compact mythology has died a public and rather unceremonious death at the hands of Congress and the U.S. Supreme Court.

[236] Hearing before a Subcommittee of the Committee on Interior and Insular Affairs, United States Senate 81st Congress, 2nd Session, on S. 3336, A Bill to Provide for the Organization of a Constitutional Government by the People of Puerto Rico, 81st Cong. 4 (1950).

[237] Hearing before a Subcommittee of the Committee on Interior and Insular Affairs, United States Senate 81st Congress, 2nd Session, on S. 3336, A Bill to Provide for the Organization of a Constitutional Government by the People of Puerto Rico, 81st Cong. 4 (1950).

[238] The federal House's report on U.S. Public Law 600, consistent with the resident commissioner's proposition, stated that "[i]t is important that the nature and general scope of S. 3336 be made absolutely clear. The bill under consideration would not change Puerto Rico's fundamental political, social and economic relationship to the United States." H.R. Rep. No. 81-2275 (1950).

38 ■ THE CONSTITUTIONAL HISTORY OF PUERTO RICO

Rico under the Territorial Clause?[239] Was Congress now unable to unilaterally modify the newly established Puerto Rico Constitution? Was the Puerto Rico Constitution simply another organic act of Congress? What was the proper scope of Congress's power with respect to Puerto Rico in the post-1952 context? Did Puerto Rico remain an unincorporated territory and, therefore, a colony even after 1952?

The U.S. Supreme Court had seldom addressed the Puerto Rican status question after the Insular Cases. On the few occasions that the federal high court had referred to it, the justices approached the issue mostly through dicta. For instance, in *Rodríguez v. Popular Democratic Party*,[240] Chief Justice Warren Burger observed that "Puerto Rico, like a state, is an autonomous political entity, sovereign over matters not ruled by the Constitution."[241] In *Examining Board of Engineers, Architects and Surveyors v. Flores de Otero*,[242] Justice Harry Blackmun noted that "Congress relinquished its control over the organization of the local affairs of the island and granted Puerto Rico a measure of autonomy comparable to that possessed by the States."[243] In *Calero-Toledo v. Pearson Yacht Leasing Co.*,[244] Justice William Brennan, writing for the court, suggested that "Puerto Rico is a political entity created by the act and with the consent of the people of Puerto Rico and joined in union with the United States of America under the terms of the compact."[245]

None of these dicta, however, altered the Supreme Court's decision in *Harris v. Rosario*,[246] in which the federal high court held that Congress, empowered under the Territorial Clause of the Constitution to "make all needful Rules and Regulations respecting the Territory . . . belonging to the United States,"[247] may treat Puerto Rico differently from the states so long as there is a rational basis for its actions.[248] The *Harris* decision, arguably, was a regurgitation of the court's holding in *Califano v. Torres*, where it held that treating Puerto Rico differently from the several states was rationally grounded.[249] Although the *Harris* and

---

[239] U.S. Const. Art. IV, § 3, Cl. 2.

[240] 457 U.S. 1 (1982).

[241] *Rodríguez v. Popular Democratic Party*, 457 U.S. 1, 8 (1982) (holding that the voting rights of Puerto Ricans are constitutionally protected to the same extent as those of all other citizens of the United States).

[242] 426 U.S. 572 (1976).

[243] *Examining Bd. of Engineers, Architects & Surveyors v. Flores de Otero*, 426 U.S. 572, 597 (1976) (holding that Puerto Rico is a state rather than a territory for purposes of Section 1983 jurisdiction).

[244] 416 U.S. 663 (1974).

[245] *Calero-Toledo v. Pearson Yacht Leasing Co.*, 416 U.S. 663, 672 (1974) (holding that the statutes of Puerto Rico are state statutes for purposes of the Three Judge Court Act (28 U.S.C. § 2281)).

[246] 446 U.S. 651 (1980).

[247] U.S. Const., Art. IV, § 3, Cl. 2.

[248] *Harris v. Rosario*, 446 U.S. 651, 652 (1980).

[249] *Califano v. Torres*, 435 U.S. 1 (1978).

Califano holdings were specifically tailored to address disparate treatment under federal assistance programs, the legal nature of Puerto Rico's status remained fraught with confusion and uncertainty.

It was Puerto Rico's bankruptcy crisis *circa* 2015–2016 that finally (and decisively) pierced the colonial veil.[250] In quick succession, the political branches in Washington, D.C., and the U.S. Supreme Court made it clear that nothing stood in the way of Congress's plenary authority to unilaterally impinge on the people of Puerto Rico's collective political right to internal self-government.[251] The compact mythology was thereafter put to rest.

---

[250] According to figures from the (now defunct) Puerto Rico Government Development Bank (GDB), as of May 31, 2014, the total outstanding debt of the island's government (including its instrumentalities and municipalities) was $72.602 billion, "equivalent to approximately 103% of the Commonwealth's gross national product for fiscal year 2013." *Commonwealth of Puerto Rico Quarterly Report*, dated July 17, 2014, 6. By then, the deficits had become so pervasive, short-term financing and liquidity sources so scarce, and the possibility of a default so real, that the credit ratings had lowered to non-investment grade ("junk status") the Commonwealth's general obligation bonds and guaranteed bonds. The writing was on the wall. Soon thereafter, in June 2015, Governor Alejandro García Padilla finally declared Puerto Rico's insolvency.

[251] All attempts at enhancing the commonwealth relationship have blatantly foundered. Therein lies the failed experiences of the 1959 Fernós-Murray bill ("A bill to provide amendments to the compact between the people of Puerto Rico and the United States," H.R. 5926, 86th Cong., 1st sess. (1959)); the 1963 Aspinall bill ("To establish a procedure for the prompt settlement, in a democratic manner, of the political status of Puerto Rico," H.R. 5945, 88th Cong., 1st sess., (1963)) (leading President Lyndon Johnson to appoint the failed status commission of 1966 (United States-Puerto Rico Commission on the Status of Puerto Rico, *Report of the United States–Puerto Rico Commission on the Status of Puerto Rico* (Washington, D.C.: Government Printing Office, 1966)); the 1973 Ad Hoc Advisory Group on Puerto Rico's Status appointed by President Richard Nixon, *see* Report of the Ad Hoc Advisory Group on Puerto Rico, October 1, 1975); and the 1989–1991 Johnson–De Lugo bills ("To provide for a referendum on the political status of Puerto Rico," S. 712, 101 Cong., 1st sess. (1989); "Puerto Rico Status Referendum Act," S. 244, 102 Cong., 1st sess. (1991); "To enable the people of Puerto Rico to exercise self-determination," H.R. 4765, 101 Cong., 2nd sess. (1990)). A closer look at the various legal opinions rendered by the Department of Justice's (DOJ) Office of Legal Counsel between the introduction of the Fernós-Murray bill in 1959 and the 1990s reveals that the DOJ's legal posture concerning the nature of the commonwealth relationship has also changed. Since the early 1990s, the DOJ has become a consistent detractor of any enhancement proposition premised on a bilateral compact of mutual consent. Contrary to its earlier, more pragmatic reading of the proprietary rights doctrine and its extension to the political status field—as evidenced in the legal opinions rendered by the Office of Legal Counsel in 1963, 1971, and 1975—the DOJ's more recent opinions have embraced the view that proprietary rights protected under the Due Process Clause of the Fifth Amendment do not vest in political status arrangements. Under this view, a compact between the people of Puerto Rico and Congress that cannot be modified without the consent of both contracting parties is unavailable as a matter of federal constitutional law. *See* Teresa Wynn Roseborough, Memorandum to the Special Representative for Guam Commonwealth, July 28, 1994; Robert Raben, letter to Frank Murkowski, Jan. 18, 2000. For the contrarian view, refer to "Memorandum Re: Power of the United States to Conclude with the Commonwealth of Puerto Rico a Compact Which Could Be Modified Only by Mutual Consent," July

40 ■ THE CONSTITUTIONAL HISTORY OF PUERTO RICO

■ *SÁNCHEZ VALLE* AND *FRANKLIN TRUST*

Chief Judge Calvert Magruder's blunt dictum in *Figueroa v. People of Puerto Rico*,[252] to the effect that the Puerto Rico Constitution was "not just another organic act of the Congress" and that there was "no reason to impute to the Congress the perpetration of such a monumental hoax,"[253] has not stood the test of time.

In *Puerto Rico v. Sánchez Valle*,[254] the Supreme Court parted ways with the First Circuit's long held view that, following the inauguration of the 1952 Constitution, Puerto Rico had become a separate sovereign for purposes of the Double Jeopardy Clause.[255] While readily admitting that, in 1952 "Puerto Rico became a new kind of political entity,"[256] the majority in *Sánchez Valle* nonetheless held that, contrary to the states and Indian tribes, the ultimate source of Puerto Rico's prosecutorial powers still derived from Congress.

The more nuanced thesis adopted by Justices Stephen Breyer and Sonia Sotomayor in their dissent, premised on the idea that in 1952 Congress had entered into a compact with Puerto Rico whereby "the source of Puerto Rico's criminal law ceased to be the U.S. Congress and had become Puerto Rico itself, its people and its constitution"[257] was rejected by the majority. This is why circumscribing *Sánchez Valle* to the Double Jeopardy inquiry is misguided. *Sánchez Valle* transcends the narrow confines of the "dual-sovereignty carve-out from the Double Jeopardy Clause."[258] Rather than embracing the compact mythology expounded upon in the dissent, the U.S. Supreme Court chose to

---

23, 1963; Office of Legal Counsel, "Memorandum Re: Micronesian Negotiations," Aug. 18, 1971; Mitchell McConnell, letter to Marlow Cook, May 12, 1975. *See also* Edward Levy, "Memorandum for the Honorable James E. Connor, Secretary to the Cabinet, Re: Report of the Ad Hoc Advisory Group on Puerto Rico," Nov. 21, 1975, Ford Presidential Library. In recent times, the DOJ has invariably adhered to the position that any mutual consent arrangement is constitutionally unviable. *See* the legal conclusions of the 2005, 2007, and 2011 reports of the President's Task Force on Puerto Rico's Status. President's Task Force on Puerto Rico's Status, Report by the President's Task Force on Puerto Rico's Status (Washington, D.C.: White House, 2005), 6–7; President's Task Force on Puerto Rico's Status, Report by the President's Task Force on Puerto Rico's Status (Washington, D.C.: White House, 2007), 7; President's Task Force, 2011 Report by the President's Task Force on Puerto Rico's Status, 26.

[252] 232 F.2d 615 (1st Cir. 1956).

[253] *Figueroa*, 232 F.2d at 620.

[254] 136 S. Ct. 1863 (2016).

[255] *Sánchez Valle*, 136 S. Ct. at 1884.

[256] *Sánchez Valle*, 136 S. Ct. at 1874.

[257] *Sánchez Valle*, 136 S. Ct. at 1884.

[258] *Sánchez Valle*, 136 S. Ct. at 1870. The position adopted by the United States, through the office of the solicitor general, is illuminating. "This case [. . .] also may affect the federal government's defense of federal legislation and polices related to Puerto Rico across a broad range of substantive areas, including congressional representation, federal benefits, federal income taxes, bankruptcy, and defense." Brief for

discard it, treating Puerto Rico, not like a state, but as a nonsovereign municipal entity.[259]

Less than a week later, in *Puerto Rico v. Franklin California Tax-Free Trust*,[260] the high court found that Puerto Rico was preempted under the Federal Bankruptcy Code from enacting "its own municipal bankruptcy scheme,"[261] even though a 1984 amendment to the federal statute had eliminated Puerto Rico from the definition of "State" "for the purpose of defining who may be a debtor under Chapter 9."[262] While *Franklin* mostly concerned the statutory construction of various provisions of the Federal Bankruptcy Code, its constitutional underpinnings should not be overlooked.

Franklin, perhaps more so than *Sánchez Valle*, uncovered the colonial dimension of Puerto Rico's asymmetric relationship with Congress. It is *Franklin* that lays bare Congress's absolute authority under the Territorial Clause. In *Franklin*, the court validated Congress's arbitrary exclusion of Puerto Rico from the definition of "State" under the Federal Bankruptcy Code's "gateway" provision,[263] despite the uniformity requirement found in the U.S. Constitution's Bankruptcy Uniformity Clause.[264] In so doing, the *Franklin* court also sanctioned Congress's contradictory inclusion of Puerto Rico in the definition of "State" for purposes of the Federal Bankruptcy Code's preemption provision.[265] The majority in *Franklin* reproduced, without saying, the same analytical framework concocted by Justice Brown in *Downes v. Bidwell*,[266] which has survived to this day alongside the Insular Cases. Because Puerto Rico, unlike a state, is not a "part" of the United States, Congress is not constitutionally required to extend to the island the structural safeguards emanating from the Bankruptcy Uniformity Clause.[267] The *Franklin* court left Puerto Rico, yet again, in the hands of an indifferent Congress, excluded from the protections of Chapter 9 and preempted from enacting its own insolvency statute.

On June 13, 2016, the same day the U.S. Supreme Court announced its decision in *Franklin*, Congress passed the highly contested Puerto Rico Oversight,

---

the United States as Amicus Curiae Supporting Respondents at 1, *Puerto Rico v. Sánchez Valle*, 136 S. Ct. 1863 (2016).

[259] *Sánchez Valle*, 136 S. Ct. at 1875.

[260] 136 S. Ct. 1938 (2016).

[261] *Franklin California Tax-Free Trust*, 136 S. Ct. at 1943.

[262] Ibid., at 1945.

[263] Ibid., at 1946.

[264] U.S. Const. Art. I, § 8, Cl. 4.

[265] *Franklin California Tax-Free Trust*, 136 S. Ct. at 1946.

[266] 182 U.S. 244 (1901).

[267] For a thoughtful analysis, *see, e.g.*, Efrén Rivera Ramos, *A Discussion of Recent Supreme Court Decisions Regarding Puerto Rico* (speech delivered at the 2016 First Circuit Judges' Workshop, October

42 ■ THE CONSTITUTIONAL HISTORY OF PUERTO RICO

Management, and Economic Stability Act (PROMESA).[268] PROMESA is a federal *lex specialis* specifically regulating territorial insolvency. Tailored to fill the statutory void the *Franklin* court found in the Federal Bankruptcy Code, PROMESA enables Puerto Rico, Guam, American Samoa, the Commonwealth of the Northern Marianas, the U.S. Virgin Islands, and their territorial instrumentalities, "to file for federal bankruptcy protection."[269]

Anchored on an expansive reading of Congress's plenary powers under the Territorial Clause, PROMESA effectively eviscerated the remaining vestiges of the compact mythology.

■ PROMESA, *AURELIUS* AND *VAELLO MADERO*

Born on the heels of *Sánchez Valle* and *Franklin*, PROMESA placed an automatic stay on all debt-related litigation against Puerto Rico and its instrumentalities, while disfiguring the island's constitutional topography.[270] More specifically, PROMESA turned upside down the proposition that in 1952 Congress entered into a compact with the people of Puerto Rico, whereby it permanently relinquished "its territorial powers over Puerto Rico's internal affairs."[271] It is precisely in the exercise of its unbridled authority under the Territorial Clause that Congress has now placed in the hands of an unelected Financial Oversight and Management Board (henceforth the Oversight Board) Puerto Rico's local governance without any consent from its people. Section 2103 of PROMESA explicitly identifies the Territorial Clause as the source of Congress's constitutional authority to enact this far-reaching insolvency regime. PROMESA is supreme in every respect "over any general or specific provisions of territory law." Pursuant to Section 2128(a), the governor and the legislature have no authority to "exercise any control, supervision, oversight, or review over the Oversight Board or its activities; or to enact, implement, or enforce any statute, resolution, policy, or rule that would impair or defeat the purposes of this chapter, as determined by the Oversight Board." Section 2141(c)(1) precludes the governor from submitting to the legislature the budget "unless the Oversight Board has certified the Territory Fiscal Plan for that fiscal year," severely limiting the governor's powers under Article IV's Section 4 of the Puerto Rico Constitution. In the event the Oversight Board makes a finding of budgetary noncompliance by the

---

20, 2016). *See also* Juan R. Torruella, "Why Puerto Rico Does Not Need Further Experimentation with Its Future: A Reply to the Notion of 'Territorial Federalism,'" *Harvard Law Review* 131 (2018): 65.

[268] 130 Stat. 549 (2016) (48 U.S.C. § 2101 *et seq.*).

[269] *Financial Oversight and Management Board for Puerto Rico v. Aurelius Investment, LLC*, 140 S. Ct. 1649, 1655 (2020).

[270] Section 2194.

[271] Rafael Hernández Colón, "The Evolution of Democratic Governance under the Territorial Clause of the U.S. Constitution," *Suffolk University Law Review* 50 (2017): 587.

island's governmental authorities, it is empowered under Section 2143(d)(1) to unilaterally "make appropriate reductions in nondebt expenditures to ensure that the actual quarterly revenues and expenditures for the territorial government are in compliance with the applicable certified Territory Budget." Not only does Section 2144(a)(2) commandeer the governor to submit to the Oversight Board for its review, "not later than 7 business days" after their enactment, all laws passed by the legislature "during any fiscal year in which the Oversight Board is in operation,"[272] it empowers the Board to suspend in its sole discretion "the enforcement or application" of any law "adversely affecting the territorial government's compliance with the Fiscal Plan."[273] It is the Oversight Board alone that certifies the island's fiscal plan and all debt-restructuring filings.[274] If the local political branches fail to present to the Board a fiscal plan amenable to it, Section 2141(d)(2) vests in the Oversight Board plenary authority to "develop and submit" to the governor and the legislature a fiscal plan of its own making. The Oversight Board's fiscal plan would then be final, enforceable, and fully binding on Puerto Rico despite its emasculation of the legislative process required under Article III of the Puerto Rico Constitution. PROMESA also shuts the door to the local judiciary: Section 2126(a) provides that "any action against the Oversight Board, and any action otherwise arising out of this chapter, in whole or in part, shall be brought in a United States district court for the covered territory."

PROMESA, moreover, vests in the Oversight Board exclusive authority for determining when to terminate its oversight of Puerto Rico. Under Section 2149, the Oversight Board shall terminate only when it certifies that Puerto Rico "has adequate access to short-term and long-term credit markets at reasonable interest rates" and that "for at least 4 consecutive fiscal years" it "has developed its budgets in accordance with modified accrual accounting standards" while keeping its expenditures during each fiscal year below its revenues for that year. Absent future amendment(s) passed by Congress, there is no end in sight, especially if seen in light of Puerto Rico's fiscal woes, magnified by such public emergencies as the

---

[272] Of significance is the fact that Congress has no commensurate authority under Article I Section 8's enumerated powers to commandeer the political branches of the states as it does the political branches of the territories (including Puerto Rico) pursuant to its plenary powers under Article IV Section 3 Clause 2's Territorial Clause. *See, e.g., Printz v. United States*, 521 U.S. 898 (1997).

[273] Note that the Oversight Board has suspended, among others, P.R. Law No. 47 of April 28, 2020 (amending the Puerto Rico Code of Tax Incentives), P.R. Law No. 181 of December 26, 2019 (adjusting compensation for firefighters), P.R. Law No. 176 of December 16, 2019 (reinstating governmental employees' sick and vacation leaves), P.R. Law No. 138 of August 1, 2019 (amending the Puerto Rico Insurance Code), and P.R. Law No. 82 of July 30, 2019 (regulating pharmacy benefit administrators). The Oversight Board's actions were fully ratified by U.S. District Judge Laura Taylor Swain on December 23, 2020. *See In re The Financial Oversight and Management Board for Puerto Rico*, 511 F. Supp. 3d 90 (D. Puerto Rico 2022). The First Circuit affirmed Judge Taylor Swain's opinion on June 22, 2022. *See* 37 F.4th 746 (1st Cir. 2022).

[274] Section 2124(j)(1).

COVID-19 pandemic, the lethal path of Hurricanes María and Fiona in 2017 and 2022 (respectively), and the 2020 earthquakes.

PROMESA, through its Board, may rule Puerto Rico's life for the foreseeable future. Not surprisingly, the constitutionality of PROMESA has been the subject of intense debate since its signing by President Barack Obama in 2016. More specifically, the question of whether Congress's enactment of PROMESA breached the self-government compact it purportedly entered into with the people of Puerto Rico, under U.S. Public Law 600, has elicited a wide-ranging universe of contending opinions. While this issue was not squarely before the U.S. Supreme Court in *Financial Oversight and Management Board for Puerto Rico v. Aurelius Investment, LLC*,[275] the court's resolution of the Appointments Clause controversy presented therein leaves little room for equivocation.[276]

In *Aurelius*, the sole question before the court was the constitutionality of PROMESA's Section 2121(e), which vests in the president exclusive authority to appoint the Oversight Board's seven members "without the advice and consent of the Senate."[277] Finding that the members of the Oversight Board are not "Officers of the United States" in the constitutional sense, but rather territorial officers exercising "the power of the local government, not the Federal Government,"[278] a unanimous court held that the strictures of the Appointments Clause did not govern how the Oversight Board members are designated.

On closer look, the high court's posture in *Aurelius* is highly problematic. Far from infusing constitutional coherence and stability into its highly dysfunctional territorial jurisprudence, an internally fractured court exacerbated even further the asymmetrical relationship between Congress and the territorial periphery.

---

[275] 140 S. Ct. 1649 (2020).

[276] In *Aurelius*, the U.S. Supreme Court suggested, without saying, that Congress's unilateral imposition of the Oversight Board is far from unconstitutional due to its plenary powers under the Territorial Clause "to create local offices" for Puerto Rico and the remaining territories. *Financial Oversight and Management Board for Puerto Rico*, 140 S. Ct. at 1654. *See also* Adriel Cepeda and Neil C. Weare, "After *Aurelius*: What Future for the Insular Cases?," *Yale Law Journal Forum* 130 (2020): 284; Christina D. Ponsa-Kraus, "Political Wine in a Judicial Bottle: Justice Sotomayor's Surprising Concurrence in *Aurelius*," *Yale Law Journal Forum* 130 (2020): 101.

[277] Pursuant to PROMESA's Section 2121(e)(2), the president alone appoints the individual members of the Oversight Board, "of which (i) the Category A member should be selected from a list of individuals submitted by the Speaker of the House of Representatives; (ii) the Category B member should be selected from a separate, non-overlapping list of individuals submitted by the Speaker of the House of Representatives; (iii) the Category C members should be selected from a list submitted by the Majority Leader of the Senate; (iv) the Category D member should be selected from a list submitted by the Minority Leader of the House of Representatives; (v) the Category E member should be selected from a list submitted by the Minority Leader of the Senate; and (vi) the Category F member may be selected in the sole discretion of the President of the United States."

[278] Section 1659.

The contention that "the Appointments Clause governs the appointment of all officers of the United States, including those located in Puerto Rico,"[279] while openly opposed by Justice Clarence Thomas in his concurrence,[280] fizzled away at the hands of the "amorphous test"[281] for determining when the Appointments Clause "restricts"[282] the appointment of "Officers of the United States" undertaking duties related to the territories. Under the *Aurelius* test, distinguishing between an "Officer of the United States with duties in or related to" an "Article IV entity" and a territorial officer whose appointment is unrestrained by the Appointments Clause hinges on whether Congress, in its sole discretion, has vested the above-referenced officer with federal responsibilities or "primarily local duties."[283]

Far from heeding Justice Anthony Kennedy's admonition in *Boumediene v. Bush*[284] that neither the president of the United States nor Congress possess "the power to switch the Constitution on or off at will,"[285] *Aurelius* seems to suggest that such dictum is wholly irrelevant in the territorial topography.

Shortly thereafter, in *United States v. Vaello Madero* (2022)[286] the Supreme Court held that Congress is not constitutionally required to extend Supplemental Security Income (SSI) to residents of Puerto Rico on an equal footing with residents of the States, despite their shared American citizenship. The Roberts Court, thus, concluded that Congress's unequal treatment of American citizens domiciled in Puerto Rico, for purposes of SSI benefits, does not run afoul of the equal protection component of the Fifth Amendment's Due Process Clause.

The *Vaello Madero* Court did not break new ground, but rather followed the precedent established in *Califano v. Torres* (1978) and *Harris v. Rosario* (1980). In so doing, the high court embraced yet again an overly expansive reading of Congress's plenary powers under the Territorial Clause—anchored to the proposition that the Territorial Clause "permits Congress to treat Puerto Rico differently from States so long as there is a rational basis for its actions."[287]

---

[279] Section 1654.

[280] Section 1666.

[281] Section 1670.

[282] Section 1661.

[283] Section 1661.

[284] 553 U.S. 723 (2008).

[285] Ibid., at 765.

[286] *United States v. Vaello-Madero*, (596 U.S. ___ (2022)). In *Vaello Madero*, the U.S. Supreme Court reversed the U.S. Court of Appeals for the First Circuit, which by voice of Judge Juan Torruella had found that "the categorical exclusion of otherwise eligible Puerto Rico residents from SSI is not rationally related to a legitimate government interest." 956 F.3d 12, 32 (1st Cir. 2020). The U.S. Supreme Court granted certiorari in *Vaello-Madero* on March 1, 2021. *See also Asociación Hospital del Maestro v. Becerra*, 10 F.4th 11 (1st Cir. 2021), where the First Circuit found that the unequal treatment of Puerto Rican hospitals, for purposes of the distribution of Medicare's "disproportionate share hospital payments" (DSH), did not run afoul of the equal protection component of the Fifth Amendment's Due Process Clause.

[287] *Vaello Madero* at 4 (citing *Harris v. Rosario*, 446 U.S. 651, 661 (1980)).

While making no distinction between the political entity known as "Puerto Rico," and the "residents of Puerto Rico" who are American citizens, the *Vaello Madero* Court conflated these two distinct legal concepts, adding credence to the problematic argument that heightened scrutiny under the equal protection component of the Fifth Amendment's Due Process Clause is unavailable to protect the American citizens residing in Puerto Rico from legislative discrimination so long as Congress acts pursuant to the Territorial Clause.[288]

At its core, *Vaello Madero*, like *Aurelius*, *Sánchez Valle* and *Franklin*, is a by-product of the same territorial powers doctrine that since the founding of the American Republic has led to an absolutist reading of Congress's authority under the Territorial Clause that is at odds with the founders' anticolonial values.[289]

■ EPILOGUE: BETWEEN SCYLLA AND CHARYBDIS

Like Odysseus on his perilous voyage to Ithaca, Puerto Rico today is navigating in a rough sea with formidable challenges on all sides, reminiscent of the Greek hero's encounter with Scylla and Charybdis. Ravaged both by a massive public debt crisis and a devastating string of public emergencies (hurricanes, earthquakes, the COVID-19 pandemic), Puerto Rico at this writing may be on the brink of major upheaval. Not only is the island's economic model obsolete, incapable of jump-starting a chronically dependent economy that has remained in a state of permanent depression for nearly fifteen years, its politico-constitutional infrastructure is in tatters.

Just as the public debt crisis pierced the island's colonial veil, bringing to the surface the inequitable and undemocratic nature of Puerto Rico's asymmetric relationship with the United States,[290] the peaceful uprising that toppled Governor Ricardo Rosselló Nevares in the summer of 2019 (in what was dubbed Puerto Rico's Arab Spring) has made it clear that the Puerto Rico Constitution of July 25, 1952, is unsuited to address the island's most pressing obstacles.

Born in the postwar period, during the waning days of the Truman administration, Puerto Rico's internal *Magna Carta* belongs to another time and place. Admittedly, the 1952 Constitution is by far Puerto Rico's most significant legal instrument since the proclamation in 1897 of the short-lived Autonomic Charter. Imbued with the postwar values of the 1948 Universal Declaration of Human Rights, the 1952 Constitution devolved to the island a significant

---

[288] Refer to Justice Thurgood Marshall's dissent in *Harris v. Rosario*, 446 U.S. 651, 654 (1980).

[289] Note that the Commerce Clause also empowers Congress to regulate activities undertaken in Puerto Rico that "substantially affect Interstate Commerce." Congress's commerce power as applied to Puerto Rico is ample indeed. *See, e.g., Hernádez Gotay v. United States* (2021) (holding that Section 12616 of the Agriculture Improvement Act of 2018, banning the sponsorship and exhibition of cockfighting matches in Puerto Rico is a legitimate exercise of the Commerce Clause power).

[290] For a careful analysis of Congress's plenary powers over Puerto Rico, *see* José Trías Monge, *Puerto Rico: The Trials of the Oldest Colony in the World* (New Haven: Yale University Press, 1997), 161–163.

quantum of political authority over its internal governance while endowing its people with a robust catalogue of fundamental rights.

Seven decades on, however, the constitutional experiment of 1952 is exhausted—not least because Puerto Rican society has undergone since then significant and irreversible changes in all orders, compounded by a technological revolution with multiple consequences. The island's unprecedented bankruptcy, the demise of its traditional political structures resulting from the ineptitude and corruption of the local political leadership, together with the rise of a cadre of new movements and individual actors demanding honesty, transparency, and competency, have irrevocably redrawn Puerto Rico's political topography. The time may be ripe for embarking on a process of constitutional restructuring that infuses democratic legitimacy and normative vitality to a worn-out constitutional arrangement.

For Puerto Rico today the challenge is twofold: on the one hand, decolonizing its endogenous constitutional repertoire; on the other, engaging Congress in the complex task of charting a clear path for its exogenous decolonization even with the sword of Damocles still hanging over its head, embodied by the debt restructuring process PROMESA has placed, for the foreseeable future, in the hands of the Oversight Board. Far from mutually exclusive propositions, the restructuring of Puerto Rico's internal constitutional infrastructure is closely intertwined with the resolution of its political status. Because Article VII's Section 3 of the Puerto Rico Constitution commands that all amendments must be compatible to U.S. Public Laws 600 and 447, as well as to the 1950 Federal Relations Act, far-reaching restructuring at the local level might require restructuring at the external level as well.

While exploring the far-reaches of Puerto Rico's status conundrum is beyond the scope of this book, some concluding observations are appropriate. First, decolonizing Puerto Rico is far from a purely legal matter. Decolonizing Puerto Rico is, above all else, a political matter requiring a bilateral dialogue between the people of Puerto Rico and the political branches in Washington, D.C. Deciding how to disentangle Puerto Rico's colonial knot is not a question for the U.S. Supreme Court, but for Congress.

Second, engaging Congress requires a new procedural mechanism. The time for nonbinding local plebiscites, denying independence and free association access to the ballot, should come to an end. From a procedural perspective, only a federal plebiscite including detailed definitions already agreed upon with Congress or a status convention elected by the people of Puerto Rico with the sole task of defining, together with Congress, the self-determination formulas to be put to the people for a definitive vote, would meet Puerto Rico's unique needs.

Third, Puerto Rico's fiscal implosion, along with its effect on the United States' municipal bond market and Washington's overall global interests in today's world (dis)order, will no doubt shape Congress's response (or lack thereof) to Puerto Rico's demands for decolonization.

Fourth, perhaps no other moment in Puerto Rico's long history has offered as fertile a terrain for transformative change as this one.

Against this background, promoting Puerto Rico's endogenous and exogenous decolonizing agenda is of the essence.

PART TWO

The Puerto Rico Constitution and Commentary

Preamble

We, the people of Puerto Rico, in order to organize ourselves politically on a fully democratic basis, to promote the general welfare, and to secure for ourselves and our posterity the complete enjoyment of human rights, placing our trust in Almighty God, do ordain and establish this Constitution for the commonwealth which, in the exercise of our natural rights, we now create within our union with the United States of America.

In so doing, we declare:

The democratic system is fundamental to the life of the Puerto Rican community.

We understand that the democratic system of government is one in which the will of the people is the source of public power, the political order is subordinate to the rights of man, and the free participation of the citizen in collective decisions is assured.

We consider as determining factors in our life our citizenship of the United States of America and our aspiration continually to enrich our democratic heritage in the individual and collective enjoyment of its rights and privileges; our loyalty to the principles of the Federal Constitution; the coexistence in Puerto Rico of the two great cultures of the American Hemisphere; our fervor for education; our faith in justice; our devotion to the courageous, industrious, and peaceful way of life; our fidelity to individual human values above and beyond social position, racial differences, and economic interests; and our hope for a better world based on these principles.

The preamble to the Puerto Rico Constitution stands as the first autochthonous declaration of general principles drafted by a body of Puerto Rican elected officials expounding on the collective values and aspirations of the people of Puerto Rico. None of the previous legal instruments regulating Puerto Rico's internal governance, first under the Spanish Crown and subsequently under the United States, included such a preamble.

The preamble confirms the existence of an indivisible body politic known as "the people of Puerto Rico." With the statement, "We, the people of Puerto Rico," the founders explicitly proclaimed the island's distinct sociological inheritance. While obliquely acknowledged by Congress in Sections 16 and 10 of the Foraker and Jones Acts, at no other point in the island's constitutional history had a cadre of Puerto Rican elected officials openly affirmed this inescapable reality. See 1900 Foraker Act, Section 16 ("[. . .] all criminal or penal prosecutions in the local courts shall be conducted in the name and by the authority of "The people of Porto Rico") and 1917 Jones Act, Section 10 ("[. . .] all penal or criminal prosecutions in the local courts shall be conducted in the name and by the authority of "The people of Porto Rico").

The preamble's nuanced language with respect to the nature of Puerto Rico's territorial relationship with the United States reflects the uneasy political compromise brokered at the constitutional convention among the delegates from the Popular Democratic Party, Statehood Party, and Socialist Party. While openly extolling the significance of Puerto Ricans' American citizenship within the island's wider political narrative, the preamble lends credence to the now-defunct compact mythology.

Seeking intellectual refuge in the natural rights theory and acknowledging Puerto Ricans' unalienable right to "ordain" and "establish" their own internal government, the preamble suggests that the Puerto Rico Constitution is the by-product of the free choice of the people of Puerto Rico and that the ultimate source of "public power" lies in the people themselves. In fact, Congress, not the people of Puerto Rico, commandeered the conception and birth of the Puerto Rico Constitution.

Contrary to the 1787 Philadelphia Convention, where the preamble to the federal Constitution was drafted without eliciting debate at the end of the proceedings, the Puerto Rico Constitutional Convention designated from the outset a specific committee under the leadership of Delegate (and Governor) Luis Muñoz Marín for drafting the preamble. The convention's record shows that the preamble committee (*Comisión de Preámbulo, Ordenanzas y Procedimientos de Enmiendas*) was designated on the third day of the proceedings (September 25, 1951). See 1 *Diario de Sesiones de la Convención Constituyente de Puerto Rico* (*Diary of Sessions of the Puerto Rico Constitutional Convention*) (San Juan: Lexis-Nexis of Puerto Rico Inc., 2003), 118–119 (henceforth *Diario*). It was composed of eleven delegates, namely Luis Muñoz Marín (president), José Trías Monge, Jorge Font Saldaña, Ernesto Ramos Antonini, Ernesto Juan Fonfrías,

Ramón Mellado Parsons, Virgilio Brunet Maldonado, Jenaro Gautier Dapena, Luis A. Ferré Aguayo, Ramiro Colón Castaño, and Antonio Reyes Delgado.

The preamble was the subject of intense and prolonged debate. The Statehood Party, dissatisfied with the initial draft, pressed for the incorporation of unequivocal language expressing the people of Puerto Rico's unwavering aspiration to statehood, while more specifically advocating for the inclusion of the word "permanent" before "union with the United States of America." Both proposals were soundly defeated.

Yet, two days before the convention's adjournment, the Statehood Party delegates struck a semantic deal with their Popular Democratic Party counterparts, agreeing on the incorporation of language extolling on the significance of the federal "rights" and "privileges" Puerto Ricans were by then already enjoying as a result of their American citizenship. The convention approved this compromise language on February 4, 1952. 4 *Diario* 2485.

Consequently, after the reference to "our citizenship of the United States of America," the following language was added: "and our aspiration continually to enrich our democratic heritage in the individual and collective enjoyment of its rights and privileges." In supporting this rhetorical compromise, Governor Muñoz Marín suggested that the wording of the preamble, far from closing any doors as to Puerto Rico's political future, left them open in case the people of Puerto Rico decided at a later time to transition to statehood or independence. Thus, to the eyes of Muñoz Marín, the language of the preamble had to remain shrouded in a cloak of status neutrality.

From a doctrinal perspective, moreover, the Puerto Rico Supreme Court made it clear in *Partido Independentista Puertorriqueño v. Comisión Estatal de Elecciones* (1988) that the Puerto Rican Preamble, contrary to its federal counterpart, which in the words of the U.S. Supreme Court "has never been regarded as the source of substantive power," *Jacobson v. Massachusetts* (1905), does constitute a source of "positive constitutional law." *Partido Independentista Puertorriqueño v. Comisión Estatal de Elecciones* (1988).

In *Partido Socialista Puertorriqueño v. Estado Libre Asociado* (1978), Chief Justice José Trías Monge argued that the preamble's status-neutral posture precluded the political branches from unilaterally changing Puerto Rico's political status vis-à-vis the United States without the people's consent. Dissenting opinions by Justices Baltasar Corrada del Río and Efraín Rivera Pérez in *Ramírez de Ferrer v. Mari Brás* (1997) and *Báez Galib v. Comisión Estatal de Elecciones* (2000), respectively, argued that the preamble's characterization of American citizenship as a "determining factor" in the lives of the Puerto Rican people, together with the aspiration delineated therein to "continually . . . enrich our . . . heritage in the collective enjoyment of its rights and privileges," gave the local political branches carte blanche to seek statehood for the island.

There can be little doubt that the Puerto Rico Supreme Court no longer follows the status-neutral approach announced in *Partido Socialista*. In *Aponte*

Rosario v. Presidente Comisión Estatal de Elecciones (2020), a majority of the court adopted the view that statehood is the island's ultimate status goal and that the political branches possess constitutional authority to pursue it. The unraveling of *Partido Socialista*'s neutrality paradigm is highly problematic. Not only does it run afoul the explicit intent of the framers, it undermines the right to self-determination of those Puerto Ricans opposing statehood and favoring sovereignty (either through independence or free association).

Article I

The Commonwealth

Section 1
The Commonwealth of Puerto Rico

The Commonwealth of Puerto Rico is hereby constituted. Its political power emanates from the people and shall be exercised in accordance with their will, within the terms of the compact agreed upon between the people of Puerto Rico and the United States of America.

Section 1 derives from the 1948 Universal Declaration of Human Rights. *See* Article 21(1) ("Everyone has the right to take part in the government of his country, directly or through freely chosen representatives.") Section 1 embodies the framers' intention to dispel the confusion already surrounding the alleged noncolonial nature of Puerto Rico's new governmental arrangement.

Originally consisting of only one sentence—"[t]he Commonwealth of Puerto Rico is hereby constituted within the terms of the compact agreed upon between the people of Puerto Rico and the United States of America"—the convention, at the behest of Delegate Víctor Gutiérrez Franqui, incorporated here what was initially intended to be the first sentence of Section 2 of the Puerto Rico Bill of Rights: "Its political power emanates from the people and shall be exercised in accordance with their will." Ideologically, the central tenet embraced by the delegation of the Popular Democratic Party was the proposition that the 1951–1952 constitution-making exercise was driven not by Congress but by the people of

Puerto Rico in the exercise of their inherent right to self-determination. Thus, the inclusion of this language was intended to reinforce the compact mythology—namely, that, in passing U.S. Public Law 600 in 1950, Congress relinquished its plenary powers over the island under the Territorial Clause. *See* U.S. Const. Art. IV, § 3, Cl. 2. This thesis, however, flies in the face of the text of PROMESA, which establishes that Congress still enjoys plenary powers over Puerto Rico. *See* PROMESA, Tit. I, § 101(b)(2) ("Constitutional basis. The Congress enacts this Act pursuant to Article IV, Section 3 of the Constitution of the United States, which provides Congress the power to dispose of and make all needful rules and regulations for territories.").

Section 2
Form of Government

The government of the Commonwealth of Puerto Rico shall be republican in form and its legislative, judicial and executive branches as established by this Constitution shall be equally subordinate to the sovereignty of the people of Puerto Rico.

In U.S. Public Law 600, Congress made it plain clear that the Puerto Rico Constitution "shall provide a republican form of government." In light of the constitutional mandate flowing from the Guaranty Clause of the U.S. Constitution, *see* U.S. Const. Art. IV, § 4 ("The United States shall guarantee to every State in this Union a Republican Form of Government [...]."), it is rather unsurprising that Congress had conditioned the viability of the island's constitution-making exercise to the establishment of a republican form of government. Section 2 must be seen in tandem with Article VII's Section 3, which establishes that "[n]o amendment to this Constitution shall alter the republican form of government established by it [...]." The convention's open reference to the subordination of the three branches of government "to the sovereignty of the people of Puerto Rico" was intended to bolster the alleged decolonizing effect of the 1952 constitutional experiment.

The Puerto Rico Supreme Court, consistent with the convention's design, has construed Section 2 as having established three separate yet coequal branches of government "in dynamic equilibrium" with one another, none of which is absolutely independent from the other. *See, e.g., Aníbal Acevedo Vilá v. José Meléndez Ortiz* (2005); *Misión Industrial v. Junta de Planificación* (1998). More specifically, in *In re Pellot Córdova* (2020), the court identified Section 2 as the source of the separation of powers mandate controlling Puerto Rico's constitutional landscape. *See Colegio de Abogados v. Estado Libre Asociado* (2010) ("the constitutional principle of the separation of powers emanates from Article I's Section 2 of the Commonwealth Constitution.").

The Puerto Rico Supreme Court revisited, yet again, the separation of powers requirement in *Senado v. Tribunal Supremo* (2021). In *Senado*, the court declared that Article 3.7(3) of the Electoral Code, which had conferred on the Supreme Court the power to appoint the president of the Puerto Rico Election Commission in case the political branches failed to agree on a nominee, was unconstitutional due to its violation of Sections 2's checks and balances mandate.

Section 3
Geographic Area

The political authority of the Commonwealth of Puerto Rico shall extend to the Island of Puerto Rico and to the adjacent islands within its jurisdiction.

The language of Article I's Section 3 constitutes a subtle, yet provocative, departure from the wording found in Article II of the Treaty of Paris ("Spain cedes to the United States the island of Porto Rico and other islands now under Spanish sovereignty in the West Indies [...]."), which was subsequently brought to bear in the recitals of the Foraker and Jones Acts.

While clearly belonging to the United States pursuant to the Treaty of Paris, the smaller adjacent islands off of Puerto Rico were now explicitly placed under the primary jurisdiction of Puerto Rico's local authorities, if only for purposes of internal governance. Again, style appeared to matter more than substance: the U.S. Navy's unilateral occupation of most of Vieques and Culebra for firing practice purposes during most of the twentieth century brought to the fore rather eloquently the lingering emptiness underlying Section 3.

Section 4
Seat of Government

The seat of the government shall be the city of San Juan.

Section 4 designates San Juan as the seat of government. This provision mirrors the language found in Sections 6 and 4 of the Foraker and Jones Acts, respectively. Section 4 should be read in tandem with Article VI's Section 17, which establishes that in case of an invasion, rebellion, epidemic, or any other extraordinary circumstance triggering a state of emergency, the governor enjoys authority to call the legislature to meet at a place other than at the Capitol and provisionally move the government away from San Juan.

Article II

The Bill of Rights

Section 1
Human Dignity and Equality; Discrimination Prohibited

The dignity of the human being is inviolable. All men are equal before the law. No discrimination shall be made on account of race, color, sex, birth, social origin or condition, or political or religious ideas. Both the laws and the system of public education shall embody these principles of essential human equality.

The Inviolability of Human Dignity

The first section of the Puerto Rico Bill of Rights is both thunderous and uniquely powerful. It proclaims that "human dignity is inviolable." The framers' understanding that the inviolability of human dignity must be accorded constitutional protection was heavily influenced by the rise, during the early stages of the postwar period, of a robust legal ideology of human rights as embodied in the 1948 United Nations' Universal Declaration of Human Rights and in the text itself of the 1949 German Constitution. *See* Article 1 of the 1949 German Basic Law ("The dignity of man shall be inviolable. To respect it and protect it shall be the duty of all state authority.").

Drawing a sharp distinction between the Puerto Rican and federal landscapes, Chief Justice José Trías Monge suggested in *Figueroa Ferrer v. Estado Libre Asociado* (1978) that the right to privacy and the protection of human dignity in

Puerto Rico "are not wandering entities in search of an author or a juridical pigeonhole." To the contrary, these protections, in the words of the *Figueroa Ferrer* court, are "consecrated in the clear text of our Constitution." Therein lies one of the more significant differences between James Madison's more discreet (and succinct) federal Bill of Rights and its Puerto Rican counterpart: the former responded to the complex dynamics of an uneasy (and incipient) system of vertical federalism at the turn of the eighteenth century, while the latter prioritized the individual as an autonomous legal subject in the aftermath of Nuremberg. The record available from the constitutional convention shows that, from the outset, the Puerto Rican framers were bent on enriching the island's constitutional repertoire with a robust catalogue of enumerated constitutional rights; some of which *circa* 1951–1952 were unavailable both under the Jones Act and the federal Bill of Rights.

At the pinnacle of the new pyramid of fundamental rights built by the local framers sits the constitutional guarantee that human dignity is inviolable. In the words of Delegate Jaime Benítez Rexach, it is the inviolability of human dignity that stands as the cornerstone of the island's newly minted bill of rights. 2 *Diario* 1103. It is, by far, the most prominent value at the heart of Puerto Rico's constitutional experiment. In *Figueroa Ferrer*, moreover, the supreme court equated "dignity" with "personhood."

Notwithstanding the obvious prominence of Section 1's dignity construct, both as a constitutional and ideological value, the supreme court has shied away from infusing it with independent life, conflating it instead with Section 8's right to privacy. Section 1's dignity clause has essentially become subsidiary to Section 8's right to privacy, devoid of any independent content. Not only does this approach run afoul of the framers' design, but it has denied the court an invaluable source of constitutional authority for protecting intrinsic aspects of an individual's "personhood" not necessarily falling under the tight boundaries of Section 8's privacy right. The "underutilization" of the dignity clause has come to the fore in various contexts. *See* Hiram Meléndez Juarbe, "Privacy in Puerto Rico and the Madman's Plight," *Georgetown Journal of Gender & Law* 9 (2008): 1.

In a long line of cases involving issues of "personhood" and "decisional autonomy," the island's high court, while invoking Section 1's dignity clause, either has found for plaintiffs solely on the basis of Section 8's right to privacy or has conflated both constitutional provisions, denying an independent existence to Section 1's dignity clause.

In *Arroyo v. Rattan Specialties, Inc.* (1986), the supreme court found that the practice of a private employer requiring its employees submit to random polygraph testing, as a compulsory condition for keeping their jobs, violated both Section 1's dignity clause and Section 8's right to privacy. Similarly, in *Ex Parte Andino Torres* (2000) and *Lozada Tirado v. Testigos de Jehová* (2010), the court embraced the plaintiffs' "personhood" claims by conflating the inviolability of human dignity guarantee with the right to privacy. In *Andino Torres*, reversing the lower courts, the supreme court ordered a change of sex on the plaintiff's birth registration. In *Lozada Tirado*, moreover, the court found that the local statute limiting the plaintiff's ability to refuse medical treatment was incompatible with the constitutional rights found in Sections 1 and 8 of the bill of rights. More recently, in *Weber Carrillo v. Estado Libre Asociado* (2014), the court found that the plaintiff did enjoy a reasonable expectation of privacy in the record of the calls made to and from his mobile phone. In so doing, the court, although timidly invoking the dignity construct, sought refuge in Section 8's right to privacy.

Not only has the court shown itself prone to construe both principles as interchangeable concepts, but on occasion it has failed to strengthen important individual liberty interests due to its apparent disinclination to infuse Section 1's dignity clause with its own textual autonomy. In *Ex Parte AAR* (2013), the court refused to adopt the "second parent adoption" doctrine, due in no small measure to the fact that the party moving the adoption application was engaged in a same-sex relationship with the minor's biological mother. The court's narrow reading of Section 8's right to privacy, which essentially mimics federal case law, could have been cured on the basis of a coherently expansive and independent application of Section 1's dignity clause. In the aftermath of *Obergefell v. Hodges* (2015), *Ex Parte AAR* can no longer stand. Along similar lines, in *Salvá Santiago v. Torres Padró* (2007), the court declined to incorporate through the right to privacy a new ground for divorce on the basis of the "irretrievable breakdown of marriage," despite its obvious dignity implications. Arguably this construction of Section 1's dignity clause also led the court in *Ex Parte Delgado Hernández* (2005) to deny plaintiff's change of sex claim, despite its order in *Ex Parte Andino Torres*.

Suspect Classes

Race or Color

In Puerto Rico, racial equality is a myth. Founded upon the twin scourges of colonialism and slavery, Puerto Rico's sociological inheritance is inextricably bound to structural racism and colorism. Since its inception early in the sixteenth century, Spanish rule in Puerto Rico was premised on racial hierarchies. Together with Cuba and Brazil, Puerto Rico remained one of the last strongholds of slavery in the Americas; abolition made a belated appearance on March 22, 1873.

The arrival of the American flag, twenty-five years later, further entrenched the island's racial caste system. The Treaty of Paris, together with the multitude of military orders enacted in the immediate aftermath of the island's occupation along with Congress's subsequent enactment of the Foraker and Jones Acts, at no point addressed the issue of race within the context of the people of Puerto Rico's individual civil rights.

A close reading of *Dottin v. Rigo & Co.* (1915), one of a handful of decisions rendered by the Puerto Rico Supreme Court on the issue of race during the first decades of American occupation, shows how the disreputable ghost of the *Civil Rights Cases* (1883) unduly influenced the court's attitudes. In *Dottin*, the court dismissed the damages claim of a black plaintiff who had been refused service at *la Mallorquina* Restaurant in Old San Juan on account of his race. The *Dottin* court showed itself utterly disinterested in articulating an autochthonous legal rule, even in the absence of local statutory protections against racial discrimination in private spaces. Not even the rudimentary 1902 bill of rights statute provided any safeguards against racial discrimination. While the local statutory vacuum was filled in 1943 with the enactment of the island's first civil rights statute, it was the framers' constitutionalization of the prohibition against racial discrimination (two years before *Brown v. Board of Education* (1954)) that finally set the island on the path of equality. In Puerto Rico, classifications based on race are inherently suspect and must meet strict scrutiny. Yet the societal traumas associated to slavery, racism, and injustice survive to this day.

Alienage

Notwithstanding that the framers did not include alienage as a suspect class under Section 1, in *Wackenhut Corp. v. Rodríguez Aponte* (1972), the Puerto Rico Supreme Court, echoing its federal counterpart's decision in *Graham v. Richardson* (1971), suggested that classifications established on the basis of alienage are suspect and must also meet strict scrutiny.

The court in *De Paz Lisk v. Aponte Roque* (1989) seemed to offer non-American citizens even greater protection than that afforded by its federal counterpart in *Ambach v. Norwick* (1979). The *De Paz Lisk* court declined to sustain the validity of the local rule, even in light of the self-governance interest exception announced by the U.S. Supreme Court in *Foley v. Connelie* (1978) and reiterated in *Ambach*. In *De Paz Lisk* a divided court found that the citizenship requirement for obtaining a teacher's certificate, mandated by local law, was unconstitutional, despite the fact that in *Ambach* the federal high court had sustained the constitutionality of an almost identical New York statutory requirement under the Fourteenth Amendment's Equal Protection Clause.

Sex

While gender equality remains an unmet goal in Puerto Rican life, the island's legal culture does reflect an evolution in that direction. One of the most significant areas of systemic transformation comes to the fore in the decisions of the Puerto Rico Supreme Court. Gone are the days of *Arbona v. Torres* (1916) and *Morales y Benet v. Junta Local de Inscripciones* (1924), when, driven by sexist stereotypes and condescending biases, the court indiscriminately validated unjustified gender classifications. Both *Arbona* and *Morales y Benet* mirrored the U.S. Supreme Court's own flawed reading of the equal protection guarantees flowing from the Fifth and Fourteenth Amendments. Contrary to the federal constitutional text, which omits any reference to gender equality, Section 1 explicitly establishes that gender is a suspect class. Rather than following the federal blueprint, the framers mirrored Article 2 of the 1948 United Nations' Universal Declaration of Human Rights, which considered gender equality a basic human right.

In *Zachry International v. Tribunal Superior* (1975), the supreme court announced that in Puerto Rico classifications premised on gender, like those based on race or alienage, must meet strict scrutiny. Not even Justice William Brennan's contemporaneous opinion in *Craig v. Boren* (1976), carving out a rather amorphous intermediate scrutiny for gender classifications, made the Puerto Rican high court veer off course. Thus, in Puerto Rico there is no intermediate scrutiny.

The available case law shows that classifications based on archaic or unfounded sexual stereotypes run afoul of the constitutional mandate. In *Comisión para los Asuntos de la Mujer v. Secretario de Justicia* (1980), the supreme court held that Rule 154 of the Rules of Criminal Procedure, requiring the corroboration of the testimony tendered by female rape victims as a precondition for the conviction of their aggressors, was unconstitutional. Because the corroboration requirement perpetuated unjustified prejudices and stereotypes against women, Rule 154 did not meet strict scrutiny. *See* PR ST T.34, App. II, § 154.

However, not all classifications based on gender will necessarily fail strict scrutiny. In *Pueblo v. Rivera Robles* (1988), the court confirmed the constitutionality of Article 99 of the 1974 Criminal Code, which assigned liability for statutory rape solely on the male aggressor and not on the similarly situated female aggressor. In *Pueblo v. Rivera Morales* (1993), following the rationale behind *Rivera Robles*, the court upheld the constitutionality of Article 95 of the 1974 Criminal Code, which defined "aggravated assault," inter alia, as an assault committed by an adult man against a woman and not the other way around.

The enactment of new Criminal Codes in 2004 and 2012 rendered the court's specific holdings in *Rivera Robles* and *Rivera Morales* irrelevant, yet the principle that disparate treatment based on gender is not unconstitutional per se remains undisturbed.

Birth

Illegitimacy classifications in Puerto Rico are suspect and, hence, must meet strict scrutiny. This is contrary to federal constitutional law, which does not view illegitimacy as suspect for purposes of equal protection. This doctrinal dissonance is perhaps one of the more significant distinctions between the island's and the mainland's catalogues of fundamental rights. In constitutionalizing illegitimacy's suspect status, the framers not only sought to redress centuries of discrimination against a historically vulnerable and neglected population but also responded to the higher values embodied in the Universal Declaration of Human Rights.

The inauguration of the constitution, however, did not put an end to the debate surrounding the rights of illegitimate children born before 1952. While it was clear that following the advent of the constitution, both matrimonial and non-matrimonial children born after 1952 enjoyed equal rights for purposes of establishing their paternity and seeking their share of the parental estate, the same was not true for pre-1952 non-matrimonial children. In the much-celebrated *Ocasio v. Díaz* (1963), the Puerto Rico Supreme Court finally disentangled an ancient Gordian knot, holding that equal treatment under the law must also be afforded to children born before 1952 regardless of whether their parents were not married at the time of their birth.

Social Origin or Condition

Under Section 1, classifications premised on social origin or condition are suspect and must be reviewed on the basis of strict scrutiny. This constitutional mandate applies *ex proprio vigore*. The inclusion of social origin or condition as a suspect class signals a significant departure from the federal constitutional rule, which establishes that classifications based on wealth are nonsuspect for purposes of equal protection. The framers' elevation of social origin or condition to the suspect class category was influenced by the text of the Universal Declaration of Human Rights. While the archival record shows that the inclusion of social origin or condition within Section 1's corpus of suspect classes did not stir debate or controversy at the convention, the Puerto Rico Supreme Court has yet to delineate with specificity its substantive contours.

Besides timidly intimating that the framers' conception of social origin or condition pertained to discrimination based on wealth, social rank, or status, the court in *Rosario v. Toyota* (2005) failed to arrive at a consensus on whether discrimination against individuals with criminal records falls under this rubric. More generally, the *Toyota* court failed to define with certainty the metes and bounds of social origin or condition in the constitutional sense.

Close to two decades later, the court faced the same issue in *Garib Bazaín v. Hospital Español Auxilio Mutuo de Puerto Rico, Inc.* (2020). The *Garib Bazaín* court followed the same conservative path the *Toyota* court had traversed and again failed to infuse doctrinal clarity, concluding over the forceful dissents of Chief Justice Maite Oronoz Rodríguez, Justice Luis Estrella Martínez, and Justice Ángel Colón Pérez that ex-convicts do not constitute a suspect class under Section 1.

Because this is an area of Puerto Rican constitutional law where the local framework offers more robust protections than its federal counterpart, its vitality will depend on whether the Puerto Rico Supreme Court is up to the task of articulating an autochthonous (and expansive) rule reflecting, not the federal approach, but rather the local framers' unwavering commitment to the inviolability of human dignity.

Political or Religious Ideas

In another deviation from the federal precedent, the Puerto Rican framers, again seeking refuge in the Universal Declaration of Human Rights, explicitly established that classifications based on political or religious ideas are inherently suspect. In *Báez Cancel v. Santos Rivera Pérez* (1972), the court suggested that this constitutional protection is both explicitly peremptory and applicable *ex proprio vigore*. The *Báez Cancel* court found that the Guaynabo Mayor's politically motivated dismissal of a cadre of irregular municipal employees violated Section 1's constitutional safeguard.

While the court appeared inclined to infuse Section 1's protection against political and religious discrimination with a life of its own, independent of the religious and expressive freedoms protected under Article II's Sections 3 and 4, the opposite has been the case. In the aftermath of *Báez Cancel*, not only has the court tended to conflate Section 1's political and religious discrimination clause with Sections 3 and 4 but local plaintiffs alleging discrimination because of their political or religious beliefs have preferred to file their complaints in federal court, claiming violations of their First Amendment rights. *See, e.g., Irizarry Robles v. José Guillermo Rodriguez* (2017), *Albino v. Municipality of Guayanilla* (2013), and *Ángel Febus Rodríguez v. Enrique Questell* (2009).

> Section 2
> Suffrage; Electoral Franchise
> The laws shall guarantee the expression of the will of the people by means of equal, direct and secret universal suffrage and shall protect the citizen against any coercion in the exercise of the electoral franchise.

The right to vote protected under Article II's Section 2 has no express equivalent in the Foraker and Jones Acts, or in the U.S. Constitution. The historical trajectory of the right to vote in Puerto Rico has not always followed a straight path. In Puerto Rico, the right to vote was nonexistent during most of the Spanish colonial period, while considerably limited in the early stages of American rule.

The archival record shows that the framers imported Section 2's language from the Universal Declaration of Human Rights. Section 2, unlike the federal constitutional text, guarantees an affirmative constitutional right to vote and establishes that the right to vote shall be universal, equal, direct, and secret, while placing on the legislature the obligation to protect voters from undue coercion.

The inclusion of this language did not give rise to opposition at the convention. Interestingly, the most significant point of contention among the framers was deciding whether Section 2 should also require compulsory voting. Following an intense debate led by Delegate Miguel Ángel García Méndez, on one side, and Delegate Jaime Benítez Rexach, on the other, the convention agreed on noncompulsory voting. 2 *Diario* 1390–1402.

In *Ramírez de Ferrer v. Mari Bras* (1997), the supreme court confirmed the right to vote as one of the fundamental guarantees available under Puerto Rico's constitutional framework. In *Pierluisi y Bhatia v. Comisión Estatal de Elecciones* (2020), the island's high court suggested, yet again, that the right to vote in a primary is as constitutionally protected as the right to vote in a general election. The *Mari Bras* court, moreover, made it clear that the scope of Section 2's right to vote is ample. The only constitutional restriction on the right to vote appears in Article VI's Section 4, which explicitly limits Puerto Rico's franchise to voters who are eighteen or older. The age requirement now found in Article VI's Section 4 was incorporated by way of a constitutional amendment passed in 1970. Before then, the constitutionally required age for voting was twenty-one or older. In Puerto Rico, moreover, inmates are not disenfranchised; their right to vote is protected by statute. *See* P.R. Law No. 3 of September 8, 1980 (PR ST T. 16, § 3001 *et seq.*). Further, Puerto Rico's framers incorporated to the constitutional text a stark prohibition against disenfranchisement based on illiteracy or lack of property ownership.

It is well settled that the final interpreter of the local electoral code is the Puerto Rico Supreme Court. *See Manny Suárez v. Comisión Estatal de Elecciones* (2004). Moreover, as the court itself has made clear, Section 2 also grants the legislature significant authority to regulate the exercise of the franchise. *See Partido Nuevo Progresista v. De Castro Font II* (2007) (regulating voters' and parties' registrations, as well as the filing of candidacies, falls within the aegis of the legislature). Nonetheless, the legislature's power in this field is not without limits. As the supreme court found in *Ortiz Angleró v. Barreto Pérez* (1980), all legislative restrictions on the right to vote must pass "vigorous judicial scrutiny," and the legislature bears the burden of showing both a compelling interest and that the challenged regulation has been narrowly tailored. *See Mari Bras, supra.*

In *Partido Nuevo Progresista v. De Castro Font II* (2007), Puerto Rico's high court made it clear that the constitutionally protected right to vote found in Section 2, in conjunction with Section 6's freedom of association, encompasses the right to participate in the political process. In *Partido Renovación Puertorriqueña v. Estado Libre Asociado* (1984), the court constitutionalized the so-called equality axiom (*axioma de igualdad*), holding that the constitution implicitly requires the legislature to treat the island's various political parties on an equal footing.

Seeking constitutional refuge in the equality axiom doctrine, Puerto Rico's high court has held, inter alia, that all political parties are constitutionally required to receive equal access to the Commonwealth's public election fund,

Partido Socialista Puertorriqueño v. Secretario de Hacienda (1980); that majority and minority parties are constitutionally entitled to co-participate in the governance of the island's Election Commission (*Comisión Estatal de Elecciones*) regardless of their share of the electorate, *Partido Socialista Puertorriqueño v. Comisión Estatal de Elecciones* (1980); that incumbents cannot use their official (state-owned) vehicles for political campaigning, *Damián Marrero v. Municipio de Morovis* (1984); and that the statutory limitation on governmental advertising during an election year also applies, as a matter of Puerto Rican constitutional law, in the context of status plebiscites and referenda, *Partido Popular Democrático v. Gobernador II* (1994).

More recently, in a 5–4 decision, the supreme court in *Burgos v. Comisión Estatal de Elecciones* (2017) overturned *Partido Popular Democrático v. Gobernador II*, 136 D.P.R. 916 (1994), holding that the statutory provision limiting the government's capacity to place ads during an election year is not applicable to status plebiscites and referenda. Because the *Burgos* court did not mince words in announcing that there is no equality axiom in the Puerto Rico Constitution, the door is now wide open for dismantling by legislative or judicial fiat some of the more egalitarian aspects of the island's electoral superstructure. As well, the court's evisceration of the constitutional protection afforded to blank ballots, and the concomitant none-of-the-above voting, has also been the subject of considerable debate.

The court's overturning of *Sánchez Vilella y Colón Martínez v. Estado Libre Asociado* (1993) in *Suárez Cáceres v. Comisión Estatal de Elecciones* (2009) appears defective both substantively and procedurally. The fractured *Suárez Cáceres* court not only insisted on answering a question not properly before it, but justified its decision to strip protest voting of the constitutional protection announced in *Sánchez Vilella y Colón Martínez* on the basis of *Burdick v. Takushi* (1992), an inapposite federal case that does not limit Puerto Rico's capacity to provide voters with a more robust repertoire of local constitutional protections, if compared to those available at the federal level.

The Puerto Rico Supreme Court has yet to address whether write-in candidates, like those candidates appearing on the ballot, must meet the statutory requirements for holding office at the time of their election or at the moment of their swearing-in. The court's refusal to grant certiorari in *Rosario Rodríguez v. Rosselló Nevares* (2021) has left this question unanswered.

Section 3
Freedom of Religion; Complete Separation of Church and State

No law shall be made respecting an establishment of religion or prohibiting the free exercise thereof. There shall be complete separation of church and state.

Puerto Rico's path to religious freedom has been particularly circuitous. The Madisonian conception of a bundle of fundamental religious rights, premised on the symmetric interaction between the right to free exercise and the separation of church and state, was utterly foreign to Puerto Rico's legal repertoire during the prolonged period of Spanish colonial domination. Ever since the founding in 1511 of the Diocese of San Juan, and Pope Julius II's appointment of the Spanish prelate Alonso Manso as its first bishop, Catholicism had remained Puerto Rico's only official religion. It was the 1898 invasion, at the hands of the U.S. military command, that finally led to the disestablishment of the Catholic Church in Puerto Rico.

Similarly, the free exercise principle remained an elusive legal concept. While the 1869 and 1876 Spanish Constitutions did provide for the free exercise of religion in the peninsula, these legal instruments did not extend that right to Puerto Rico; neither did it apply *ex proprio vigore* to the island.

The right to the free exercise of religion, on the Madisonian model, made its first appearance in the Puerto Rican landscape with the signing of the 1898 Treaty of Paris and with the subsequent enactment of the 1902 local civil rights statute. *See* Section 1 of P.R. Law No. 42 of February 27, 1902 (PR ST T. 1, § 9). Congress finally exported to the island the exact language found in the First Amendment (including its disestablishment mandate) with the enactment of the Jones Act. *See* Section 2 of the Jones Act.

By the time the convention met in 1951, and in keeping with the values of the postwar world, there was unanimous consensus among the framers on the need to constitutionalize the religious freedoms then available under the Jones Act. Not only does Section 3 of the Puerto Rico Bill of Rights reproduce the language found in the religious clauses of the First Amendment, it also adds that "[t]here shall be complete separation of church and state"—a command that does not exist in the federal constitutional text.

The archival record shows that the framers designed Section 3 as the local corollary to the First Amendment's Establishment and Free Exercise Clauses. This is why the Puerto Rico Supreme Court, in tracing Section 3's scope and boundaries, has shown itself less inclined than in other areas to carve out an autochthonous analytical framework but, instead, has shown a marked propensity to mirror in full the U.S. Supreme Court's religious jurisprudence.

Despite the doctrinal infirmities surrounding the three-part test announced by Chief Justice Warren Burger in *Lemon v. Kurtzman* (1971), the Puerto Rico Supreme Court appears to have adopted it for purposes of issues arising under Section 3's establishment clause. In *Diócesis de Arecibo v. Secretario de Justicia* (2014), the court openly suggested that claims alleging an establishment violation are to be decided on the basis of *Lemon*. Thus, under Section 3's establishment clause, the challenged governmental action will only survive if it has a secular purpose, its primary effect neither advances nor inhibits religion, and it does not create an "excessive entanglement" between church and state.

Determining the proper test to apply under Section 3's free exercise clause has proved more problematic. Because Puerto Rico, unlike the fifty states, is a "covered entity" under the Religious Freedom Restoration Act (RFRA), *see* 42 U.S.C. § 2000bb-2, it is required to apply a free exercise test that does not coincide with the standard favored by the U.S. Supreme Court in *Church of the Lukumi Babalu Aye, Inc. v. City of Hialeah* (1993). Yet Puerto Rico's high court has never applied the free exercise test required under RFRA, choosing instead to seek refuge in *Church of the Lukumi*. These standards are incompatible and irreconcilable. While under *Church of the Lukumi* a law that is "neutral and of general applicability need not be justified by a compelling government interest even if the law has an incidental effect on burdening a particular religious practice," the same is not true under RFRA, which requires the showing of a compelling government interest "even if the burden results from a rule of general applicability." Solving this doctrinal asynchrony will require fresh thinking.

Recently, in *Roman Catholic Archdiocese of San Juan v. Acevedo Feliciano* (2020), the door was open for the U.S. Supreme Court to explore the penumbras of the First Amendment's Free Exercise Clause in light of a decision rendered by the Puerto Rico Supreme Court implicating the internal governance of the Catholic Church. In that case, the Puerto Rico high court found that the Archdiocese of San Juan (1511), together with the Dioceses of Ponce (1924), Arecibo (1960), Caguas (1964), Mayagüez (1976), and Fajardo-Humacao (2008), and all Catholic parishes, orders, and schools (unincorporated under Puerto Rico law) were "merely indivisible fragments of the legal personality that the Catholic Church has." *Acevedo Feliciano* was arguably premised on an erroneous reading of canon law. It is well settled that the five dioceses established in Puerto Rico in the post-1898 period by direct mandate of the Pope, in his unique role as Supreme Pontiff, acceded to the same legal status the San Juan Archdiocese has enjoyed since the sixteenth century. Each diocese is endowed with a distinct, unique, and independent legal personality with complete administrative and juridical autonomy, answerable only to the Holy See in Rome not to the San Juan Archdiocese.

While the U.S. Supreme Court reversed its Puerto Rican counterpart solely on jurisdictional grounds, in a concurring opinion Justices Samuel Alito and Clarence Thomas asserted that the local court's disfigurement of the Catholic Church's canonical governance raised "difficult questions" under the First Amendment's Free Exercise Clause.

Section 4
Freedom of Speech and Press; Peaceful Assembly; Petition for a
Redress of Grievances

No law shall be made abridging the freedom of speech or of the press, or the right of the people peaceably to assemble and to petition the government for a redress of grievances.

Mostly nonexistent throughout the four hundred years of Spanish colonial rule, the freedoms of speech, press, assembly, and petition in Puerto Rico have followed a rather tortuous path. But for those very few outbursts of Spanish constitutionalism in the wake of the 1812 Cádiz Constitution, the 1820–1823 liberal triennium, and the 1873 republican hiatus, these fundamental expressive freedoms were unavailable to Puerto Ricans during the chaotic nineteenth century. The 1898 U.S. invasion did not cure this systemic deficiency.

Moreover, in enacting the 1900 Foraker Act, Congress failed to grant to Puerto Rico any of the expressive freedoms available under the First Amendment. Unlike in the Philippines, where by 1902 Congress had statutorily extended the protections found in the First Amendment, *see* 32 Stat. 691 (1902), Puerto Rico's first exposure to the freedoms of speech, press, assembly and petition came by way of local legislation in 1902, *see* Section 3 of P.R. Law No. 42 of February 27, 1902 (PR ST T.1, § 3), and, subsequently, through Congress's enactment of the Jones Act a decade and a half later.

While the framers argued that they had designed a bill of rights significantly more advanced than the federal one, *see Estado Libre Asociado v. Hermandad de Empleados* (1975), attuned to the more progressive legal values of the postwar period, in the zone of expressive rights they followed the blueprint set out in the First Amendment. *See 4 Diario* 2564. Unsurprisingly, in drawing the boundaries of Section 4's substantive content, the Puerto Rico Supreme Court has followed very closely the U.S. Supreme Court's jurisprudence. Thus, as a threshold matter, the constitutional inquiry under Section 4 must examine whether the action or omission undertaken by the relevant governmental entity is content neutral, with respect to the particular ideas or viewpoints that have been expressed or to the impact this speech (expressive or symbolic) might have on a specific audience. Note that under Section 4, as under the First Amendment, the following speech is not constitutionally protected: speech that incites to imminent lawless action, obscenity (if prurient, offensive, and lacking any serious literary, artistic, political or scientific value), child pornography, defamatory speech, and false or misleading commercial speech.

In *Muñiz v. Administrador del Deporte Hípico* (2002), the supreme court reiterated that any governmental action burdening expressive activities on the basis of their content is presumed unconstitutional (regardless of the place of the speech) and can only survive if it meets strict scrutiny. Following the U.S. Supreme Court's approach in *New York Times v. United States* (1971), the island's high court in *Aponte Martínez v. Lugo* (1971) reversed a lower court's order enjoining the publication of a report authored by the accountant of the San Juan Archdiocese. The *Aponte Martínez* court held that the ruling issued by the judge below was a constitutionally impermissible prior restraint and, thus, could not stand.

Content-neutral restrictions are subject to time, place, and manner regulations. In *Pacheco Fraticelli v. Cintrón Antonsanti* (1988), the court characterized streets (including sidewalks), parks, and squares as public fora. Along similar lines, in *Coss y la Universidad de Puerto Rico v. Comisión Estatal de Elecciones* (1995), the court suggested that a designated or limited public forum is one not historically opened to speech-related activities but that the government has opened, by practice or policy, for those purposes. Pursuant to Puerto Rico's constitutional law, access to public fora and to designated or limited public fora enjoys the same protection. Content-neutral regulations of speech and assembly in public fora, and in designated or limited public fora, must be narrowly tailored to serve an important governmental interest while leaving open alternative channels of communication.

In *Universidad de Puerto Rico v. Laborde* (2010), the Puerto Rico Supreme Court found that the University of Puerto Rico, the island's only public higher learning institution, is not a public forum, but rather a limited public forum for purposes of time, place, and manner regulations. In *Unidad Nacional de Trabajadores de la Salud v. Soler Zapata* (1993), the court not only found that government-owned hospitals are nonpublic fora but, more generally, suggested that most public property is nonpublic in the context of time, place, and manner regulations. The *Soler Zapata* court, paying heed to federal case law, found that the Puerto Rico Department of Health's regulation prohibiting the distribution of leaflets and literature in those areas of public health care facilities where patients receive treatment was reasonably related to a legitimate governmental purpose. Thus, content-neutral governmental restrictions of speech or assembly in nonpublic fora, contrary to those applicable in public or designated fora, are susceptible to minimum scrutiny.

Together with the right to free speech, the freedom of the press sits at the forefront of the pantheon of expressive liberties safeguarded under Section 4. In *Disidente Universal de Puerto Rico v. Departamento de Estado* (1998), the supreme court outlined the scope of Section 4's freedom of the press. Seeking doctrinal refuge in local and federal authorities, including American legal treatises, the high court suggested that the protection of the press found in Section 4 precludes the government from arbitrarily restricting or restraining publications solely on the basis of their content or viewpoint, regardless of their "veracity, popularity or affinity." The *Disidente Universal* court intimated that one of the more basic values at the heart of Section 4 is the freedom of the press to decide what and when to print, while protecting the people's unalienable right to access this information in the way the press decides to publish it.

Interestingly, while Puerto Rico's high court has followed the federal path in delineating the contour of Section 4's expressive freedoms, it has parted ways with the U.S. Supreme Court's construction of the First Amendment in at least one significant way. In *Soto v. Secretario de Justicia* (1982), the court announced that, within the freedoms found in Section 4, there is also an implied right to access public information. In *Kilómetro O, Inc. v. Pesquera López* (2021), the court reminded the parties that, while the right to access public information is fundamental, it is not absolute. Restrictions on access to public information must meet strict scrutiny. *See also Ortiz v. Directora Administrativa de los Tribunales* (2000).

The government, on the one hand, must demonstrate it has legal authority to issue such a directive; and, on the other, it must show that it pursues a compelling (content-neutral) interest and that the measure adopted has been narrowly tailored. It was against this background that the Puerto Rico Court of First Instance in *Eva Prados Rodríguez v. Thomas Rivera Schatz* (2020), issued a writ of mandamus ordering the president of the senate to release the salaries of all senate employees, including those working in committees and as legislative aids.

Finally, the substantive content of the rights to assembly and petition available under Section 4, like the freedoms of speech and the press, also mirror the First Amendment. In *Estado Libre Asociado v. Hermandad de Empleados* (1975), the court indicated that the right to peaceably assemble is intimately intertwined to free speech. Because the right to freedom of speech would be meaningless and empty in the absence of an audience, the right to assembly is an indivisible corollary of free speech.

Similarly, in constitutionalizing the right to petition the government for the redress of grievances, the framers also intended to import the federal high court's relevant case law. A close inspection of the convention's records shows that, far from articulating an autochthonous, more robust, configuration of the First Amendment's right to petition, the framers clearly intended to import the federal version as it stood. In *Defendini Collazo v. Estado Libre Asociado* (1993), the court not only found that the right to petition is independent of Section 6's right to free association but that it is closely connected to the right to access the justice system.

Despite the framers' apparent commitment to the evolution of a culture of civil liberties in the island, within the framework of a robust corpus of expressive freedoms, the historical record confirms their omissions in this specific aspect of their constitution-making exercise. By the time the founders inaugurated the constitutional convention in 1951, that same leadership, also at the helm of the local legislature, had enacted P.R. Law No. 53 of June 10, 1948 (PR ST T.33, § 1471), which was an endogenous version of the Smith Act. *See* 18 U.S.C. § 2385. Not only did P.R. Law No. 53 remain in full force and effect following the inauguration of the 1952 Constitution but even after its abrogation in 1957 the island's law enforcement agencies continued with their systematic surveillance of the independence movement. And while this illegal practice was dismantled by the Puerto Rico Supreme Court in 1988, *see Noriega v. Gobernador* (1988), and *Noriega v. Gobernador II* (1992), the scars from that episode in Puerto Rican life have yet to fully heal. Preventing a sequel to that collective tragedy will require, in the Jeffersonian proverb, "eternal vigilance."

Section 5
Public Education

Every person has the right to an education which shall be directed to the full development of the human personality and to the strengthening of respect for human rights and fundamental freedoms. There shall be a system of free and wholly non-sectarian public education. Instruction in the elementary and secondary schools shall be free and shall be compulsory in the elementary schools to the extent permitted by the facilities of the state. Compulsory attendance at elementary public schools to the extent permitted by the facilities of the Commonwealth, as herein provided, shall not be construed as applicable to those who receive elementary education in schools established under non-governmental auspices. No public property or public funds shall be used for the support of schools or educational institutions other than those of the state. Nothing contained in this provision shall prevent the state from furnishing to any child non-educational services established by law for the protection or welfare of children.

In constitutionalizing the right to education, Puerto Rico's framers not only parted ways with their federal counterparts but also with the island's historical experience. At no point during the nineteenth century did the Spanish Crown extend to the people of Puerto Rico a right to education or any commensurate prerogative. Following the 1898 invasion, no right to education followed the American flag. Besides providing for the appointment by the president of the United States (with the advice and consent of the federal Senate) of a commissioner of education, none of the organic acts provided for an affirmative right to education. Thus, the ideological source of Section 5 cannot be found in any of the legal instruments Madrid or Washington extended to Puerto Rico, but rather in the Universal Declaration of Human Rights.

A close perusal of the language found in Section 5 shows that it coincides in significant ways with the text of Article 26 of the United Nations' Declaration. *See* Article 26 ("(1) Everyone has the right to education. Education shall be free, at least in the elementary and fundamental stages. Elementary education shall be compulsory [...]; (2) Education shall be directed to the full development of the human personality and to the strengthening of respect for human rights and fundamental freedoms.").

The archival record shows, moreover, that Puerto Rico's Constitutional Convention was wedded to the idea that education is not a privilege, but an unalienable human right, which the state is constitutionally bound to provide. *See Meléndez de León v. Keleher* (2018). This is precisely why the framers agreed to constitutionally require the establishment of a public and free education system, where elementary schooling is compulsory.

Nonetheless, in *Asociación de Academias y Colegios Cristianos de Puerto Rico v. Departamento de Educación* (1994), the supreme court found that the right to education announced in Section 5 is exclusively limited to elementary schooling and does not extend to university education. And even then, the island's high court seemed to suggest in *Asociación de Academias* that the government's constitutionally required obligations under Section 5 are contingent on the availability of the necessary public funds.

74 ■ THE PUERTO RICO CONSTITUTION AND COMMENTARY

By far the most puzzling aspect of Section 5 resides in deciphering the proper scope of its supporting clause (*cláusula de sostenimiento*). Section 5's supporting clause prohibits, in unequivocal terms, the use of public funds and property for the support of schools, or educational institutions, other than those of the government. While the supporting clause itself was not completely foreign to Puerto Rico's (and the mainland's) legal architecture *circa* 1952, defining its breadth has been the subject of intense constitutional (and political) debate.

Confronted with the question of whether the government can award publicly funded scholarships to students attending private schools, the supreme court in *Asociación de Maestros v. José Arsenio Torres* (1994) held that such a scheme was incompatible with Section 5's supporting clause. Yet, two decades later, in *Asociación de Maestros v. Departamento de Educación* (2018), a different court facing the same issue reversed course. The new court found that the supporting clause does not preclude the government from granting financial aid to students attending private schools. Besides the obvious public policy dimension of this debate, from a purely constitutional law perspective, the question before the court was the same in both cases: namely, whether Puerto Rico's own supporting clause ought to be construed independently and more robustly than the First Amendment's Establishment Clause or simply mirror it. In the aftermath of *Departamento de Educación*, the supporting clause has been considerably diluted. Under the new reading, the supporting clause is only triggered if the local government were to entirely replace the public school system with a private one, or substantially finance the private school system. Anything short of this, according to *Departamento de Educación*, would not run afoul of the supporting clause.

Besides limiting the government's entanglement with sectarian and nonsectarian private education, Section 5 explicitly suggests that the political branches do enjoy ample constitutional authority to pass legislation granting non-educational services to both public and private school children. While the framers did not provide an exhaustive list of constitutionally viable non-educational services, it is clear that they did refer, inter alia, to school cafeterias, milk stations, dental care, and transportation. *See* 2 *Diario* 1480, 1487.

Not only has the doctrinal construction of Section 5 been surrounded by vigorous debate but its ultimate ratification by Congress was also the subject of painstaking negotiations in Washington, D.C. In approving the constitution, Congress made it clear that Section 5 would have no force and effect until the people of Puerto Rico, by means of a constitutional amendment, incorporate language establishing that Section 5's requirement of compulsory elementary education could be met both at public and private (including sectarian) schools. Section 5 was amended retroactively by the voters on November 4, 1952, nearly four months after the inauguration of the constitution.

Section 6
Freedom of Association

Persons may join with each other and organize freely for any lawful purpose, except in military or quasi-military organizations.

Unlike the architects of the 1787 Philadelphia Convention, Puerto Rico's framers constitutionalized a distinct and independent right to free association. Unavailable during the Spanish colonial period, the right to free association remained invisible even after Congress's enactment of the Jones Act, which made no reference to it. Interestingly, the Puerto Rican founders' elevation to the bill of rights of a self-contained right to free association, autonomous from the right to free speech, antedated by six years Justice John Marshall Harlan's pathbreaking opinion in *NAACP v. Alabama* (1958).

The archival record shows that the framers' inclusion of this provision, together with their specific choice of words, was heavily influenced by the relevant texts of the Universal Declaration of Human Rights, as well as the American Declaration on the Rights and Duties of Man. Despite their ideological allegiance to the corpus of international human rights emerging in the postwar period, the framers explicitly exempted "military or quasi-military organizations" from the protective aegis of Section 6's right to free association. Thus, a literal reading of Section 6 would lead to the rather anomalous conclusion that in Puerto Rico there is no freedom to associate in "military or quasi-military organizations," even if that advocacy is not "directed to inciting or producing imminent lawless action and is not likely to incite or produce such action." *Brandenburg v. Ohio* (1969). Because this result would directly contravene federal doctrine, the framers' inclusion of this subordinate clause at the end of Section 6 is, arguably, without any legal merit. Sociologically, however, the incorporation into Section 6 of this subordinate clause shows how the framers, in the heyday of McCarthyism, succumbed to their biases against Puerto Rico's nationalist movement in the aftermath of the 1950 revolt.

In construing the right to free association, the Puerto Rico Supreme Court has shown a tendency to follow the federal blueprint. Pursuant to the mandate flowing from Section 6, a governmental measure significantly affecting the ability of a group engaged in "expressive association" to advocate its viewpoints must pass strict scrutiny. *See, e.g., Boy Scouts of America v. Dale* (2000).

In *Partido Nuevo Progresista v. De Castro Font* (2007), the island's high court posited that the right to free association protects a person's decisional autonomy to join with others in the furtherance of common goals, such as political advocacy. Furthermore, in *Rivera Schatz v. Estado Libre Asociado* (2014), not only did the court invalidate attorneys' mandatory membership to the Puerto Rico Bar Association (*Colegio de Abogados y Abogadas de Puerto Rico*) but it reminded the litigants that the right not to associate is as fundamental as the right to associate. In construing the proper dimension of the right not to associate, the court did

76 ■ THE PUERTO RICO CONSTITUTION AND COMMENTARY

not rely on First Amendment federal case law. Instead, seeking refuge in the "adequate and independent state grounds" doctrine, *Michigan v. Long* (1983), the court rendered its own autochthonous reading of Section 6's associational right pursuant to Puerto Rico's domestic constitutional law.

> Section 7
> Right to Life, Liberty, and Enjoyment of Property; No Death Penalty;
> Due Process; Equal Protection of Laws; Impairment of Contracts;
> Exemption of Property from Attachment
>
> The right to life, liberty and the enjoyment of property is recognized as a fundamental right of man. The death penalty shall not exist. No person shall be deprived of his liberty or property without due process of law. No person in Puerto Rico shall be denied the equal protection of the laws. No laws impairing the obligation of contracts shall be enacted. A minimum amount of property and possessions shall be exempt from attachment as provided by law.

Prohibition of the Death Penalty

The convention constitutionalized the prohibition of the death penalty. Despite the framers' opposition to capital punishment, the death penalty was not completely foreign to Puerto Rico's legal landscape. Both the 1879 and 1902 Criminal Codes, first under Spain and then under the United States, provided for the application of the death penalty to those individuals who committed the most heinous of crimes. The death penalty was finally abolished by local statute in 1929. *See* P.R. Law No. 42 of April 26, 1929 (PR ST T.34, § 995).

Deciding whether to constitutionalize the then existing statutory abolition of the death penalty gave rise to a lively debate at the convention. On the one hand, Delegates José Gelpí Bosch and Miguel Ángel García Méndez argued that, while the prohibition of the death penalty should be elevated to the constitutional text, the legislature should also be granted constitutional authority to decide whether to reinstate it. Others, such as Delegates Leopoldo Figueroa Carreras and Ramón Barreto Pérez, opposed this approach, advocating instead for an absolute constitutional prohibition of the death penalty. The latter position won the day. In the post-Nuremberg world, having embraced the higher values of the Universal Declaration of Human Rights embodied in the inviolability of human dignity, nothing short of the constitutional abolition of the death penalty would have met the demands of most delegates.

Yet the debate over the death penalty in Puerto Rico continues. The enactment in 1994 of the Federal Death Penalty Act, *see* 18 U.S.C. §§ 3591–3598, which authorizes the application of the death penalty to defendants across the fifty states and the territories charged with various types of federal crimes, has led to a dilution of the anti-death penalty mandate flowing from Section

7. Interestingly, in *U.S. v. Acosta Martínez* (2000), the U.S. District Court for the District of Puerto Rico found that the Federal Death Penalty Act was "locally inapplicable" under the 1950 Federal Relations Act due to Section 7's constitutional prohibition. Shortly thereafter, the U.S. Court of Appeals for the First Circuit reversed, holding that nothing in the Puerto Rico Constitution stands in the way of Congress's "ability to impose penalties for federal crimes" committed in the island. *U.S. v. Acosta Martínez* (2001) ("[T]he argument made by defendants and amici," the court observed, "is a political one, not a legal one.").

Due Process

As a threshold matter, it is important to note that the Fifth Amendment's Due Process Clause did follow the American flag to Puerto Rico in 1898. Because the rights emanating from the federal Due Process Clause are "fundamental" in nature (contrary to those emanating from the structural provisions of the federal Constitution), they have applied *ex proprio vigore* in the island from the time of the 1898 invasion pursuant to the doctrine of territorial incorporation arising under the Insular Cases. *See Balzac v. Puerto Rico* (1922) ("[t]he guaranties of certain fundamental personal rights declared in the Constitution, as, for instance, that no person could be deprived of life, liberty, or property without due process of law, had from the beginning full application in the Philippines and Porto Rico [...]"). Further, in enacting the Jones Act, Congress superimposed therein the same language found in the federal Due Process Clause. *Mora v. Mejías* (1953) ("No doubt under the Organic Act of 1917 the insular government was subject to the Due Process Clause of the Fifth Amendment.").

Textually, Section 7's due process clause is almost identical to its Jones Act's predecessor, with the only exception that the Puerto Rican provision makes reference only to liberty and property interests. Because the framers believed the constitutional prohibition of the death penalty made redundant the inclusion of the life component of the federal Due Process Clause, it was not reproduced in the text.

The ghost of *Lochner v. New York* (1905), in which the U.S. Supreme Court read into the Due Process Clauses of the Fifth and Fourteenth Amendments the protection of socioeconomic interests, was not lost on the Puerto Rican framers. In delineating the contours of Section 7's due process clause, some voices within the convention insisted on adding a supplemental subclause establishing that the substantive due process protections ingrained therein could not be invoked by the courts in order to annul on a whim socioeconomic legislation. Although this proposal died a quiet death, the post-1952 Puerto Rico Supreme Court case law shows how the local judiciary has afforded great deference to the legislature's intervention in socioeconomic matters.

78 ■ THE PUERTO RICO CONSTITUTION AND COMMENTARY

In *Rivera Rodriguez & Co. v. Stowell Taylor* (1993), the Puerto Rico high court reiterated that Section 7's due process clause encompasses two distinct, yet intertwined, dimensions: one procedural and the other substantive. Mimicking the standard applied by its federal counterpart under the Due Process Clauses of both the Fifth and Fourteenth Amendments, the Puerto Rico Supreme Court has consistently applied rational basis review to socioeconomic legislation (or regulations). For instance, in *Marina Industrial, Inc. v. Brown Boveri Corporation* (1983) the court upheld the constitutionality of Puerto Rico's local distribution statute on the basis of minimum scrutiny; having found that P.R. Law No. 75 of June 24, 1964 (PR ST T.10, § 278 *et seq.*) bore a rational relationship to a legitimate state interest; namely, infusing stability and certainty to the legal relationships binding local distributors and dealers with their respective principals or suppliers.

Perhaps the most significant distinction between Puerto Rico's due process clause and its federal counterparts is the fact that the former is not considered the constitutional source of the local right to privacy, the source of which is found in Article II's Section 8.

Unsurprisingly, the panoply of procedural due process protections flowing from Section 7 also mirror their federal counterparts. Similarly, their activation will depend on whether the challenged governmental action (or omission) intrudes on an individual's protected liberty or property interests. *Rivera Santiago v. Secretario de Hacienda* (1987). In *McConnell v. Palau* (2004), the court reiterated that adversarial governmental proceedings, implicating an individual's protected liberty or property interests, must afford the affected party proper notice, a transparent hearing before an impartial judge, as well as an opportunity to be heard, to cross-examine opposing witnesses, to examine the evidence against him or her, to retain legal counsel, and to have a decision made on the available record.

Equal Protection

The equal protection safeguards found in the federal Constitution, like the due process rights emanating from it, followed the American flag in the aftermath of the invasion of 1898. Because equal protection under the law is a fundamental federal right, it applied to Puerto Rico *ex proprio vigore* under the constitutional doctrine concocted by the Fuller Court in the Insular Cases. It was against this background that Congress included an equal protection clause in the catalogue of individual rights attached to Section 2 of the Jones Act.

The incorporation into the Puerto Rico Bill of Rights of an autochthonous equal protection clause did not stir significant debate at the convention. While Section 1 of the bill of rights declares that "[a]ll men are equal before the law" and, contrary to its federal counterpart, explicitly identifies a list of suspect classes, the framers nonetheless agreed to place an endogenous equal protection provision right next to Section 7's due process clause. Since the equality language found in Section 1 was framed in the context of natural persons, it was believed that the inclusion of an equal protection provision (following the federal model) would send a clear signal that legal persons are also protected under Section 7's equal protection clause.

In *Defendini Collazo v. Estado Libre Asociado* (1993), the Puerto Rico Supreme Court reiterated that, under Section 7, there is no intermediate scrutiny. Thus, governmental classifications based on gender and birth, like those motivated by race, color, alienage, social origin or condition, political, or religious ideas, must all meet strict scrutiny, which ideologically responds to the higher constitutional values ingrained in the inviolability of human dignity. The *Defendini Collazo* court further suggested that strict scrutiny is also constitutionally required when the legislative action infringes on the exercise of rights as fundamental as the right to vote, the right to religious freedom and free speech, the right to life, the right to privacy, and the right to access the criminal and civil courts.

In *Rodríguez Pagán v. Departamento de Servicios Sociales* (1993), the island's high court not only intimated that legislative actions placing undue burdens on the constitutional rights to counsel and interstate travel must meet strict scrutiny but held that governmental measures infringing on the right of minors placed in foster homes to seek child support must also pass muster under the strict scrutiny standard.

One of the more relevant, yet unfinished, debates surrounding the proper scope of Section 7's equal protection clause revolves around the issue of whether a facially neutral statute, administered in a nondiscriminatory manner, can be found unconstitutional solely for having an unintended "disproportionate impact" on a protected constitutional class. Arguably, the blind extrapolation of the rule announced by the U.S. Supreme Court in *Washington v. Davis* (1976), which requires a showing of "invidious discriminatory purpose," might run counter to the structural and ideological designs of the Puerto Rican framers. While as a matter of federal constitutional law, Puerto Rico is bound, at a minimum, to offer the same quantum of protection available under the Fifth and Fourteenth Amendments' Equal Protection Clauses, it is well settled that nothing in the federal constitutional text prevents Puerto Rico from extending even greater and more robust protections under Section 7's equal protection clause.

Contracts Clause

In Puerto Rico, the constitutional protection against the impairment of contracts followed a different historical path as compared to the due process and equal protection safeguards. Contrary to the 1902 Philippines Organic Act (32 Stat. 691 (1902)), the Foraker Act did not provide an analogous provision to the federal Contracts Clause. *See* U.S. Const. Art. 1, § 10, Cl. 1. Until the enactment of the Jones Act in 1917, it was not at all clear whether the territorial legislature was precluded from impairing (under certain circumstances) both public and private contracts. This legal lacuna was finally filled by Congress with the incorporation to the Jones Act of a locally applicable contracts clause.

Despite the waning significance of the federal Contracts Clause as a matter of federal constitutional law *circa* 1952, constitutionalizing the local contracts clause met with the approval of the framers, who viewed it as a tool for infusing further stability and legal certainty to the island's wide commercial traffic.

More recently, the Puerto Rico Supreme Court has reacquainted itself with Section 7's contracts clause. In *Trinidad Hernández v. Estado Libre Asociado* (2013), the court, in validating the constitutionality of the modifications made by the government to the retirement benefits of public employees, reviewed the analytical framework behind Section 7's contracts clause. The *Trinidad Hernández* court made it clear that the governmental impairment of contracts between (or among) private parties must be rationally related to a legitimate state interest. Furthermore, the government's impairment of its own contractual obligations must meet a higher standard: it must be necessary to achieve an important governmental interest. In *Asociación de Maestros v. Sistema de Retiro* (2014), while reiterating these principles, the Puerto Rico Supreme Court found that the changes made to the pension plans of public school teachers ran afoul of Section 7's contracts clause.

PROMESA has, still more recently, eroded the vitality of Puerto Rico's contracts clause.

Exemption of Property from Attachment

Puerto Rico's local legal framework had long afforded natural persons a minimum degree of protection from embargoes or attachments to their property. *See* P.R. Law No. 107 of March 12, 1903 (PR ST T.32, § 2907). By the time the framers inaugurated the constitutional convention in 1951, the applicable statute exempted from embargo the first $500 stemming from the execution of an individual's primary home (*hogar seguro*). *See* P.R. Law No. 87 of May 13, 1936 (PR ST T.31, § 1851). Consistent with the then existing statutory design, and in furtherance of the ideological values informing the Puerto Rico Bill of Rights, the framers decided to constitutionalize the legislature's authority to exempt from attachment a minimum quantum of real estate and personal property. *See Money's People Inc. v. Julia López* (2019).

Section 8
Protection against Attacks on Honor, Reputation, and Private Life

Every person has the right to the protection of law against abusive attacks on his honor, reputation and private or family life.

Paramount among the enumerated rights in Puerto Rico's bill of rights is the right to privacy. In explicitly incorporating the right to privacy into the constitutional text, the framers parted ways not only with the federal Bill of Rights but with most of the state constitutions in full force and effect *circa* 1952. A close textual inspection of Section 8 shows that the language chosen by the framers mirrors the values enshrined both in the United Nations' Universal Declaration of Human Rights and in the American Declaration of the Rights and Duties of Man.

Constitutionalizing the right to privacy not only signaled a clear break from the Jones Act's ideological straitjacket but opened the door to the importation into Puerto Rico of postwar conceptions of individual freedoms then unavailable in the federal landscape. From a comparative law perspective, the framers read Section 8's right to privacy as superimposing on the island the protections found in the American common law, together with the new catalogue of individual rights then evolving in the European legal culture. *See, e.g., Cortés Portalatín v. Hau Colón* (1975).

In Puerto Rico, as the supreme court reiterated in *Castro v. Tiendas Pitusa* (2003), the right to privacy is self-executing and, therefore, operates *ex proprio vigore*. Moreover, Puerto Rico's domestic right to privacy is not limited by the labyrinthic state action doctrine and may be triggered, instead, by the actions of public and private actors alike. *Castro v. Tiendas Pitusa* (2003); *see also Siaca v. Bahía Beach Resort* (2016).

In *Diócesis de Arecibo v. Secretario de Justicia* (2014), the island's high court suggested that, in order to successfully prosecute a right to privacy claim, the plaintiff must show, prima facie, he or she enjoys a reasonable expectation of privacy within the specific factual context of the case. A constitutionally viable expectation of privacy must be both subjectively and objectively reasonable, meaning that the expectation of privacy entertained by the plaintiff must also seem reasonable within a wider community standard.

The universe of supreme court decisions addressing Section 8's right to privacy involves cases touching upon an individual's fundamental right to exercise his or her own decisional autonomy as well as controversies surrounding his or her right to control the disclosure of his or her personal information. *See López Vives v. Policía de Puerto Rico* (1987). Invoking Section 8's right to privacy, the court in *Belk Arce v. Martínez* (1998) reminded the parties that the right to marry belongs to that pantheon of fundamental rights implicating an individual's privacy interest. More specifically, the *Belk Arce* court held that private employers cannot discriminate against their employees on the basis of their marital status. Similarly, in *Siaca v. Bahía Beach Resort* (2016), the court held that private employers cannot unduly burden a woman's capacity to breastfeed; doing so would run afoul of their right to privacy under Section 8. In *Indulac v. Central General de Trabajadores* (2021), the court held that an employee's installation of a hidden camera in the office of a co-worker violated that co-worker's right to privacy.

The Puerto Rico Supreme Court has also found that individuals enjoy an expectation of privacy, inter alia, in their banking statements, *RDT v. Contralor I* (1996); their mobile phone records, *Weber Carrillo v. Estado Libre Asociado* (2014); information surrounding sexual abuse claims, *Diócesis de Arecibo v. Secretario de Justicia* (2014); and their own image, *Vigoreaux Lorenzana v. Quizno's* (2008).

Section 8's right to privacy offers women an independent basis for the constitutional protection of their reproductive rights in the aftermath of *Dobbs v. Jackson Women's Health Organization* (2022). *See Pueblo v. Duarte* (1980).

Section 9
Just Compensation for Private Property

Private property shall not be taken or damaged for public use except upon payment of just compensation and in the manner provided by law. No law shall be enacted authorizing condemnation of printing presses, machinery or material devoted to publications of any kind. The buildings in which these objects are located may be condemned only after a judicial finding of public convenience and necessity pursuant to procedure that shall be provided by law, and may be taken before such a judicial finding only when there is placed at the disposition of the publication an adequate site in which it can be installed and continue to operate for a reasonable time.

The eminent domain authority is well established. The protection against takings embodied in Section 9 antedates the 1952 Constitution. The Spanish Constitution of 1876, and more specifically the 1879 *Ley de Expropiación Forzosa*, Law of January 10, 1879, provided (at least de jure) safeguards against the illegal confiscation of private property at the hands of governmental entities. Because by the time the McKinley Administration consummated the 1898 invasion of Puerto Rico, the U.S. Supreme Court had already held in *Chicago, B. & Q. R.R. Co. v. Chicago* (1897) that the right to just compensation under the Fifth Amendment was fundamental and applicable to the states through the Due Process Clause of the Fourteenth Amendment, it is safe to conclude that this protection was enforceable *ex proprio vigore* in the island from the outset of American rule.

Both the 1902 Civil Code, Article 355 of the 1902 Civil Code, and the 1903 locally enacted law of expropriation, *see* P.R. Law of March 12, 1903 (PR ST T.32, § 2907), soon regulated the procedural strictures governing the legislature's exercise of its formidable power of eminent domain. Congress, for its part, appended to the Jones Act's incipient bill of rights a takings clause, identically worded to its Fifth Amendment counterpart. In drafting Puerto Rico's takings clause, the framers insisted on extrapolating to the new constitutional text the Fifth Amendment's Madisonian language, in an effort to infuse Section 9 with clarity and interpretative coherence.

Determining what constitutes "public use" under Section 9, the supreme court concluded in *Estado Libre Asociado v. Aguayo* (1958), falls under the exclusive aegis of the legislature. On the other hand, defining just compensation, pursuant to Section 9, falls exclusively on the judiciary, as the court reiterated in *Municipio de Guaynabo v. Adquisición* (2010). *See also Autoridad de Carreteras v. Adquisición de 8,554.741 Metros* (2007).

The government's (full or partial) physical taking of private property immediately triggers the safeguards available under Section 9. *Plaza de Descuentos v. Estado Libre Asociado* (2010). Regulatory takings must also pass muster under Section 9. In *Torres Marrero v. Alcaldesa de Ponce* (2017), the Puerto Rico Supreme Court concluded that, whenever a governmental regulation denies "all economically beneficial use of land," Section 9 is activated, requiring that the government pays just compensation to the aggrieved party.

In deciding whether Section 9 requires the payment of just compensation for a partial regulatory taking, where the government's actions are only temporary or not sufficiently burdensome to deny "all economically beneficial use of the land," the Puerto Rico Supreme Court has engaged in a case by case balancing test. *Hampton Development v. Estado Libre Asociado* (1996). The test distinguishes between a valid exercise of the legislature's police powers and a constitutionally impermissible invasion of private property rights through the use of its eminent domain authority. In drawing this nuanced distinction, the court has been inclined to apply the test announced by Justice William Brennan in *Penn Central Transportation v. New York City* (1978), paying heed to the character of the governmental regulation and its economic impact on the private proprietary interests involved. *See Torres Marrero, supra.*

The island's high court made it clear in *Autoridad de Carreteras v. Adquisición de 8,554.741 Metros* (2007) that the payment of interests is an essential component of just compensation under Section 9. Section 9, moreover, requires that the interest rate be reasonable. The court in *Autoridad de Carreteras* announced that awards for just compensation must follow the interest rates set by Puerto Rico's Commissioner of Financial Institutions.

In *Administración de Terrenos de Puerto Rico v. Ponce Bayland Enterprises* (2021), the court held that evidence of environmental contamination and remediation costs are relevant for determining the fair market value of the condemned property and is, therefore, admissible in the expropriation proceedings subject to the requirements of the Puerto Rico Rules of Evidence.

Following Congress's enactment of PROMESA in 2016, the Puerto Rico Supreme Court stayed all pending claims against the government for just compensation under Section 9. Seeking refuge in PROMESA's automatic stay of litigation, *see* PROMESA's Section 405(b), the court has indefinitely postponed the vindication of litigants' constitutional rights under Section 9.

Unlike the Fifth Amendment, Article II's Section 9 also prohibits the condemnation of printing presses and their machinery and publication materials.

84 ■ THE PUERTO RICO CONSTITUTION AND COMMENTARY

This prohibition, originally proposed by the delegates of the Socialist Party, is absolute. Similarly, those buildings housing printing presses are constitutionally protected. Section 9 explicitly establishes that their condemnation requires a judicial decree of public convenience and necessity, except for those cases where an alternative facility has already been identified. Section 9, thus, severely limits the legislature's power of eminent domain in the context of printing presses.

> Section 10
> Searches and Seizures; Wiretapping; Warrants
>
> The right of the people to be secure in their persons, houses, papers and effects against unreasonable searches and seizures shall not be violated.
>
> Wire-tapping is prohibited.
>
> No warrant for arrest or search and seizure shall issue except by judicial authority and only upon probable cause supported by oath or affirmation, and particularly describing the place to be searched and the persons to be arrested or the things to be seized.
>
> Evidence obtained in violation of this section shall be inadmissible in the courts.

Searches and Seizures

Prior to the 1952 Constitution, the protection against unreasonable searches and seizures was statutory in nature. Unavailable during most of the Spanish colonial period, it made its first appearance on Puerto Rican soil in 1902. *See* Section 2 of P.R. Law No. 42 of February 27, 1902 (PR ST T.1, § 10). Congress elevated this local statutory safeguard into the Jones Act.

By the time the framers constitutionalized the protection against unreasonable searches and seizures, the U.S. Supreme Court had already incorporated the bulk of the Fourth Amendment into the Fourteenth Amendment's Due Process Clause. In drafting Section 10's search and seizure protection, the Puerto Rican framers, as the archival record shows, sought to import the same language found in the federal provision.

In *Puerto Rico v. Coca Cola* (1984), the Puerto Rico Supreme Court announced that, except for decisions of the U.S. Supreme Court setting forth the minimum standard required under the Fourth Amendment, all other federal case law is but persuasive. Thus, on occasion, the Puerto Rico Supreme Court in construing Section 10 has parted ways with the federal high court, extending to local defendants a more robust repertoire of constitutional protections. For instance, in *Pueblo v. Vélez Bonilla* (2013), the court refused to mimic the federal rule announced in *Arizona v. Youngblood* (1988) establishing that the government's failure to preserve potentially exculpatory evidence would only violate due process on a showing of bad faith. Under *Vélez Bonilla*, governmental negligence alone constitutes a violation of the defendant's due process rights under Section 7 above.

Moreover, in *Pueblo v. Dolce* (1976), the island's high court openly rejected the "full search" rule announced in *United States v. Robinson* (1973), thereby limiting the scope of a warrantless search incident to a valid arrest. In *Dolce*, the court found that only a superficial search is reasonable in this context. Under *Coca Cola*, the government bears the burden of rebutting the presumption that a warrantless search or seizure is unreasonable per se and, hence, violative of Section 10. *See Coca Cola, supra.*

Interestingly, the Puerto Rico Supreme Court has yet to decide whether the federal doctrine of stop and frisk announced in *Terry v. Ohio* (1968) is compatible with the letter and spirit of Section 10. The court, moreover, has not shied away from incorporating into the local legal milieu the ample corpus of exceptions to the Fourth Amendment's warrant requirement, as carved out by its federal counterpart.

It is well settled that a warrantless search incident to a valid arrest does not run afoul of the strictures of Section 10. *See, e.g., Pueblo v. Riscard* (1967). Section 10, moreover, does not require a warrant if the person to be searched, or whose belongings are to be searched, so consents. In *Pueblo v. Acevedo Escobar* (1982), the island's high court conceded that such consent could be explicitly or tacitly tendered. Although it remains unclear whether the Puerto Rico Supreme Court will embrace the automobile exception adopted by its federal counterpart, it is well settled that the police may search a vehicle incident to a valid arrest only when the suspect is unsecured and within reaching distance of the passenger compartment at the time of the search. *Pueblo v. Malavé González* (1988).

Furthermore, in *Pueblo v. Ortiz Martínez* (1985), the court reiterated that Section 10 does not require a warrant for searching or seizing evidence abandoned by a suspect. Similarly, in *Pueblo v. Lebrón* (1979), the court suggested that warrants are not required for searching abandoned structures. As well, the *Lebrón* court intimated that the "open fields" doctrine, originally announced by Justice Oliver Wendell Holmes in *Hester v. United States* (1924), appears to be fully applicable in Puerto Rico.

Likewise, as the court explained in *Pueblo v. Malavé González* (1988), objects in plain view are susceptible to warrantless searches or seizures. Inventory searches of vehicles, *see Pueblo v. Rodríguez Rodríguez* (1991), along with administrative searches in "closely regulated industries," *Pueblo v. Ferreira Morales* (1998), are also exempted from Section 10's warrant requirement. In *Pueblo v. Rivera Collazo* (1988), the court indicated that Section 10 does not require a search warrant "to prevent a shooting or to bring emergency aid to an injured person." In *Pueblo v. Báez López* (2013) and in *Pueblo v. Díaz Medina* (2009), the Puerto Rico Supreme Court adopted the plain feel and plain smell doctrines, respectively. Yet, contrary to the federal rule, under *Báez López* and *Díaz Medina* the police must have discovered the contraband inadvertently. Otherwise, the seized evidence could be susceptible to suppression.

86 ■ THE PUERTO RICO CONSTITUTION AND COMMENTARY

Notwithstanding the above-referenced exceptions to the warrant requirement, the scope of Section 10's constitutional protection is commensurate with the safeguards available under the Fourth Amendment. In *Pueblo v. Soto Soto* (2006), for example, the Puerto Rico Supreme Court imported the federal standard for drawing the boundaries of the "curtilage" adjoining the property to be searched, where the interested party might enjoy a legitimate expectation of privacy.

Prohibition against Wiretapping

The framers' explicit prohibition against wiretapping, unavailable under the Jones Act, finds no counterpart in the federal Constitution. In *Puerto Rico Telephone Company v. Martínez* (1983), the Puerto Rico Supreme Court, paying heed to Delegate José Trías Monge's admonition, *see* 3 *Diario* 1586, found that Section 10's wiretapping prohibition is a corollary of Section 8's right to privacy. The framers' decision to constitutionalize the prohibition against wiretapping notably preceded the U.S. Supreme Court's enlargement of the Fourth Amendment's protection from "unreasonable searches and seizures" to cover wiretapping. Not only does Section 10's wiretapping prohibition antedate *Katz v. United States* (1967), it offers a far more robust protection from governmental intrusion than the rule announced in *Katz*.

Section 10's wiretapping prohibition is close to absolute. Not even a court order can undo its rather strict mandate, as the island's high court held in *Pueblo v. Santiago Feliciano* (1995). Only the consent of the telephone call's participants, accompanied by a supporting court order, can trump Section 10's explicit wiretapping prohibition. *See id.*

Section 10's wiretapping prohibition, moreover, is exclusively circumscribed to telephone conversations. *See id.* All other modalities of oral communications, as the *Santiago Feliciano* court announced, are susceptible to governmental intrusion if preceded by a court order substantiated on probable cause. *See id.* Nonetheless, in *United States v. Quiñones* (1985), the U.S. Court of Appeals for the First Circuit made it clear that Section 10's wiretapping prohibition did not preclude the applicability to the island of Congress's Omnibus Crime Control Act, which allows the admission in federal court of "consensually recorded" telephone conversations that would have been preempted under Puerto Rico's Constitution. *See* 82 Stat. 212 (1968), as amended.

Warrants Shall Issue upon Probable Cause Supported by Oath or Affirmation

Section 10, mirroring the Fourth Amendment, establishes that search and arrest warrants must be based on "probable cause," supported by oath or affirmation and describe with "particularity" the places to be searched or the persons (or things) to be seized. By the time the constitutional convention met in 1951, the "probable cause" requirement was already available under the Jones Act. Yet the framers' most significant contribution was elevating it to the constitutional text.

In *Pueblo v. Muñoz, Colón y Ocasio* (1992), the Puerto Rico Supreme Court found that Section 10 requires that a determination of probable cause be premised on an affirmation from a declarant on his or her perception of the facts; on information produced by a third party; or on a combination of both. The *Muñoz, Colón y Ocasio* court further suggested that Section 10 requires a careful examination of the veracity of the information proffered by an anonymous informant. In *Pueblo v. Ortiz Alvarado* (1994), the court adopted the federal rule enunciated in *Illinois v. Gates* (1983), requiring that the police officer confirms the veracity of the anonymous tip through personal observation or against information received from independent (and reliable) sources.

Section 10's warrant requirement, however, is not absolute. In *Pueblo v. Martínez Torres* (1988), the court reiterated that a warrantless arrest does not always run afoul of Section 10. In *Martínez Torres*, the court suggested that a police officer does not need a warrant to arrest a person who commits a crime in his or her presence; nor is a warrant required to arrest a suspect if the officer has a "reasonable belief" (*motivos fundados*) that the suspect has committed or is about to commit a felony (*delito grave*).

Structurally, Section 10's warrant requirement parted ways with the Jones Act and the *Código de Enjuiciamiento Criminal* in force during the pre-1952 period. In constitutionalizing the principle that issuing a search or arrest warrant is the exclusive province of a judge, the framers put an end to the pernicious practice whereby a district attorney (*fiscal*), beholden to the *Procurador General* and the executive branch, was also entrusted with statutory authority to issue warrants. Separating the judicial branch from the executive branch was a policy imperative for the framers. *See* 4 *Diario* 2568.

The Exclusionary Rule and the Fruit of the Poisonous Tree

Unlike the Fourth Amendment, Section 10 explicitly prohibits the government from introducing evidence resulting from an unreasonable search or seizure. Interestingly, the exclusionary rule was not altogether foreign to Puerto Rico's legal culture prior to its constitutional elevation. While unavailable under the limited catalogue of individual rights found in the Jones Act, the exclusionary rule had already been adopted locally by judicial fiat in *Pueblo v. Capriles* (1941). Thus, one of the framers' more significant contributions to Puerto Rico's legal landscape was constitutionalizing the exclusionary rule. The superimposition of the exclusionary safeguard to the island's constitutional text antedated *Mapp v. Ohio* (1961), where the U.S. Supreme Court held that the federal exclusionary principle announced in *Weeks v. United States* (1914) was enforceable against the states pursuant to the Fourteenth Amendment's Due Process Clause.

In Puerto Rico, as the court explained in *Pueblo v. Fernández Rodríguez* (2013), the exclusionary rule has been used to suppress ill-gotten evidence, along with

88 ■ THE PUERTO RICO CONSTITUTION AND COMMENTARY

the poisonous fruit derived therefrom, in a variety of settings. The *Fernández Rodríguez* court, seeking refuge in a long line of federal case law, held that Section 10's exclusionary directive is only available to suppress evidence gathered by the government in the course of unreasonable searches and seizures. Against this background, Section 10 does not require the exclusion of evidence derived from the breach of an evidentiary privilege. *See id.* In *Toll v. Adorno Medina* (1992), the court concluded that Section 10's exclusionary rule is inapplicable in civil cases involving private parties alone. Under the principle announced in *Adorno Medina*, Section 10's exclusionary rule is only available in those civil cases where the government (including its agencies or instrumentalities) appears as a party and the contested evidence is the fruit of an unreasonable search or seizure attributable to a public officer. Under *Adorno Medina*, the exclusionary rule is also triggered if the challenged evidence in the civil litigation where the government appears was collected by force or brutality or by breaching the opposing party's constitutionally guaranteed right to privacy.

Section 11
Criminal Prosecutions; Jury Trial; Self Incrimination; Double Jeopardy; Bail; Imprisonment

In all criminal prosecutions, the accused shall enjoy the right to have a speedy and public trial, to be informed of the nature and cause of the accusation and to have a copy thereof, to be confronted with the witnesses against him, to have compulsory process for obtaining witnesses in his favor, to have assistance of counsel, and to be presumed innocent.

In all prosecutions for a felony the accused shall have the right of trial by an impartial jury composed of twelve residents of the district, who may render their verdict by a majority vote which in no case may be less than nine.

No person shall be compelled in any criminal case to be a witness against himself and the failure of the accused to testify may be neither taken into consideration nor commented upon against him.

No person shall be twice put in jeopardy of punishment for the same offense.

Before conviction every accused shall be entitled to be admitted to bail.

Incarceration prior to trial shall not exceed six months nor shall bail or fines be excessive. No person shall be imprisoned for debt.

Right to a Speedy Trial

The right to a speedy trial was first incorporated into the Puerto Rican legal landscape through the local enactment of the 1902 Code of Criminal Procedure (*Código de Enjuiciamiento Criminal*). *See* Article 11(1) of the 1902 Code of Criminal Procedure. Fifteen years later, Congress included the right to a speedy trial in the Jones Act's limited catalogue of individual rights. When the constitutional convention first met in September 1951, the right to a speedy trial was purely statutory in nature: the U.S. Supreme Court had yet to establish that the Sixth Amendment's right to a speedy trial was fundamental and enforceable against the states under the Due Process Clause of the Fourteenth Amendment. Thus, at the time, there was no constitutional right to a speedy trial in Puerto Rico. Therein lies the significance of Section 11's speedy trial clause.

In construing the metes and bounds of Section 11's right to a speedy trial, the Puerto Rico Supreme Court has strictly adhered to the dictates of the federal high court. In *Pueblo v. Rivera Tirado* (1986), a divided court found that the right to a speedy trial is activated as soon as the suspect is arrested or indicted and held to answer. In so doing, the *Rivera Tirado* court followed the federal approach, which also limits the right to a speedy trial to the post-arrest context.

The Puerto Rico Supreme Court has shied away from adopting a more autochthonous approach to its application of the right to a speedy trial, despite the fact that nothing in the federal Constitution stands in the way of the court's authority to carve out a more robust protection as a matter of Puerto Rico constitutional law. In furtherance of Section 11's mandate, Rule 64(n) of the Puerto Rico Rules of Criminal Procedure establishes specific timetables for the unfolding of the criminal justice proceedings. *See* PR ST T.34, Ap. II, § 64.

The right to a speedy trial is not absolute. *See Pueblo v. Rivera Tirado* (1986). In determining the viability of a defendant's motion to dismiss for breach of the right to a speedy trial under Section 11, the inferior courts will engage in a balancing test weighing the following elements: the duration of the delay, the reasons for the delay, defendant's responsibility (if any) in the delay, his or her consent to it, and the prosecution's showing of just cause for the delay. Lastly, the lower courts will look at the overall prejudices resulting from the delay. While waivable, constitutional rights such as the right to a speedy trial must be renounced expressly and explicitly, not tacitly. *Pueblo v. Arcelay Galán* (1974).

In *Pueblo v. Camacho Delgado* (2008), the court held that the remedy for a breach of the right to a speedy trial is the dismissal of the criminal action against the defendant. The prosecution must then decide whether to again seek a determination of probable cause for arrest under Rule 6 of the Rules of Criminal Procedure. PR ST T.34, Ap. II, § 6.

Right to a Public Trial

The right to a public trial, initially found in the 1902 Code of Criminal Procedure and subsequently in the Jones Act, *see* Article 11(1) of the 1902 Code of Criminal Procedure, was constitutionalized by the framers in Section 11. Unlike the right to a speedy trial, the Sixth Amendment's right to a public trial was at the time deemed fundamental by the U.S. Supreme Court, *see In re Oliver* (1948), and, hence, incorporated into the Fourteenth Amendment's Due Process Clause, enforceable against the states and the unincorporated territories (including Puerto Rico) before the inauguration of the 1952 Constitution.

The framers' constitutionalization of a local right to a public trial means the island's judiciary, while required to afford defendants the minimum federal standard under the Sixth Amendment, is not precluded from crafting an endogenous balancing test for weighing the right of the defendant to an impartial jury (free from prejudicial media coverage) versus the right of the public and the press to access judicial proceedings. Nonetheless, not only has the Puerto Rico Supreme Court shown itself disinclined to tailor a more progressive doctrine but, in some instances, it has construed the content of the right to a public trial more restrictively than the federal high court.

In *El Vocero de Puerto Rico v. Puerto Rico* (1992), the court upheld the constitutionality, under Section 11, of a local rule of criminal procedure requiring that all preliminary criminal hearings be closed to the public and the press. The U.S. Supreme Court reversed *El Vocero*, finding that its holding ran afoul of the dictates of the First Amendment. *El Vocero de Puerto Rico v. Puerto Rico* (1993).

In the aftermath of *El Vocero*, the Puerto Rico Supreme Court adopted the blueprint laid out by Justice Lewis Powell in *Waller v. Georgia* (1984), *see Pueblo v. Pepín Cortés* (2008), whereby a party's petition to close a preliminary criminal hearing must pass strict scrutiny. Thus, the party seeking closure must possess a compelling interest and show that the closure will be narrowly tailored to serve that compelling interest. The court, for its part, must consider other alternatives and make adequate findings to support the closure. *See Pepín Cortés, supra.*

Right to Be Informed of the Nature and Cause of the Accusation and to Have a Copy Thereof

The right to be informed of the nature and cause of the accusation antedates the Puerto Rico Constitution. It was statutorily extended to Puerto Rico under the Jones Act, subsequently becoming a fundamental right under the U.S. Constitution following the U.S. Supreme Court's decision in *In re Oliver* (1948) ("A person's right to reasonable notice of a charge against him . . . [is] basic in our system of jurisprudence.").

In *Pueblo v. Vélez Rodríguez* (2012), the Puerto Rico high court made it clear that Section 11 requires that the prosecution include in the indictment (*pliego acusatorio*) all the constitutive elements of the crime(s) imputed to the defendant. An accusation lacking this information is fatally flawed and must be dismissed.

Section 11 requires that the defendant be presented with a copy of the accusation as a matter of right. Moreover, under Rule 52 of the Rules of Criminal Procedure, the prosecution is required to attach to the accusation the list of witnesses it intends to produce at trial. *See* PR ST T.34, App. II,

§ 52. In *Pueblo v. Rodríguez López* (2001), the Puerto Rico Supreme Court reiterated that the defendant's right to be informed of the nature and cause of the accusation (and to have a copy thereof) does not attach to the sworn statements used by the prosecution at the preliminary hearing for determining cause for arrest under Rule 6 of the Rules of Criminal Procedure. *See* PR ST T.34, Ap. II, § 6.

Right to Confront Witnesses against Him or Her

The framers constitutionalized in Section 11 the right of the defendant in a criminal proceeding to confront and cross-examine the witnesses brought against him or her. The right to confrontation is only triggered at trial, as the Puerto Rico Supreme Court reiterated in *Pueblo v. Santiago Cruz* (2020). Thus, the constitution does not require that the accused be given the opportunity to confront opposing witnesses at preliminary hearings. Although Congress had extended the right to confrontation to Puerto Rico by legislative fiat, the right to confrontation and cross-examination only attained constitutional status upon the inauguration of the 1952 Constitution.

In construing the extent of this constitutional right, the Puerto Rico Supreme Court has paid heed to the doctrinal ruminations of its federal counterpart. In *Pueblo v. Pérez Santos* (2016), the court suggested that Section 11 provides three procedural safeguards: the right of the criminal defendant to directly face opposing witnesses, to cross-examine them, and to exclude hearsay.

At the height of the COVID-19 pandemic, the court in *Pueblo v. Daniel Cruz Rosario* (2020) held that the use of face masks by opposing witnesses does not violate a defendant's constitutional right to confrontation under Section 11.

Right to Have Compulsory Process for Obtaining Witnesses in His or Her Favor

A criminal defendant's right to have compulsory process for obtaining witnesses in his or her favor predates the constitution. This right was first incorporated into Puerto Rico law with the enactment of the 1902 Code of Criminal Procedure. *See* Article 11(3) of the 1902 Code of Criminal Procedure; *see also Pueblo v. Román* (1903). It was later imported through the Jones Act. The framers' constitutionalization of the right to compulsory process antedated its incorporation into the Fourteenth Amendment in *Washington v. Texas* (1967).

The right to compulsory process is not without limits. In *Pueblo v. Lausell Hernández* (1988), the Puerto Rico Supreme Court held that Section 11 does not require the summoning of witnesses whose testimonies are devoid of any pertinence or relevance. The defendant bears the burden of establishing that such testimony is both "material and favorable to his defense."

Right to Counsel

By the time the Puerto Rican framers constitutionalized the right to counsel, its Sixth Amendment's counterpart was only enforceable against the states in capital cases. *See Powell v. Alabama* (1932). The U.S. Supreme Court's gradual federalization of the right to counsel with regard to all criminal defendants facing prison terms came to fruition over a decade after the elevation of the right to counsel to the Puerto Rico Bill of Rights. Notwithstanding the pre-constitutional existence of the right to counsel, under both the 1902 Code of Criminal Procedure and the Jones Act, its scope was considerably limited prior to the inauguration of the constitution. In the pre-1952 landscape, a criminal defendant's right to counsel was not activated at the investigative stage of the proceedings. It was only triggered at a later time, with the reading of the indictment in open court.

Section 11's right to counsel today is as ample as its Sixth Amendment counterpart. In *Pueblo v. Santiago Cruz* (2020), the Puerto Rico Supreme Court made it clear that a criminal defendant's right to counsel under Section 11 is activated at the outset of the criminal prosecution and extends to the appellate phase. *See Pueblo v. Ortiz Couvertier* (1993). In *Santiago Cruz*, the court reiterated that the constitution does not require the assistance of counsel at every step of the proceedings, but only in those more "critical stages," where there is a genuine possibility of substantial harm to the defendant: when the law enforcement investigation turns adversarial, at the preliminary hearing, and at the reading of the charges. In determining when a defendant has been deprived of the right to effective assistance of counsel, requiring the reversal of a conviction and a new trial, the moving party must show that counsel's errors were "so serious as to deprive the defendant of a fair trial, a trial whose result is reliable." *Strickland v. Washington* (1984).

While it is well settled that defendants charged with felonies have a constitutional right to counsel, it remains unclear whether the right to counsel enjoyed by defendants charged with misdemeanors is constitutional or statutory in nature. Regardless, the right belongs to the defendant not to the attorney; in the words of the *Santiago Cruz* court, the attorney is the "tool" used by the defendant "in the process of building a robust defense."

Confronted with the unique challenges posed by the COVID-19 pandemic, the court in *Santiago Cruz* concluded that the constitution does not foreclose the possibility of holding by videoconference a preliminary hearing under Rule 23 of the Rules of Criminal Procedure (PR ST T.34, Ap. II, § 23). Holding a virtual hearing does not conflict with Section 11's right to counsel, or with Section 7's right to due process, so long as the procedural safeguards of Rule 23 are met and the defendants and their attorneys see and hear the opposing parties, while communicating confidentially with each other through a direct telephone line or any other court-approved technical device. *See Santiago Cruz, supra.*

Right to Be Presumed Innocent

Unlike the framers of the U.S. Constitution, the delegates to the Puerto Rican Convention explicitly constitutionalized the presumption of innocence. Although the presumption of innocence had been available by legislative fiat since the local enactment of the 1902 Code of Criminal Procedure, its transformation into a fundamental right came as a direct result of its incorporation into Section 11 of the bill of rights. In *Pueblo v. Santiago* (2009), the Puerto Rico Supreme Court affirmed the principle that the prosecution bears the burden of proving every element of a crime beyond a reasonable doubt. The *Santiago* court, moreover, found that the term "reasonable doubt" is not tantamount to any possible or speculative doubt, but rather refers to doubt substantiated on a fair and impartial scrutiny of the totality of the admissible evidence.

Right to Jury Trial

Both the Foraker and Jones Acts were silent on the right to jury trial. The right to jury trial, nonexistent under Spanish rule, was first introduced to Puerto Rico in 1901 pursuant to local legislation. *See* P.R. Law of January 12, 1901 (PR ST T.34, Ap. II, § 111). By the time the constitutional convention met, the Sixth Amendment's right to jury trial had not been incorporated to the states. Thus, the constitutionalization of Puerto Rico's right to jury trial antedated the federal Supreme Court's decision in *Duncan v. Louisiana* (1968).

In *Pueblo v. Agudo Olmeda* (2006), the Puerto Rico Supreme Court, following the rule announced in *Baldwin v. New York* (1970), found that the right to jury trial under Section 11 attaches to all criminal proceedings where the defendant potentially faces a prison term exceeding six months. The Puerto Rican framers, however, did not require unanimous convictions. Under Section 11, a three-fourths majority of the jury (9 out of 12) was sufficient to reach a conviction. Interestingly, the unanimity requirement was not foreign to the framers. From 1901 until 1948, unanimous convictions were required as a matter of local law. Conviction, thereafter, only required a three-fourths majority. Rather than resurrecting the then defunct unanimity requirement, the framers constitutionalized the 1948 provision. *See* P.R. Law No. 11 of August 19, 1948 (PR ST T.34, App. II, § 112).

In *Ramos v. Louisiana* (2020), the U.S. Supreme Court held that the right to a unanimous verdict is fundamental and enforceable against the states (and unincorporated territories) through the Due Process Clause of the Fourteenth Amendment. Shortly thereafter, in *Pueblo v. Torres Rivera* (2020), the Puerto Rico Supreme Court unanimously confirmed that Section 11's non-unanimous verdict rule ran afoul of *Ramos* and could no longer stand. Because *Ramos* effectively amended Section 11, Puerto Rico's criminal defendants now enjoy a fundamental right to unanimous convictions. The court went further in *Pueblo v. Nelson Daniel Centeno* (2021), holding that not-guilty verdicts in criminal cases must also be unanimous. Since Section 11 does not explicitly require identical numerical symmetry between guilty and not guilty verdicts, the *Centeno* court's ruling seems highly problematic, as it does not appear to reflect the intention of the framers or the letter of the constitutional text.

The framers of Section 11 declined to incorporate into Puerto Rico's legal topography the Fifth Amendment's grand jury mechanism and the Seventh Amendment's right to jury trial in civil cases. Neither is available as a matter of Puerto Rico's constitutional law, and the U.S. Supreme Court has never held these protections to be "fundamental" for purposes of their incorporation through the Due Process Clause of the Fourteenth Amendment.

Right Not to Be Compelled in Any Criminal Case to Be a Witness against Himself or Herself

The Silence of the Defendant Shall Not Be Used against Him or Her

The right against self-incrimination, originally statutory in nature, was first introduced in Puerto Rico pursuant to the 1902 Code of Criminal Procedure and subsequently through the Jones Act. The Puerto Rican framers finally constitutionalized it under Section 11. *See Pueblo v. Nieves Vives* (2013). Interestingly, its inclusion in the island's bill of rights preceded by a decade the U.S. Supreme Court's incorporation of the Fifth Amendment's right against self-incrimination to the Due Process Clause of the Fourteenth Amendment. *See Malloy v. Hogan* (1964).

Unlike the Fifth Amendment, Section 11 explicitly protects a criminal defendant's silence, which the government cannot use to secure the defendant's conviction or to impeach his or her credibility. *See, e.g., Pueblo v. Santiago Lugo* (1993). In *Pueblo v. González Colón* (1981), the Puerto Rico Supreme Court held that the right to remain silent is activated as soon as the party of interest becomes a suspect and the government's investigation is centered on him or her. Thus, as the court suggested in *Pueblo v. Santiago Lugo*, the right to remain silent under Section 11 accompanies the defendant through the various phases of the criminal proceedings; it is an indispensable corollary to the defendant's constitutionally protected presumption of innocence.

Nonetheless, in *Meléndez, F.E.I.* (1994), the Puerto Rico Supreme Court opined that the defendant's right to remain silent does not extend to physical evidence derived from the person of the defendant, such as blood, hair, voice, physical features, fingerprints, photographs, or calligraphy, among others. The *Meléndez* court echoed a principle the court had announced as early as *Pueblo v. Aspurúa* (1943).

Right Not to Be Subject to Double Jeopardy for the Same Offense

Although both the 1902 Code of Criminal Procedure and the Jones Act statutorily protected criminal defendants from double jeopardy, it was the framers who constitutionalized this most basic right. By the time the convention met to draft the constitution, the U.S. Supreme Court had yet to hold that the Fifth Amendment's double jeopardy protection was fundamental and, hence, applicable to the states through the Due Process Clause of the Fourteenth Amendment.

In construing the reach of Section 11's double jeopardy protection, the Puerto Rico Supreme Court has closely mirrored the dictates of its federal counterpart. In *Pueblo v. Santos Santos* (2013), the court suggested the double jeopardy safeguard only attaches to criminal proceedings; its sole purpose being the protection of criminal defendants from a subsequent retrial for the same offense(s) following an acquittal or a conviction, and from the imposition of multiple penalties for the same offense. The *Santos Santos* court further explained that a double jeopardy claim can only succeed if the first proceeding was undertaken on the basis of a valid indictment and by a competent court with jurisdiction over the subject matter and the person of the defendant. The first trial must have been concluded or, at a minimum, commenced for the activation of Section 11's double jeopardy protection. *See id.* In *Plard Fagundo v. Tribunal Superior* (1973), the court made clear that, pursuant to Section 11, a case cannot be tried a third time following two hung juries.

The test applied by the court to determine whether there is only one or two offenses for double jeopardy purposes mimics the federal standard, which is centered on whether "each provision requires proof of a fact which the other does not." *Pueblo v. Rivera Cintrón* (2012) (citing *Blockburger v. United States* (1932)).

In *Commonwealth of Puerto Rico v. Sánchez Valle* (2016), the U.S. Supreme Court held that Puerto Rico and the United States are not separate sovereigns for double jeopardy purposes, putting an end to a line of First Circuit cases holding the opposite; namely, "that Puerto Rico is to be treated as a state for purposes of the Double Jeopardy Clause." *United States v. López Andino* (1987).

Right to Bail

The right of criminal defendants to bail, nonexistent in the federal Bill of Rights, was constitutionalized by the framers in Section 11. In the pre-1952 period, the right to bail under the Jones Act was statutory in nature and not available in those capital cases where "the proof was evident or the presumption great." The framers' abrogation of the death penalty and explicit inclusion of the presumption of innocence in the bundle of fundamental rights available under Section 11 rendered the Jones Act's limitations on the right to bail inapposite. As the Puerto Rico Supreme Court held in *Pueblo v. Colón Rodríguez* (2004), the right to bail must be read in tandem with the defendant's constitutionally protected presumption of innocence.

The issue of whether Section 11's fundamental right to bail ought to be limited or abolished altogether has been the subject of intense public debate. On November 6, 1994, the Puerto Rican electorate rejected a constitutional amendment proposal that would have eliminated the right to bail of criminal defendants charged with first-degree murder and other related felonies. Almost eighteen years later, on August 19, 2012, Puerto Rico's voters again turned down a new attempt at severely curtailing the right to bail through a constitutional amendment referendum.

Incarceration Prior to Trial Shall Not Exceed Six Months

Section 11's limitation on preventive detentions exceeding six months, while nonexistent in the Jones Act or the federal constitutional text, stands as one of the framers' more novel contributions to Puerto Rico's criminal justice system. Soon after the constitution's adoption, the Puerto Rico Supreme Court, in *Sánchez v. González* (1955), announced that this protection is not waivable. Thus, the mandate emanating from Section 11 requires the immediate release of the criminal defendant who, unable to post bail, has been incarcerated while awaiting trial for 181 days or longer.

Under Section 11, the trial must begin within 181 days from the day the defendant was incarcerated due to failure to post bail. *See Ex Parte Ponce Ayala* (2010). Otherwise, in the words of Delegate Arcilio Alvarado Alvarado, "he walks," 3 *Diario* 1595, pending trial. *See Iglesias v. Secretaria de Corrección* (1994). In *Pueblo v. Aponte Ruperto* (2018), Chief Justice Maite Rodríguez Oronoz made it clear that natural disasters, such as 2017's hurricanes Irma and María, do not constitute just cause to suspend Section 11's fixed six-month deadline. Further, the chief justice suggested that Section 11's preventive detention protection has but two exceptions; namely, when the defendant by fraudulent or illegal means hijacks the prosecution, or when the defendant is under custody in a mental institution for lack of capacity to stand trial.

There Shall Be No Excessive Bails and Fines

The prohibition against excessive bails and fines, while available under the Jones Act, was constitutionalized by the framers. The elevation of these safeguards to Section 11 antedated the U.S. Supreme Court's holdings in *Schilb v. Kuebel* (1971) and *Timbs v. Indiana* (2019), where the federal high court incorporated into the Fourteenth Amendment's Due Process Clause the prohibition against excessive bails and fines.

Rule 218 of the Rules of Criminal Procedure requires that in setting bails, judges carefully consider, among other elements, the specific nature of the charges against the defendant, the links (if any) binding the defendant to the community (including employment and family relations), the defendant's character, state of mind, dangerousness, financial condition, record of previous appearances, and compliance with court orders, as well as the evaluations prepared by the local office of pretrial services. *See* PR ST T.34, Ap. II, § 218.

No Person Shall Be Imprisoned for Debt

Section 11's prohibition of imprisonment for debt finds no counterpart in the federal Constitution. *See Bearden v. Georgia* (1983) (holding "that if a probationer cannot pay the fine for reasons not of his own fault, the sentencing court must at least consider alternative measures of punishment other than imprisonment, and may imprison the probationer only if the alternative measures are deemed inadequate to meet the State's interests in punishment and deterrence."). The historical record shows that the framers of the Puerto Rico Constitution imported this safeguard from the Jones Act and the island's 1902 Civil Code.

In *Viajes Lesana, Inc. v. Saavedra* (1984), the Puerto Rico Supreme Court concluded that Section 11 prohibits the use of the imprisonment mechanism to vindicate private interests. Section 11's prohibition, however, is not absolute. In *Díaz Aponte v. Comunidad San José, Inc.* (1992), the court held that imprisonment for failure to obey a court-ordered child support award is exempted from Section 11's strictures.

Section 12
Slavery; Involuntary Servitude; Cruel and Unusual Punishments; Suspension of Civil Rights for Prisoners; Ex Post Facto Laws; Bills of Attainder

Neither slavery nor involuntary servitude shall exist except in the latter case as a punishment for crime after the accused has been duly convicted. Cruel and unusual punishments shall not be inflicted. Suspension of civil rights including the right to vote shall cease upon service of the term of imprisonment imposed.

No ex post facto law or bill of attainder shall be passed.

Slavery and Involuntary Servitude

The substantive rights found under Section 12 were imported from the Jones Act. The framers' most significant innovation here consisted of constitutionalizing the right of inmates to resume the free exercise of their civil rights upon the extinguishment of their terms of imprisonment. The prohibition of slavery in Puerto Rico is absolute and antedates American sovereignty. The first Spanish Republic had abolished slavery in the island on March 22, 1873, twenty-five years before the outbreak of the Spanish-American War.

Once Spain ceded Puerto Rico to the jurisdiction of the United States, as required under the Treaty of Paris, the slavery prohibition of the federal Constitution's Thirteenth Amendment was made applicable to Puerto Rico *ex proprio vigore*. Because of the amendment's ample geographic scope, which makes it binding in "the United States, or any place subject to their jurisdiction," the inclusion of a commensurate provision in the Puerto Rico Constitution, while relevant from an ideological and public policy perspective, is not legally indispensable. The federal mandate in this respect accordingly is supreme. And yet, while not legally indispensable, Section 12's anti-slavery prohibition offers Puerto Rican society the opportunity to constitutionalize far broader protections against involuntary servitude than those provided by federal constitutional law. It is well settled that the federal Constitution establishes the floor, not the ceiling, with respect to fundamental rights.

The significance of including an explicit anti-slavery provision in the bill of rights was not lost on the delegates to the constitutional convention. Delegate Jaime Benítez Rexach was adamant in suggesting that Section 12 not only prohibits the conventional practice of slavery (as historically construed prior to its formal abolition) but all other modalities of de facto involuntary servitude. 3 *Diario* 1603.

The constitutional protection from involuntary servitude available under Section 12 also stems from the language of the Thirteenth Amendment, as made clear by the Puerto Rico Supreme Court in *Brunet Justiniano v. Hernández Colón* (1992). In defining involuntary servitude, the court paid heed to the jurisprudence emerging from the U.S. Supreme Court. The *Brunet Justiniano* court found that involuntary servitude may be enforced by the use or threatened use of physical force or legal coercion to compel an individual to work against his or her will to the benefit of a third party.

The court has warned that involuntary servitude may encompass a far broader class of suspect activities than slavery. *See id.* In *Ramos Acevedo v. Tribunal Superior* (1993), the court held that the court-ordered appointment of attorneys to represent criminal defendants on a pro bono basis is no infringement of Section 12's protection against involuntary servitude.

Cruel and Unusual Punishments

The protection from cruel and unusual punishments found in Section 12 has its origins in the Eighth Amendment to the U.S. Constitution, *Brunet Justiniano, supra*, and was imported to Puerto Rico through the Jones Act. In *Pueblo v. Negrón Rivera* (2011), the Puerto Rico Supreme Court suggested that only disproportionate and arbitrary sentences run afoul of the constitutional safeguard. As the court had explained earlier, in *Pueblo v. Pérez Méndez* (1961), Section 12 requires that the punishment be proportionate to the social ill it was designed to address. It is well settled, for instance, that an additional penalty for recidivism does not amount to cruel and unusual punishment in the constitutional sense. *See id.*

Ex Post Facto Laws and Bills of Attainder

Section 12, furthermore, establishes that the legislature cannot pass ex post facto laws or bills of attainder. In construing the reach of the ex post facto prohibition, the Puerto Rico Supreme Court has shown an inclination to follow the dictates of the federal high court. In *Pueblo v. Candelario Ayala* (2005), the court reiterated that the constitutional prohibition against ex post facto laws extends only to penal (not civil) legislation. More specifically, Section 12's safeguards apply exclusively in the context of penal laws that criminalize actions that were perfectly legal when perpetrated; that retroactively increase penalties for crimes after their commission or that retrospectively decrease the burden of proof required for conviction. Interestingly, the *Calendario Ayala* court left the door open to extending the ex post facto prohibition to the retroactive application of those procedural laws significantly affecting the substantive rights of criminal defendants. In so doing, the court refused to follow its federal counterpart's approach in *Collins v. Youngblood* (1990).

The normative architecture of Section 12's bill of attainder also mimics its federal counterpart. It is well settled that a bill of attainder impermissibly diminishes the principle of separation of powers, while running to the ground the due process rights of its victims. In *Pueblo v. Basilio Figueroa Pérez* (1968), the court, following the test applied by the federal high court in *United States v. Lovett* (1946), announced that legislation targeting an individual (or a class of individuals) for punishment is tantamount to a bill of attainder.

Suspension of Civil Rights for Prisoners

Section 12, moreover, incorporates an additional layer of constitutional protection (unavailable under the Jones Act) for those individuals convicted of criminal offenses. It commands the automatic restoration of their civil rights as soon as their sentences are extinguished. P.R. Op. § Just. 1960-33 (July 6, 1960). Enabling executive action is no longer required. P.R. Op. § Just. 1958-26 (May 29, 1958). Against this background, the question of whether the legislature acted unconstitutionally by extending to the island's inmates a statutory right to vote, while unexplored by the island's high court, must be answered in the negative. Section 12's mandate is solely concerned with the restoration of convicts' civil rights. Determining the legal viability or public policy desirability of extending to inmates a statutory right to vote appears to be an issue for the legislature alone, unrelated to the constitutional objectives associated with Section 12.

Section 13
Habeas Corpus; Military Authority Subordinate

The writ of habeas corpus shall be granted without delay and free of costs. The privilege of the writ of habeas corpus shall not be suspended, unless the public safety requires it in case of rebellion, insurrection, or invasion. Only the Legislative Assembly shall have the power to suspend the privilege of the writ of habeas corpus and the laws regulating its issuance.

The military authority shall always be subordinate to civil authority.

The writ of habeas corpus made its first appearance on Puerto Rican soil long before the inauguration of the constitution. Initially established by General George Davis, pursuant to U.S. General Order No. 71 (dated May 31, 1899), the writ of habeas corpus remained a seminal component of the island's criminal justice system following its inclusion by Congress in both the Foraker and Jones Acts. One of the framers' most significant contributions was redesigning the procedural configuration surrounding the writ. Under Section 13, suspending the writ of habeas corpus is no longer the exclusive province of the governor. Such power is now exclusively vested in the legislature, and this authority is only available in cases of rebellion, insurrection, invasion or whenever the island's public safety is threatened.

Interestingly, the convention's committee on the bill of rights had initially suggested the governor alone should have the power to unilaterally suspend the habeas writ. 4 *Diario* 2572. Under this design, the governor would then have been required to convene the legislature within five days of the suspension proclamation to confirm or revoke the suspension directive. The governor could then reinstate the writ of habeas corpus at a time of his or her own choosing without seeking further legislative authorization. *See id.* This approach was finally rejected by the convention; widespread consensus emerged among the delegates around the desirability of bypassing the governor altogether and entrusting this power in the legislature alone. 3 *Diario* 1863.

Section 13 provides that the habeas writ must be adjudicated speedily and free of costs. 3 *Diario* 1605. The inclusion of Section 13's last clause, requiring the subordination of the military to civilian authorities, while arguably unnecessary given U.S. Public Law 600's republican government requirement, was the byproduct of unanimous consensus among the delegates. 2 *Diario* 1385.

Section 14
Titles of Nobility; Gifts from Foreign Countries

No titles of nobility or other hereditary honors shall be granted. No officer or employee of the Commonwealth shall accept gifts, donations, decorations or offices from any foreign country or officer without prior authorization by the Legislative Assembly.

The sources of Section 14's foreign emoluments clause are found in the Jones Act and in the U.S Constitution. *See* U.S. Const., Art. I, § 9, Cl. 8. The Jones Act imported almost in its entirety the federal Foreign Emoluments Clause, with the caveat that the limitations imposed under the organic act were only applicable to those persons "holding any office of profit or trust" under the territorial government.

Structurally, Section 14 is identical to the Jones Act's provision, with the sole distinction that the former vests in the local legislature, and not in Congress, the power to authorize officers or employees of the Commonwealth to accept foreign presents, emoluments, titles (including those of nobility), and offices. Pursuant to its powers under Section 14, the island's legislature has set out a procedural framework regulating their acceptance. Under P.R. Law No. 9 of March 8, 1955 (PR ST T.3, § 578), a foreign power granting any such distinction on an officer or employee of the government of Puerto Rico must do so through the Puerto Rico State Department. Upon the legislature passing a concurrent resolution authorizing the acceptance of the foreign award, it will be the Puerto Rico State Department that bestows on the Commonwealth's officer or employee the appropriate distinction. This procedural framework is only applicable when the receiving public officer or employee is still in office at the time he or she is presented with the foreign award. A former elected official, to whom a foreign government grants a present, emolument, or title, is not required to seek legislative authorization before tendering his or her acceptance if no longer holding office. *See* P.R. Op. § Just. 1969-3 (Jan. 30, 1969) (finding that former San Juan Mayor Felisa Rincón de Gautier was not required to seek legislative authorization under Article II's Section 14 for accepting a distinction tendered to her by the Spanish Kingdom because she was no longer in office).

Section 15
Employment and Imprisonment of Children

The employment of children less than fourteen years of age in any occupation which is prejudicial to their health or morals or which places them in jeopardy of life or limb is prohibited.

No child less than sixteen years of age shall be kept in custody in jail or penitentiary.

Not only did the Puerto Rican founders import to the bill of rights the safeguards available under the Jones Act with respect to child labor, they also constitutionalized the prohibition against the imprisonment of juveniles under sixteen years of age. The archival record shows that the child labor language, which was initially proposed by Delegate Antonio Reyes Delgado, was incorporated to the constitution on the basis of far-reaching consensus among the delegates. 3 *Diario* 1622.

102　■　THE PUERTO RICO CONSTITUTION AND COMMENTARY

While Section 15 prohibits the employment of minors aged fourteen years or under in any occupation endangering their health or morals, or that in any way threatens their life or limb, the legislature has statutorily extended this protection to minors under eighteen. On May 12, 1942, Puerto Rico's legislature enacted P.R. Law No. 230 (PR ST T.29, § 431), regulating the employment of minors. This statute remained in full force and effect upon the constitution's inauguration. In the post-1952 period, the local legislature has remained particularly active in this field, amending the 1942 statute on various occasions. *See* P.R. Op. § Just. 1997-10 (March 26, 1997).

The inclusion of Section 15's final clause, regarding minors' ineligibility for incarceration in adult prisons, was also the byproduct of overwhelming consensus at the convention. Delegate Francisco Paz Granela's proposal was premised on the statutory rule found in P.R. Law No. 37 of March 11, 1915 (PR ST T.34, § 1941), in full force and effect on the island by the time the convention met, which precluded the imprisonment of minors under sixteen years of age in adult prisons. 3 *Diario* 1590–1591.

In furtherance of the constitutional mandate announced in Section 15, and pursuant to its power to legislate for the general welfare under Article II's Section 19, the local legislature has put in place a juvenile justice system that bypasses the ordinary criminal justice system. P.R. Law No. 88 of July 9, 1986 (PR ST T.34, § 2201). In *Pueblo v. Wilfredo Suárez Alers* (2006), the supreme court found that in establishing a juvenile justice system the government exercises its "*parens patriae*" authority over the delinquent minors for the fundamental purpose of achieving their rehabilitation. P.R. Law No. 88, however, leaves outside its coverage minors aged fifteen or older accused of first-degree murder (with malice aforethought) or felony murder.

Section 16
Rights of Employees

The right of every employee to choose his occupation freely and to resign therefrom is recognized, as is his right to equal pay for equal work, to a reasonable minimum salary, to protection against risks to his health or person in his work or employment, and to an ordinary workday which shall not exceed eight hours. An employee may work in excess of this daily limit only if he is paid extra compensation as provided by law, at a rate never less than one and one-half times the regular rate at which he is employed.

Section 16 is unique to Puerto Rico, with no counterpart in the federal Constitution or any provision of the Jones Act. In drafting Section 16, the framers constitutionalized the bundle of labor rights found in Articles 23 and 24 of the Universal Declaration of Human Rights.

Because the state action doctrine is inapplicable with respect to the labor rights found in Sections 15 through 18 of the bill of rights, these provisions bind both governmental and private entities. Moreover, these labor rights are self-executing: parties seeking to vindicate their labor rights under Section 16 need not wait for enabling legislation before bringing their claims against their public or private employers.

In construing the right of every employee to choose his or her occupation freely (and to freely resign therefrom), the supreme court in *Ortiz Cruz v. Junta Hípica* (1973) suggested that this constitutional protection is intertwined with an employee's due process rights. In *Beltrán Cintrón v. Puerto Rico* (2020), the island's high court made it clear that a claim under Section 16's equal pay for equal work clause must be based on concrete and particularized allegations. The reach of the equal pay for equal work clause, which the framers incorporated to the constitutional text attempting to winnow down gender inequality in the labor market, is not without bounds. *See Mercado Vega v. Universidad de Puerto Rico* (1991). In *Zachry International v. Tribunal Superior* (1975), the island's high court found that the equal pay for equal work clause is gender neutral in its application; it protects both female and male employees from disparate treatment.

The convention agreed that Section 16 does not preclude all dissimilar treatment among similarly situated employees. 4 *Diario* 2574. As the court posited in *Ortiz v. Departamento de Hacienda* (1987), selective promotions premised on productivity or years of service and maternity (or paternity) leaves, among others, are not incompatible with the constitutional mandate. This principle was reiterated in *Rivera Padilla v. OAT* (2013), where the court found that salary discrimination among those similarly situated could survive constitutional scrutiny if the employer successfully shows that there is an "objective" justification for the discrepancy in compensation.

In their attempt to further stabilize labor rights, the framers also constitutionalized the right of all workers (public and private) to a reasonable minimum wage. *A.D. Miranda, Inc. v. Secretario de Justicia* (1961). In so doing, the framers elevated to the constitutional text the statutory framework then available in Puerto Rico under P.R. Law No. 8 of April 5, 1941 (PR ST T.29, § 211). The minimum wage clause establishes a self-executing right, binding on public and private employers. Under the framers' design, the legislature enjoys considerable deference in establishing a minimum wage metric based on a standard of "reasonability." This is, by definition, an elastic standard, which enables the legislature to review (and increase) the minimum wage over time, based on the fundamentals of the island's economy.

In *García v. Aljoma Lumber* (2004), the court reiterated that the protection workers enjoy under Section 16 from risks to their health and personal integrity applies *ex proprio vigore* and is enforceable against governmental and private parties. The *Aljoma Lumber* court, moreover, suggested that a heightened scrutiny will be applied to measures exposing workers to such dangers. Although the records from the convention do not shed light on whether the framers construed "health" and "personal integrity" as interchangeable concepts, the *Aljoma Lumber* court held that these are dissimilar concepts. The former stands for physical well-being, while the latter relates to a workers' private life, thoughts, values and beliefs. Thus, Section 16's health and personal integrity clause protects workers from risks to their physical and psychological fitness. This protection, however, is not limitless; it only extends to injuries occurring in the workplace.

Section 16, moreover, constitutionalized the eight-hour workday, available only statutorily by the time the constitutional convention was elected in 1951. *See* P.R. Law No. 379 of May 15, 1948 (PR ST T.29, § 271). Section 16 requires extra remuneration for extra hours, which can never be less than one and half times the regular compensation rate. From a policy perspective, the framers saw the time and half requirement as a tool for deterring exploitative labor practices. *See Green Giant Co. v. Tribunal Superior* (1975). Section 16, however, does not require the payment of extra pay to executives, administrators, or other professionals (as these terms are defined under Puerto Rico's domestic labor legislation) working longer than eight hours per day. In *Malavé v. Oriental Bank & Trust* (2006), the supreme court made it clear that it is the employee, not the employer, who bears the burden of persuasion in claims for extra compensation. The worker-claimant must not only demonstrate he or she worked overtime but must show the court, with particularity, the number of extra hours he or she worked. *See id.*

While Section 16 sets the floor or minimum standard of constitutional protection, the legislature remains free to set the ceiling, and in the exercise of such authority it has enacted a rather robust tapestry of labor laws and regulations prohibiting, for instance, unjustified dismissals, *see* P.R. Law No. 80 of May 30, 1976 (PR ST T.29, § 185); sexual harassment, *see* P.R. Law No. 17 of April 22, 1988 (PR ST T.29, § 155); and discrimination in the (private and public) workplace on the basis of age, race, color, religion, gender, national origin, or social condition, *see* P.R. Law No. 100 of June 30, 1959 (PR ST T.29, § 146).

Section 17
Right to Organize and Bargain Collectively

Persons employed by private businesses, enterprises and individual employers and by agencies or instrumentalities of the government operating as private businesses or enterprises, shall have the right to organize and to bargain collectively with their employers through representatives of their own free choosing in order to promote their welfare.

Section 18.
Right to Strike, Picket, and Other Legal Concerted Activities

In order to assure their right to organize and to bargain collectively, persons employed by private businesses, enterprises and individual employers and by agencies or instrumentalities of the government operating as private businesses

ARTICLE II ▪ 105

or enterprises, in their direct relations with their own employers shall have the right to strike, to picket and to engage in other legal concerted activities.

Nothing herein contained shall impair the authority of the Legislative Assembly to enact laws to deal with grave emergencies that clearly imperil the public health or safety or essential public services.

The labor rights available under Sections 17 and 18 are nonexistent under the federal Constitution. *See, e.g., Dorchy v. State of Kansas* (1926) ("Neither the common law, nor the Fourteenth Amendment, confers the absolute right to strike."). Unsurprisingly, Congress did not incorporate any of these labor protections into the Foraker or Jones Acts. Their first appearance on Puerto Rican soil came by way of local legislation. Puerto Rico's first legislation regulating strikes and pickets was enacted on March 1, 1902 (PR ST T.29, § 41).

By the time the constitutional convention first met in 1951, Puerto Rico's legislature had already made available to the island's private workers, as well as to those workers employed by governmental instrumentalities operating as private businesses, the rights to organize, to collective bargaining, to strike, and to picket. Ideologically driven by the Universal Declaration of Human Rights, the framers elevated to the bill of rights the statutory framework then available under the local 1945 Labor Relations Act. *See* P.R. Law No. 130 of May 8, 1945 (PR ST T.29 § 61 *et seq.*).

The convention vested in the legislature substantial residual power to limit workers' exercise of these rights in the event of "grave emergencies that clearly imperil the public health or safety or essential public services." This legislative check on the right to strike, which had not been included in the first draft of the bill of rights, was only incorporated (without debate) into its final version at the urging of Delegate Víctor Gutiérrez Franqui. 3 *Diario* 2220. Arguably, any local statute curbing the exercise of any of these labor rights, on the basis of the legislature's residual power under Section 18's final clause, must face strict scrutiny. *Morales Morales v. Estado Libre Asociado* (1990). The Puerto Rico high court's application of strict scrutiny in this context departs from the rule announced in *Lyng v. International Union* (1988), where the U.S. Supreme Court applied minimum scrutiny to an analogous provision of the 1981 Food Stamp Act making households where any of its members was on strike ineligible for benefits.

These labor rights found in Article II's Sections 17 and 18 are not without limits. In *U.T.I.E.R. v. Junta de Relaciones del Trabajo de Puerto Rico* (1970), for instance, the court reiterated that a strike undertaken in violation of a valid collective bargain agreement is illegal and, thus, unprotected under Section 18.

By far the most controversial issue surrounding the incorporation into the constitution of these labor rights was determining which governmental instrumentalities would be bound by them. In *Junta de Relaciones del Trabajo v. Asociación de Servicios Médicos Hospitalarios de Yauco* (1984), the Puerto

106 ■ THE PUERTO RICO CONSTITUTION AND COMMENTARY

Rico Supreme Court held that Article IV's executive departments and their subdivisions are not subject to the constitutional strictures of Sections 17 and 18. Only those employees of governmental instrumentalities operating as private businesses are constitutionally protected under Sections 17 and 18. *See also* P.R. Op. § Just. 1993-7 (March 12, 1993) (employees of the Puerto Rico Health Department do not enjoy a constitutional right to organize, to collectively bargain and to strike under Sections 17 and 18); P.R. Op. § Just. 1992-9 (April 27, 1992) (public school teachers do not enjoy a constitutional right to strike under Section 18); and P.R. Op. § Just. 1960-13 (March 8, 1960) (the members of the police force do not enjoy a constitutional right to strike under Section 18).

Consequently, as the island's high court found in *Hernández Estrella v. Junta de Apelaciones del Sistema de Educación Pública* (1999), public school teachers do not enjoy a constitutional right to strike under Section 18. Along similar lines, the supreme court suggested in *Universidad de Puerto Rico v. Laborde* (2010) that the students at the University of Puerto Rico have no constitutional right to strike under Section 18. Section 18, however, does not preclude the legislature from statutorily extending this bundle of labor rights to public workers in the executive departments and their dependencies. The framers left this door open. *See Hernández Estrella* (1999). It was precisely against this background, that in 1998 the legislature passed a statute extending these protections to all public employees in all executive departments and agencies not operating as private businesses. *See* P.R. Law No. 45 of February 25, 1998 (PR ST T.3, § 1451).

Interestingly, the reach of the labor rights constitutionalized under Sections 17 and 18 have been significantly eroded in recent times. In enacting PROMESA, Congress considerably impaired the exercise of these constitutional rights. PROMESA explicitly empowers the Oversight Board with plenary authority to modify, adjust, or vacate altogether rights and benefits already agreed upon by the contracting parties to a collective bargain. The reach of these constitutional provisions is shrouded in legal uncertainty.

Section 19
Liberal Construction of Rights of People and Powers of Legislative Assembly

The foregoing enumeration of rights shall not be construed restrictively, nor does it contemplate the exclusion of other rights not specifically mentioned which belong to the people in a democracy. The power of the Legislative Assembly to enact laws for the protection of the life, health and general welfare of the people shall likewise not be construed restrictively.

Section 19 embodies two distinct principles. First, Section 19 establishes that the textual enumeration of individual rights under Article II does not preclude the existence of other unenumerated rights. 4 *Diario* 2575–2576. Second,

Section 19 makes it clear that the local legislature, unlike Congress, does have authority to legislate for the general welfare.

Resembling the U.S. Constitution's Ninth Amendment, Section 19 confirms the dynamic nature of the Puerto Rico Constitution's bill of rights. In her dissent in *Burgos v. Comisión Estatal de Elecciones* (2017), Justice Anabelle Rodríguez suggests that, in drafting Section 19, the framers, far from endorsing a textualist or strict constructionist approach to the bill of rights, embraced a far more holistic and flexible canon of interpretation, arguably opening the door to the charter's organic evolution.

Determining the specific content of Section 19's first clause has been the subject of intense debate. In *Partido Socialista Puertorriqueño v. Estado Libre Asociado* (1978), Chief Justice José Trías Monge, writing for the court, announced that the right to self-determination is among those unenumerated rights exclusively reserved to the people under Section 19. The *Partido Socialista Puertorriqueño* court accordingly found that Section 19 bars the legislature from passing measures affecting or modifying Puerto Rico's political status. Legislative activity in this area, according to *Partido Socialista Puertorriqueño*, is constitutionally permissible only when the people have explicitly issued their specific consent.

In *Partido Independentista Puertorriqueño v. Comisión Estatal de Elecciones* (1988), *Báez Galib v. Comisión Estatal de Elecciones* (2000), and *Aponte Rosario v. Presidente Comisión Estatal de Elecciones* (2020), the supreme court distanced itself from Chief Justice Trías Monge's dictum in *Partido Socialista Puertorriqueño*, announcing that Section 19 places no intrinsic limit on the power of the political branches to enact legislation intended to disentangle Puerto Rico's status conundrum.

Section 19's second prong also deserves careful attention. Because Section 19's last clause explicitly bestows on the legislature the power to legislate for the general welfare (concomitant with its police powers), *see Partido Independentista Puertorriqueño v. Comisión Estatal de Elecciones* (1988); *Báez Galib v. Comisión Estatal de Elecciones* (2000), the political branches sought refuge in its language to enact emergency legislation in the wake of Hurricanes María and Fiona, the 2020 earthquakes, and the COVID-19 pandemic. Yet Section 19's grant of legislative authority is not boundless or infinite. It is clearly limited by the bill of rights and, more generally, by the constitution in toto.

Section 19 makes it clear that the local legislature, unlike Congress, does have authority to legislate for the general welfare.

Article III

The Legislature

Section 1
Legislative Assembly

The legislative power shall be vested in a Legislative Assembly, which shall consist of two houses, the Senate and the House of Representatives whose members shall be elected by direct vote at each general election.

Unlike Congress, the radius of action of Puerto Rico's legislature is not limited by a corpus of enumerated powers. In *Nogueras v. Hernández Colón* (1990), the Puerto Rico Supreme Court made it clear that the legislature enjoys far-reaching authority to legislate on all matters not explicitly or implicitly prohibited under the 1952 Constitution.

Deciding whether the island's legislature should be bicameral or unicameral was, by far, the most divisive issue before the convention's committee on the legislative branch. 4 *Diario* 2579. While by the time the constitutional convention met in 1951, various modalities of bicameralism had been in existence in the island for over half a century, there was widespread disagreement among the framers on this seminal issue. Drawing a distinction between the local landscape and the federal topography, the unicameralists argued that, since representation in each of the local legislative chambers would be apportioned on the basis of population, there was no need to duplicate constituencies and number of legislators. 4 *Diario* 2579. Those voices

110 ■ THE PUERTO RICO CONSTITUTION AND COMMENTARY

arguing for the superimposition of Nebraska's unicameral model suggested, moreover, that having only one legislative chamber would guarantee procedural economy and cost efficiency. *See id.*

Interestingly, the cadre of scholars housed at the University of Puerto Rico's School of Public Administration, together with Delegate Jaime Benítez Rexach (by then Chancellor of the University of Puerto Rico) and the Convention's Vice President María Libertad Gómez, all advocated for the adoption of a unicameral system. The minority delegations, for their part, clung to the bicameral approach, contending that bicameralism would guarantee an internal (and indispensable) check and balance between the legislative chambers that could lead to legislation of higher quality, while guaranteeing the legislature's independence from factions or interest groups that might find it easier to manipulate and control one single chamber. 4 *Diario* 2579. More importantly, during this period bicameralism had won very powerful allies in the persons of Governor Luis Muñoz Marín, Speaker Ernesto Ramos Antonini, Senate President Samuel R. Quiñones, and Resident Commissioner Antonio Fernós Isern. The top brass of the Popular Democratic Party believed any structural departure from the federal design might imperil the constitution's ultimate ratification in Congress. Thus, unicameralism was put in cold storage; only to be resurrected on July 10, 2005, when 464,010 voters cast their ballots demanding the island's legislative assembly initiate the constitutional process for replacing the island's bicameral system with a unicameral one. Notwithstanding the failure of this effort, the bicameral-unicameral debate remains alive today.

Besides delineating the legislature's structure, the framers also made it clear in Article III's Section 1 that the island's senators and representatives would be elected on the basis of the "first past the post" system, not unlike the federal and state governments under their respective constitutions.

Section 2
Number of Members

The Senate shall be composed of twenty-seven Senators and the House of Representatives of fifty-one Representatives, except as these numbers may be increased in accordance with the provisions of § 7 of this Article.

Section 3
Senatorial and Representative Districts; Senators and Representatives at Large

For the purpose of election of members of the Legislative Assembly, Puerto Rico shall be divided into eight senatorial districts and forty representative districts. Each senatorial district shall elect two Senators and each representative district one Representative.

There shall also be eleven Senators and eleven Representatives elected at large. No elector may vote for more than one candidate for Senator at Large or for more than one candidate for Representative at Large.

Because the framers chose to preserve the fundamental trappings of the island's pre-1952 legislative structure, the convention only slightly altered the composition of the bicameral legislature. The constitution left unchanged the quadrennial electoral cycle found in Section 29 of the Jones Act. The most significant modifications undertaken by the delegates at the convention were increasing by one the number of senatorial districts, while adding five new house districts. Thus, the constitution fixed the number of senatorial and house districts at eight and forty, respectively. Each senatorial district, moreover, comprises five house districts. Following the same formula used by Congress under the Jones Act, the framers established an apportionment system whereby the voters in each senatorial district elect two senators for a total of sixteen district senators, two more than under the Jones Act. Similarly, the number of senators at large was set at eleven, six more than under the Jones Act, with the caveat that each voter can only vote for one senator at large. Against this background, the constitution fixed at twenty-seven the total number of senators.

In the house of representatives, the number of representatives at large was increased from four, under the Jones Act, to eleven. Each of the forty house districts, furthermore, elects one representative. Hence, the total number of representatives was fixed at fifty-one, twelve more house members than under the Jones Act.

Section 4
Board to Revise Senatorial and Representative Districts

In the first and subsequent elections under this Constitution the division of senatorial and representative districts as provided in Article VIII shall be in effect. After each decennial census beginning with the year 1960, said division shall be revised by a Board composed of the Chief Justice of the Supreme Court as Chairman and of two additional members appointed by the Governor with the advice and consent of the Senate. The two additional members shall not belong to the same political party. Any revision shall maintain the number of senatorial and representative districts here created, which shall be composed of contiguous and compact territory and shall be organized, insofar as practicable, upon the basis of population and means of communication. Each senatorial district shall always include five representative districts.

The decisions of the Board shall be made by majority vote and shall take effect in the general elections next following each revision. The Board shall cease to exist after the completion of each revision.

Constitutionalizing a redistricting board, fully independent from the long (and occasionally treacherous) tentacles of the political branches, stands as one of the more innovative contributions of the 1952 experiment. In creating a mechanism that *circa* 1952 was completely foreign to the island's redistricting experience, the framers broke new ground. Since the days of the first municipal election under the American flag in 1899, until the inauguration of the 1952

Constitution, Puerto Rico only underwent two redistricting exercises—in 1900 and 1917, respectively—both under the firm grip of the executive council. In both instances the council failed to observe the statutory standards of contiguity and compactness required by the Foraker and Jones Acts, let alone pay heed to the 1910 federal census in carving out districts on the basis of population equality. The framers put an end to the antediluvian and inequitable practices of the now defunct executive council.

Following the federal blueprint, see U.S. Const. Art. I, § 2, Cl. 3., Section 4 has made it a constitutional requirement for all senate and house districts to undergo boundary reviews every ten years on the basis of the federal census. This task now falls to an independent board made up of the island's chief justice, and two additional members who cannot belong to the same political party and must be appointed by the governor with the advice and consent of the senate. The framers' decision to designate the chief justice of the Puerto Rico Supreme Court president of Section 4's redistricting board still is the subject of debate. Authoritative voices, such as Chief Justice Víctor Pons Núñez and Virgilio Ramos González, have openly argued for re-examining the desirability of having the chief justice on the board. Because in all likelihood legal challenges to the board's decisions will find their way to the supreme court, the chief justice might be forced to recuse himself or herself, depriving the court and the parties from his or her decisive vote in case of a tie.

Modeled on the structure of the English Boundary Commission, Puerto Rico's Redistricting Board is a *sui generis* constitutional body exercising, in the words of the Puerto Rico Supreme Court, a purely legislative function. In *Partido Estadista Republicano v. Junta Constitucional* (1964), the island's high court reinforced the board's independence, finding there is nothing in the constitution requiring the board to hold public hearings. The board's existence, moreover, is episodic; it only comes to life as soon as the census results are duly certified by the relevant federal agencies and ceases to exist once the redistricting task is completed. By the time the next decennial review comes under way, the sitting governor will be free to appoint new additional members with the advice and consent of the senate.

Despite its structural independence, the board is required to conduct its redistricting mandate with strict adherence to a multipronged constitutional standard. All senate and house districts must be contiguous, compact, and organized on the basis of population equality and access to means of communications. Furthermore, the timely rise of a new corpus of federal jurisprudence in the wake of *Baker v. Carr* (1962), *Reynolds v. Sims* (1964), and their progeny, has added yet another level of scrutiny to the actions of the redistricting board.

Although the board enjoys authority to redraw the boundaries of the island's eight senate districts and forty house districts, it cannot increase or decrease the number of districts; neither can it modify the constitutional formula requiring that each senate district include five house districts. Any such arithmetic restructuring requires a constitutional amendment.

Section 5
Qualifications of Members of Legislative Assembly

No person shall be a member of the Legislative Assembly unless he is able to read and write the Spanish or English language and unless he is a citizen of the United States and of Puerto Rico and has resided in Puerto Rico at least two years immediately prior to the date of his election or appointment. No person shall be a member of the Senate who is not over thirty years of age, and no person shall be a member of the House of Representatives who is not over twenty-five years of age.

Following the blueprint of most state constitutions, the Puerto Rican framers elevated to the constitutional text the qualifications senators and representatives must meet. The constitutional convention left the age, residency, and literacy requirements relatively unchanged, as compared to those established under the Jones Act. Candidates for the house of representatives must be, at least, twenty-five years old by the time of their swearing-in on the house floor. *See Tonos Florenzán v. Bernazard* (1981). Those running for the senate must, at a minimum, be thirty years old by the time of their swearing-in on the senate floor. *See id.*

While the two-year Puerto Rico residency required under the Jones Act was kept intact for those seeking a senate seat, it was increased from one year to two years for candidates seeking a house seat. Interestingly, the framers kept intact the literacy requirement in effect in Puerto Rico since the enactment of the 1900 Foraker Act, even though by the time the convention convened in 1951 all but two states (Washington and Arizona) had abolished it. To this day, candidates seeking election to the legislature must read and write in Spanish or English, unlike the governor, whose literacy in English or Spanish is not a requisite for eligibility under Article IV's Section 3.

Perhaps the most significant distinction between Section 5 and the related provisions of the defunct organic acts is the former's explicit requirement that senators and representatives, like the governor, must be U.S. and Puerto Rico citizens. While not uncommon to require American citizenship, considering the stateside precedents, the prerequisite of Puerto Rican citizenship, which was also made with respect to the governor, only refers to domicile in the island.

Section 6
Residence in District

No person shall be eligible to election or appointment as Senator or Representative for a district unless he has resided therein at least one year immediately prior to his election or appointment. When there is more than one representative district in a municipality, residence in the municipality shall satisfy this requirement.

Similar to Sections 26 and 27 of the Jones Act, Article III's Section 6 establishes that no person shall be elected to the legislature to represent a senate or house district unless he or she has resided in that district for at least one year before his or her election or appointment. While the inclusion of Section 6 did not meet opposition at the convention, a close look at the historical record shows that the framers were unwilling to resurrect the delocalized approach of the Foraker Act. For the founding generation there was indeed a direct correlation between district residence and district loyalty.

This constitutional requirement, however, includes a narrow exception. If there are two or more house districts in the same municipality, *bona fide* residency in the municipality, and not in the specific house district the candidate intends to represent, suffices. Whether this exception is only available to candidates seeking a house district seat, as opposed to a senate district seat, remains unclear. In *Merle Feliciano v. Comisión Estatal de Elecciones* (2020), Puerto Rico's Appellate Court opined that Section 6's limited exception applies both to senate and house district seats. However, a careful look at the framers' constitutional design leads to the conclusion that Section 6's residency exception should only apply in the context of house district seats. Holding otherwise would defeat the founders' carefully wrought apportionment calculus. Arguably, the Puerto Rico Supreme Court's refusal to grant certiorari and review the inferior court's decision in *Merle Feliciano* has left in place a distorted construction of a constitutional provision that goes to the heart of the island's representative democracy.

Section 7
Representation of Minority Parties; Additional Members

If in a general election more than two-thirds of the members of either house are elected from one political party or from a single ticket, as both are defined by law, the number of members shall be increased in the following cases:

(a) If the party or ticket which elected more than two-thirds of the members of either or both houses shall have obtained less than two-thirds of the total number of votes cast for the office of Governor, the number of members of the Senate or of the House of Representatives or of both bodies, whichever may be the case, shall be increased by declaring elected a sufficient number of candidates of the minority party or parties to bring the total number of members of the minority party or parties to nine in the Senate and to seventeen in the House of Representatives. When there is more than one minority party, said additional members shall be declared elected from among the candidates of each minority party in the proportion that the number of votes cast for the candidate of each of said parties for the office of Governor bears to the total number of votes cast for the candidates of all the minority parties for the office of Governor.

When one or more minority parties shall have obtained representation in a proportion equal to or greater than the proportion of votes received by their respective candidates for Governor, such party or parties shall not be entitled to additional members until the representation established for each of the other minority parties under these provisions shall have been completed.

(b) If the party or ticket which elected more than two-thirds of the members of either or both houses shall have obtained more than two-thirds of the total number of votes cast for the office of Governor, and one or more minority parties shall not have elected the number of members in the Senate or in the House of Representatives or in both houses, whichever may be the case, which corresponds to the proportion of votes cast by each of them for the office of Governor, such additional number of their candidates shall be declared elected as is necessary in order to complete said proportion as nearly as possible, but the number of Senators of all the minority parties shall never, under this provision, be more than nine or that of Representatives more than seventeen.

In order to select additional members of the Legislative Assembly from a minority party in accordance with these provisions, its candidates at large who have not been elected shall be the first to be declared elected in the order of the votes that they have obtained, and thereafter its district candidates who, not having been elected, have obtained in their respective districts the highest proportion of the total number of votes cast as compared to the proportion of votes cast in favor of other candidates of the same party not elected to an equal office in the other districts.

The additional Senators and Representatives whose election is declared under this section shall be considered for all purposes as Senators at Large or Representatives at Large.

The measures necessary to implement these guarantees, the method of adjudicating fractions that may result from the application of the rules contained in this section, and the minimum number of votes that a minority party must cast in favor of its candidate for Governor in order to have the right to the representation provided herein shall be determined by the Legislative Assembly.

Section 7 guarantees the political rights of minority parties. It requires that, whenever a majority party wins over two-thirds of the seats in the senate or in the house of representatives, the minority parties must be allocated extra seats amounting to a third of the senate's and house's total number of seats. Hence, under Section 7, minority parties are collectively guaranteed nine seats in the senate and seventeen seats in the house in the event of a majority party landslide. The rationale behind the framers' thinking was relatively simple. On the one hand, they were genuinely concerned with strengthening the parliamentary participation of minority parties; on the other, they believed the introduction of this mechanism would further clear the way for Congress's subsequent ratification of the constitution.

The historical record shows that, following the elections of 1944 and 1948, the presence of minority parties in the legislature was meager, bearing no proportionality to their island-wide vote. Throughout the period from January 1945 through December 1952, the Statehood and Socialist Parties only had one seat each, in a senate of nineteen seats, despite polling collectively more than 30 percent of the island-wide votes. Similarly, in the house of representatives, during this same period, there was only one seat for the Statehood Party out of a total of thirty-nine seats. It was precisely against this background that Delegate Luis Negrón López moved for the adoption of this rather novel mechanism, unavailable under the Foraker and Jones Acts.

Triggering the constitutional procedure for allocating extra minority seats requires a landslide victory by one of the majority parties *and* that the gubernatorial candidate of each of the eligible minority parties gets at least 3 percent of the total votes for governor cast in the election. As the supreme court reiterated in *Fuster v. Busó* (1974), only minority parties meeting the gubernatorial threshold will be eligible to receive an additional allocation of legislative seats under Section 7.

In filling these extra seats, the Puerto Rico Election Commission is required, under Section 7, to first seat the unelected at large candidates of the eligible minority parties. If there still are any seats available, these must go to the minority party's unelected district candidates. These allocations, as the constitutional text requires, shall follow a pecking order based on the number of votes these unelected candidates received. In *Suárez v. Comisión Estatal de Elecciones* (2009), the court made it clear that in choosing between two or more unelected district candidates, the Puerto Rico Election Commission shall compare their respective voting percentages, including the decimals if these are of 0.49 or higher. Otherwise, the Election Commission shall eliminate the decimals, and if a tie results, a new election shall be held, as required under Puerto Rico's electoral law.

Section 8
Terms of Office; Vacancies

The term of office of Senators and Representatives shall begin on the second day of January immediately following the date of the general election on which they shall have been elected. If a vacancy occurs in the office of Senator or Representative for a district, such vacancy shall be filled as provided by law. When the vacancy occurs in the office of a Senator at Large or a Representative at Large, the presiding officer of the appropriate house shall fill it, upon recommendation of the political party to which belonged the Senator or Representative causing the vacancy, with a candidate selected in the same manner as that in which his predecessor was selected. A vacancy in the office of a Senator or Representative at Large elected as an independent candidate, shall be filled by an election in all districts. [As amended by the voters at a referendum held Nov. 3, 1964.]

In drafting Section 8, the framers left unchanged the terms of office of senators and representatives as provided under Section 30 of the Jones Act, pursuant to which new elected legislators also took possession of their seats on January 2 of the year following their election.

Besides setting out the terms of office of senators and representatives, Section 8 provides a framework for filling vacancies in the house of representatives and the senate, a subject that under the organic acts had remained fraught with uncertainty.

The Foraker Act had not established a specific method for filling vacancies in the house of delegates. The Jones Act, for its part, required that vacancies in the house of representatives and the senate be filled by holding special elections in the relevant districts pursuant to regulations enacted by the legislature itself, making no distinction between district and at large vacancies. Congress further amended the Jones Act in 1938, at the behest of Resident Commissioner Santiago Iglesias Pantín, eliminating the special election requirement to provide that, going forward, all legislative vacancies (both district and at large) would be filled by the governor "upon the recommendation of the central committee of the political party of which such senator or representative was a member [...]." The Jones Act made no special provisions for filling seats vacated by independent legislators not affiliated to any political party.

Distancing themselves from the replacement mechanism available under the 1938 amendment to the Jones Act, the framers came up with a hybrid approach: one for district vacancies and another for at-large vacancies. In the case of district seats left vacant at least fifteen months before a general election, the governor would call a special election in the affected district. If the district seat became vacant less than fifteen months prior to a general election, then the seat would be filled by the speaker of the house or the president of the senate with someone selected in the same manner as his or her predecessor upon the recommendation of the previous holder's political party.

The framers extended the latter approach to all at-large vacancies, regardless of whether they occurred at the beginning or end of the legislature's four-year term. The application of disparate treatment to district and at large vacancies, while facing the eloquent opposition of Delegate Cruz Ortiz Stella, 3 *Diario* 2032–2033, did not stir much debate at the convention. The rationale for treating at-large and district vacancies differently was best summed up by Delegate Luis Negrón López, who argued that filling at-large vacancies, as opposed to district vacancies, required a more robust involvement of the political party on whose ticket the previous holder had been elected. 2 *Diario* 1316–1317. Because at-large seats are often reserved for those leaders with higher name recognition, more attuned to the party's policies and strategies, the framers drew a distinction between them and district seats for purposes of the replacement method. Even more decisively, the fact that minority parties, without local political structures at the district level, only tend to elect at-large legislators convinced the framers that the replacement of an at-large legislator, as opposed to a district one, required a more active participation from the political parties. 2 *Diario* 1317.

118 ■ THE PUERTO RICO CONSTITUTION AND COMMENTARY

A constitutional amendment was passed on November 3, 1964, removing from Section 8 the requirement that district vacancies occurring fifteen months before a general election be filled on the basis of a special vote in the relevant district. The 1964 amendment assigned to the legislature alone the responsibility for determining the applicable replacement mechanism. In *Rodríguez v. Popular Democratic Party* (1982), the U.S. Supreme Court held that the framework adopted by the island's legislature for filling district vacancies was not either "constitutionally defective" or "foreclosed" under the U.S. Constitution.

Section 9
Powers of Each House

Each house shall be the sole judge of the election, returns and qualifications of its members; shall choose its own officers; shall adopt rules for its own proceedings appropriate to legislative bodies; and, with the concurrence of three-fourths of the total number of members of which it is composed, may expel any member for the causes established in § 21 of this Article, authorizing impeachments. The Senate shall elect a President and the House of Representatives a Speaker from among their respective members.

Section 9 confers on the legislature the twin powers of exclusion and expulsion.

The power of exclusion was not completely foreign to the island's parliamentary topography by the time the constitutional convention first assembled in 1951. To the contrary, the Foraker Act explicitly granted the old house of delegates the power to exclude delegates who did not meet the qualifications required by Congress in the organic statute. Likewise, the Jones Act entrusted the house of representatives and the senate with similar authority.

In construing the metes and bounds of the legislature's power of exclusion, the Puerto Rico Supreme Court has paid heed to the constitutional framework articulated by the U.S. Supreme Court in *Powell v. McCormack* (1969), finding that the political question doctrine is inapplicable in this context despite the fact that Section 9 explicitly suggests that each house "shall be the sole judge of the legal capacity of its members, their returns and elections."

In *Santa Aponte v. Hernández* (1977), the island's high court ordered the seating of senator-elect Jesús Santa Aponte, notwithstanding the senate's refusal to sit him pending a vote recount. In *Tonos Florenzán v. Bernazard* (1981), Justice Antonio Negrón García, writing for the court, suggested that despite their role as "sole" judges of their members' legal capacity, neither the house of representatives nor the senate has any authority to ignore or subvert the age requirements legislators must meet by the time their terms of office begin on January 2 of the year following their election. And, in *Corujo Collazo v. Viera Martínez* (1981), the supreme court determined that the speaker of the house and the president of the senate have no power to unilaterally exclude representatives or senators. The

Corujo Collazo court made it clear that Section 9 vests the power of exclusion in each legislative body.

Unlike the power of exclusion, Congress did not explicitly grant the power of expulsion to the local legislature under either organic act, though in *José De Diego v. Cámara de Delegados* (1904), the Puerto Rico Supreme Court appeared to suggest that under the Foraker Act the local legislature did enjoy an implied power of expulsion. The power of expulsion under Section 9 offers the island's legislature less latitude than its federal counterpart grants Congress. *See* U.S. Const. Art. I, § 5, Cl. 2. At the insistence of Delegate Leopoldo Figueroa Carreras, *see* 2 *Diario* 815, expulsion from the house of representatives or the senate requires not a two-thirds majority of those legislators present, but rather a three-fourths majority of all house or senate members.

The framers added yet another check on the legislature's expulsion power: expulsion is only available if the actions or omissions of the indicted legislator rise to the level of impeachable offenses as defined under Article III's Section 21. This limitation is nonexistent at the federal level, where each house of Congress enjoys broader discretion in the exercise of its power under the federal Expulsion Clause.

The Puerto Rico Supreme Court's treatment of the legislature's expulsion power, under Section 9, raises more questions than answers. As evidenced by *Nogueras v. Rexach Benítez* (1996), not only has the court shown itself prone to review *de novo* determinations made by the legislature as "sole judge" of the expulsion process, but it has failed to clarify what constitutes an impeachable offense under Article III's Section 21.

Section 9 also endows the house of representatives and the senate with absolute power over their respective internal governance, including control over their bureaucracies and budgets. At this writing, it remains to be seen whether the enactment of PROMESA, together with Congress's appointment of an Oversight Board with plenary power over the island's fiscal life, undermines the legislature's erstwhile unchallenged autonomy over its internal affairs.

Section 10
Regular and Special Sessions

The Legislative Assembly shall be deemed a continuous body during the term for which its members are elected and shall meet in regular session each year commencing on the second Monday in January. The duration of regular sessions and the periods of time for introduction and consideration of bills shall be prescribed by law. When the Governor calls the Legislative Assembly into special session it may consider only those matters specified in the call or in any special message sent to it by him during the session. No special session shall continue longer than twenty calendar days.

One of the framers' more prominent contributions was transforming a diminished legislature, severely hampered by the straitjacket of tight timetables, into a continuous legislative body with ample and independent authority to undertake its own constitutional responsibilities. From the time the first fully elective legislative body under the American flag was inaugurated in 1900, up until the establishment of the 1952 Constitution, Puerto Rico's legislature only met sparingly, unable to infuse continuity to the complex task of systematically studying and unraveling the wide-ranging challenges then enveloping the island in the pre-industrial period. Under the Foraker Act, for instance, the house of delegates could only convene for a maximum of sixty days per year. Far from unlocking the straitjacket, the Jones Act went further, providing that the successor house of representatives and newly established senate could only meet once every two years. And, while this specific provision of the Jones Act was amended by Congress in 1927, *see* 44 Stat. 1420 (1927), reverting the island's legislature to annual sessions beginning on the second Monday of February and adjourning no later than April 15 of the same year, the discontinuity of the legislature's calendar had considerably eroded its capacity to effect leadership within the context of a checks and balances system.

In discarding the Jones Act's approach, the framers constitutionalized the starting date of the legislature's ordinary session. Article III's Section 10 establishes that the house of representatives and the senate must both convene on the second Monday of January of each calendar year, leaving the legislature free to determine by statute the adjournment date of its ordinary session. Consequently, the length of the ordinary session was expanded by a month and a half as compared to the timetable available under the Jones Act. Shortly after the adoption of the constitution, local legislation was passed changing the adjournment date from April 15 to April 30 of each calendar year. *See* P.R. Law No. 9 of April 9, 1954 (PR ST T.2, § 1a).

In construing the breadth and depth of Section 10's continuity clause, the court in *Hernández Agosto v. Ortiz Montes* (1984) found that legislative activity does not come to an abrupt end at the expiration of each ordinary (or extraordinary) session. Rather, the work of the legislative committees continues even in the face of intersession recesses. In *Ortiz Montes*, the court made it clear that, contrary to Sections 29 and 33 of the Foraker and Jones Acts, respectively, Section 10 insulates legislative committees from unwarranted interruptions arising in the context of intersession adjournments. Thus, Section 10 adds an extra layer of protection to the legislature in the exercise of its constitutional powers.

Legislation was passed in 1988 adding a second ordinary session to the legislature's annual calendar, *see* P.R. Law No. 138 of July 22, 1988 (PR ST T.2, § 1a). The Puerto Rico Supreme Court validated the constitutionality of the second session in *Nogueras v. Hernández Colón* (1990). In 1995, a rather controversial statute was passed making Puerto Rico's lawmakers full time legislators. *See* P.R. Law No. 235 of December 16, 1995 (PR ST T.2, § 28). These laws, while still the source of intense public debate, have served to provide some balance to the historically asymmetric relationship between the legislature and the executive.

At this writing, the island's legislative calendar has been considerably expanded, as compared to its length during the period immediately following the constitution's adoption. The first ordinary session is now sixty days longer, ending on June 30, while the second ordinary session, unavailable on election years, begins on the third Monday of August and ends on the Tuesday preceding the third Thursday of November. *See* P.R. Law No. 9 of April 9, 1954 (PR ST T.2, § 1a). During the remaining fifteen weeks of intersession recess, there are no constitutional impediments precluding the legislative committees from carrying on with their work at full throttle.

The framers left relatively unchanged the structural framework of the extraordinary session. Deciding if and when to convene an extraordinary session of the legislature, along with determining the bills or issues to be considered therein, remains the exclusive province of the governor. The governor cannot call an extraordinary session lasting more than twenty days. This constitutional limitation, however, does not preclude the governor from calling successive extraordinary sessions of twenty days during the same intersession recess if the need arises.

More recently, the legislature, and in particular the senate, has embraced the proposition that it can call itself into extraordinary session *sua sponte*, independently of the governor. In *Nieves Huertas v. García Padilla* (2013), the court, in a fractured and highly contested decision, found that the senate need not wait for the governor's call-in order to self-convene into extraordinary session to, among other things, consider appointments made by the governor during the preceding ordinary session. While provocative, *Nieves Huertas* rests on a rather dubious reading of the constitutional text, which explicitly establishes that the legislature can self-convene only in two extraordinary instances: in considering articles of impeachment under Article III's Section 21 and in deciding whether to ratify or nullify the governor's declaration of the martial law pursuant to Article IV's Section 4. Given its reading of the text, *Nieves Huertas* stands potentially to upset the framers' carefully wrought balance between the island's political branches.

Section 11
Open Sessions

The sessions of each house shall be open.

Section 12
Quorum

A majority of the total number of members of which each house is composed shall constitute a quorum, but a smaller number may adjourn from day to day and shall have authority to compel the attendance of absent members.

Section 13
Place of Meeting; Adjournment

The two houses shall meet in the Capitol of Puerto Rico and neither of them may adjourn for more than three consecutive days without the consent of the other.

The incorporation into the constitutional text of Article III's Sections 11, 12, and 13 did not stir considerable debate at the convention. Their elevation to the constitution, moreover, reveals the framers' tendency to mimic the federal text, perhaps fearing that doing otherwise might have led Congress to reject their constitutional project. It was against this background, guided by a deep-seated commitment to transparency, that the framers incorporated into the new constitution the directive that the sessions of the house of representatives and the senate shall always be open to the public. By then, thirty-five state constitutions offered identical guarantees to their citizens. Notwithstanding the axiomatic and self-explanatory nature of Section 11's language, the legislative leadership has only recently put to the test the reach of this constitutional mandate. In *Asociación de Fotoperiodistas de Puerto Rico v. Thomas Rivera Schatz* (2011), the opinions of Chief Justice Federico Hernández Denton and Justice Anabelle Rodríguez both suggest that the constitutional mandate flowing from Section 11 leaves no room for equivocation.

Furthermore, the text of the quorum and adjournment clauses is almost identical to the language used by the federal framers. *See* U.S. Const. Art. I, § 5. In both contexts, a majority of the total members of each house is required to conduct business. Even though Congress had not appended to the Jones Act a quorum provision, the convention did not shy away from incorporating this language into the island's constitution. 3 *Diario* 1932–1933. By the time the convention met, the U.S. Constitution, along with forty-four state constitutions, contained identical language.

The adjournment provision, together with its three-day rule, mirrored both the language found in the Jones Act and in the federal constitutional text, with the proviso that the framers designated the island's Capitol (*el Capitolio*) as the place where both legislative chambers must conduct their business.

Section 14
Privileges and Immunities of Members

No member of the Legislative Assembly shall be arrested while the house of which he is a member is in session, or during the fifteen days before or after such session, except for treason, felony or breach of the peace. The members of the Legislative Assembly shall not be questioned in any other place for any speech, debate or vote in either house or in any committee.

Section 14 constitutionalizes the privileges and immunities of Puerto Rico's legislators. At no point during the period preceding 1952 did Congress extend to the island's lawmakers such protections. *See Romero Barceló v. Hernández Agosto* (1984). Contrary to the organic acts enacted by Congress for Hawaii—*see* Sections 28 and 29 of 1900 Hawaii Organic Act (31 Stat. 141); Alaska, *see* Section 12 of the 1912 Alaska Organic Act (37 Stat. 512); and even the Philippines, *see* Section 18 of the 1916 Philippines Organic Act (39 Stat. 545)—neither the Foraker nor Jones Acts provided any such immunities. Legislative immunities were first introduced in Puerto Rico by way of local legislation on February 21, 1902 (PR ST T.2, §§ 12 and 13).

Section 14 closely mirrors the language in the U.S. Const. Art. I, § 6, Cl. 2, with the only caveat that the island's legislators, as opposed to their federal counterparts, enjoy immunity from arrest for misdemeanors (other than breach of the peace) not only when the house of representatives or the senate is in session but also fifteen days before the session's commencement and fifteen days after its adjournment. 2 *Diario* 758.

The Puerto Rico Supreme Court made it clear in *Presidente del Senado* (1999) that, in construing the metes and bounds of legislators' parliamentary immunity under Section 14, it has been guided by the decisions of the U.S. Supreme Court. In a line of decisions beginning with *Romero Barceló v. Hernández Agosto* (1984), the island's high court has established that immunity under Section 14 only extends to legitimate "legislative activities," pertaining to a legislator's words, speeches, deliberations, written committee reports, investigations, resolutions, votes, and other activities essential to the legislative process. In *Diaz Carrasquillo v. García Padilla* (2014), the high court found that distinguishing between genuine legislative activities, protected under Section 14, and other unprotected legislative pursuits requires a determination of whether the specific legislative activity in question is closely related to the deliberative and voting processes inherent to the legislative role.

Furthermore, in *Silva v. Hernández Agosto* (1986), the court extended Section 14's immunity to legislative aides undertaking protected legislative activities, as well as to the work of the legislative committees. Thus, pursuant to Section 14, Puerto Rico's legislators (and their aides) are immune from actions seeking pecuniary damages, injunctive relief, oral testimony at trial, and document production requests (*subpoena duces tecum*), among other claims, if exclusively based on their undertaking of protected legislative duties.

While the constitutionalization of the doctrine of parliamentary immunity has strengthened the separation of powers arrangement at the heart of the island's governmental structure, this immunity is far from absolute. Delineating its outer limits falls to the judiciary alone. *See Diaz Carrasquillo, supra.*

Section 15
Membership Incompatible with Other Offices

No Senator or Representative may, during the term for which he was elected or chosen, be appointed to any civil office in the Government of Puerto Rico, its

124 ■ THE PUERTO RICO CONSTITUTION AND COMMENTARY

> municipalities or instrumentalities, which shall have been created or the salary of which shall have been increased during said term. No person may hold office in the Government of Puerto Rico, its municipalities or instrumentalities and be a Senator or Representative at the same time. These provisions shall not prevent a member of the Legislative Assembly from being designated to perform functions ad honorem.

The immediate source of the constitution's so-called incompatibilities clause is found in Section 30 of the Jones Act, which was subsequently amended by Congress in 1938. *See* 52 Stat. 595 (1938). While the Jones Act was exclusively concerned with preventing legislators from accepting positions in the executive branch during the term for which they were elected, the framers articulated a more nuanced approach. Mirroring, for the most part, the language found in the federal Incompatibilities Clause, *see* U.S. Const. Art. I, § 6, Cl. 2, Section 15 contains three complementary subclauses, each of which deserves careful attention.

The first subclause precludes the appointment of senators and representatives to any civil office in the Commonwealth's government, municipalities and/or instrumentalities, that was either created, or the salary of which was increased, during the term for which they were elected to the legislature. The reach of this mandate, however, is somewhat uncertain.

In *González v. Alcalde de Utuado* (1973), the supreme court reiterated that municipal legislators are subject to these same limitations and that the prohibition covers the full term for which the legislator (island-wide or municipal) was elected. Yet the court has not examined whether a legislator can cure or bypass this constitutional prohibition simply by waiving the salary increase in case of appointment to a position that was in existence prior to his or her election to the legislature. The issue of whether it is constitutional for a legislator who resigns his or her seat in the house or the senate to accept a post in the executive or the judiciary, so long as he or she waives the salary increase legislated during the term for which he or she was elected, remains unanswered. The legislature attempted to answer this question statutorily P.R. Law No. 5 of April 1, 1992 (PR ST T.2, § 20), enabling the appointment of resigning legislators to other governmental positions, regardless of whether the salaries and emoluments coming with their new positions have been increased (or will be increased) during the legislative term for which they were elected. So long as the outgoing legislator resigns with the salary increases legislated during his or her legislative term, he or she is free to accept the new position. This proposition, while ingenious, arguably runs afoul of the framers' intent and seems to be unconstitutional.

The archival record shows that the framers were not merely or exclusively concerned with the pecuniary aspect of the equation. 2 *Diario* 781. The framers shared the Hamiltonian concern of stamping out conflicting interests and of shielding the legislative branch from "office hunters." The supreme court failed to address these critical issues head on when it declined to hear the *quo warranto* actions filed by the Puerto Rico Attorney General in 2001, arising out of a series of irregular appointments of legislators to judicial posts whose salaries had been improved during their respective legislative terms.

The second subclause found in the incompatibilities clause establishes that no one shall simultaneously hold an office in the Commonwealth's government, municipalities, or instrumentalities while serving as a senator or representative. Here again the terrain is far from settled. The issue of whether an unpaid leave cures the constitutional defect has become the source of an unfinished debate; the stricter approach seems more consistent with the intent of the framers. *See* 2 *Diario* 780.

The final subclause of Section 15 leaves the door open to other types of more limited extracurricular activities, by establishing that senators and representatives shall be able to serve in *ad honorem* positions. In so doing, the framers made it clear that *ad honorem*, for purposes of Section 15, does not mean an "unpaid leave" from a salaried position but from a position for which there is no salary or pecuniary remuneration. *See* 2 *Diario* 780. Accordingly, refusing payment or seeking unpaid leaves of absence does not necessarily cure the constitutional deficiency.

Section 16
Power to Change Executive Departments

The Legislative Assembly shall have the power to create, consolidate or reorganize executive departments and to define their functions.

Section 16 must be read in tandem with Article IV's Section 6. The constitutional mandate flowing from both sections grants the legislature power to create, consolidate, and reorganize executive departments. For the first time in Puerto Rico's constitutional history under the American flag, the island's legislature was vested with authority to engage in the active restructuring of the executive branch. Under the Foraker and Jones Acts, the insular legislature had no such authority. From 1900 until 1952, the design of the executive branch remained exclusively in the hands of the political branches in Washington, D.C. More specifically, the Jones Act made it clear that the creation of executive departments required congressional action. Under Section 37 of the Jones Act, however, their consolidation or abolition required instead the authorization of the president of the United States. Interestingly, the history behind this specific provision throws light on the vagaries and arbitrariness of the United States' territorial policy. While consistently denied to Puerto Rico's legislature until the enactment of the 1952 Constitution, Congress had conferred this same power on the Philippines's legislature since 1916. *See* Section 22 of the 1916 Philippines Organic Act (39 Stat. 545).

126 ■ THE PUERTO RICO CONSTITUTION AND COMMENTARY

The framers sought to constitutionalize the legislature's authority to create, consolidate, and reorganize executive dependencies, while affording the legislature enough flexibility to undertake these responsibilities on its own, without the need to resort in future to the constitutional amendment mechanism. Under Section 16, the legislature's reach in this area is broad. Both constitutional and nonconstitutional executive departments fall under its aegis, with the caveat that those executive departments established under Article IV's Section 6, while susceptible to legislative consolidation and reorganization, are immune from abolition absent a constitutional amendment. *See Comisión Independiente de Ciudadanos v. Ética Gubernamental* (2004).

Section 17
Legislative Proceedings

No bill shall become a law unless it has been printed, read, referred to a committee and returned therefrom with a written report, but either house may discharge a committee from the study and report of any bill and proceed to the consideration thereof. Each house shall keep a journal of its proceedings and of the votes cast for and against bills. The legislative proceedings shall be published in a daily record in the form determined by law. Every bill, except general appropriation bills, shall be confined to one subject, which shall be clearly expressed in its title, and any part of an act whose subject has not been expressed in the title shall be void. The general appropriation act shall contain only appropriations and rules for their disbursement. No bill shall be amended in a manner that changes its original purpose or incorporates matters extraneous to it. In amending any article or section of a law, said article or section shall be promulgated in its entirety as amended. All bills for raising revenue shall originate in the House of Representatives, but the Senate may propose or concur with amendments as on other bills.

Because Section 17 reproduces in its entirety the legislative process found in Section 34 of the Jones Act, it is the least innovative provision found under Article III. As a threshold matter, each of the procedural requirements the framers incorporated into Section 17 closely mirrors those already available under the Jones Act. None of these was new to the Puerto Rican parliamentary landscape: the printing of all bills, their referral to committee, the keeping of a journal for the recording of proceedings (including the votes cast for and against bills), the confinement of every bill to only one subject (except in the case of appropriation bills), the voidance of any part of a statute whose subject has not been expressed in its title, the requirement that no bill shall be amended in a manner that changes its original purpose, and the explicit requirement that all revenue raising bills originate not in the senate but in the house of representatives.

Despite the fact that some of these requisites, such as the keeping of the journal and the house's original jurisdiction with respect to revenue raising legislation, followed the federal blueprint; the remainder came from the Jones Act except for the publication of a daily record and the requirement that no bill can become law unless it has been read in both houses and returned from a committee with a written report. While these latter requisites were unavailable under the Jones Act and only incorporated into the constitutional text due to the advocacy of Delegates Leopoldo Figueroa Carreras and Lino Padrón Rivera, *see* 2 *Diario* 853–854, the reality is that, by the time the convention assembled in 1951, several state constitutions already contained similar requirements with respect to the reading of bills and their referral to committee.

Section 17 has kept the legislative branch tied to a painstakingly specific procedural straitjacket, affording it little room to reinvent itself. Nonetheless, one of the more significant aspects of Section 17 is its constitutionalization of legislative committees, with the concomitant effect of strengthening the legislature's power to investigate executive departments and officers. In *Silva v. Hernández Agosto* (1986), the supreme court confirmed that legislative committees are constitutional in nature and that the source of their constitutional authority is found under Article III's Sections 14 and 17. The *Silva* court made it abundantly clear that the constitution requires the participation of legislators from the minority parties in the work of the committees. While the Puerto Rico Supreme Court has yet to address the issue of whether an independent legislator possesses a constitutional right to participate in all committees, a careful reading of *Silva*, attentive to the intention of the framers as evidenced in the convention's diary, appears to confirm the existence of such an implied right.

Section 17 elevates to the constitutional text a blanket prohibition of legislative riders. In adding the anti-rider provision to Section 17, which requires that all bills be limited to one subject clearly established in their respective titles, the framers were adamant, as Justice Pierce Butler put it in his opinion in *Posados v. Warner, Barnes & Co.* (1929) when describing the rider prohibition Congress had incorporated into Section 3 of the 1916 Philippines Organic Act (39 Stat. 545), to "prevent the inclusion of incongruous and unrelated matters in the same measure and to guard against inadvertence, stealth and fraud in legislation." *See* 2 *Diario* 879. In construing a test for determining when any part of a statute whose subject has not been expressed in the title shall be void, the Puerto Rico Supreme Court in *Dorante v. Wrangler de Puerto Rico* (1998) adopted a flexible rule. The island's high court found that Section 17 does not require that the title of a statute include an overly detailed description of the legislation. A succinct title explaining in general terms the statute's overall purpose meets the constitutional standard. *See id.*

The framers' cautious (and conservative) approach in drafting Section 17, as evidenced by their reluctance to depart from the byzantine procedural requirements found in the Jones Act, shows their continued resolve to avoid, whenever possible, significant structural departures from the Jones Act that could endanger the constitution's chances of final ratification in Congress.

Section 18
Joint Resolutions

The subjects which may be dealt with by means of joint resolution shall be determined by law, but every joint resolution shall follow the same legislative process as that of a bill.

The inclusion of this provision in Article III responded to the framers' genuine concern for textual clarity. The joint resolution made its first appearance in Puerto Rico with the enactment of the Jones Act. *See* Section 34. The Foraker Act, before it, had not explicitly provided for joint resolutions.

Unlike the Jones Act's vague and imprecise treatment of joint resolutions, which failed to offer any guidance as to their procedural and substantive nature, Section 18 constitutionalizes the legislature's authority to determine by law their scope. Further, Section 18, unlike Section 34 of the Jones Act, makes it clear that the consideration of joint resolutions and bills is susceptible to the same legislative process: approval in the house of representatives and the senate by a majority of the members of each chamber and the governor's signature. Clearly, the legislature can also override a gubernatorial veto of a joint resolution.

Shortly after the adoption of the constitution, the legislature passed P.R. Law No. 2 of March 4, 1953 (PR ST T.2, § 200) establishing that joint resolutions are available in the context of legislation "which is to become ineffective upon the carrying out of the work or the fulfillment of the work sought by it." Not surprisingly, the most typical joint resolution of the legislative cycle is the island's budgetary legislation.

In his concurring opinion in *C.R.I.M v. Méndez Torres* (2008), Chief Justice Federico Hernández Denton, exploring more fully the constitutional trajectory and structural contours of the joint resolution, suggested that the legislature cannot achieve the suspension or abrogation of a law by passing a joint resolution.

Section 19
Passage of Bills; Approval by Governor

Every bill which is approved by a majority of the total number of members of which each house is composed shall be submitted to the Governor and shall become law if he signs it or if he does not return it, with his objections, to the house in which it originated within ten days (Sundays excepted) counting from the date on which he shall have received it.

When the Governor returns a bill, the house that receives it shall enter his objections on its journal and both houses may reconsider it. If approved by two-thirds of the total number of members of which each house is composed, said bill shall become law.

If the Legislative Assembly adjourns sine die before the Governor has acted on a bill that has been presented to him less than ten days before, he is relieved of the obligation of returning it with his objections and the bill shall become law only if the Governor signs it within thirty days after receiving it.

Every final passage or reconsideration of a bill shall be by a roll-call vote.

Contrary to their federal counterparts, the Puerto Rican framers included in the constitutional text a particularly detailed legislative process. While following the blueprint set out by Congress in Section 34 of the Jones Act, Section 19 effected significant modifications to the organic act's legislative provision; chief among them was the conferral on the legislature of the power to override the governor's vetoes, which was nonexistent under both the Jones and Elective Governor Acts. Seldom used, the legislative override requires the approval of two-thirds of the total number of members of the house of representatives and the senate. Interestingly, the Puerto Rican legislature has only recently begun to use its override authority, likely due in no small measure to the island's pervasive balkanization among warring political factions. The legislature's first override of a gubernatorial veto took place in 2005 during the uneasy cohabitation of Governor Aníbal Acevedo Vilá of the Popular Democratic Party and a legislature in the hands of the opposing New Progressive Party. In 2016 and 2018, legislatures controlled by their respective political parties overrode express vetoes issued by Governors Alejandro García Padilla and Ricardo Rosselló Nevares.

Section 19, moreover, regulates the governor's power to block legislation by way of express and pocket vetoes. Although imported from the Foraker and Jones Acts, both veto modalities underwent important technical modifications at the convention. First, under Section 19, the ten-day period available to the governor to expressly veto a measure, while the legislature is still in session, starts to run on the same day the bill arrives at *La Fortaleza*, not the next day as was the old rule under the organic acts. And, second, Section 19 makes it clear that, if the ten-day period is interrupted by a legislative recess, the governor is under no obligation to return the vetoed bill along with his or her objections to the house of origin. The bill will only become law if the governor signs it within the ensuing thirty days.

Contrary to Sections 31 and 34 of the Foraker and Jones Acts, respectively, Section 19 establishes that legislation enters into full force and effect upon the governor's signature, unless the bill itself provides otherwise. Thus, the constitutional convention did away with the ninety-day waiting period required under the organic acts. The convention, however, kept the rule first introduced in 1900 pursuant to the Foraker Act; namely, that the passage of legislation requires the vote of a majority of the total number of members of each legislative chamber. In *Acevedo Vilá v. Aponte Hernández* (2006), the supreme court clarified a significant constitutional lacuna, making it clear that, once a bill is passed by the house of representatives and the senate, the legislature must present it forthwith to the governor. The legislature's indefinite and unwarranted withholding from

130 ■ THE PUERTO RICO CONSTITUTION AND COMMENTARY

the governor's desk of a bill approved by both houses contravenes the presentment requirement and is, therefore, unconstitutional. *See id.*

Section 20
Line-item Veto

In approving any appropriation bill that contains more than one item, the Governor may eliminate one or more of such items or reduce their amounts, at the same time reducing the total amounts involved.

The line-item veto made its debut in Puerto Rico under Section 34 of the Jones Act. While unavailable at the federal level, the line-item veto was not foreign to the American territorial landscape. By the time the line-item veto made its initial appearance in Puerto Rico, Congress had already endowed the territorial governor of the Philippines with similar authority under both the 1902 and 1916 Philippines Organic Acts. When the constitutional convention met in 1951, thirty-nine state constitutions provided their respective governors with some modality of a line-item veto, with California, Massachusetts, and Missouri explicitly conferring on their respective chief executives the authority not only to veto but to reduce appropriations altogether.

In constitutionalizing the line-item veto, the Puerto Rican framers parted ways with the "finely wrought" presentment procedure found in the federal constitutional text. *Clinton v. New York* (1998). Despite the initial unease of the minority parties' delegations and the open misgivings of the academicians at the University of Puerto Rico's School of Public Administration, the convention entrusted the island's newly elected governor with the same line-item authority his predecessors had enjoyed under the Jones Act. *Díaz Saldaña v. Acevedo Vilá* (2006).

Contrary to Section 34 of the Jones Act, Article III's Section 20 explicitly confers on the governor additional authority to reduce specific appropriations passed by the legislature, thus elevating to the newly minted constitutional text a prerogative that the appointed governors had only enjoyed by judicial fiat.

Structurally, the line-item veto stands as a class of its own as compared to the express and pocket vetoes. Nothing stands in the way of the governor's capacity to use the line-item veto whenever an appropriation bill, *containing more than one item*, sits on his or her desk. The governor's use of the line-item veto is not subject to the same temporal restrictions applicable to the express and pocket vetoes. Although the governor has no authority to increase the quantum of the appropriations put before his or her consideration, only to reduce or eliminate them, his or her authority in this respect is unrivaled. The legislature has no authority under the constitution to override the governor's line-item veto. *See 2 Diario* 879.

Interestingly, the convention agreed it was best to leave the governor's appropriation vetoes undisturbed as a policy tool to fend off logrolling and other pernicious legislative practices leading to the artificial manufacturing of wasteful spending measures.

Under PROMESA's Section 2142, Congress has effectively endowed the Oversight Board with a long-handed appropriation veto that surpasses the reach of the governor's constitutional line-item authority. The constitutional asymmetries and discontinuities flowing from this rather atypical (and utterly undemocratic) arrangement may well have undermined the framers' carefully delineated design.

Section 21
Impeachment Proceedings

The House of Representatives shall have exclusive power to initiate impeachment proceedings and, with the concurrence of two-thirds of the total number of members of which it is composed, to bring an indictment. The Senate shall have exclusive power to try and to decide impeachment cases, and in meeting for such purposes the Senators shall act in the name of the people and under oath or affirmation. No judgment of conviction in an impeachment trial shall be pronounced without the concurrence of three-fourths of the total number of members of which the Senate is composed, and the judgment shall be limited to removal from office. The person impeached, however, may be liable and subject to indictment, trial, judgment and punishment according to law. The causes of impeachment shall be treason, bribery, other felonies, and misdemeanors involving moral turpitude. The Chief Justice of the Supreme Court shall preside at the impeachment trial of the Governor.

The two houses may conduct impeachment proceedings in their regular or special sessions. The presiding officers of the two houses, upon written request of two-thirds of the total number of members of which the House of Representatives is composed, must convene them to deal with such proceedings.

The impeachment mechanism finally adopted by the framers departed, albeit slightly, from the one available under the Elective Governor Act. Under Section 21, impeachment is no longer exclusively confined to the governor; both the justices of the supreme court and the comptroller are also susceptible to removal by impeachment. Unlike the Elective Governor Act, which adopted in its entirety the impeachment language found in the federal constitutional text, the Puerto Rican framers limited the scope of impeachable misdemeanors only to those involving moral turpitude and did not require the disqualification of the removed officer from any future office of honor, trust, and profit in the island's government.

The supreme court suggested in *Nogueras v. Rexach Benítez* (1996) that a prior conviction is not indispensable for initiating an impeachment proceeding, and it held that an "impeachable" offense must always refer to a crime or fault found in the Criminal Code or in special legislation, limiting the legislature's discretion and, accordingly, departing in significant respects from the Hamiltonian blueprint. Although the impeachment and removal processes are political in nature, the impeached officer still enjoys the full panoply of due process rights arising under Section 7 of the Puerto Rico Bill of Rights. *See id.*

Besides treason and bribery, Section 21 also identifies as "impeachable" offenses "other felonies and misdemeanors involving moral turpitude." Defining what those "other felonies" are, determining what "moral turpitude" means in this context, and deciding whether it falls exclusively on the legislative branch to settle these questions has proven a source of an unfinished debate at the heart of the court.

In *Nogueras,* one of the very few cases where the court has been required to decide on the proper scope of Section 21, the court did not arrive at a discernible consensus. On the one hand, Justices Federico Hernández Denton and Baltasar Corrada Del Río argued that only those felonies involving moral turpitude or depravity implicating a breach of the public trust were impeachable. Justice Antonio Negrón García, on the other, argued that making such determination was the exclusive province of the legislature and not of the judicial branch.

In a clear departure from the federal paradigm, the *Nogueras* court showed an interest in scrutinizing the constitutionality of the removal proceeding. Far from embracing the political question doctrine, *see, e.g., Nixon v. United States* (1993), the *Nogueras* court engaged in a *de novo* review of the legality of Senator Nicolás Nogueras's expulsion. The court's unwarranted invasion of a process where there is a "textually demonstrable constitutional commitment" to the senate seems contrary to the framers' design. *See Baker v. Carr* (1962). Delegate José Trías Monge, for example, argued that impeachment is a political process, in no way reviewable by a court of law. 3 *Diario* 1801. The events of the summer of 2019, leading to the resignation of Governor Rosselló Nevares only after the house of representatives had begun considering articles of impeachment, serve as a reminder that the constitutional lacunae surrounding the island's impeachment machinery require further clarification.

Section 22
Comptroller

The Governor shall appoint a Comptroller with the advice and consent of a majority of the total number of members of which each house is composed. The Comptroller shall meet the requirements prescribed by law and shall hold office for a term of ten years and until his successor has been appointed and qualifies. The Comptroller shall audit all the revenues, accounts and expenditures of the Commonwealth, of its agencies and instrumentalities and of its municipalities, in order to determine whether they have been made in accordance with law. He shall render annual reports and any special reports that may be required of him by the Legislative Assembly or by the Governor.

> In the performance of his duties the Comptroller shall be authorized to administer oaths, take evidence and compel, under pain of contempt, the attendance of witnesses and the production of books, letters, documents, papers, records and all other articles deemed essential to a full understanding of the matter under investigation.
>
> The Comptroller may be removed for the causes and pursuant to the procedure established in the preceding section.

The comptroller established under the constitution is the successor of the auditor, a territorial position inaugurated in 1900 pursuant to Section 23 of the Foraker Act. Under Section 20 of the Jones Act, the auditor simultaneously enjoyed *accounting* and *auditing* authority to oversee the revenues and receipts of both the insular and municipal governments, including public trust funds and funds derived from bond issues. A presidential appointee, the auditor was an officer of the executive branch under "the general supervision of the governor," whose decisions or actions were subject to appeal to the governor alone.

In designing the position of comptroller, the convention parted with the organic acts in significant ways. The framers understood that the comptroller, unlike the auditor, should only wield *post-auditing* authority, leaving all *pre-auditing* oversight to the newly established Treasury Department (*Departamento de Hacienda*). *See* 2 *Diario* 920. Under their blueprint, the *pre-auditing* power belonged to the executive branch, while the *post-auditing* power belonged to the legislative branch. To their eyes maintaining both responsibilities in the same pair of hands could engender insurmountable conflicts of interest. *Id.* at 921. Not surprisingly, the comptroller was squarely placed under the aegis of the legislative branch and no longer reported to the governor.

The comptroller, at least theoretically, enjoys considerable independence from the vagaries of political or partisan factionalism. Appointed by the governor to a ten-year term, with the possibility of an indefinite holding over tenure, the comptroller, like the governor and the justices of the supreme court, is only removable by impeachment and his or her salary cannot be decreased during his or her term.

Along with the secretary of state, the comptroller is the only other officer whose appointment requires, by constitutional mandate, the advice and consent of the house of representatives and the senate. However, unlike the secretary of state, the text of the constitution explicitly requires that confirmation of the comptroller must pass by an absolute majority of the total number of members of both legislative chambers. As referenced under Article IV's Section 5 below, no such language is found in the constitution with respect to the confirmation of the secretary of state.

The local comptroller also parts ways, in important respects, from the federal comptroller, whose legal existence is statutory and, unlike the island's comptroller, has no independent authority to *post-audit* the financials of the federal legislative and judicial branches. The radius of action enveloping the Puerto Rican comptroller is wide: so long as a transaction involving public funds (including movable property and real estate) has been consummated by any public or quasi-public actor belonging to any branch of government (including the municipalities), the comptroller has *carte blanche* to examine its legality.

In *Zequeira v. Universidad de Puerto Rico* (1954), the Puerto Rico Supreme Court made it clear that the comptroller's oversight mission begins only *after* the disbursement of public funds has been made. In *Puerto Rico Telephone Company v. Ramón Rivera Marrero* (1983), the island's high court found that the comptroller does have authority to oversee the use of public funds in the hands of public-private partnerships.

In the exercise of his or her constitutional prerogatives, the comptroller enjoys formidable investigative powers, such as authority to issue subpoenas, to summon witnesses, and to require the production of evidence under penalty of contempt. In *H.M.C.A. (P.R.), Inc. v. Contralor* (1993), the supreme court suggested that the comptroller has authority under the constitution to request information from private parties, if relevant to the exercise of his or her unique oversight responsibilities. The comptroller's powers, however, are not limitless. In *RDT Const. Corp. v. Contralor I* (1996), the court invalidated a *subpoena duces tecum* issued by the comptroller against Santander Bank requesting the disclosure of private banking information belonging to a private party doing business with the government. The court held that the comptroller's failure to put the private contractor on notice violated the latter's right to privacy.

Article IV

The Executive

Section 1
Governor

The executive power shall be vested in a Governor, who shall be elected by direct vote in each general election.

Puerto Rico's governorship, both as a historical and politico-constitutional construct, has undergone significant transformations since the era of the Spanish *capitanes generales*. From the days of Juan Ponce de León, designated by the Spanish Crown in 1508 as Puerto Rico's first governor, up until the belated enactment of the 1897 Autonomic Charter, the island was ruled by military governors vested with plenary powers over the life of the colony. Under the short-lived Autonomic Charter, an absolutist military governor gave way to a constitutional governor general in the British mold whose authority was counterbalanced by a local bicameral parliament.

The colossal implosion of the Autonomic Charter in the face of the 1898 invasion led to yet another swing of the pendulum, as American military governors soon ruled Puerto Rico by decree in absolutist fashion. The arrival of civil government to the island two years later with the enactment of the Foraker Act not only put an end to the plenary powers enjoyed by the American military governors but led to a considerably weakened chief executive. On the eve of Congress's enactment of the Elective Governor Act, only five years before

136 ■ THE PUERTO RICO CONSTITUTION AND COMMENTARY

the inauguration of the 1952 Constitution, the island's governor had become an isolated and somewhat ceremonial figure. Appointed by the president of the United States, with the advice and consent of the U.S. Senate, American civilian governors were detached from the intense dynamics of the island's tumultuous party politics. Thus, during this period the center of political gravity turned to the seat of the legislature at the Capitol.

The period spanning from 1900 until 1948 saw the governor as the unwitting arbitrator among the island's warring political factions nested in the elected legislature. Moreover, the configuration itself of the executive branch, where the principal officers like the attorney general and the commissioner of education (similar to the governor) were appointed by the president of the United States, took away considerable authority from the chief executive, who was surrounded by presidential appointees who did not respond directly to him. *See El Pueblo v. Arrillaga* (1922) ("In case of a conflict, it is the duty of each head of department to defend the position that in his judgement is appropriate. If the head of department does not prevail [...] there is within the executive branch an even higher station: the president."). As well, an ill-designed web of considerably autonomous public utility companies and governmental agencies, unresponsive to the governor, further eroded the governor's capacity to articulate coherent public policies under his undivided leadership.

By the time Luis Muñoz Marín was elected governor in November 1948, there was a clear need to transform the executive branch in light of the challenges then besieging the island. It was against this background that the framers of Puerto Rico's constitutional experiment designed a robust and unitary executive branch led by an elected governor enjoying formidable powers. Not surprisingly, Puerto Rico's political life gravitates around *La Fortaleza*.

Unlike the delegates attending the Philadelphia Convention one hundred sixty-five years earlier, the architects of the Puerto Rico Constitution were determined from the outset to bestow on an elected chief executive significant politico-constitutional authority. Unlike the president, moreover, the governor is elected by the direct vote of the people.

The language of Section 1, constitutionalizing the elective nature of the governorship, mirrors the text of the Elective Governor Act. While structurally succinct, the drafting of this specific provision was not devoid of controversy at the heart of the convention. Determining whether the executive branch should be unitary or collective in nature, as well as deciding on the desirability of placing gubernatorial term limits, ignited important debates among the delegates. Some of these unfinished debates are as relevant today as they were in 1952.

The delegates from the Socialist and Statehood Parties opposed the concentration of all executive power in the hands of the governor. Under their respective proposals the island's executive power would be vested in the governor *and* in his or her cabinet. The Popular Democratic Party's majority, then in control of the executive branch under Governor Muñoz Marín was bent on strengthening the chief executive's capacity to press ahead with the island's industrial transformation and opposed the minority viewpoint. Needless to say, the latter approach, which was not inconsistent with the federal precedent, prevailed. In *Santana v. Gobernadora* (2005), the Puerto Rico Supreme Court found that "our Constitution, therefore, adopted a unitary executive power by vesting in one official alone—the governor—supreme authority over the executive branch without any class of limitations."

Section 2
Terms of Office; Residence and Office

The Governor shall hold office for the term of four years from the second day of January of the year following his election and until his successor has been elected and qualifies. He shall reside in Puerto Rico and maintain his office in its capital city.

Article IV's Section 2 borrows from the organic acts. Both the Foraker and Jones Acts, as amended by the Elective Governor Act, required that the governor reside in Puerto Rico while maintaining his or her office at the seat of government, namely, in San Juan. The governor's quadrennial term, moreover, antedates the Elective Governor Act. Section 17 of the Foraker Act had already established that the governor "shall hold his office for a term of four years and until his successor is chosen and qualified unless sooner removed by the President." Furthermore, the governor's inauguration date of January 2 was extrapolated from the language of the Elective Governor Act.

One of the more interesting, and relevant, aspects of the debate involving this provision revolved around the issue of gubernatorial term limits. Of significance is the rich debate that ensued at the convention pitting Delegates Luis A. Ferré Aguayo, Celestino Iriarte Miró, José Veray Hernández, and José Gelpí Bosch against Delegates Samuel R. Quiñones and Jaime Benítez Rexach. 1 *Diario* 653–657; 670–672. Both the recent ratification in the United States of the Twenty-Second Amendment (only seven months prior to the Puerto Rico Constitutional Convention) and Governor Muñoz Marín's unparalleled political ascendancy served as backdrop for the minority delegations' proposal aimed at precluding the governor from seeking re-election more than once. Mirroring the language of the Twenty-Second Amendment, the Statehood and Socialist Parties alike suggested no person should be elected to the office of governor more than twice, for a maximum tenure of eight years.

While the gubernatorial term limits proposal died a swift death at the convention, the test of time has proven it still commands widespread appeal across the island's public opinion.

Section 3
Qualifications of Governor

No person shall be Governor unless, on the date of the election, he is at least thirty-five years of age, and is and has been during the preceding five years a citizen of the United States and a citizen and bona fide resident of Puerto Rico.

The eligibility requirements established under Section 3 closely mirror the language of the organic acts. The archival record shows that the minority delegations did not contest the incorporation of these requisites into the constitutional text. The Elective Governor Act, in full force and effect by the time the constitutional convention met in 1951, had established that "[n]o person shall be eligible to election as Governor unless [...] at least thirty years of age." The convention's slight modification, raising the minimum age to thirty-five, coincided with the federal requirement, *see* U.S. Const. Art. II, § 1, Cl. 5, thus paving the way for unanimous consensus.

Similarly, the framers amended the citizenship, residency, and language requirements available under the Elective Governor Act pursuant to which no person was eligible to serve as governor "unless at the time of the election" he or she was a citizen of the United States. The constitution embraced a somewhat stricter construction of this directive, requiring that candidates have both American and Puerto Rico citizenship (i.e., bona fide residency) for at least five years prior to their election. Reading and writing the English language, however, would no longer be required as a precondition for election as governor.

Section 4
Powers and Duties of Governor

The Governor shall execute the laws and cause them to be executed.

He shall call the Legislative Assembly or the Senate into special session when in his judgment the public interest so requires.

He shall appoint, in the manner prescribed by this Constitution or by law, all officers whose appointment he is authorized to make. He shall have the power to make appointments while the Legislative Assembly is not in session. Any such appointments that require the advice and consent of the Senate or of both houses shall expire at the end of the next regular session.

He shall be the commander-in-chief of the militia.

He shall have the power to call out the militia and summon the *posse comitatus* in order to prevent or suppress rebellion, invasion or any serious disturbance of the public peace.

He shall have the power to proclaim martial law when the public safety requires it in case of rebellion or invasion or imminent danger thereof. The Legislative Assembly shall meet forthwith on their own initiative to ratify or revoke the proclamation.

He shall have the power to suspend the execution of sentences in criminal cases and to grant pardons, commutations of punishment, and total or partial remissions of fines and forfeitures for crimes committed in violation of the laws of Puerto Rico. This power shall not extend to cases of impeachment.

He shall approve or disapprove in accordance with this Constitution the joint resolutions and bills passed by the Legislative Assembly.

He shall present to the Legislative Assembly, at the beginning of each regular session, a message concerning the affairs of the Commonwealth and a report concerning the state of the Treasury of Puerto Rico and the proposed expenditures for the ensuing fiscal year. Said report shall contain the information necessary for the formulation of a program of legislation.

He shall exercise the other powers and functions and discharge the other duties assigned to him by this Constitution or by law.

The governor of Puerto Rico possesses wide and far-reaching powers. Not only is he or she the head of the island's body politic, but the supreme administrator of the executive branch and, arguably, the island's chief legislator. The governor is the only political actor that, due to his or her constitutional role, speaks for the island as a whole as the personification of a "unitary" executive branch. *See Santana v. Gobernadora* (2005).

The list of executive powers enumerated under Section 4 is nonexhaustive. Governors enjoy a panoply of inherent powers, concomitant with their unique role as sole constitutional leaders of the executive branch. *See Noriega v. Hernández Colón* (1990) ("The chief executive enjoys a series of inherent powers not specifically enumerated under the Constitution or the law"). The Puerto Rico Supreme Court has yet to elucidate the full reach of the executive's inherent powers.

The governor's power to call the legislative assembly (both the house and the senate), or the senate alone, into extraordinary session antedates the constitution. Both the Foraker and Jones Acts bestowed on the governor similar authority. This power, however, is not without limits. While the constitution is silent with respect to the formalities surrounding the convocation by the governor of an extraordinary session of the legislature, it has been common for governors to call these special sessions by signing an executive order. The governor's executive order must specify the matters the legislature must address in its extraordinary session, which has a maximum duration of twenty calendar days and allows for the consideration of no issues other than those explicitly dictated by the governor in his or her order.

In *Nieves Huertas v. García Padilla* (2013), the Puerto Rico Supreme Court found that the governor is not constitutionally required to include the names of his or her appointees, or their designated positions, in an executive order calling for an extraordinary session in order to have them confirmed; the mere inclusion of language suggesting that among the matters to be addressed

140 ■ THE PUERTO RICO CONSTITUTION AND COMMENTARY

in the extraordinary session are appointments awaiting advice and consent suffices.

The powers of appointment and removal are among the governor's most formidable. The Puerto Rican constitutional text departs from its federal counterpart to the extent it makes no explicit distinction between principal and inferior officers of the executive branch. In this area, while persuasive, the decisions of the U.S. Supreme Court with respect to the federal Appointments Clause, *see* U.S. Const. Art. II, § 2, Cl. 2, are not controlling with regard to local gubernatorial designations. *See Hernández Agosto v. López Nieves* (1983) ("With respect to this issue the Constitution of the Commonwealth of Puerto Rico and part of our legislation are based on American texts. This, however, does not mean that the interpretation of those texts controls the meaning of ours. Their historical context is different and, on occasion, produces different rules."). However, the Puerto Rico Supreme Court has shown itself prone to adhere the federal doctrine. In *Santana v. Gobernadora* (2005), the court, applying the federal rule announced in *Humphrey's Executor v. United States* (1935) held that the governor enjoys unfettered discretion to remove purely executive officers not undertaking quasi-legislative and/or quasi-judicial duties.

In *Guzmán v. Calderón* (2005), the supreme court found that the legislature has the authority to limit the governor's capacity to fire the chairman of the Puerto Rico Broadcasting Corporation and can require the governor to make a showing of cause prior to removing an officer having quasi-legislative and/or quasi-judicial responsibilities. Similarly, in *Díaz Carrasquillo v. García Padilla* (2014), the court posited that the statutory limitation precluding the governor from firing at will, and without cause, the ombudsman for people with disabilities did not run afoul of the constitutional doctrine of the unitary executive nor did it undermine the separation of powers principle at the heart of the island's constitutional design.

The delegates to the convention also vested in the governor the power to make appointments while the legislature is not in session. A governor's recess appointment expires at the end of the legislature's next ordinary session. Unlike the president, who can only make recess appointments to fill vacancies that occur while the U.S. Senate is not in session, *see* U.S. Const. Article II, § 2, Cl. 3, the governor has constitutional authority to make recess appointments even if the vacancy arose before the expiration of the legislature's ordinary session. This, together with the uncontested fact that the ordinary sessions of the island's legislature tend to be shorter than their federal counterparts, has enabled the governor to use this constitutional tool with far more flexibility and effectiveness than the president.

In striking a balance between the governor's unique role as head of the executive branch and the senate's obligation to tender its advice and consent, the Puerto Rico Supreme Court held in *Hernández Agosto v. López Nieves* (1983) that the governor can fill a vacancy in the cabinet with an interim unconfirmed appointee only until the expiration of the legislature's subsequent ordinary session. Similarly, in *Betancourt v. Gobernador* (1987), the court, paying heed to the separation of powers doctrine, found that the governor cannot replace a holdover executive officer whose commission has already expired with a recess appointee. Moreover, in *Nogueras v. Hernández Colón* (1991), the court made it clear that the governor cannot cling to holdover officers indefinitely; their tenures expire at the end of the subsequent ordinary session at which point the vacancy can only be filled by whomever the governor nominates and garners the confirmation of the senate.

While the governor remains the commander-in-chief of the militia and the police, this military authority has been considerably diminished if compared to the authority Congress had vested in the appointed governors under the organic acts. The governor can no longer call upon the commanders of the military and naval forces of the United States on the island, unilaterally declare the martial law, or suspend the writ of habeas corpus, which now requires legislative action.

Likewise, the governor's power to issue pardons, while far-reaching, was also streamlined if seen in light of the language of the Foraker and Jones Acts. Executive clemency is no longer available for violations of the laws of the United States. Under the constitution, pardons are only available for offenses against the laws of Puerto Rico. *See Pueblo v. Albizu* (1955); *see also Emanuelli v. Tribunal* (1953).

Not only has the Puerto Rico Supreme Court found that the legislature cannot usurp the governor's unique constitutional responsibility of faithfully executing the laws, *see Noriega v. Hernández Colón II* (1994) (finding that the legislature's pork barrel spending mechanism unconstitutionally usurped the governor's obligation to execute the laws) but it has suggested that the governor does possess authority to use public funds for the articulation of new legislation and policies that might lead to the abrogation of existing ones. *See Noriega v. Hernández Colón* (1990).

The governor's leadership in framing the public policy debate is further strengthened by his or her constitutional obligation to deliver an annual message to the legislature on the "affairs of the Commonwealth," together with an in-depth fiscal report detailing the government's projected revenues and its proposed expenditures for the next fiscal year. Unlike the president who is only constitutionally required "to give to the Congress Information of the State of the Union" "from time to time," *see* U.S. Const. Art. II, § 3, the governor must appear before the legislature annually. Paying heed to the debates held at the constitutional convention, *see* 2 *Diario* 882, the court in *Hernández Torres v. Hernández Colón* (1992) suggested that Section 4 requires that the governor identify in the budget report all surpluses (if available), estimates of unpaid taxes, value of bonds placed on the municipal market, quantum of federal aid, including any other source of revenue.

The governor's directives are, more often than not, issued through executive orders, some of which, if based on an explicit grant of constitutional power or on a delegation of legislative authority, carry force of law. Nevertheless, the governor's capacity to commandeer the various components of the island's governmental structure through the use of the executive orders is not without limits. While it is apparent that the governor lacks authority to issue executive orders dictating terms to the island's municipalities or to those administrative agencies statutorily tasked with quasi-judicial or quasi-legislative responsibilities, there also seems to be a consensus among commentators that the governor does not have power to commandeer public corporations by executive order when the directives decreed therein stand in contravention to their own endogenous organic acts.

The COVID-19 pandemic brought to the fore the issue of whether the governor, in addition to the enumerated powers found in Article IV's Section 4, is also vested with inherent powers in the exercise of the unique role as head of the island's executive branch. For example, can the governor alone, in the absence of a specific grant of constitutional authority or without an explicit delegation of legislative power, decree an island-wide lockdown, a face mask mandate, or an indefinite curfew? At this writing, the scope of the governor's inherent powers is far from clear. In *Noriega v. Hernández Colón* (1990), then Associate Justice Federico Hernández Denton insinuated, without elaborating, that the governor possesses inherent powers that the founders did not enumerate in the constitutional text. Yet the text of Section 4's final clause, establishing that the governor "shall exercise the other powers and functions and discharge the other duties assigned to him by this Constitution or by law," does not seem to bestow on the governor an indefinite reservoir of inherent powers. Following the *Youngstown* framework as articulated in the concurring opinion of Justice Robert Jackson, it seems safe to conclude that the governor's authority is at its "highest ebb" when he or she acts in the exercise of an express grant of constitutional authority or pursuant to an explicit delegation of power from the legislature. *See Youngstown v. Sawyer* (1952). When the governor acts independently of the legislature, in the absence of either a constitutional or legislative grant of authority, his or her power is at its "lowest ebb." *Id.* This explains, in part, why the body of executive orders signed by Governor Wanda Vázquez at the beginning of the COVID-19 emergency imposing lockdowns, curfews, and face mask mandates, and those signed by Governor Pedro Pierluisi Urrutia in the summer of 2021 requiring COVID-19 vaccinations for public employees were all premised not on their inherent powers but on authority delegated to them by law. *See, e.g.,* OE-2021-58.

Delegations of legislative authority to the governor also are not without bounds, as demonstrated by the COVID-19 crisis. For example, Governor Vázquez's unilateral extension of liability immunity to healthcare providers and facilities for the duration of the pandemic, through an executive order signed on April 22, 2020, appears to have surpassed her constitutional and statutory powers. The legislature's retroactive ratification of this specific provision of the governor's order, through the enactment of new legislation granting liability immunity to healthcare stakeholders, *see* P.R. Law No. 53 of May 26, 2020 (amending Article 2 of P.R. Law No. 104 of June 29, 1955 (PR ST T.32, § 3077)), seemed to confirm the legal infirmity of the governor's unilateral course of action.

Finally, PROMESA has likely eroded the governor's constitutional prominence both with respect to the framing and execution of the island's fiscal policies and its overall governance.

Section 5
Appointment of Secretaries; Council of Secretaries

For the purpose of exercising executive power, the Governor shall be assisted by Secretaries whom he shall appoint with the advice and consent of the Senate. The appointment of the Secretary of State shall in addition require the advice and consent of the House of Representatives, and the person appointed shall fulfill the requirements established in § 3 of this Article. The Secretaries shall collectively constitute the Governor's advisory council, which shall be designated as the Council of Secretaries.

Section 6.
Executive Departments

Without prejudice to the power of the Legislative Assembly to create, reorganize and consolidate executive departments and to define their functions, the following departments are hereby established: State, Justice, Education, Health, Treasury, Labor, Agriculture and Commerce, and Public Works. Each of these executive departments shall be headed by a Secretary.

The governor enjoys full authority to appoint, with the advice and consent of the senate, all cabinet secretaries. The appointment of the secretary of state, moreover, also requires the advice and consent of the house of representatives due to the latter's status as the governor's constitutional successor in case of a temporary or permanent absence; the only other officer requiring dual confirmation is the comptroller. In *Acevedo Vilá v. Meléndez* (2005), the Puerto Rico Supreme Court left unresolved the issue of whether the constitution requires an absolute or simple majority in both houses for the confirmation of the secretary of state.

Unlike the federal framers, who did not enumerate (let alone describe) the "executive departments" in the constitutional text, the Puerto Rican delegates provided for a corpus of cabinet positions following, for the most part, the design already available under the organic acts. The executive departments established under the constitution, except for the State, Treasury, and Public Works

Departments, mirrored those in place pursuant to the Foraker and Jones Acts, with a slight change in nomenclature.

Unlike the organic acts, the constitution does not bind cabinet secretaries to fixed terms of office. *See* 3 *Diario* 2268–2270. The secretaries serve at the pleasure of the governor, who can retain them in their cabinet posts without the need to resubmit their nominations to the senate for its advice and consent if he or she were to win re-election. An incoming governor might be able to maintain members of his or her predecessor's cabinet without returning to the senate. Although in practice governors who have chosen to retain their secretaries of state have resubmitted their nominations to the legislature for yet another round of advice and consent, *see Hernández Agosto v. Romero Barceló* (1982), the constitution does not appear to require this action. Under the island's constitutional design, the legislature lacks authority to limit or abridge the term of office of a cabinet secretary. In *Hernández Agosto,* the Puerto Rico Supreme Court dismissed a writ of mandamus filed by the president of the senate, soon after the re-election of Governor Carlos Romero Barceló, demanding that the governor send to the senate the cabinet members "chosen to hold over for a second term" for its advice and consent.

With respect to their legal personality, the court in *Cirino González v. Administración de Corrección* (2014), found that an executive department does not enjoy a separate identity from the Commonwealth of Puerto Rico and, hence, cannot sue or be sued independently from it. More recently, in *Hernández Montañez v. Rosselló Nevares* (2018), the Puerto Rico Appellate Court, seeking refuge in the political question doctrine, refused to determine whether the Office of Recovery and Reconstruction established by the governor through an executive order was an "executive department" for purposes of Article IV's Section 6. The court concluded that it is incumbent on the political branches to make this determination.

The drafting of Sections 5 and 6 of Article IV was not exempt from debate at the convention. Both the composition of the governor's cabinet, along with the method for selecting its members, soon became significant points of contention among the delegates. While the Statehood and Socialist Parties pressed for the direct election of all cabinet secretaries to four-year terms, the Popular Democratic Party's majority had no appetite to deviate from the federal model. Similarly, the proposal put forward by the University of Puerto Rico's School of Public Administration, advocating for the inclusion of the legislative leadership in the governor's cabinet met the opposition of the majority delegation, which was inclined to mimic the federal precedent.

Paying heed to the minority delegates' deep-seated concern with legislative overreach, and in an attempt at brokering a compromise, the majority made it clear that under the new constitutional arrangement the legislature would have no power to abolish the eight executive departments established under Section

6. *See* 3 *Diario* 1767. The framers, however, agreed to endow the legislature with explicit authority not only to create new executive departments but to reorganize, consolidate, and redefine the functions of the eight existing constitutional departments. *See* 3 *Diario* 1792–1793. The quantum of authority entrusted to the legislature with respect to the structuring of the executive departments surpassed, by far, the Jones Act. The duties of the executive departments would no longer be exclusively defined by the governor subject to the approval of the president.

The balkanization of the executive branch, due in no small measure to political patronage and overbureaucratization, has led the island's governors (most poignantly, Muñoz Marín's successors) to rely more heavily on a coterie of assistants who liaise with the cabinet secretaries and the legislative leadership. The framers' idea that the cabinet secretaries would collectively become an advisory body to the governor (styled "council of secretaries") was made impracticable by the geometric growth of Puerto Rico's executive branch. The executive branch today is made up of a discontinuous and ineffective labyrinth of hundreds of governmental agencies, each for the most part independent of the others and devoid of any internal coherence.

Section 7
Succession to Office of Governor—Permanent Vacancy

When a vacancy occurs in the office of Governor, caused by death, resignation, removal, total and permanent incapacity, or any other absolute disability, said office shall devolve upon the Secretary of State, who shall hold it for the rest of the term and until a new Governor has been elected and qualifies. In the event that vacancies exist at the same time in both the office of Governor and that of Secretary of State, the law shall provide which of the Secretaries shall serve as Governor.

Section 8
Temporary Vacancy

When for any reason the Governor is temporarily unable to perform his functions, the Secretary of State shall substitute for him during the period he is unable to serve. If for any reason the Secretary of State is not available, the Secretary determined by law shall temporarily hold the office of Governor.

Section 9
Election by Legislative Assembly in Advance of Qualified Successor

If the Governor-elect shall not have qualified, or if he has qualified and a permanent vacancy occurs in the office of Governor before he shall have appointed a Secretary of State, or before said Secretary, having been appointed, shall have qualified, the Legislative Assembly just elected, upon convening for its first

> regular session, shall elect, by a majority of the total number of members of
> which each house is composed, a Governor who shall hold office until his suc-
> cessor is elected in the next general election and qualifies.

The issue of gubernatorial succession, to this day, has proved to be one of the more intractable challenges besieging Puerto Rico's constitutional topography. The archival record shows that the language of Sections 7, 8, and 9 was the byproduct of a compromise struck at the heart of the convention. For the framers, the point of contention was determining whether the constitutional successor to the governor ought to be an elected or an appointed officer. The convention's committee on the executive branch recommended that a lieutenant governor, elected by the direct vote of the people, replace the governor in case of a permanent vacancy at *La Fortaleza. See* 1 *Diario* 701. Both the Statehood and Socialist Parties' delegations at the convention supported the proposition of having an elected official, as opposed to an appointed civil servant, succeed the governor. The idea of incorporating an elected successor to Puerto Rico's politico-constitutional repertoire was not completely foreign to the island's political leadership; the U.S. Senate's Committee on Territories and Insular Affairs had already broached the subject in 1943 in anticipation of the enactment in 1947 of the Elective Governor Act.

The implementation of such a proposal, however, would have marked a clear departure from the island's incipient constitutional experience thus far. Under Spain, and subsequently under the Foraker, Jones, and Elective Governor Acts, the succession to the governorship befell on an appointed official.

The lieutenant governor proposal met the opposition of Governor Muñoz Marín and other influential members of his Popular Democratic Party. Unsurprisingly, the initial draft put forward by the committee on the executive branch was soon substituted with the language found today in Section 7: a secretary of state appointed by the governor would replace the lieutenant governor as the constitutional successor. Because placing an unelected official first in the line of succession would, no doubt, lead to a democratic deficit, the framers insisted the secretary of state ought to be confirmed by both the island's senate and house of representatives. *See* 3 *Diario* 2312, 2315–2316. Besides designating the secretary of state as the governor's constitutional successor in case of his or her temporary or permanent absence, Section 7 entrusts the legislature with authority to define the line of succession in case both the governor and the secretary of state were simultaneously unavailable due to death, resignation, impeachment, or incapacity.

Section 8, mimicking Section 7, establishes that the secretary of state steps in whenever there is a temporary absence at the helm. Section 9 reproduces a similar arrangement to the one then available under Section 24 of the Elective Governor Act; establishing that a permanent vacancy occurring prior to the governor-elect's inauguration and/or prior to the nomination or swearing in of the secretary of state is to be filled by the direct vote of the island's representatives and senators.

The unprecedented resignation of Governor Ricardo Rosselló Nevares, on August 2, 2019, triggered an *unparalleled* constitutional crisis centered on the metes and bounds of Section 7. Two days prior to his abrupt departure, the outgoing governor appointed a new secretary of state in the midst of a legislative recess. Following the governor's belated call for an extraordinary session of the legislature, to be held on August 1, 2019, the secretary of state nominee while confirmed by the house of representatives was denied a hearing in the senate until August 5, 2019. Although the senate's advice and consent was still pending, the designated secretary of state took the oath of office as governor at 5:00 p.m. on August 2, 2019. In so doing, Secretary Pedro Pierluisi Urrutia sought refuge in a 2005 amendment to the succession statute, *see* P.R. Law No. 7 of May 2, 2005 (PR ST T.3, § 9), which provided that the secretary of state, unlike other cabinet members in line to succeed, could ascend for the remainder of the outgoing governor's term without the advice and consent of both legislative chambers. Shortly thereafter, on August 7, 2019, the Puerto Rico Supreme Court unanimously declared the above-referenced amendment to the succession legislation unconstitutional. *See Senado de Puerto Rico v. Gobierno de Puerto Rico* (2019). The governorship, thus, came upon the third in line pursuant to the succession statute; namely, the island's attorney general. It is clear now that no one, not even the secretary of state, can accede to *La Fortaleza* to fill an absolute vacancy without confirmation from both the senate and the house of representatives.

Section 10
Removal of Governor

The Governor may be removed for the causes and pursuant to the procedure established in § 21 of Article III of this Constitution.

Section 10, while cross-referencing Article III's Section 21, superimposes on the island's constitution an impeachment mechanism that did not exist under the Foraker and Jones Acts. From 1900 until 1947, the governor was only removable by the president of the United States. For close to half a century, the local legislature had no role to play in the removal of the governor. While the impeachment provision of the Elective Governor Act forms the basis of the constitution's removal mechanism, the framers modified it rather slightly.

The archival record shows that the Statehood and Socialist Parties' delegations did not dispute the desirability of incorporating to the constitutional text an impeachment protocol. Their problems with the model finally adopted by the convention were more of style than of substance.

Similar to its federal counterpart, the island's constitutional text bestows on the house of representatives the sole power of impeachment. *See* P.R. Const. Art.

III, § 21. While the federal House enjoys authority to impeach the president of the United States on the basis of a simple majority of those members present at the proceedings, *see* U.S. Const., Art. I, § 2, Cl. 5, the Puerto Rican lower chamber can only impeach on the concurrence of two-thirds of the majority of all the representatives. *See* P.R. Const. Art. III, § 21.

If the impeachment threshold is met in the house, the senate then exercises its sole power to try the impeachment of the governor under the watchful eye of the island's chief justice. But in a departure from the Philadelphia precedent, the Puerto Rican framers raised the bar further by requiring not a two-thirds but a three-fourths majority of all members of the senate for the conviction and removal of the governor.

At no point since the adoption of the constitution has the local legislature impeached, let alone removed, a sitting governor. The political crisis that erupted in the summer of 2019, however, led to its first rehearsal as Governor Rosselló Nevares's abrupt resignation put an end to the house of representatives' imminent vote on articles of impeachment.

Article V

The Judiciary

Section 1
Judicial Power; Supreme Court; Other Courts

The judicial power of Puerto Rico shall be vested in a Supreme Court, and in such other courts as may be established by law.

At the pinnacle of Puerto Rico's judicial branch sits the supreme court, the island's only constitutional court. Section 1 reproduces the structure of Article III of the U.S. Constitution, whereby all inferior federal courts are established by legislation and not in the federal constitutional text itself. *See* U.S. Const. Art. I, § 8, Cl. 9 ("The Congress shall have power to constitute tribunals inferior to the Supreme Court.").

The adoption of this structure was the subject of intense debate. There was no initial consensus among the convention delegates as to whether to entrust the political branches with unhindered authority to unilaterally create and abolish inferior courts. The minority delegates representing the Statehood and Socialist Parties made the case for establishing in the constitutional text itself the complete universe of lower courts. Pursuant to the Statehood Party's proposal, those inferior courts already in existence under the 1950 Judiciary Act, P.R. Law No. 432 of May 15, 1950 (PR ST T.4, § 301), would rise to the level of constitutional courts. On this view, the justice of the peace courts, the municipal courts, and the district courts (including the tax court (*Tribunal de Contribuciones de Puerto*

150 ■ THE PUERTO RICO CONSTITUTION AND COMMENTARY

Rico)) would be effectively insulated from the vagaries of the legislative process. Additionally, the Socialist delegation advocated elevating to constitutional rank the then existing court of eminent domain (*Tribunal de Expropiaciones de Puerto Rico*). *See* Proposition Nos. 94 and 319 in *Proposiciones y Resoluciones de la Convención Constituyente de Puerto Rico* (San Juan: Academia Puertorriqueña de Jurisprudencia y Legislación, 1992), 198, 534.

The academicians at the University of Puerto Rico's School of Public Administration espoused the opposite view. Seeking intellectual refuge in the federal Constitution, the state constitutions of Maine, Oregon, Rhode Island, and Tennessee, and even the debates of the 1934 Filipino Constitutional Convention, the School of Public Administration suggested the constitution should only make explicit reference to the supreme court, leaving the establishment of all other inferior courts to the legislature's discretion. From a policy perspective, the aim was to endow the political branches with the necessary flexibility with which to redraw the island's judicial architecture, particularly at a time when there seemed to be widespread consensus across the political spectrum that the 1950 Judiciary Act should be replaced with new legislation more attuned to the strictures of the constitution that was soon to take effect. In the final analysis, this more restrained approach prevailed as Section 1's crisp language shows.

In construing Section 1, the Puerto Rico Supreme Court has suggested that it is the island's only constitutional court. *See, e.g., Alvarado Pacheco v. Estado Libre Asociado de Puerto Rico* (2013); *see also Cosme v. Hogar Crea* (2003). Nonetheless, the 1952 Constitution did not do away with the authority of the U.S. Court of Appeals for the First Circuit to review the writs of error and appeals from the final judgments and decrees rendered by the Puerto Rico Supreme Court. The appeal as of right to the First Circuit was finally abrogated by Congress in 1961. Since then, the final judgments and decrees of the Puerto Rican Supreme Court are only reviewable by the U.S. Supreme Court.

From a purely historical perspective, Puerto Rico's experience with an endogenous appellate court had been somewhat limited. For the first three hundred years of Spanish colonization, more specifically between 1511 and 1800, the court with immediate appellate jurisdiction over Puerto Rico was *la Real Audiencia de Santo Domingo*. Appeals to Santo Domingo were discontinued in 1800 following Spain's cession of today's Dominican Republic to France pursuant to the Treaty of Basel. From then on, immediate appellate jurisdiction over Puerto Rico's colonial courts fell to *la Real Audiencia de Puerto Príncipe* in Cuba. In the meantime, the medieval *Real y Supremo Consejo de Indias* in Spain would remain as the island's court of last resort up to 1834, when it was finally replaced with Spain's newly minted *Supremo Tribunal de Justicia*. Puerto Rico had to wait until 1832 for the inauguration of its own *Audiencia Territorial*, which, as the historical record shows, came about as a collateral consequence of the significant increase in commercial and demographic traffic experienced in the island due in no small measure to the enactment of the 1815 *Real Cédula de Gracias.*

The configuration of the island's appellate jurisdiction underwent a profound transformation following Spain's relinquishment of its sovereignty over Puerto Rico. Shortly after the inauguration, on October 18, 1898, of the U.S. military government on the island, *la Audiencia Territorial* and *el Tribunal de lo Contencioso Administrativo* were abolished, soon to be replaced with a supreme court of justice. This new court of last resort, predecessor of today's supreme court, parted ways with the *Audiencia's* European foundations. No longer acting as a court of cassation, the newly established supreme court adopted the structural trappings of a typical Anglo-American appellate court. Its internal underpinnings, with respect to jurisdiction, competence, and composition, remained mostly unchanged until the establishment of the 1952 Constitution.

Section 2
Unified Judicial System; Creation, Venue, and Organization of Courts

The courts of Puerto Rico shall constitute a unified judicial system for purposes of jurisdiction, operation and administration. The Legislative Assembly may create and abolish courts, except for the Supreme Court, in a manner not inconsistent with this Constitution, and shall determine the venue and organization of the courts.

Section 2 represents one of the more effective and innovative features of the island's judicial system; namely, the complete unification of the judiciary for purposes of jurisdiction, operation, and administration. In the words of Chief Justice José Trías Monge, this provision in itself amounts to the "nerve" of Article V. José Trías Monge, *Historia Constitucional de Puerto Rico* vol. 3 (Río Piedras: Editorial de la Universidad de Puerto Rico, 1982), 90.

Section 2 put an end to the jurisdictional fragmentation that had rendered Puerto Rico's justice system, since the days of the U.S. military government, particularly inefficient and procedurally defective. By the time the convention began drafting the new constitutional text, Puerto Rico's court system was made up of a discontinuous hotchpotch of district courts, municipal courts, and justice of the peace courts lacking jurisdictional cohesion. While civil and criminal cases originally tried in the district courts were appealable as a matter of right to the Puerto Rico Supreme Court, those actions originally tried in the municipal and justice of the peace courts were subjected to de novo trial at the district court level and only reviewable by the supreme court by means of a writ of certiorari. Actions were, for instance, susceptible to dismissal on the basis of intrajurisdictional conflicts. Against this background, by the time the report of the judicial branch committee was submitted to the convention, *see* 4 *Diario* 2608–2609, both the majority and minority delegates supported the incorporation of this provision to the constitutional text. *See* 1 *Diario* 471.

152 ■ THE PUERTO RICO CONSTITUTION AND COMMENTARY

In construing Section 2, the supreme court has made it clear that, while the legislature can modify the court's competence or venue (*"competencia"*), it cannot alter its jurisdiction as the island's court of last resort. *Trinidad Hernández v. Estado Libre Asociado de Puerto Rico* (2013). This means that, while the constitution explicitly delegates authority to the legislature to establish the appropriate competence of the island's courts, that authority is limited by the constitution's requirement of a unified court system for purposes of jurisdiction. Accordingly, under Section 2, as the court explained in *Misión Industrial v. Junta de Planificación de Puerto Rico* (1998), the legislature cannot preclude the supreme court from exercising its jurisdiction as court of last resort; neither can the legislature undo the jurisdictional unification that binds together the various components of the island's court of general justice (*"Tribunal General de Justicia"*). The framers of Puerto Rico's constitutional experiment broke away from the old practice, enshrined in the Foraker and Jones Acts, whereby the exclusive power "to modify, or rearrange the courts and their jurisdiction" resided in the legislature. *Suárez Martínez v. Tugwell* (1947). The Puerto Rico Constitution has no analogous provision to the Exceptions Clause of the U.S. Constitution, U.S Const., Art. II, § 2, Cl. 2., pursuant to which Congress alone enjoys full authority to regulate the appellate jurisdiction of the federal Supreme Court. *See, e.g., Ex Parte McCardle* (1869). Unlike its federal counterpart, *see* U.S. Const., Art. III, § 2, the Puerto Rico Constitution has no "case or controversy" requirement. *See Asociación de Periodistas v. González* (1991). Yet, in *Estado Libre Asociado v. Aguayo* (1958), the supreme court voluntarily imported to Puerto Rico the federal rules of justiciability—including the political question doctrine, which it first applied in *Córdova v. Cámara de Representantes* (2007) and the court of first instance, more recently, invoked in *Gobierno de Puerto Rico v. Elizabeth Torres Rodríguez* (2022) to dismiss the claim brought forth by the Puerto Rico Department of Justice requesting the removal from office of one of the island's shadow territorial delegates in the U.S. House of Representatives.

The 2003 Judiciary Act (as amended) complies with Section 2's mandate by establishing that "the Commonwealth of Puerto Rico shall be constituted in one sole judicial district, over which the Court of General Justice shall exercise jurisdiction and authority." Hence, as things currently stand, the island's court of general justice is made up of the Puerto Rico Supreme Court, the Appellate Court, and the Court of First Instance.

Section 3
Supreme Court as Court of Last Resort; Composition

The Supreme Court shall be the court of last resort in Puerto Rico and shall be composed of a Chief Justice and four associate justices. The number of justices may be changed only by law upon request of the Supreme Court.

Besides confirming that the supreme court is the island's sole constitutional court, Section 3 establishes a rather sui generis mechanism for determining the prospective composition of Puerto Rico's high court. Unlike its federal counterpart, the Puerto Rico Constitution explicitly establishes that there shall be a chief justice who shall sit alongside four associate justices. In so doing, the Puerto Rican framers intended for the court to be composed, at a minimum, of five justices (including the chief justice). This arrangement left intact the number of justices sitting on the island's high court since the time of its inception in 1899 pursuant to General Davis's General Order No. 118. The delegates to the convention, however, added a caveat: rather than setting in stone the number of justices at five, they added a certain degree of flexibility. By superimposing on the Puerto Rican landscape the mechanism found in Article 98 of the 1946 Brazilian Constitution, the framers agreed to leave in the hands of the justices themselves the power to determine when and under what circumstances to request from the legislature a change in the size of the court. No other jurisdiction under the American flag, at the time, had included in its constitutional text or organic act a similar provision.

The incorporation into Section 3 of this rather unprecedented procedure was the subject of intense debate at the convention. The School of Public Administration had recommended against it, and Delegate Jaime Benítez Rexach rose to oppose it. *See* 1 *Diario* 525. The basis for their opposition was the rather reasonable concern that taking away from the political branches the primary decision-making authority for determining the size of the court could very well undermine the legitimacy of the judiciary in the eyes of the people, particularly if a stubborn court were able to maintain its size even in the face of widespread public demands for either its expansion or contraction.

Opposing this argument, Delegate Ernesto Ramos Antonini opined that the failure of the island's political class to do away with patronage and undue influence in the judiciary made it necessary to guarantee the court's independence while, at the same time, strengthening the separation of powers. *See* 1 *Diario* 552. Ramos Antonini, furthermore, argued that taking away from the politicians the decision of whether to modify the size of the court also meant that in Puerto Rico there could be, in future, no attempt at court packing along party lines. *See id.*

While this mechanism was approved on the floor of the convention without amendments, it has since remained a source of controversy. It was first used shortly after the inauguration of the constitution in August 1952 when, at the behest of a unanimous court, the legislature added two seats. Nine years later, in 1961, the legislature, again at the request of a unanimous court, increased the court's membership to nine by adding two associate justices. By 1975, having finally stabilized its calendar and decongested its caseload, a unanimous court once again requested that the legislature modify its size, this time by eliminating two seats and leaving the court at seven justices.

154 ■ THE PUERTO RICO CONSTITUTION AND COMMENTARY

Almost two decades later, in 1994, a changed political climate led Governor Pedro Rosselló González to propose an amendment to Section 3. Pursuant to the governor's proposal, the number of justices would have been permanently set at nine and the court would no longer have any say on its future size. This proposal was put to the people in a referendum held on November 6, 1994, and soundly defeated. The number of justices accordingly remained unchanged. Sixteen years later, a bitterly divided court requested the legislature to add two additional justices. The legislature passed the appropriate legislation on November 10, 2010. *See* P.R. Law No. 169 of November 10, 2010 (PR ST T. 4, § 24r). At this time, the Puerto Rico Supreme Court is made up of one chief justice and eight associate justices.

Section 4
Sessions and Decisions of Supreme Court; Judicial Review

The Supreme Court shall sit, in accordance with rules adopted by it, as a full court or in divisions composed of not less than three justices. No law shall be held unconstitutional except by a majority of the total number of justices of which the Court is composed in accordance with this Constitution or with law.

[As amended by referendum held at the time of the General Election of Nov. 8, 1960.]

Section 4 brings to the fore additional distinctions between Puerto Rico's constitutional text and its federal counterpart. The island's constitution empowers the high court to sit in panels and explicitly vests in the court the power of judicial review.

By the time the constitutional convention assembled, the idea of enabling the court to sit in panels had already received considerable attention, as evidenced in the School of Public Administration's *travaux préparatoires* and in the recommendations made by some of the more influential delegates at the convention. A chronically overcrowded docket made it necessary, in the eyes of the framers, to vest in the court the power to decide when and how to use the panel mechanism, which until that time was foreign to Puerto Rico.

Because at the time of the constitution's inauguration the court's size remained at five justices and the language requiring that *all* of its decisions "be concurred in by a majority of its members" was in full force and effect, the panel mechanism did not become fully operational. In fact, it remained virtually unused until 1961. It was not until the elimination of the second sentence of Section 4, by means of a constitutional amendment successfully put to the people on November 8, 1960, and the addition of two extra seats on May 6, 1961, that the justices of Puerto Rico's high court began to sit, albeit sparingly, in panels of three.

In furtherance of its constitutional mandate, the supreme court has adopted a corpus of internal rules governing both its *en banc* and panel proceedings. *See In re Reglamento del Tribunal Supremo de Puerto Rico* (2011). In *Dimas Zayas v. Levitt & Sons* (1992), the court confirmed its authority to issue discretionary and mandatory writs when sitting in panels.

The court's use of the panel mechanism has been the subject of intense debate. Although widely used by the Negrón Fernández Court at the height of its overcrowding crisis between 1961 and 1972, the practice of distributing the caseload among panels made up of three justices has proven, for the most part, ineffective in alleviating the court's backlog. And, furthermore, as Chief Justice José Trías Monge and Justice Antonio Negrón García both suggested, the indiscriminate use of the panel mechanism by the island's high court, if left unchecked, might very well lead to internal doctrinal inconsistencies triggered by panel splits, effectively weakening the court's capacity to infuse legal certainty and uniformity across the island's justice system. *See, e.g.,* Antonio Negrón García, "Práctica Apelativa: Aspectos Constitucionales, Legales y Reglamentarios," *Revista Jurídica de la Universidad Interamericana* 42 (2007): 1. The debate on the proper positioning of the panels within the court's wider constitutional mandate is still alive today. *See In re Reglamento del Tribunal Supremo* (2011) (concurring and dissenting opinions by Justice Rafael Martínez Torres and Justice Anabelle Rodríguez, respectively).

Neither the Foraker Act nor the Jones Act explicitly or implicitly conferred on the island's courts the power of judicial review. The doctrine made its appearance on Puerto Rican soil by judicial fiat in a seminal line of cases, starting with *Marimón v. Pelegrí* (1902), where the court announced that all laws or ordinances (including military orders issued prior to the entry into force of the organic act) running afoul the Foraker Act were null and void. Section 4 constitutionalizes the judicial review authority of the island's courts (thus departing from the federal precedent) and establishes that no law shall be declared unconstitutional *unless a majority of the total* number of justices sitting on the court concur. This means that if (as is the case at this writing) the total number of seats (required by statute) on the court is nine but there are, for instance, two vacancies, a majority of at least five justices will be required under Section 4 to declare a law unconstitutional. *See, e.g., Pueblo de Puerto Rico v. Terry Terrol* (1977). A plurality will be insufficient to issue a declaration of unconstitutionality. This requirement, however, does not extend to municipal ordinances or administrative regulations. *See Partido Independentista Puertorriqueño v. Estado Libre Asociado* (1980). Nonetheless, the supreme court's powers under Article V (except for its judicial review authority) are in no way diminished if, and when, vacancies arise. *See Sánchez Rodríguez v. López Jiménez* (1985).

Section 5
Original Jurisdiction of Supreme Court

The Supreme Court, any of its divisions, or any of its justices may hear in the first instance petitions for habeas corpus and any other causes and proceedings as determined by law.

156 ■ THE PUERTO RICO CONSTITUTION AND COMMENTARY

Section 5 establishes that the Supreme Court may hear habeas corpus petitions on the basis of its original competence. At the convention there was no consensus on whether it was necessary to explicitly refer here to the writ of habeas corpus. Because in enacting U.S. Public Law 600, Congress had incorporated into the Federal Relations Act Section 48 of the Jones Act, Delegate José Trías Monge, for instance, described Section 5's habeas corpus reference as "unnecessary." *See* 48 U.S.C., § 734 (2003) ("The supreme and district courts of Puerto Rico and the respective judges thereof may grant writs of habeas corpus in all cases in which the same are grantable by the judges of the district courts of the United States.").

The minority parties at the convention disagreed. Both the Statehood and Socialist Parties advocated for the incorporation of explicit language bestowing on the court original competence to hear not just habeas corpus petitions but also writs of prohibition, writs of quo warranto, and writs of mandamus. The cadre of legal scholars assembled by the University of Puerto Rico's School of Public Administration only favored the court's exercise of original competence with respect to the writs of habeas corpus and quo warranto.

In the meantime, Delegates Ernesto Ramos Antonini and Víctor Gutiérrez Franqui argued for more streamlined language. *See* 1 *Diario* 592; *see also* 3 *Diario* 1652. To their eyes, the court's original competence should be limited to hearing habeas corpus petitions. Because most delegates saw the need to tackle the court's chronically crowded docket, the latter approach prevailed.

By limiting the universe of cases where the constitution requires the court's review on the basis of its original competence, the framers sought to decompress the court's clogged pipeline. Unlike Article III, Section 2, Cl. 1 of the U.S. Constitution, which sets in stone the U.S. Supreme Court's original jurisdiction, Section 5 (except for habeas corpus petitions) leaves the court's original competence in the hands of the legislature, which can regulate or modify it by ordinary legislation.

Pursuant to Article 3.002 of the Judiciary Act (PR ST T.4, § 24 *et seq.*), Puerto Rico's legislature has also empowered the island's high court to hear, on an original basis, writs of mandamus, habeas corpus, quo warranto, and prohibition. The available caselaw shows that the island's high court has historically shown relative self-restraint in exercising its original competence under Article V's Section 5.

In *Chamberlain v. Delgado* (1960), the court warned litigants that it would not use its original competence to hear habeas petitions in the absence of compelling circumstances. Moreover, in *Acevedo Vilá v. Aponte Hernández* (2006), the court made it clear that the writ of mandamus is a "highly privileged" procedural mechanism, wholly discretionary in nature. In his dissent in *Hernández López v. Santana Ramos* (1998), Justice Antonio Negrón García argued that the court should be "very careful" in deciding when to issue a writ of prohibition, which has as its sole purpose precluding inferior tribunals from overstepping their competence. While the supreme court, under Puerto Rico's Land Law, enjoys exclusive original competence to issue writs of quo warranto in matters arising under this statute, *see* PR ST T.28, § 421, its use of the quo warranto remedy in other areas where it enjoys complete discretion has been somewhat scant.

In more recent years the court has shown a somewhat concerning proclivity to use the procedural mechanism of the "intrajurisdictional certification" (of legislative origin) to bypass the inferior courts. *See* PR ST T.32, Ap. V, R. 52.2. The applicable legislation establishes that the intrajurisdictional certification is only available in cases pending before the inferior courts, implicating a compelling public interest, constitutional issues of first impression, or conflicts among the various circuits of the appellate court. Through this mechanism, the supreme court effectively exercises original competence in a panoply of matters going beyond the scope of the traditional extraordinary remedies. *See Torres Montalvo v. Gobernador* (2016), *Rivera Schatz v. Estado Libre Asociado y Colegio de Abogados* (2014), *Alvarado Pacheco v. Estado Libre Asociado* (2013), and *Nieves Huertas v. García Padilla* (2013). Determining the proper place of the "intrajurisdictional certification," within the island's wider constitutional design, remains the subject of intense debate. *See Alvarado Pacheco v. Estado Libre Asociado* (2013) (dissenting opinion of Chief Justice Federico Hernández Denton).

Section 6
Rules of Evidence and of Civil and Criminal Procedure

The Supreme Court shall adopt for the courts rules of evidence and of civil and criminal procedure which shall not abridge, enlarge or modify the substantive rights of the parties. The rules thus adopted shall be submitted to the Legislative Assembly at the beginning of its next regular session and shall not go into effect until sixty days after the close of said session, unless disapproved by the Legislative Assembly, which shall have the power both at said session and subsequently to amend, repeal or supplement any of said rules by a specific law to that effect.

Section 6 constitutionalizes the rule-making authority of Puerto Rico's Supreme Court and, in so doing, makes a clean break from the past. Before and after the transfer of sovereignty, rules of procedure came by legislative fiat. Both the Law of Civil Procedure (*Ley de Enjuiciamiento Civil*) and the Law of Criminal Procedure (*Ley de Enjuiciamiento Criminal*), which were in full force and effect in Puerto Rico by the time of the 1898 invasion, were enacted by the *cortes* in Madrid. Shortly thereafter, General George Davis decreed new rules of civil and criminal procedure. *See* U.S. General Order No. 118 (August 16, 1899). The inauguration of the island's civil government, first under the Foraker Act and then under the Jones Act, left the rule-making authority within the grip of the legislative branch. Not surprisingly, the importation to Puerto Rico of the 1902 Code of Criminal Procedure and the 1904 Code of Civil Procedure was the byproduct of legislative transactions.

Determining the proper roles of the judiciary and legislature in the rule-making process soon became a point of contention at the constitutional convention. Delegate Miguel Ángel García Méndez and his Statehood Party delegation advocated for the complete suppression of the legislature's rule-making authority, arguing the supreme court alone should be constitutionally vested with such power. *See* Proposition No. 319 in *Proposiciones y Resoluciones de la Convención Constituyente de Puerto Rico* (San Juan: Academia Puertorriqueña de Jurisprudencia y Legislación, 1992), 536–537. Delegates Ernesto Ramos Antonini and Víctor Gutiérrez Franqui and their Popular Democratic Party's caucus, on the other hand, argued for the cohabitation of both the judiciary and the legislature in the rule-making process.

By the time the convention met, the supreme court was uneasy with the legislature's arbitrary handling of the rule-making power. Having delegated full authority to the court in 1941, the legislature only took it away in 1948. *See González Vélez v. Tribunal Superior* (1953) ("For obvious reasons, this court has not proposed any additional rules in its new role as ghostwriter for the legislature."). Thus, constitutionalizing the court's power to adopt rules of civil and criminal procedure (including rules of evidence) was immediately perceived as an indispensable corollary to the unified court system designed under Article V's Section 2.

The compromise reached at the convention struck a fine balance between the judiciary and the legislative branches. Section 6 undoubtedly vests in the supreme court the constitutional authority to initiate and lead the rule-making process. The legislature can no longer abrogate or arbitrarily diminish the court's rule-making ascendancy. Only the high court can produce the full corpus of civil, criminal, and evidentiary rules applicable across the island's unified court system. *See* 3 *Diario* 1661. Yet Section 6 also endows the legislature with residual oversight authority.

The supreme court, under Section 6, is required to put the legislature on notice regarding the scope of the new rules. *See* 1 *Diario* 611–612; *see also In re Sesión Especial del Tribunal Supremo sobre el Proyecto de Reglas de Procedimiento Criminal de 2018* (2019). Those rules become enforceable sixty days after the expiration of the legislative session at which they were introduced, unless the legislature votes them down, amends them, or complements them. Section 6 grants the legislature authority to abrogate, amend, or complement any of these rules at any subsequent time by "specific legislation." As Chief Justice Cecil Snyder suggested in *González Vélez v. Tribunal Superior de Puerto Rico* (1953), this legislative prerogative, which operates as a necessary check on the court's otherwise unrestrained power, should only be invoked "on rare occasions and only in light of compelling reasons."

The legislature's recent addition of Rule 8.9 to the Rules of Civil Procedure, requiring nongovernmental entities litigating in the island's courts to fully disclose the existence of any parent corporation owning 10 percent or more of their stock, would seem to fall squarely within Chief Justice Snyder's standard. *See* P.R. Law No. 190 of August 5, 2018 (PR ST T.32, Ap. V, R 8.9). The historical experience shows that the relatively slow pace of the supreme court's rule-making exercise justifies, on occasion, the legislature's swift action in order to address pressing regulatory needs, without overstepping the neatly drawn constitutional boundaries that Section 6 delineates.

Section 7
Rules of Administration; Chief Justice to Direct Administration and Appoint Administrative Director

The Supreme Court shall adopt rules for the administration of the courts. These rules shall be subject to the laws concerning procurement, personnel, audit and appropriation of funds, and other laws which apply generally to all branches of the government. The Chief Justice shall direct the administration of the courts and shall appoint an administrative director who shall hold office at the will of the Chief Justice.

Section 7 put an end to the ancient, yet unfortunate, practice of placing in the hands of the executive branch the administration of the island's court system. At no point during the Spanish period had the insular courts exercised any endogenous administrative authority, not even under the much-celebrated Autonomic Charter of 1897. All administrative directives had come from Madrid in the guise of special legislation. The transfer of sovereignty did not lead to the devolution of administrative authority to the courts. To the contrary, shortly after the U.S. invasion, General Guy Henry put the courts under the watchful eye of the newly established Puerto Rico Department of Justice. *See* U.S. General Order No. 12 (February 6, 1899). The executive branch's control over the court system remained unchanged under both the Foraker and Jones Acts.

On the eve of the constitutional convention, there was widespread consensus among the island's political forces that there could be no genuine judicial independence so long as the courts remained under the attorney general's administrative yoke. *See* 1 *Diario* 616–617. All three political parties represented at the convention agreed that the constitution should vest in the chief justice of the supreme court the administration of the judicial branch.

The Statehood Party went as far as calling for the inclusion in the constitutional text of unequivocal language designating the chief justice as "administrative chief" (*jefe administrativo*) of the judiciary, with the same powers then enjoyed by the attorney general. The option of delegating the administration of the courts to a collective body, such as the quasi-public Judicial Council (*Consejo Judicial*) as initially suggested by the University of Puerto Rico's School of Public Administration, gained no traction at the convention.

A close perusal of the convention diaries shows that the framers' deepseated commitment to the twin principles of separation of powers and judicial independence, *see* 1 *Diario* 617, was inextricably bound to their conception of a robust chief justice with unquestioned authority over all administrative matters. *See* 1 *Diario* 616 and 3 *Diario* 1666, 1667. To their eyes, decolonizing the island's frail court system from the executive branch required delegating to the chief justice the administration of the judicial branch.

The structural design of Section 7 puts in place an internal check and balance within the supreme court itself. *In re Aprobación de las Reglas para los procedimientos de investigaciones especiales independientes de la Rama Judicial* (2012). While the full court establishes the regulatory framework, in areas like the codes of judicial conduct and disciplinary enforcement, attorney admissions, continuing legal education, procurement standards, methods of alternative dispute resolution, rules of evidence, civil and criminal procedure, as well as the internal governance of the inferior courts (among others), the chief justice alone is the administrative head of the judiciary. Thus, the full court legislates while the chief justice executes, like concentric circles, each gravitating within its own constitutional orbit. *See* 3 *Diario* 1667, 1669.

Only recently Section 7 has been the subject of debate within the supreme court. *See In re Aprobación de las Reglas para los procedimientos de investigaciones especiales independientes de la Rama Judicial, supra.* A majority of the justices has now embraced an arguably revisionist reading of Section 7, contending that the full court, as opposed to the chief justice, enjoys overriding administrative authority. *In re Designación del Secretario del Tribunal Supremo* (2021). The reverberations surrounding this debate led the legislature to significantly curtail the chief justice's administrative prerogatives. *See* P.R. Law No. 120 of December 15, 2017 (PR ST T.4, § 73). The court's reconfiguration of Section 7 appears to have unraveled the framers' original intent.

Section 8
Appointment of Judges, Officers, and Employees

Judges shall be appointed by the Governor with the advice and consent of the Senate. Justices of the Supreme Court shall not assume office until after confirmation by the Senate and shall hold their offices during good behavior. The terms of office of the other judges shall be fixed by law and shall not be less than that fixed for the term of office of a judge of the same or equivalent category existing when this Constitution takes effect. The other officials and employees of the courts shall be appointed in the manner provided by law.

By placing in the hands of the elected governor the appointment of justices to the supreme court, Section 8 charted a new path for the island. For the first time in its constitutional trajectory, the nomination of the magistrates of the high court would be made by locally elected officials. Under the Foraker, Jones, and Elective Governor Acts, the justices of the supreme court were nominated by the president of the United States, with the advice and consent of the federal Senate.

Under Section 8, moreover, the appointment of the lower court judges remained the exclusive prerogative of the governor, who would still be required to seek the advice and consent of the local senate. Having turned down the choice of electing judges, the critical issue before the convention became determining the scope of the governor's nominating authority. The option of limiting that power by requiring the governor to designate only judicial candidates already preselected by a nonpolitical third party, while enticing to the Statehood Party delegation, was also discarded. Interestingly, the possibility of excluding the governor from the appointment of the chief justice was flatly rejected. *See Torres Montalvo v. Gobernador* (2016) (dismissing the bizarre proposition that Section 8 does not bestow on the governor the power to nominate the chief justice). Thus, the power to nominate all judges, including the chief justice, vests in the governor alone. This authority, however, is limited by unavoidable checks and balances. Section 8 requires the senate's ratification of all judicial appointments. Moreover, the prerequisites for holding judicial office in Puerto Rico's Appellate and First Instance Courts are determined by ordinary legislation.

Section 8 is distinguishable from the federal precedent in two important ways. First, it does not provide for lifetime appointments. Appellate court judges enjoy tenure for sixteen years, while first instance judges serve for twelve years. Upon the expiration of their terms, the governor can renominate them if he or she so wishes, so long as the judges have not reached the compulsory retirement age of seventy years established under Section 10. The renomination of an inferior judge also requires the advice and consent of the senate.

Second, Section 8 shuts the door to recess appointments to the supreme court. If extrapolated to the federal landscape, this would have meant that the infamous John Rutledge and both Earl Warren and William Brennan (to name but a few) would have been unable to take their places at the U.S. Supreme Court as they did—that is, prior to the U.S. Senate's confirmation vote. (President George Washington appointed Rutledge chief justice during the summer recess of 1795, and Rutledge took his commission on June 30, 1795; six months later, the U.S. Senate rejected his nomination. President Dwight Eisenhower nominated Earl Warren as chief justice and William Brennan as associate justice during the fall recesses of 1953 and 1956, respectively; they were both subsequently confirmed by the U.S. Senate.) These scenarios are all incompatible with Article V's Section 8, which precludes the governor from making recess appointments to the supreme court.

Section 9
Qualifications of Justices of Supreme Court

No person shall be appointed a justice of the Supreme Court unless he is a citizen of the United States and of Puerto Rico, shall have been admitted to the practice of law in Puerto Rico at least ten years prior to his appointment, and shall have resided in Puerto Rico at least five years immediately prior thereto.

162 ■ THE PUERTO RICO CONSTITUTION AND COMMENTARY

Unlike the federal constitutional text, and contrary to the precedent established by the organic acts, Section 9 spells out the qualifications supreme court nominees must possess at the time of their nomination. If compared to the constitutions of the various states *circa* 1952, the requirements listed under Section 9 are far from unusual. By then, sixteen state constitutions required American citizenship, twelve demanded five years of state residency, and three explicitly called for ten years of admission to the local bar.

The archival record shows that the inclusion of the American citizenship requirement was proposed by Delegate Miguel Ángel García Méndez, 1 *Diario* 518, and that its incorporation into the constitution was intended to diffuse any concerns Congress might raise at the ratification stage about the future composition of the court. 1 *Diario* 519. The addition of both the five-year residency and the ten-year bar admission requirements was intended to disincentivize carpetbaggers, while placing an additional check on the governor's formidable nominating power. Interestingly, the convention made it plain clear that the admission requirement did not mean ten years of active nonstop legal practice. It merely meant, at a minimum, ten years of bar membership. 1 *Diario* 517. Thus, the door was left wide open for governors to construe a widely diverse and intellectually rich court made up of lower court judges, practitioners, and academicians. 1 *Diario* 639.

Section 10
Retirement of Judges

The Legislative Assembly shall establish a retirement system for judges. Retirement shall be compulsory at the age of seventy years.

A novel feature of the framers' design was the constitutional protection extended to the judiciary's retirement system. No other public pension plan is guaranteed by the constitution. By the time the convention met in September 1951, there was no independent pension plan for the judges. Their pensions were commingled with those of all other public employees under the government's newly established retirement system. In disentangling the judiciary's pension plan, the framers, in the words of the supreme court, intended to strengthen the judiciary's independence from the political branches. *García Martínez v. Gobernador* (1979).

Puerto Rico's bankruptcy and Congress's enactment of PROMESA has brought to the fore the legal and policy complexities surrounding Section 10. In *Brau v. Estado Libre Asociado* (2014), the court struck down as unconstitutional some of the more seminal provisions incorporated to P.R. Law No. 162 of December 24, 2013 (PR ST T.3, § 757), which attempted to retroactively modify the pensions of retired judges. Seeking refuge in the separation of powers doctrine, Chief Justice Federico Hernández Denton, writing for a unanimous court, found that the retroactive provisions included in P.R. Law No. 162 of 2013 contravened the constitutional mandate.

More recently, the island's debt restructuring process has exacerbated the debate revolving around Section 10, pitting the Puerto Rico Supreme Court against PROMESA's Oversight Board. On March 13, 2017, the Board certified a fiscal plan that retroactively reduced the pensions of the judiciary, in violation of the court's holding in *Brau*. On July 2, 2019, U.S. District Judge Laura Taylor Swaine refused to lift the automatic stay of the litigation filed by the *Asociación Puertorriqueña de la Judicatura* against the Oversight Board, *In re The Financial Oversight and Management Board for Puerto Rico as representative of the Commonwealth of Puerto Rico* (2019), which, invoking *Brau*, sought to shield the judiciary's retirement system from any retroactive modifications.

Contrary to the Foraker and Jones Acts, Section 10 also establishes a mandatory retirement age for all judges, including those sitting in the supreme court. They must all retire upon reaching their seventieth birthday.

Section 11
Removal of Judges

Justices of the Supreme Court may be removed for the causes and pursuant to the procedure established in § 21 of Article III of this Constitution. Judges of the other courts may be removed by the Supreme Court for the causes and pursuant to the procedure provided by law.

Section 11 underscores the framers' adherence to the twin principles of separation of powers and judicial independence. Not only does this section grant to the legislature the sole power to impeach and remove the justices of the supreme court, it eliminates all vestiges of executive meddling in the removal of lower court judges, thus strengthening the unitary framework of the island's judiciary.

In the pre-1952 period, under the Foraker and Jones Acts, the justices of the Puerto Rico Supreme Court were presidential appointees only removable by the president of the United States on the basis of inefficiency, neglect of duty, or malfeasance in office. The removal of inferior court judges required the full involvement of the executive branch. Only the governor could remove, on the recommendation of the Puerto Rico Supreme Court, district court judges charged with prevarication, bribery, immoral conduct, moral turpitude, gross negligence, or manifest incapacity in the discharge of his or her judicial functions. *See* Section 40 of the 1950 Judiciary Act (PR ST T.4, § 301). All other judicial officers, including municipal and peace court judges, prosecutors, and marshals, could be removed by the governor alone, without any participation of the supreme court. The independence of the judicial branch required putting an end to the executive branch's trespassing.

In its approach to the removal of Puerto Rico Supreme Court justices, Section 11 mirrors the dictates of the U.S. Constitution, pursuant to which the

164 ■ THE PUERTO RICO CONSTITUTION AND COMMENTARY

federal justices are only removable by way of impeachment. *See* U.S. Const., Art. II, § 4. Article V's Section 11, however, parts ways with the federal precedent to the extent lower court judges are removable not by legislative impeachment but by the supreme court itself. *See In re Reinaldo Santiago Concepción* (2013) (removing judge on charges of drug abuse and domestic violence).

The structural design of Section 11 did not elicit intense debate at the convention. There was widespread consensus among delegates of all political persuasions that the power to remove lower court judges should be vested in the supreme court, while exclusive authority to remove supreme court justices should be placed in the hands of the legislature by means of impeachment.

The only point of contention was determining whether to define with specificity the metes and bounds of an impeachable offense for the purpose of removing a supreme court justice. Delegate Lionel Fernández Méndez proposed the inclusion of such degree of detail in Section 11, but this idea was rejected. *See* 3 *Diario* 623–624.

The final text of Section 11 simply states that the members of the high court may be removed for the same causes, and pursuant to the same proceedings, as the governor; namely, treason, bribery, other felonies, and misdemeanors involving moral turpitude. Because impeachment is political in nature, falling under the exclusive jurisdiction of the legislative branch, the framers left the task of defining what constitutes an impeachable offense to the house of representatives and the senate. At this writing, no justice of the Puerto Rico Supreme Court has been impeached. The impeachment of a supreme court justice requires a two-thirds majority of all house members and a three-fourths majority of all senate members for removal.

Section 12
Political Activity by Judges

No judge shall make a direct or indirect financial contribution to any political organization or party, or hold any executive office therein, or participate in a political campaign of any kind, or be a candidate for an elective public office unless he has resigned his judicial office at least six months prior to his nomination.

Section 12 constitutes yet another mechanism to insulate the judiciary from the entanglements of the political process. The mandate flowing from Section 12 is nowhere to be found in the federal Constitution. By the time the Puerto Rico Convention met, only Missouri and New Jersey had incorporated analogous provisions to their constitutional texts. The historical record shows that, prior to the adoption of the 1952 Constitution, judges were at liberty to fundraise for political parties. Moreover, judges seeking political office were not statutorily required to resign prior to winning their party's nomination. Section 12 brought an end to these practices. This constitutional prohibition extends, arguably, to judges' law clerks and their spouses.

The inclusion of Section 12 in the constitution did not stir controversy. Only the lonely voice of Delegate Celestino Iriarte Miró opposed the constitutional banning of judges' political fundraising activities. Iriarte's attempt at eliminating this language from the constitutional text was decisively defeated at the convention floor. *See* 1 *Diario* 624–627.

In Puerto Rico's highly politicized society, defining what constitutes an impermissible political activity under Section 12 has, on occasion, proven a rather complex task. In *In re Zaida Hernández Torres* (2006), the supreme court, seeking refuge in Section 12 and Canon 28 of the Code of Conduct for Puerto Rico Judges (*Cánones de Ética Judicial*), made it clear that judges must not only refrain from fundraising and engaging in partisan politics but must also abstain themselves from expressing their political views.

Section 13
Tenure of Judge of Changed or Abolished Court

In the event that a court or any of its divisions or sections is changed or abolished by law, the person holding a post of judge therein shall continue to hold it during the rest of the term for which he was appointed and shall perform the judicial functions assigned to him by the Chief Justice of the Supreme Court.

Section 13 offers the judiciary yet an additional layer of insulation from the political thicket. Although the 1950 Judiciary Act (PR ST T.4, § 301) had put an end to the practice of removing lower court judges by stealth, simply by abolishing or reorganizing the courts where they sat, only to favor the ambitions of the party controlling the political branches; the delegates to the convention unanimously decided to constitutionalize this statutory protection. 1 *Diario* 633.

Section 13 places a check on the legislature's constitutional authority. While the constitution endows the legislative branch with authority to create, abolish, and reorganize the inferior courts, it denies legislators the power to remove the judges sitting in the abolished tribunals. Section 13 requires that the now bereft judges serve in the judiciary on new tasks assigned to them by the chief justice until the expiration of their terms of office. *See In re Reglas para la creación y funcionamiento de la Unidad Especial de Jueces de Apelaciones* (1993).

Of special significance is the fact that Section 13 vests full authority in the chief justice alone to rearrange the judicial and administrative tasks delegated to the stray judges. Section 13 accordingly confirms the framers' conception of a robust chief justice with unquestioned administrative and executive authority.

Article VI

General Provisions

Section 1
Municipalities

The Legislative Assembly shall have the power to create, abolish, consolidate and reorganize municipalities; to change their territorial limits; to determine their organization and functions; and to authorize them to develop programs for the general welfare and to create any agencies necessary for that purpose.

No law abolishing or consolidating municipalities shall take effect until ratified in a referendum by a majority of the qualified electors voting in said referendum in each of the municipalities to be abolished or consolidated. The referendum shall be conducted in the manner determined by law, which shall include the applicable procedures of the election laws in effect when the referendum law is approved.

Finding the proper place for Puerto Rico's municipalities within the island's constitutional landscape remains a hotly contested issue. Voices as authoritative as Harvard's Carl Friedrich have suggested that the founders' failure to constitutionalize the devolution to the municipalities of a robust quantum of administrative power over local affairs, immune from the whims of the legislature, stands as the most salient omission of the 1951–1952 constitution-making exercise. The Puerto Rico Constitution, like the organic acts preceding it, establishes that the municipalities are creatures of the legislature. A careful examination of the language found in Sections 32 and 37 of the Foraker and Jones Acts, respectively,

167

168 ■ THE PUERTO RICO CONSTITUTION AND COMMENTARY

shows that the framers' approach to local government did not fundamentally deviate from the treatment afforded to that issue under the *ancien régime*.

Despite Delegate José Gelpí Bosch's proposal for constitutionalizing municipal autonomy over those local issues not exclusively ruled by the Commonwealth's government, *see* 3 *Diario* 2040, the convention chose instead to design a highly centralized governmental structure where the legislature sits at the pinnacle, wielding plenary power over the municipalities. Under Article VI's Section 1, the legislature alone is entrusted with authority to create and reorganize municipalities, to modify their territorial limits, and to determine their internal organization. The legislature, moreover, may delegate to the municipalities the power to develop programs for the general welfare and to create the necessary administrative agencies for carrying out that goal.

In *López v. Municipio de San Juan* (1988), the Puerto Rico Supreme Court, evoking the principle it had embraced in *Cabassa v. Rivera* (1948), reiterated that municipal ordinances cannot run afoul of legislation enacted by the island's political branches. Thus, as the court itself insinuated in *Domínguez Castro v. Estado Libre Asociado* (2010), the municipalities do not appear to enjoy an inherent police power independent from the legislature.

Nothing in the constitutional text precludes the legislature from delegating its police power to the municipalities for safeguarding the health, safety, welfare, and morals of their inhabitants. Following the legislature's enactment of the far-reaching municipal reform of 1991, *see* P.R. Law No. 81 of August 30, 1991 (PR ST T.21, § 4001 *et seq.*), the Puerto Rico Supreme Court in *Municipio de Ponce v. Autoridad de Carreteras* (2000) held that a covenant entered into by a municipality and an instrumentality or agency of the central government is fully binding and susceptible to regulation under local contract law.

The only area of significance where the framers parted ways with the organic acts was in the limitation on the legislature's power to unilaterally abolish and consolidate municipalities. Unlike the pre-1952 landscape, where municipalities could be abolished or consolidated by legislative fiat alone, under Article VI's Section 1 any such legislative abrogation requires that the inhabitants of each of the affected municipalities ratify the measure in a referendum.

At this writing, Puerto Rico's bankruptcy, along with the economic devastation brought about by Hurricanes María and Fiona in 2017 and 2022 (respectively), the COVID-19 pandemic, and the slew of earthquakes affecting most southwestern towns in 2020, brought the issue of municipal restructuring to the fore.

Section 2
Power of Taxation; Power to Contract Debts

The power of the Commonwealth of Puerto Rico to impose and collect taxes and to authorize their imposition and collection by municipalities shall be exercised as determined by the Legislative Assembly and shall never be surrendered or suspended. The power of the Commonwealth of Puerto Rico to contract and to authorize the contracting of debts shall be exercised as determined by the Legislative Assembly, but no direct obligations of the Commonwealth for money borrowed directly by the Commonwealth evidenced by bonds or notes for the payment of which the full faith, credit and taxing power of the Commonwealth shall be pledged shall be issued by the Commonwealth if the total of (i) the amount of principal of and interest on such bonds and notes, together with the amount of principal of and interest on all such bonds and notes theretofore issued by the Commonwealth and then outstanding, payable in any fiscal year and (ii) any amounts paid by the Commonwealth in the fiscal year next preceding the then current fiscal year for principal or interest on account of any outstanding obligations evidenced by bonds or notes guaranteed by the Commonwealth, shall exceed 15 percent of the average of the total amount of the annual revenues raised under the provisions of Commonwealth legislation and covered into the Treasury of Puerto Rico in the two fiscal years next preceding the then current fiscal year; and no such bonds or notes issued by the Commonwealth for any purpose other than housing facilities shall mature later than 30 years from their date and no bonds or notes issued for housing facilities shall mature later than 40 years from their date; and the Commonwealth shall not guarantee any obligations evidenced by bonds or notes if the total of the amount payable in any fiscal year on account of principal of and interest on all the direct obligations referred to above theretofore issued by the Commonwealth and then outstanding and the amounts referred to in item (ii) above shall exceed 15 percent of the average of the total amount of such annual revenues.

The Legislative Assembly shall fix limitations for the issuance of direct obligations by any of the municipalities of Puerto Rico for money borrowed directly by such municipality evidenced by bonds or notes for the payment of which the full faith, credit and taxing power of such municipality shall be pledged; Provided, however, That no such bonds or notes shall be issued by any municipality in an amount which, together with the amount of all such bonds and notes theretofore issued by such municipality and then outstanding, shall exceed the percentage determined by the Legislative Assembly, which shall be not less than five per centum (5%) nor more than ten per centum (10%) of the aggregate tax valuation of the property within such municipality.

The Secretary of the Treasury may be required to apply the available revenues including surplus to the payment of interest on the public debt and the amortization thereof in any case provided for by § 8 of this Article VI at the suit of any holder of bonds or notes issued in evidence thereof.

Section 2 lies at the heart of the Commonwealth's fiscal architecture. It bestows on the legislature the power to tax and to issue public debt. Section 2, however, is silent with respect to all matters pertaining to commerce with foreign jurisdictions. Because Puerto Rico belongs to the customs territory of the United States, all issues involving customs duties on imports and exports remain under Congress's unilateral control.

The taxing power of Puerto Rico's legislature antedates the 1952 Constitution. The origins of the legislature's "power to destroy," in the stark words of Chief Justice John Marshall, *see M'Culloch v. Maryland* (1819), are found in Sections 38 and 3 of the Foraker and Jones Acts, respectively. Similarly, in enacting the organic acts, Congress also entrusted the local legislature with the power to issue bonds.

In *Rodríguez v. Secretario de Hacienda* (1994), the Puerto Rico Supreme Court made it clear that the legislature enjoys an "inherent" taxing power. Such "inherent" taxing power, which the text itself of Section 2 describes as unalienable, can only be surrendered in a handful of exceptional circumstances. In *R.C.A. v. Gobierno de la Capital* (1964), the court warned that the judiciary should nullify a legislative measure enacted in furtherance of Section 2's taxing power only if it runs afoul of the Puerto Rico Constitution (especially the fundamental rights enshrined therein) or any of the fiscal provisions found in the 1950 Federal Relations Act.

As the island's high court suggested in *Lukoil Pan Americas v. Municipality of Guayanilla* (2015), Section 2 also grants the legislature authority to delegate its taxing prerogatives to the municipalities. Yet the scope of municipal taxation is particularly limited. In *Compañía de Turismo v. Municipality of Vieques* (2010), the court declared null and void a municipal room tax that was clearly incompatible with the Puerto Rico Internal Revenue Code. A municipal tax will necessarily fail if it impermissibly invades a regulatory area preempted by the Commonwealth's government. *See id.*

While the framers constitutionalized the legislature's formidable power to issue triple tax-free bonds against the Commonwealth's full faith and credit, the debt ceiling formula remained in the hands of Congress until 1961. This is precisely why the original version of Section 2 made no reference to the debt ceiling calculus, which, following the inauguration of the constitution in 1952, was regulated under the 1950 Federal Relations Act.

Congress's devolution to the local legislature of the power to set the debt ceiling requires particular attention. The debt ceiling formula incorporated into Puerto Rico's Constitution in 1961 established a legally sound fiscal framework. It did away with the rule that had survived since 1900, whereby the island's debt ceiling was fixed at 7 percent of the aggregate tax valuation of its property. Under the new formula, the Commonwealth's debt ceiling cannot exceed 15 percent of the average revenue for the two immediate fiscal years preceding the current one.

Despite its legal coherence, the framers' debt management mechanism has failed. Puerto Rico's bankruptcy has brought the debt management debate full circle. The irresponsible (and in some instances illegal) issuance of so-called "extra-constitutional debt" by an avalanche of public corporations and other quasi-public legal entities not bound by Section 2's constitutional limitations was a catalyst behind Puerto Rico's implosion. Puerto Rico's constitutional design is no longer equipped to infuse legal certainty into its fiscal labyrinth.

Section 3
Rule of Taxation to be Uniformed

The rule of taxation in Puerto Rico shall be uniform.

The Puerto Rico Constitution, like its federal counterpart, requires tax uniformity. *See* U.S. Const., Art. 1, § 8, Cl. 1. Initially imported to Puerto Rico's legal landscape in 1917, following Congress's enactment of the Jones Act, the text of Section 3's tax uniformity clause reproduces the language found in the second organic act. Not only was its inclusion in the constitutional text devoid of any significant debate at the convention, but the Puerto Rico Supreme Court has yet to draw with precision its doctrinal boundaries.

On one of the very few occasions the court has examined the tax uniformity clause, it has held that Section 3 does not require "intrinsic uniformity," but rather "geographic uniformity." *See Miranda v. Secretario de Hacienda* (1954). Thus, in the exercise of its wide taxing power, the legislature enjoys ample discretion to treat taxpayers differently. Section 3 does not require equal treatment with respect to tax liabilities, credits, deductions, and any other number of tax-related classifications. Section 3 only requires that the legislature uniformly apply the same tax criteria across the Puerto Rican geography.

Section 4
Elections

General elections shall be held every four years on the day of November determined by the Legislative Assembly. In said elections there shall be elected a Governor, the members of the Legislative Assembly, and the other officials whose election on that date is provided for by law.

Every person over eighteen years of age shall be entitled to vote if he fulfills the other conditions determined by law. No person shall be deprived of the right to vote because he does not know how to read or write or does not own property.

All matters concerning the electoral process, registration of voters, political parties and candidates shall be determined by law.

Every popularly elected official shall be elected by direct vote and any candidate who receives more votes than any other candidate for the same office shall be declared elected. [As amended by the voters at a referendum held Nov. 1, 1970.]

Section 4 complements the constitutional mandate contained in Article II's Section 2. It establishes that the right to vote in Puerto Rico is universal and, therefore, immune from invidious literacy or property ownership restrictions, though this section explicitly limits the franchise to voters who are eighteen years or older on election (or primary) day.

Mirroring Article II's Section 2, Article VI's Section 4 delegates to the legislature significant power to regulate the island's electoral process with very few limitations. While Section 4 requires that a general election for governor, senators, and representatives takes place every four years in the month of November, it leaves it to the legislature to decide when in November to hold it.

172 ■ THE PUERTO RICO CONSTITUTION AND COMMENTARY

Section 4 is silent on the election of mayors and municipal legislators. Determining the timing of municipal elections is a matter left entirely in the hands of the legislature. Similarly, Section 4 omits any reference to the election of the resident commissioner. At the insistence of Delegate Antonio Fernós Isern (then serving as Puerto Rico's resident commissioner in Washington, D.C.), *see* 3 *Diario* 2067, 2072, the convention removed from Section 4's first draft any reference to the election of the resident commissioner in an overly cautious attempt at avoiding any interpretative conflicts with the 1950 Federal Relations Act. *See* 4 *Diario* 2620. Consequently, the election of Puerto Rico's resident commissioner is regulated under federal law.

Section 4 explicitly constitutionalizes the "first past the post" principle intimated by the framers in Article III's Section 1, and together with Article IX's Section 6 and Article III's Sections 7 and 8, extends to Puerto Rico's political parties a distinct constitutional personality susceptible to legislative regulation.

Section 5
Promulgation of Laws; Effective Date

The laws shall be promulgated in accordance with the procedure prescribed by law and shall specify the terms under which they shall take effect.

The Puerto Rico Constitution, unlike the Jones Act, places no structural limits on the legislature's power to determine the effective date of its own legislation. A fuller understanding of Article VI's Section 5 requires a closer look at Article III's Section 19. The former supplements the latter. In designing a more robust and agile legislature, the framers were bent on extirpating from the Puerto Rican legislative landscape the fatal defect Congress had injected into the Jones Act—the provision whereby local legislation (with the exception of the island's budget) could only become fully effective until ninety days after its passage. Section 5 put an end to that procedural straitjacket. Determining the effective date of legislation, as the Puerto Rico Supreme Court found in *Herrero y Otros v. Estado Libre Asociado* (2010), is an "inherent aspect" of the legislature's constitutional prerogatives. *See also Rodríguez Quintana v. Rivera Estrada* (2015).

Section 6
Failure to Make Appropriations

If at the end of any fiscal year the appropriations necessary for the ordinary operating expenses of the government and for the payment of interest on and amortization of the public debt for the ensuing fiscal year shall not have been made, the several sums appropriated in the last appropriation acts for the objects and purposes therein specified, so far as the same may be applicable, shall continue in effect item by item, and the Governor shall authorize the payments necessary for such purposes until corresponding appropriations are made.

Section 6 is at the core of the constitution's fiscal provisions. Its origins may be traced to an amendment to the Foraker Act passed by Congress in 1909 known as the Olmsted Act. *See* 36 Stat. 11 (1909). At first glance, Section 6 stands for a relatively simple proposition: if, at the start of the fiscal year, the political branches have failed to enact the necessary appropriations for the operating expenses of the government and the payment of the public debt, the relevant sums appropriated for the previous fiscal year shall remain in full force and effect solely with respect to operating costs and debt amortization alone. Of significance is the fact that, unlike the Olmsted and Jones Acts, Section 6 provides for the automatic reappropriation of the sums assigned "for the payment of interest on and amortization of the public debt."

Section 6, moreover, leaves the door open to the brokering of fiscal compromises between the governor and the legislature. At the behest of Delegate Miguel Ángel García Méndez, *see* 2 *Diario* 890, the Convention incorporated into Section 6 an additional provision establishing that the sums appropriated for the previous fiscal year shall cease to apply as soon as a deal is brokered among the political branches and new appropriations are made. Thus, the activation of the safeguards found in Section 6 in no way binds the island for the remainder of the current fiscal year to the sums appropriated for the preceding fiscal year.

Notwithstanding its apparent textual clarity, the full scope of Section 6 is unclear. Issues of mootness and standing have led the Puerto Rico Supreme Court to dismiss as nonjusticiable a handful of cases implicating the complex interplay among Article VI's Sections 6, 7, 8, and 9. *See Presidente de la Cámara v. Gobernador* (2006); *see also Hernández Torres v. Hernández Colón* (1992).

Chief among the unanswered questions is, what happens if, resulting from an impasse between the political branches, Section 6 is triggered but the projected revenues for the new fiscal year are insufficient to cover the operating costs of the government and the debt service at the level they were appropriated for the previous fiscal year? Is this an event of default triggering Section 8's debt priority ranking? Bearing in mind that Section 7 requires a balanced budget, is there any constitutional impediment under Section 6 precluding the governor (in light of a legislative gridlock) from unilaterally modifying the appropriations for governmental expenses and debt service from the previous fiscal year? Can the governor effectively modify the appropriations belonging to the budgets of the legislative and judicial branches? Is the line-item veto found under Article III's Section 20 available to the governor in this context? Or is the governor's role under Section 6 exclusively limited to authorizing, by executive order, the disbursements of those appropriations approved in the preceding fiscal year?

In *Presidente de la Cámara, supra,* the supreme court, facing the above-referenced issues for the first time, dismissed the claimants' cause of action on justiciability grounds. In a dissenting opinion, Justice Anabelle Rodríguez intimated that Section 6 does not vest in the governor the extraordinary power

174 ■ THE PUERTO RICO CONSTITUTION AND COMMENTARY

to unilaterally modify the budget appropriated to the legislative branch in the previous fiscal year. Rather, Justice Rodríguez characterized the mechanism found in Section 6 as "transitory" in nature, limited to the disbursement of only the most essential sums for the operation of the government and the service of the public debt. *See id.* (Rodríguez, J., dissenting).

Revisiting the substantive issues raised in *Presidente de la Cámara* might lead to different conclusions, particularly in light of the fact that nothing in the constitutional text appears to prevent the governor from using his or her line-item veto authority whenever an appropriation bill containing more than one item reaches his or her desk. Arguably, a symmetrical reading of Article VI's Sections 6, 7, 8, and 9 requires a more robust construction of the governor's unique role in infusing constitutional certainty to the island's fiscal landscape in times of gridlock.

Section 7
Appropriations not to Exceed Revenues

The appropriations made for any fiscal year shall not exceed the total revenues, including available surplus, estimated for said fiscal year unless the imposition of taxes sufficient to cover said appropriations is provided by law.

Unlike the federal founders, the delegates to the Puerto Rico Constitutional Convention incorporated into the island's constitutional text a balanced budget requirement. Section 7 effectively constitutionalized the balanced budget rule found in the Jones Act, with the caveat that the balanced budget formula found in the second organic act underwent significant modifications at the constitutional convention. Whereas Section 34 of the Jones Act explicitly established that governmental expenditure could not exceed the island's total tax revenue (including any accumulated surplus from previous fiscal years), Section 7 significantly expanded the definition of governmental revenue, to include not only income derived from local taxes but also income generated from the sale of triple tax-free bonds and other governmental property, the transfer of federal grants-in-aid, the payment of royalties to quasi-public corporations, and a host of other sources. *See* P.R. Op. § Just. 1974-15 (May 21, 1974).

Thus, the constitutionally required expenditure-to-income ratio under Section 7 affords the island's political branches substantial latitude for designing (at least theoretically) a comprehensive annual budget for fully addressing some of the island's more intractable socio-economic ills (i.e., inequality, poverty, a decaying infrastructure, and the failure of its public health and education systems). Section 7, however, has proven highly ineffectual. The Commonwealth's massive bankruptcy shows how the political branches have breached their constitutional obligations under Section 7, perhaps encouraged by the Puerto Rico Supreme Court's inclination to dismiss, on justiciability grounds, legal actions predicated on the political branches' violation of Section 7. *See, e.g., Hernández Torres v. Hernández Colón* (1992).

Section 8
Priority of Disbursements if Revenues Insufficient

In case the available revenues including surplus for any fiscal year are insufficient to meet the appropriations made for that year, interest on the public debt and amortization thereof shall first be paid, and other disbursements shall thereafter be made in accordance with the order of priorities established by law.

In the aftermath of the Commonwealth's fiscal implosion, one of the more scrutinized, yet lesser explored (let alone enforced), constitutional provisions is Article VI's Section 8. The framers' decision to constitutionalize a debt priority ranking, to be activated in case of insolvency, should be seen as a necessary corollary to Section 2's debt ceiling limitations, Section 6's transitory budget mechanism, and Section 7's balanced budget requirement.

The framers envisioned Section 8 as an indispensable component of the constitution's delicate fiscal framework. While the notion of incorporating a debt priority ranking was imported from the Jones Act, Section 8 parts ways, both substantively and structurally, with the second organic act. No longer endowed with overriding authority to unilaterally bypass the debt priority ranking, the governor under Section 8 has no power to suspend or rearrange the order of priorities established therein. Unlike the Jones Act, which placed at the pinnacle both "the ordinary expenses of the legislative, executive and judicial departments," together with "the interest on any public debt," Section 8 solely prioritizes "interest on the public debt and amortization thereof." Accordingly, in case of insolvency, the payment of all other governmental expenditures (including the financing of essential services) is subordinated to the service of the public debt.

Arguably, public debt under Section 8 only refers to those obligations issued against the Commonwealth's full faith and credit, pursuant to the strictures of Section 2. The convention's adoption of Section 8 was preceded by a rather revealing debate between Delegates José Gelpí Bosch and Víctor Gutiérrez Franqui. Gelpí Bosch suggested the constitution ought to explicitly endow the legislature with authority to bypass Section 8's debt priority order by declaring a debt moratorium in case of a national emergency. *See 3 Diario* 1962. Gutiérrez Franqui, for his part, opposed the explicit inclusion of any such provision in the constitutional text, but openly suggested that despite Section 8's silence on this issue, the legislature enjoys "inherent" authority to suspend the payment of the public debt (both interest and amortization of principal) in the event of insolvency. *See id.*

The convention's defeat of Gelpí Bosch's proposal did not put to rest the issue of whether the legislature enjoys inherent authority to declare a debt moratorium. By 2014, at the height of the Commonwealth's debt crisis, the legislature enacted the Puerto Rico Corporation Debt Enforcement and Recovery Act, P.R. Law No. 71 of June 28, 2014 (PR ST T.13, § 111), which effectively led to the suspension of debt service and the initiation of a locally regulated debt modification procedure.

In the midst of the debt crisis, Section 8 (like Section 7) has proved irrelevant, insulated from judicial review by the Puerto Rico Supreme Court's sense of self-restraint. In addressing the recent debt crisis, the political branches bypassed the constitutional path designed by the framers, choosing instead to plod along an extra-constitutional road that, in turn, was found unconstitutional (on preemption grounds) by the U.S. Supreme Court in *Commonwealth of Puerto Rico v. Franklin California Tax-Free Trust* (2016).

Section 9
Use of Public Property and Funds

Public property and funds shall only be disposed of for public purposes, for the support and operation of public institutions, and pursuant to law.

By incorporating Section 9 into the constitutional text, the framers placed an important limitation on the legislature's spending power. Section 9 establishes that "public property and funds" shall only be used for "public purposes" as well as "for the support and operation of public institutions, and pursuant to law."

Public spending, under Section 9, requires legislative action. The language found in Section 9 is derived from the religious supporting clause Congress added to the Jones Act in 1921, *see* 41 Stat. 1096 (1921), and should be read in tandem with the education supporting clause available under Section 5 of the Puerto Rico Bill of Rights.

By far the more contentious issue at the convention, with respect to Section 9, was determining whether to describe with specificity the meaning of "public purposes" and "public institutions" in the constitutional text itself, or whether to leave that task in the hands of the judiciary. At the urging of Delegate Víctor Gutiérrez Franqui, and despite the opposition of Delegate Leopoldo Figueroa Carreras, the convention chose the latter path. *See* 2 *Diario* 903, 913–914.

In retrospect, the absence of a clear constitutional standard establishing the proper scope of Section 9's substantive content has led to the rendering of a hodgepodge of judicial decisions devoid of a clear doctrinal focus. In *Partido Popular Democrático v. Gobernador* (1995), a divided court, in an attempt to provide clarity, announced that "public purposes" under Section 9 are found "in any public or quasi-public activity safeguarding the health, safety, morals and general welfare of the people, promoting the interests and objectives of governmental institutions consistent with their respective public policies and statutory obligations, or furthering programs, services, opportunities, rights or any other social, civic, cultural, economic or sporting cause." If anything, the amorphous rule emerging from *Partido Popular* brings to the fore the significant deference the judiciary extends to the legislature in defining what amounts to "public purposes" under Section 9.

A systematic review of the available jurisprudence shows how the absence of a bright line rule has proven particularly problematic in borderline cases involving the expenditure of public monies for the political gain of the party in power. *See, e.g., Marrero v. Municipio de Morovis* (1984) (holding that the use by public officers of government vehicles for political campaigning is unconstitutional under Section 9). Furthermore, local legislation authorizing the use of public funds for the financing of statehood referenda, presidential primaries, and even the election of presidential delegates to the Electoral College, has rendered the Puerto Rico Supreme Court incapable of tracing a doctrinally coherent path. In *Partido Socialista Puertorriqueño v. Estado Libre Asociado* (1978), the high court found that Section 9 prohibited the use of public monies for financing the internal elections of the local Democratic and Republican National Committees. Yet, two years later, in *Partido Independentista Puertorriqueño v. Estado Libre Asociado* (1980), an evenly split court validated the use of local public funds for holding presidential primaries in the island, despite the indisputable fact that Puerto Rican voters do not send presidential electors to the Electoral College. The court reaffirmed its limited reading of Section 9 in *Partido Independentista Puertorriqueño v. Comisión Estatal de Elecciones* (1988), concluding that the use of public monies for holding local presidential primaries did not run afoul the constitutional mandate. In so doing, the court distanced itself once again from the conclusions drawn by the *Partido Socialista* court.

In *Báez Galib v. Comisión Estatal de Elecciones* (2000), the court declared that the legislature's appropriation of public funds for the local selection of presidential electors to the Electoral College was unconstitutional under Section 9. Because Puerto Rico residents have no presidential vote and Puerto Rico (unlike the fifty states and the District of Columbia) has no participation in the Electoral College, the *Báez Galib* court found the legislature's appropriation of public monies for this political ploy devoid of any "public purpose." Not surprisingly, the court concluded that Section 9 required declaring P.R. Law No. 403 of September 10, 2000 (PR ST T.16, § 961) null and void.

More recently, Section 9 has been the subject of significant litigation, due in no small measure to the ideological balkanization of the island's political jigsaw puzzle.

In the run-up to the 2020 election, the Puerto Rico Supreme Court revisited *Báez Galib*, as it faced the issue of whether the use of public monies for holding a nonbinding "yes or no" statehood vote on election day ran afoul of Section 9's constitutional limitations. In *Aponte Rosario v. Presidente Comisión Estatal de Elecciones* (2020), a deeply fractured court found that funding the local status referendum with public monies, as required under P.R. Law No. 51 of May 16,

2020 (PR ST T.16, § 975), did pursue a public purpose as required under Section 9. Not only did the court's analysis in *Aponte Rosario* significantly veer off to the political arena but its conclusions flew in the face of the legal findings of the U.S. Department of Justice, which had previously refused to "obligate" federal funds for holding the statehood referendum precisely because "the ballot and related materials" were not compatible "with the Constitution, laws, and public policies of the United States". *See* Letter of Deputy Attorney General Jeffrey Rosen, July 29, 2020.

The complex uncertainties surrounding Puerto Rico's relationship with the United States are likely in the future to engender further debate regarding the proper scope of Section 9's limitations.

Section 10
Extra Compensation for Services; Extension of Term or Decrease of Salary of Public Officer; Salary for More than One Office

No law shall give extra compensation to any public officer, employee, agent or contractor after services shall have been rendered or contract made. No law shall extend the term of any public officer or diminish his salary or emoluments after his election or appointment. No person shall draw a salary for more than one office or position in the government of Puerto Rico.

Section 11
Salaries of Officials; Increase or Decrease

The salaries of the Governor, the Secretaries, the members of the Legislative Assembly, the Comptroller and Judges shall be fixed by a special law and, except for the salaries of the members of the Legislative Assembly, shall not be decreased during the terms for which they are elected or appointed. The salaries of the Governor and the Comptroller shall not be increased during said terms. No increase in the salaries of the members of the Legislative Assembly shall take effect until after the expiration of the term of the Legislative Assembly during which it is enacted. Any reduction of the salaries of the members of the Legislative Assembly shall be effective only during the term of the Legislative Assembly which approves it.

Not only do Sections 10 and 11 share a common source, they are intimately intertwined both structurally and substantively. A detailed reading of Section 34 of the Jones Act shows that the framers extrapolated from the second organic act, almost verbatim, the constitutional command enunciated in Section 10. Section 10, similar to Section 9, limits the legislature's spending power, explicitly prohibiting the appropriation of public funds for awarding "extra compensation to any public officer, employee, agent or contractor after services shall have been rendered or contract made."

Drawing the proper boundaries of this constitutional prohibition was a point of contention at the convention. Delegate Sigfrido Vélez González, with the blessing of Delegate Luis Negrón López, proposed expanding the reach of Section 10 in order to explicitly preclude executive agencies from retroactively awarding extra compensation from the public monies appropriated to them by the legislature. *See* 3 *Diario* 1976–1977. While the convention defeated Delegate Vélez González's proposed amendment, *see* 3 *Diario* 1983, it is well settled that the legislature enjoys ample authority to regulate the way in which the agencies and instrumentalities of the executive branch use public monies.

In *Landfill Technologies v. Municipio de Lares* (2013), seeking validation in a statement proffered by Delegate Luis Muñoz Rivera, *see* 3 *Diario* 1979, the Puerto Rico Supreme Court suggested that Section 10 in no way limits the legislature's power to appropriate public funds for the payment of additional services even if related to those already under contract. The constitutional impediment lies in appropriating public monies, ex post facto, for the payment of services already rendered or under contract.

Section 10 further limits the legislature's powers by establishing that no law shall diminish the salary or emoluments of any "public officer" or extend his or her term of office after his or her election or appointment. Pursuant to Section 10, there is a distinction of constitutional magnitude between the terms "public officer" and governmental "employee, agent or contractor." In distinguishing these terms, the framers paid heed to the available jurisprudence *circa* 1952. The archival record shows that the framers understood the term "public officer" (*funcionario*) to include the principal officers of the executive and judicial branches. *See* 2 *Diario* 928–930. Insulating those "public officers" from the arbitrariness of the legislative process, while strengthening their independence with respect to the legislature, stood as the framers' guiding principle.

Nonetheless, the double salary prohibition found in Section 10 makes no distinction between "public officer" and "employee, agent or contractor." It applies across the board. Since the adoption of the constitution, Puerto Rico's attorney general has only episodically opined on the reach of Section 10's double salary prohibition. On those few occasions, the attorney general has concluded that this constitutional prohibition is not applicable to public employees whose salaries are funded with federal monies, *see* P.R. Op. § Just. 1972-25 (Sept. 1, 1972); or to those who might receive a *per diem* allowance for services rendered to other public entities outside their regular hours of work, *see* P.R. Op. § Just. 1962-30 (May 28, 1962).

Section 11 strengthens the constitutional values embodied in Section 10 by placing another check on the power of the purse entrusted to the legislature. Structurally similar to the Compensation Clause found in the federal Constitution, *see* U.S. Const., Art. III, § 1, Section 11 protects the salaries of the governor, comptroller, cabinet secretaries, and judges from diminution for the duration of their mandates.

Section 11 is silent with respect to the salaries and emoluments of mayors and other municipal officers, leaving this subject in the hands of the legislature.

Whereas Section 11 requires that the salaries of the governor and the comptroller remain unchanged throughout the course of their respective terms, nothing in the constitution bars the legislature from increasing the compensation of the cabinet secretaries and the judges while they are in office.

In designing Section 11, the framers crafted a rather ingenious arrangement whereby any increase in the salaries of senators and representatives can only take effect following the election of their successors. On the other hand, diminution of legislative salaries shall take effect immediately.

Section 11 explicitly commands that the salaries of the governor, the cabinet secretaries, the judges, and the comptroller "be fixed by a special law." Nonetheless, in recent years succeeding governors have implemented the irregular practice of fixing the salaries of cabinet secretaries, not pursuant to special legislation as required under Section 11 but by contract. Their attempt at bypassing the explicit mandate emanating from Section 11 is arguably unconstitutional.

Section 12
Residence of Governor

The Governor shall occupy and use, free of rent, the buildings and properties belonging to the Commonwealth which have been or shall hereafter be used and occupied by him as chief executive.

Section 12 stands for a relatively simple proposition: the governor, if he or she wishes, shall live in *La Fortaleza*, rent-free for the duration of his or her term. A UNESCO World Heritage Site and U.S. National Historic Landmark, *La Fortaleza* is the most ancient executive mansion in continuous use in the Western Hemisphere. Its construction began in 1533 during the reign of Emperor Charles V and, together with the fortresses of *San Felipe del Morro* and *San Cristóbal*, stood as one of the more valuable military assets of the Spanish Crown on the island. It has been the official residence of Puerto Rico's governors to this day. *See* Eugenio Fernández Méndez, *Crónicas de Puerto Rico* (Río Piedras: Editorial de la Universidad de Puerto Rico, 1969), 128, n. 42.

The same principle applies to the governor's use, while in office, of other governmental properties for residential or recreational purposes. This language was imported from the Foraker and Jones Acts, with only minor modifications.

Section 13
Franchises, Rights, Privileges, and Concessions

The procedure for granting franchises, rights, privileges and concessions of a public or quasi-public nature shall be determined by law, but every concession of this kind to a person or private entity must be approved by the Governor or by the executive official whom he designates. Every franchise, right, privilege or concession of a public or quasi-public nature shall be subject to amendment, alteration or repeal as determined by law.

Section 13 effectively devolves to the legislature the power to regulate the procedure "for granting franchises, rights, privileges and concessions of a public or quasi-public nature," as well as the power to "amend, alter or repeal" them.

Of significance is the fact that the legislature's power under Section 13 is not without limits. The framers specifically vested in the governor the power to approve "every concession of this kind to a person or private entity."

In constitutionalizing this mechanism, the framers modified the framework found in the organic acts. Whereas the Foraker Act vested authority in the executive council, on the approval of the governor, to grant "franchises, rights, privileges and concessions of a public or quasi-public nature," *see* Section 32, the Jones Act established a public service commission (made up of the heads of the executive departments and two elected commissioners) to grant "franchises, rights and privileges" with the governor's authorization. *See* Section 38 of the Jones Act. Under both organic acts, however, Congress had explicitly reserved for itself plenary power "to annul or modify" any of the above-referenced grants. *Id.*

Upon the inauguration of the constitution, such authority was devolved to the local legislature per the strictures of Section 13. Following Congress's enactment of PROMESA, there can be little doubt that Congress, in the exercise of its plenary powers under the U.S. Constitution's Territorial Clause, *see* U.S. Const. Art. IV, § 3, Cl. 2, retains to this day overriding authority to unilaterally modify, or even annul, any franchise, right, privilege, and concession of a public or quasi-public nature awarded by the local legislature.

Section 14
Land Holding by Corporations

No corporation shall be authorized to conduct the business of buying and selling real estate or be permitted to hold or own real estate except such as may be reasonably necessary to enable it to carry out the purposes for which it was created, and every corporation authorized to engage in agriculture shall by its charter be restricted to the ownership and control of not to exceed five hundred acres of land; and this provision shall be held to prevent any member of a corporation engaged in agriculture from being in any wise interested in any other corporation engaged in agriculture. Corporations, however, may loan funds upon real estate security, and purchase real estate when necessary for the collection of loans, but they shall dispose of real estate so obtained within five years after receiving the title. Corporations not organized in Puerto Rico, but doing business in Puerto Rico, shall be bound by the provisions of this section so far as they are applicable. These provisions shall not prevent the ownership, possession, or management of lands in excess of five hundred acres by the Commonwealth, its agencies or instrumentalities.

182 ■ THE PUERTO RICO CONSTITUTION AND COMMENTARY

Section 14 constitutionalizes, with few modifications, the 500-acre restriction Congress enacted for Puerto Rico by Joint Resolution on May 1, 1900. *See* 31 Stat. 716 (1900). While intended to prevent land concentration in the hands of absent sugar companies, the 500-acre restriction was mostly unenforced. Efforts at the local level to curb corporate land grabbing were further strengthened with the signing of P.R. Law No. 26 of April 12, 1941 (PR ST T.28, § 241); this local statute, together with Congress's 1900 Joint Resolution, served as the catalysts for Section 14.

Section 14 establishes that corporations duly authorized to engage in agriculture in Puerto Rico cannot own and control more than 500 acres of land. Nonagricultural corporations doing business in the island, while not limited by the 500-acre restriction, are constitutionally precluded from buying, selling, holding, or owning real estate, except as "rationally" required to further the purposes for which they were created. *See, e.g.*, P.R. Op. § Just. 1968-6 (March 12, 1968).

Contrary to Congress's 1900 Joint Resolution, Section 14 exempts the Commonwealth, along with its agencies and instrumentalities, from the 500-acre limitation. Accordingly, nothing in Section 14 prevents public entities from owning, possessing, or managing lands exceeding 500 acres.

Section 15
Flag, Seal, and Anthem

The Legislative Assembly shall determine all matters concerning the flag, the seal and the anthem of the Commonwealth. Once determined, no law changing them shall take effect until one year after the general election next following the date of enactment of said law.

Section 15 brings to the fore one of the more sensitive aspects of Puerto Rico's constitution-making exercise. Puerto Rico's first endogenous flag was designed by Ramón Emeterio Betances and sewed by Mariana Bracetti in 1868 in anticipation to the short-lived *Grito de Lares* of that same year. The so-called *Lares* flag was kept alive in separatist circles as a symbol of nationalist resistance against Spanish colonialism. Similarly, the lyrics and music of Puerto Rico's first anthem were composed by the renowned poet Lola Rodríguez de Tió and Félix Astol, respectively, during the 1868 revolutionary cycle.

The *Lares* flag, however, was eclipsed as the symbol of the Puerto Rican nation in 1895 with the design and adoption of the island's current flag by the Puerto Rico Committee of the Cuban Revolutionary Party, which José Martí had founded in New York City in 1892 before his untimely death. The new flag, like the *Lares* emblem before it, came to life clandestinely, proscribed by the Spanish and Americans authorities alike. Similarly, the revolutionary lyrics of Lola Rodríguez de Tío's anthem were erased from the national conscience, as they were irreconcilable with the island's unfortunate colonial condition.

Soon after the 1898 invasion, Manuel Fernández Juncos drafted new lyrics devoid of any heroic or revolutionary penchant. It was Fernández Juncos' sanitized lyrics that the local legislature chose as Puerto Rico's official anthem on the eve of the constitution's inauguration in 1952. P.R. Law No. 2 of July 24, 1952 (PR ST T.1, § 39).

A slightly modified version of the 1895 flag, with a dark blue triangle as opposed to the historical light blue one, was adopted by the local legislature as the Commonwealth's official standard. In the interim, however, from 1898 until 1952, Puerto Rico's flag was not displayed in public buildings or used on official holidays. During this period, the U.S. flag was Puerto Rico's only official flag. Notably, Puerto Rico's coat of arms has remained relatively unchanged since it was first promulgated by a royal decree signed by King Ferdinand of Aragon and his daughter Queen Juana of Castile on November 8, 1511. *See* P.R. Law No. 7 of August 8, 1952 (PR ST T.1, § 34).

Fully aware of the political sensitivity of these issues, the convention chose not to constitutionalize the specific design and content of the Commonwealth's official symbols. Instead, it vested in the legislature the power to determine all matters concerning Puerto Rico's flag, coat of arms, and anthem. It was pursuant to that authority that the legislature enacted P.R. Laws Nos. 1 and 2 of July 24, 1952, and P.R. Law No. 7 of August 8 of the same, establishing the characteristics of Puerto Rico's flag, coat of arms and anthem, respectively (PR ST T.1, §§ 32, 34, and 38).

The legislature's power under Section 15 is not absolute. Any law modifying, or altogether, changing the flag, coat of arms, or anthem shall not immediately enter into full force and effect. It would only take effect one year after the next general election. Section 15 accordingly requires a cooling off period for the voters to weigh in on the wisdom (or lack thereof) of any such modification.

Section 16
Oath of Public Officials and Employees

All public officials and employees of the Commonwealth, its agencies, instrumentalities and political subdivisions, before entering upon their respective duties, shall take an oath to support the Constitution of the United States and the Constitution and laws of the Commonwealth of Puerto Rico.

The oath requirement constitutionalized by the framers in Section 16 finds its roots in Section 16 of the Foraker Act, and was subsequently reproduced in Section 10 of the Jones Act. Because Section 10 of the Jones Act survives to this day in the 1950 Federal Relations Act, the constitutional text must be read in tandem with the federal statute. The provision found in the Federal Relations Act requires that all officials of the government of Puerto Rico "shall be citizens of the United States, and, before entering upon the duties of their respective offices, shall take an oath to support the Constitution of the United States and the laws of Puerto Rico." *See* 48 U.S.C., § 874. Section 16, for its part, complements the congressional mandate emanating from the Federal Relations Act by extending the oath requirement to all public employees, including those working in the Commonwealth's agencies, instrumentalities, and political subdivisions. Under the organic acts, however, only "public officials" (as opposed to "public employees") were required to take such an oath as a condition precedent to acceding to their posts.

Perhaps the more interesting aspect of Section 16 is the framers' silence with respect to the American citizenship requirement found in the Federal Relations Act for all "public officials" that first appeared under Section 10 of the Jones Act, and which remains alive in the Federal Relations Act. Despite Section 16's omission, it is well settled that the American citizenship requirement found in the Federal Relations Act is binding on all Commonwealth officials.

Section 17
Removal of Seat of Government in Emergency

In case of invasion, rebellion, epidemic or any other event giving rise to a state of emergency, the Governor may call the Legislative Assembly to meet in a place other than the Capitol of Puerto Rico, subject to the approval or disapproval of the Legislative Assembly. Under the same conditions, the Governor may, during the period of emergency, order the government, its agencies and instrumentalities to be moved temporarily to a place other than the seat of the government.

Section 17 garnered attention during the COVID-19 pandemic. It establishes that, in case of an invasion, rebellion, epidemic, or any other extraordinary circumstance triggering a state of emergency, the governor enjoys authority to call the legislature to meet at a place other than at its constitutional seat in the Capitol. The governor's calling, however, will only become effective if the legislature consents. Section 17 also vests in the governor the power to provisionally move the government, along with its agencies and instrumentalities, from its constitutional seat in San Juan to another location in the event of an emergency. Accordingly, in times of extraordinary upheaval, Section 17 appears to empower the governor with the authority to temporarily suspend the command found in Article I's Section 4 establishing that the seat of government shall be the city of San Juan.

The archival record shows the initial version of Section 17 was significantly modified at the convention. At the urging of Delegate Leopoldo Figueroa Carreras, *see* 3 *Diario* 2122, the framers rejected Section 17's first draft, which would have granted the governor plenary authority to call the legislature into session outside of the Capitol without the latter's consent. The framers amended the initial language; legislative consent would now be required for the governor's emergency calling to have any effect. The importation of this internal check and balance into Section 17's first clause seems appropriate if seen in light of the command emanating from Article III's Section 13, which designates the Capitol as the constitutional seat of the legislative branch.

Section 17, still untouched by the Puerto Rico Supreme Court at this writing, leaves unanswered many questions. It remains unclear whether "government," for purposes of the governor's unchecked relocation authority under Section 17's second clause, is limited to the executive branch, or whether it also includes the legislative and judicial branches. Moreover, it is not clear whether the legislative consent required under Section 17's first clause is exclusively limited to the specific instance when the governor calls the legislature into session. Should Section 17 be read as bestowing on the governor sole authority to move the government, including the legislative and judicial branches, away from its constitutional seat while denying him or her the power to unilaterally call the legislature into session in a place other than the Capitol? Section 17, furthermore, seems to suggest that the governor alone decides if there is a state of emergency calling for extraordinary measures.

Finding answers to these questions requires unearthing the archival record, which seems to show that Section 17 implicitly authorizes the governor to act independently of the legislative and judicial branches with respect to the provisional relocation of the government (including the other two coequal branches). Yet a broader look at the constitutional text calls into question the conception that the governor becomes a constitutional Leviathan in times of emergency. The Hobbesian paradigm is difficult to reconcile with the framers' exclusive grant of constitutional authority to the legislature to take charge of the most pressing societal emergencies. It is the legislature alone that can ratify or suspend the governor's declaration of the martial law under Article IV's Section 4. Only the legislature can suspend the writ of habeas corpus pursuant to Article II's Section 13. It is the legislature, not the governor, the branch with constitutional authority to curtail the labor rights available under Article II's Section 18 in cases of emergency. In times of emergency, it remains unclear what the proper constitutional balance is between the roles of the governor and the legislature.

Section 18
Criminal Actions Conducted in Name of People of Puerto Rico

All criminal actions in the courts of the Commonwealth shall be conducted in the name and by the authority of 'The People of Puerto Rico' until otherwise provided by law.

The immediate source of Section 18 is found in Sections 16 and 10 of the Foraker and Jones Acts, respectively. The adoption of this language, however, came with a caveat: in future, criminal actions would be heard, not in "local courts" as described under the organic acts, but rather "in the courts of the Commonwealth of Puerto Rico." Yet the remainder of Section 18 reproduces in toto the language found in the organic acts. Criminal actions would still "be conducted in the name and by the authority of The People of Puerto Rico," not the "Commonwealth of Puerto Rico."

Congress's decision not to repeal Section 10 of the Jones Act, which survives today as part of the 1950 Federal Relations Act, meant that the convention had little choice but to reproduce the same language found in the organic acts in an effort to infuse consistency to the constitutional text. However, in the aftermath of *Puerto Rico v. Sánchez Valle* (2016), Section 18 has lost its relevance. It is now clear that the ultimate source of Puerto Rico's prosecutorial powers derives, not from the people of Puerto Rico, but from Congress.

Section 19
Natural Resources; Historic or Artistic Sites; Penal Institutions; Delinquents

It shall be the public policy of the Commonwealth to conserve, develop and use its natural resources in the most effective manner possible for the general welfare of the community; to conserve and maintain buildings and places declared by the Legislative Assembly to be of historic or artistic value; to regulate its penal institutions in a manner that effectively achieves their purposes and to provide, within the limits of available resources, for adequate treatment of delinquents in order to make possible their moral and social rehabilitation.

Section 19 constitutionalizes a corpus of noble, yet unmet aspirations. This section did not meet universal approval at the convention. To the contrary, its incorporation ignited a vigorous debate among the framers. Delegate Jaime Benítez Rexach, on the one hand, forcefully argued against constitutionalizing this text. Because the Puerto Rico legislature, unlike Congress, possesses authority to legislate for the general welfare unencumbered by a catalogue of enumerated powers, Benítez Rexach argued that the elevation of these policy guideposts to the constitutional text was utterly unnecessary. *See* 3 *Diario* 2114. To Benítez Rexach's eyes, the legislature (under Article II's Section 19 and Article III's Section 1) was already endowed with sufficient authority to take all necessary and proper measures for protecting the environment, conserving the island's historic and artistic heritage and investing in the rehabilitation of convicts. *See* 3 *Diario* 2114–2115. Opposing Benítez Rexach's view, Delegate Santiago Polanco Abreu pressed for the adoption of Section 19. Seeking support in the constitutions of various Latin American sovereigns, including Mexico and Brazil, as well as in the constitutional text of states such as New York, Massachusetts, and Arizona, Polanco persuaded the convention to incorporate this provision as an expression of its underlying values. *See* 3 *Diario* 2115–2116.

Structurally, Section 19 amounts to one long sentence with three clauses. Each clause addresses a separate subject and deserves careful and separate consideration.

The Environmental Clause

The language chosen by the framers in drafting Section 19's environmental clause is both "terse and unconditional." *Misión Industrial de Puerto Rico, Inc. v. Junta de Planificación* (1998). It announces that protecting the environment for the general welfare shall be the public policy of the Commonwealth. In furtherance of this constitutional mandate, and in the exercise of its authority under Article III's Section 16, the legislature created in 1972 the Puerto Rico Department of Natural Resources. P.R. Law No. 23 of June 20, 1972 (PR ST T.3, § 151). Besides adding an extra layer of bureaucracy to the island's top-heavy governmental structure, the Department of Natural Resources has proven a failure. Not only have the political branches failed to live up to the values inspiring Delegate Pablo Morales Otero's environmental clause proposal, but the Puerto Rico Supreme Court's more recent decisions addressing the subject have proven devastating to the constitutional ideal.

Refusing to pay heed to the principle that the Puerto Rico Constitution ought to be construed broadly and, in some instances, independently from its federal counterpart, the court has failed to make sense of the constitutional obligations emanating from Section 19's environmental clause. The court's narrow reading of the rules of standing have limited the capacity of environmental groups to sue and seek redress on behalf of Puerto Rico's more vulnerable communities. The more cogent approach announced by Chief Justice José Trías Monge in *Salas Soler v. Secretario de Agricultura* (1974) has been replaced without any doctrinal justification. *See, e.g., Municipios de Aguada y Aguadilla v. Junta de Calidad Ambiental* (2014); *Lozada Sánchez v. Junta de Calidad Ambiental* (2012). Far from articulating an endogenous standing rule for environmental claims in light of Section 19's indisputable mandate, the court has mimicked the federal rule of standing, which is not constitutionally required and fails to address the uniqueness of Puerto Rico's constitutional topography. *See Fundación Surfrider Inc. v. ARPE* (2010). Similarly, the incipient rule intimated by the court in *Municipio de San Juan v. Junta de Calidad Ambiental* (2000), requiring a more rigorous review of the environmental determinations rendered by administrative agencies, has also been unceremoniously discarded.

The Conservation Clause

The wording of the conservation clause, unlike the environmental clause, is conditional in nature. *See Misión Industrial de Puerto Rico, Inc. v. Junta de Planificación* (1998). Under the conservation clause, the legislature is only bound to conserve and maintain those buildings and places it declares of historic or artistic value. During the course of the convention debates, Delegate Santiago Polanco Abreu confirmed that statues and monuments also fell under the aegis of the conservation clause. *See* 3 *Diario* 2119.

The immediate legislative consequence of the conservation clause's incorporation into Section 19 was the founding in 1955 of the Puerto Rican Institute of Culture (*Instituto de Cultura Puertorriqueña*). *See* P.R. Law No. 89 of June 21, 1955 (PR ST T.18, § 1195). Despite the language found in Section 19, the legislature's radius of action in this area is considerably limited by the federal regulatory framework emanating from the National Historic Preservation Act. *See* 16 U.S.C. 470 (1966).

The Penal Rehabilitation Clause

Similar to the wording of the conservation clause, the language of the penal rehabilitation clause is conditional. The Commonwealth's obligations under the penal rehabilitation clause are contingent on its "available resources." The worthy aspiration enshrined in this provision, conceived by Delegate José Veray Hernández and vigorously advocated by Delegate Yldefonso Solá Morales, *see* 3 *Diario* 2145, has never been met. Despite a mounting correctional bureaucracy, led by the Corrections and Rehabilitation Department, the state of Puerto Rico's prison system remains deficient. *See Morales Feliciano v. Romero Barceló* (1979) (illustrating the failure of a system that far from rehabilitating convicts blatantly transgresses the boundaries of human dignity).

Article VII

Amendments to the Constitution

Section 1
Proposal of Amendments

The Legislative Assembly may propose amendments to this Constitution by a concurrent resolution approved by not less than two-thirds of the total number of members of which each house is composed. All proposed amendments shall be submitted to the qualified electors in a special referendum, but if the concurrent resolution is approved by not less than three-fourths of the total number of members of which each house is composed, the Legislative Assembly may provide that the referendum shall be held at the same time as the next general election. Each proposed amendment shall be voted on separately and not more than three proposed amendments may be submitted at the same referendum. Every proposed amendment shall specify the terms under which it shall take effect, and it shall become a part of this Constitution if it is ratified by a majority of the electors voting thereon. Once approved, a proposed amendment must be published at least three months prior to the date of the referendum.

The process of designing Article VII's amendment mechanism led to one of the more contentious episodes in Puerto Rico's constitution-making process. The authority to modify the island's legal framework had always been off limits to local political actors. The power to amend the Foraker and Jones Acts resided in Congress alone. Not even the relatively liberal 1897 Autonomic Charter granted Puerto Rico's leadership authority to unilaterally alter the legal instrument binding the island to the Spanish Kingdom. The constitutional convention's inclusion of Section 1's amendment procedure, while indispensable from the framers' vantage point, was fraught with controversy and pitted the Puerto Rican leadership against powerful congressional voices.

Structurally, Article VII mimics the federal model. It vests in the legislative branch the authority to determine when to activate the amendment mechanism. Likewise, the possibility of amending the constitutional text solely by means of a popular initiative is also nonexistent. Under Article VII, as is the case under Article V of the federal Constitution, there are only two paths to proposing constitutional amendments: either by passing a concurrent resolution in both the house and the senate or by calling yet another constitutional convention. Both procedural vehicles are under the jurisdiction of the legislative branch.

The Puerto Rican model, however, departs from the federal approach in significant ways. In the federal context, passing the concurrent resolutions requires the vote of two-thirds of those members "present and voting" in the U.S. House of Representatives and the Senate. Article VII's Section 1, for its part, establishes that the concurrent resolutions must garner the approval of two-thirds of the total number of members of the house of representatives and the senate. While federal amendments "are not incorporated into the existing text" of the U.S. Constitution, but rather appended to the original document, amendments under Article VII are interwoven into the body of the constitution.

Unlike the federal landscape, where the power to ratify resides in the state legislatures, in Puerto Rico such authority is directly vested in the people, who can either ratify or reject on a referendum the amendment proposals. The governor, like the president, has no constitutional role in the elaboration of proposals for constitutional amendments; the gubernatorial veto power is unavailable in this context. At the ratification stage, however, the governor, unlike the president, plays an accessory role by signing or vetoing the enabling legislation that calls for the holding of a ratification referendum.

Article VII's Section 1 also places procedural limits on the legislature. It can only present to the electorate a maximum of three proposed amendments in the same referendum, each of which must be published at least three months before the date of the referendum. Each proposed amendment must be voted separately and must specify its effective date. A proposed amendment will only be ratified if a majority of the voters casting their ballots in the referendum approve it.

The timing of the referendum is also in the hands of the legislature. Holding a constitutional amendment referendum on election day requires the vote of at least three-fourths of the total number of members of the house of representatives and the senate. Thus, the internal political composition of each legislative chamber could potentially impact the ratification timeline.

In *Berríos Martínez v. Gobernador* (1994), the supreme court suggested the framers limited to three the number of proposed constitutional amendments to be put to the people in a single referendum in an effort to stamp out voter manipulation, confusion, and logrolling. In *Berríos Martínez*, the legislature had passed three concurrent resolutions, with the required two-thirds vote, proposing to modify Article II's Section 11 (limiting a defendant's right to bail); Article V's Section 3 (increasing the number of justices of the Puerto Rico Supreme Court to nine while vesting in the legislature alone the power to increase or decrease the court's size); and adding a new Section 20 to Article VI (establishing term limits for governor, senators, representatives, and mayors). Because two out of the three concurrent resolutions addressed more than one matter, the issue before the court was determining whether the legislature was in fact presenting to the voters more than three amendment proposals, in violation of the constitutional limitations set forth under Article VII's Section 1. In answering this first impression question, the island's high court embraced the "sole purpose" (*propósito único*) doctrine, whereby an amendment proposal covering more than one issue will be deemed as one, for purposes of Article VII's limitations, if the implementation of all the issues presented therein is indispensable to achieving the "sole purpose" behind the proposed constitutional amendment. *See id.* Against that background, a divided court found that the proposal limiting the terms of office of the governor, senators, representatives, and mayors ran afoul of the constitutional limitation and, hence, could not be included in the upcoming referendum alongside the remaining proposed amendments.

Reiterating the legislature's exclusive control of the amendment mechanism, the court in *Córdova v. Cámara de Representantes* (2007) dismissed a mandamus petition requesting that the house of representatives pass a concurrent resolution for amending Article III so as to replace the bicameral legislature established under it with a unicameral parliament.

In *Partido Independentista Puertorriqueño v. Estado Libre Asociado* (2012), the court announced that Article VII requires that the two-thirds majority of "total seats" in the house of representatives and the senate also include vacant seats resulting from temporary or permanent absences. Further, the court found that, unlike a bill, a concurrent resolution underlying a proposed amendment need not be confined to only one subject, and that a concurrent resolution lacking the required two-thirds majority of the total number of seats of both legislative chambers could nonetheless be retroactively cured and put to the people pursuant to a subsequent concurrent resolution passed in both houses by the required two-thirds majority.

Since its adoption in 1952, the Puerto Rico Constitution has been amended only rarely. Immediately following its ratification, the island's constitutional text underwent two modifications at the urging of Congress: Article II's Section 5 was amended to explicitly safeguard the right to elementary education in nongovernmental schools, and an additional sentence was added to Article VII's Section 3, establishing, in no uncertain terms, that no constitutional amendment can contravene U.S. Public Law 600, U.S. Public Law 447, the Puerto Rico

1950 Federal Relations Act, and the U.S. Constitution. Both amendments were approved by a majority of the Puerto Rican electorate on November 4, 1952.

Article V's Section 4 was also amended on November 8, 1960, providing that the Puerto Rico Supreme Court could decide cases in panels of no fewer than three justices. A subsequent amendment to Article VI's Section 2, increasing the island's debt ceiling, was approved by the voters in a referendum held on December 10, 1961. Three years later, on November 3, 1964, Article III's Section 8 was modified, vesting in the legislature the power to decide how to fill vacant district seats. The most recent amendment to the island's constitution was passed on November 1, 1970, lowering the minimum voting age from twenty-one to eighteen years. *See* P.R. Const. Art. VI, § 4.

None of these amendments was proposed by a constitutional convention, but rather by the legislature itself, pursuant to its unique power under Article VII's Section 1.

Section 2
Revision of Constitution by Constitutional Convention

The Legislative Assembly, by a concurrent resolution approved by two-thirds of the total number of members of which each house is composed, may submit to the qualified electors at a referendum, held at the same time as a general election, the question of whether a constitutional convention shall be called to revise this Constitution. If a majority of the electors voting on this question vote in favor of the revision, it shall be made by a Constitutional Convention elected in the manner provided by law. Every revision of this Constitution shall be submitted to the qualified electors at a special referendum for ratification or rejection by a majority of the votes cast at the referendum.

In Puerto Rico, like in the United States, the convention mechanism available under Article VII's Section 2 has never been used. Unlike the United States, where the road to the constitutional convention is driven not by Congress but by the states, in Puerto Rico that path is also under the control of the legislature.

The journey leading to the convention requires legislative action at various critical stages. A two-thirds majority of the total number of senators and representatives must first pass a concurrent resolution in order to hold a referendum asking the people to decide whether to call a convention "to revise" the present constitution. If the people vote for the convention, then the legislature steps in, yet again, passing an enabling statute that sets forth the legal framework for the election of the delegates and the internal structuring of the convention.

Enacting the enabling legislation will require, unlike the passing of the concurrent resolution, the governor's signature. Immediately after the convention completes the revision of the constitutional text, the legislature will retake the lead, passing new legislation for holding a second referendum where the people will either ratify or reject the convention's proposed revisions.

Ostensibly, the outer penumbras of the convention mechanism remain unclear. There seems to be no consensus within Puerto Rico's legal academia on whether the legislature can limit beforehand, in its enabling statute, the scope of the convention's revision only to certain specific subjects or areas. The question of whether the framers intended for the convention to act independently from the legislature remains unanswered. Is it constitutional for the legislature to place limits on the convention's agenda? Can the convention revise all aspects of the existing constitution if it so chooses? Even in the face of legislative opposition? Even if this means violating the legal mandate emanating from the enabling legislation? Would the Puerto Rico Supreme Court remove from the ratification referendum's ballot ultra vires proposals put forward by a runaway convention?

These textual lacunae lend credence to the idea that the convention mechanism available under Section 2 could very well unlock a Pandora's box, with unforeseeable consequences for the island's institutional stability. Nonetheless, and considering the recent collapse of the island's political and fiscal stability, at this writing the time may be ripe for treading the convention's uncharted path. The convention alone, as opposed to the more limited mechanism available under Article VII's Section 1, offers the people of Puerto Rico the possibility of engineering far-reaching structural modifications of the 1952 Constitution.

Section 3
Limitation of Amendments

No amendment to this Constitution shall alter the republican form of government established by it or abolish its Bill of Rights. Any amendment or revision of this Constitution shall be consistent with the resolution enacted by the Congress of the United States approving this Constitution, with the applicable provisions of the Constitution of the United States, with the Puerto Rican Federal Relations Act, and with Public Law 600, of the Eighty-first Congress, adopted in the nature of a compact. [As amended at General Election of Nov. 4, 1952, effective Jan. 29, 1953.]

Section 3 establishes Article VII's outer limits. The text suggests that the power of the people of Puerto Rico to amend their own constitutional instrument is significantly constrained. The entrenchment of the amendment provisions responded, not to the framers' design, but rather to Congress's overriding political and geostrategic interests.

Section 3 contains two distinct, yet interrelated, sentences: the first one was added by the framers at the convention and the second incorporated by way of a constitutional amendment at the urging of Congress shortly after the constitution's adoption. The original version of Section 3, as drafted by the convention's committee on preamble and amendments, only contained one sentence: "No amendment to this Constitution shall alter the republican form of government established by it or abolish its bill of rights." Unsurprisingly, the framers chose to constitutionalize the language found in Section 2 of U.S. Public Law 600, whereby Congress authorized the people of Puerto Rico to draft their own constitution on the condition that it "provide[s] a republican form of government and [...] a bill of rights." 64 Stat. 319 (1950). These guideposts seem somewhat elusive. Determining what constitutes a "republican form of government" is a nonjusticiable political question. *See Luther v. Borden* (1849), while the panoply of rights enshrined in the bill of rights are indeed susceptible to amendment. Only the abolition of the charter in toto is constitutionally prohibited.

The limits set out in Section 3's last sentence bring to the surface Washington's more basic geopolitical concerns as Congress prepared to review the constitutional text put forward by the convention. The sentence highlights the constitutional straitjacket limiting Puerto Rico's capacity to fully exercise its unalienable right to self-determination by establishing that no future amendment to the 1952 Constitution may ever run afoul of the strictures of U.S. Public Law 600, U.S. Public Law 447, the 1950 Federal Relations Act, and the U.S. Constitution. Besides reiterating the supremacy of the U.S. Constitution, this language appears to bind Puerto Rico rather inextricably to its territorial condition, ruling out the possibility of constitutional modifications that could upset its asymmetric relationship with the United States.

Article VIII

Senatorial and Representative Districts

Section 1
Boundaries of Senatorial and Representative Districts

The senatorial and representative districts shall be the following:

I. SENATORIAL DISTRICT OF SAN JUAN, which shall be composed of the following Representative Districts:

Representative District 1.—Old San Juan, and the following census tracts of barrio Santurce: 9-15, 16.01, 16.02, 17.01, 17.02, 18, 19, 20.01, 20.02, 22, 23, 25-31, 41, 42.01, 42.02 and 40.

Representative District 2.—Census tracts 24 and 32-39, of barrio Santurce; census tracts 43, 65 and 68 of barrio Hato Rey Norte; from census tract 43, blocks 101-107, 201-206, 218 and 221-223 are included; from census tract 68, blocks 101-118, 201-218, 301-319, 401-406, 410-414, 418 and 420-422 are included; census tracts 44, 45, 62 and 63 of barrio Hato Rey Central, and blocks 101 and 103-106 of census tract 61.01; census tracts 46-48 and 60 of barrio Oriente, and blocks 101-107 of census tract 59.

Representative District 3.—Barrio Sabana Llana Norte; census tract 50 of barrios, Oriente and Sabana Llana Norte (population corresponding to each, barrio was included therewithin); census tract 56 of barrios, Oriente and Sabana Llana Sur (population of barrio Oriente included only); census tract 49 of barrio Oriente; from census tract 59 of barrio Oriente, blocks 108, 109 and 201-208 are included; census tract 58 of barrios Oriente and Universidad; census tract 90 of barrio Oriente; census tract 61.02 of barrios, Universidad and Hato Rey Central; census tract 64 of barrio Hato Rey Central; blocks 107-110, 112, 201 and 202 of census tract 61.01 of barrio Hato Rey Central; census tracts 66 and 87 of barrio Hato Rey Sur; from census tract 67 of barrios Hato Rey Norte and Hato Rey Sur, blocks 101-107, 201-203, 205, 207-210, 401-409 and 415 are included; and barrio Pueblo.

Representative District 4.—Barrio Gobernador Pinero; census tract 70 of barrios Hato Rey Norte and Gobernador Pinero (the portion belonging to barrio Hato Rey Norte has no population); from census tract 43 of barrio Hato Rey Norte, blocks 221, 220, 225, 226 and 224 are included); census tract 68 of barrio Hato Rey Norte (block 419 without population, included); from census tract 67 of barrio Hato Rey Sur blocks 301-310 are included; census tract 86.01 of barrios Hato Rey Sur and El Cinco; census tract 86.02 of barrios Hato Rey Sur, El Cinco and Monacillo Urbano; census tract 86.03 of barrio El Cinco; census tract 97 of barrios Monacillo Urbano, El Cinco and Gobernador Pinero (population corresponding to barrio Monacillo Urbano was included, the portion of barrio El Cinco included has no population and population of barrio Gobernador Pinero was included therein); from census tract 81 of barrio Monacillo Urbano, blocks 102-106, 108-111, 201-205 and 303-311 are included; from census tract 80 of barrios Monacillo Urbano and Gobernador Pinero, blocks 101, 104-108, 201-205, 301-304, 306 and 505-507 are included; and census tract 79 of barrios Monacillo Urbano and Gobernador Pinero (population corresponding to barrio Monacillo Urbano was included, population of barrio Gobernador Pinero was included therein).

Representative District 5.—Barrios Quebrada Arenas, Tortugo, Caimito, Cupey and Monacillo; blocks 301, 302, 401-404 of census tract 81 of barrio Monacillo Urbano; blocks 307, 401, 403-406, 408-410 and 501-504 of census tract 80 of barrio Monacillo Urbano; census tract 98 of barrio Monacillo Urbano; census tracts 96.01, 96.02 and 96.03 of barrios El cinco and Monacillo Urbano; census tract 95 of barrios El Cinco, Pueblas and Sabana Llana Sur (population of barrio, El Cinco included only); and census tract 96.04 of barrios Monacillo Urbano and Monacillo.

II. SENATORIAL DISTRICT OF BAYAMON, which shall be composed of the following Representative Districts:

Representative District 6.—Municipality of Guaynabo.

Representative District 7.—Municipality of Toa alta, and barrios Nuevo, Guaraguao Arriba, Guaraguao Abajo, Dajaos, Santa Olaya, Buena Vista and part of census tract 311.03 of barrio Pajaros; section of census tract 313 of barrio Cerro Gordo and census tracts 317.02, 317.03 and 317.04 corresponding to barrio Minillas of Bayamon.

Representative District 8.—Census tract 317.01, which is part of barrios Minillas and Juan Sanchez; census tracts 316.12, 316.32, 316.11, 316.21, 316.31, 316.22, 316.41, which is part of barrio Minillas; census tract 304, which is part of barrio Bayamon Pueblo (block 103 of this tract belongs to barrio Juan Sanchez); census tracts 314.03, 314.01, 314.02, 315.01 which are part of barrio Cerro Gordo; census tracts 315.02 and 315.03, which are part of barrios Cerro Gordo and Bayamon Pueblo; census tract 307, part of barrios Bayamon Pueblo and Pajaros; census tract 308, part of barrios Bayamon Pueblo and Pajaros; census tract 309.03, part of barrio Pajaros; census tracts 312.03, 312.02, 311.01, 309.04, which are part of barrio Pajaros of; Bayamon census tract 312.01, part of barrios Pajaros and

Bayamon Pueblo; census tract 311.02, part of barrios Pajaros and Hato Tejas (population of barrio Pajaros included); census tract 310.03, population included in barrio Pajaros.

Representative District 9.—Municipality of Catano and barrio Juan Sanchez (not including block 103 of census tract 304); census tracts 302, 303 and 305 of barrio Bayamon Pueblo, portion of census tract 306 belonging to barrio Bayamon Pueblo; barrio Hato Tejas (not including census tract 310.02).

Representative District 10.—Municipality of Toa Baja and census tract 310.02 of barrio Hato Tejas of Bayamon.

III. SENATORIAL DISTRICT OF ARECIBO, which shall be composed of the following Representative Districts:

Representative District 11.—Municipalities of Dorado and Vega Alta, and barrios Puerto Nuevo, Cabo Caribe, Cibuco, Ceiba, Almirante Norte, Almirante Sur, Rio Arriba, Vega Baja Pueblo and Rio Abajo of Vega Baja.

Representative District 12.—Municipalities of Manati and Morovis, and barrios Yeguada, Algarrobo, Pugnado Afuera, Pugnado Adentro and Quebrada Arenas of Vega Baja.

Representative District 13.—Municipalities of Ciales, Florida and Barceloneta and barrios Cambalache, Islote, Factor, Garrochales, Santana, Domingo Ruiz, Arenalejos, Miraflores, Sabana Hoyos, Arrozal, Carreras, Rio Arriba and Hato Viejo of Arecibo.

Representative District 14.—Municipality of Hatillo and barrios Hato Abajo, Hato Arriba, Dominguito, Esperanza, Tanama and Arecibo Pueblo.

Representative District 15.—Municipalities of Isabela, Quebradillas and Camuy.

IV. SENATORIAL DISTRICT OF MAYAGUEZ, which shall be composed of the following Representative Districts:

Representative District 16.—Municipality of Aguadilla, and barrios Moca, Aceitunas, Centro, Rocha, Cuchilla, Pueblo, Capa, Voladoras, Cruz, Naranjo, Marias and Moca Pueblo.

Representative District 17.—Municipalities of Aguada, Rincon and Anasco, and barrios Cerro Gordo and Plata of Moca, and barrios Sabanetas, Rio Canas Abajo, Quemado and Leguisamo of the municipality of Mayaguez.

Representative District 18.—Urban barrios Candelaria, Carcel, Marina Meridional, Marina Septentrional, Rio and Salud; barrios Miradero, Mayaguez, Arriba, Quebrada Grande, Sabalos, Juan Alonso, Algarrobo, Guanajibo and Rio Hondo of the municipality of Mayaguez.

Representative District 19.—Municipalities of San Sebastian, Las Marias, Hormigueros and Maricao; and barrios Rio Canas Arriba, Bateyes, Naranjales, Montoso, Limon, Rosario and Malezas of Mayaguez; and barrios Rosario Bajo, Duey Bajo, Duey Alto, Hoconuco Bajo, Hoconuco Alto, Rosario Alto and Rosario Penon of the municipality of San German.

Representative District 20.—Municipalities of Cabo Rojo and Lajas; barrios San German Pueblo, Cain Alto, Cain Bajo, Guama, Minillas, Retiro, Ancones,

Maresua, Sabana Grande Abajo, Sabana Eneas, Cutui and Tuna of San German; Mona Island and Monito Islet.

V. SENATORIAL DISTRICT OF PONCE, which shall be composed of the following Representative Districts:

Representative District 21.—Municipalities of Sabana Grande, Guanica and Yauco; barrios Consejo, Llano, Sierra Baja, Pasto and Jagua Pasto of Guayanilla.

Representative District 22.—Municipalities of Lares, Utuado and Adjuntas.

Representative District 23.—Municipality of Penuelas; barrios Guayanilla, Quebrada Honda, Barrero, Macana, Quebradas, Jaguas, Magas, Cedro, Boca, Indios, Rufina, Playa and Guayanilla Pueblo; and barrios Canas, Magueyes Urbano, Quebrada Limon, Portugues, Magueyes, Marueno, Tibes, Monte Llano, Guaraguao and San Patricio of Ponce.

Representative District 24.—Barrios Playa, Canas Urbano and Portugues Urbano; barrios First through Sixth of Ponce.

Representative District 25.—Municipality of Jayuya; and barrios Anon, Maraguez, Real, Machuelo Arriba, Machuelo Abajo, San Anton, Cerrillos, Coto Laurel, Sabanetas, Capitanejo, Vayas and Bucana of the municipality of Ponce.

VI. SENATORIAL DISTRICT OF GUAYAMA, which shall be composed of the following Representative Districts:

Representative District 26.—Municipalities of Villalba and Juana Diaz, and barrios Santa Isabel Pueblo, Playa, Boca Velazquez and Descalabrado of Santa Isabel.

Representative District 27.—Municipalities of Orocovis and Coamo, and barrios Algarrobo, Pasto, Asomante, Llanos and Caonillas of Aibonito, and barrios Honduras, Helechal, Palo Hincado, Barrancas, Canabon and Pueblo of Barranquitas.

Representative District 28.—Municipalities of Corozal, Naranjito, Comerio, and barrios Quebradilla and Quebrada Grande of the municipality of Barranquitas.

Representative District 29.—Municipality of Cidra, and barrios Aibonito Pueblo, Plata, Robles and Cuyon of the municipality of Aibonito; and barrios Cayey Pueblo, Beatriz, Vegas, Rincon Monte Llano, Toita, Quebrada Arriba, Sumido, Lapa, Pedro Avila, Pasto Viejo, Piedras, Maton Abajo and Maton Arriba of the municipality of Cayey.

Representative District 30.—Municipalities of Guayama and Salinas; and barrios Guavate, Farallon, Cedro, Culebras Bajo, Culebras Alto, Jajome Alto, Jajome Bajo and Cercadillo of the municipality of Cayey; and barrios Felicia 1, Felicia 2, Jauca 1 and Jauca 2 of the municipality of Santa Isabel.

VII. SENATORIAL DISTRICT OF HUMACAO, which shall be composed of the following Representative Districts:

Representative District 31.—Municipality of Aguas Buenas; barrios San Antonio, Rio Canas, Bairoa, Canabon, Canaboncito and Beatriz of Caguas and census tracts 2011, 2029 and portion of census tracts 2004, 2005, 2013 and 2015 of barrio Pueblo of Caguas.

Representative District 32.—Municipality of Gurabo; and the barrios of Castro, Turabo, Borinquen, San Salvador and census sectors 2006, 2008, 2009, 2017, 2018 and 2015; census sectors 2010, 2010 and 2016 of barrio Pueblo Caguas.

Representative District 33.—Municipalities of Juncos, San Lorenzo and Las Piedras.

Representative District 34.—Municipalities of Yabucoa, Maunabo Patillas and Arroyo.

Representative District 35.—Municipalities of Humacao, Naguabo and Ceiba.

VIII. SENATORIAL DISTRICT OF CAROLINA, which shall be composed of the following Representative Districts:

Representative District 36.—Municipalities of Fajardo, Luquillo, Culebra and Vieques; barrios Rio Grande Pueblo, Herrera, Guzman, Abajo, Guzman Arriba, Cienaga Alta, Zarzal, Jimenez and Mameyes Segundo of Rio Grande.

Representative District 37.—Municipalities of Loiza and Canovanas; and barrios Canovanillas, Santa Cruz, Barrazas, Carruzos and Cedros of Carolina; and barrio Cienaga Baja of Rio Grande.

Representative District 38.—Barrios Carolina Pueblo, Hoyo Mulas, San Anton, Martin Gonzalez, Trujillo Bajo and Cacao of the municipality of Carolina; and barrios Dos Bocas, La Gloria, Quebrada Negrito and Quebrada Grande of the municipality of Trujillo Alto.

Representative District 39.—Barrios Cangrejo Arriba and Sabana Abajo of Carolina.

Representative District 40.—Barrio Sabana Llana Sur of the municipality of San Juan; and barrios Trujillo Alto Pueblo, Cuevas and Carraizo of Trujillo Alto.

Section 2
Electoral Zones in San Juan

Electoral zones numbers 1, 2, 3 and 4 included in three representative districts within the senatorial district of San Juan are those presently existing for purposes of electoral organization in the second precinct of San Juan.

Article VIII established the boundaries of all senate and house districts for the 1952, 1956, and 1960 elections. With the publication of the 1960 federal census, this task devolved to the constitutional redistricting board, as required under Article III's Section 4.

In drafting Article VIII, the framers' most significant and long-lasting contribution was increasing by one the number of senate districts and by five the number of house districts, fixing at eight the number of senate districts and at forty the number of house districts. Under Article VIII, Bayamón was separated from San Juan, becoming its own separate senate district. Hence, the additional five house districts, apportioned pursuant to Article VIII, were assigned to the new Bayamón senate district, as required under Article III's Section 3, which established that each senate district would also include five house districts.

Article VIII is now inoperative. Succeeding redistricting boards, while observing the constitutional fixture of eight senate districts and forty house districts, have redrawn Puerto Rico's electoral map in significant ways.

Article IX

Transitory Provisions

Section 1
Laws, Rights, and Liabilities

When this Constitution goes into effect all laws not inconsistent therewith shall continue in full force until amended or repealed, or until they expire by their own terms.

Unless otherwise provided by this Constitution, civil and criminal liabilities, rights, franchises, concessions, privileges, claims, actions, causes of action, contracts, and civil, criminal and administrative proceedings shall continue unaffected, notwithstanding the taking effect of this Constitution.

Section 2
Existing Officers Continued in Office

All officers who are in office by election or appointment on the date this Constitution takes effect shall continue to hold their offices and to perform the functions thereof in a manner not inconsistent with this Constitution, unless the functions of their offices are abolished or until their successors are selected and qualify in accordance with this Constitution and laws enacted pursuant thereto.

The framers added Article IX's transitory provisions in order to infuse stability into the island's legal and administrative framework, amid the transition to a new constitutional order. Unsurprisingly, almost every state constitution *circa* 1952 contained similar language. Article IX's Sections 1 and 2 reproduce the

202 ∎ THE PUERTO RICO CONSTITUTION AND COMMENTARY

same type of transitory language found in Sections 57 and 8 of the Jones and Foraker Acts, respectively, as well as in the military orders rendered by General Nelson Miles in the aftermath of the 1898 invasion.

Under Section 1, the vast corpus of Puerto Rico laws enacted prior to July 25, 1952, remained in full force and effect, except for those statutes and regulations repugnant to the new constitutional instrument. Section 2, for its part, guaranteed administrative continuity. It represents a measure of self-restraint on the part of the majority party, precluding its political bosses from using the adoption of the new constitutional order as an excuse to remove, without cause, civil servants, and elected officials from minority parties.

Section 3
Existing Judges Continued in Office

Notwithstanding the age limit fixed by this Constitution for compulsory retirement, all the judges of the courts of Puerto Rico who are holding office on the date this Constitution takes effect shall continue to hold their judicial offices until the expiration of the terms for which they were appointed, and in the case of justices of the Supreme Court during good behavior.

Section 3 insulated the island's judiciary from the vagaries of the interim period. Inferior court judges, regardless of the seventy-year age limit established under Article V's Section 10, would serve the full terms for which they were appointed, and Puerto Rico Supreme Court justices appointed prior to the constitution's adoption would continue in their positions during good behavior, unaffected by the constitutional age limitation. The composition of the island's high court accordingly remained unchanged upon the adoption of the 1952 Constitution.

Section 4
Commonwealth of Puerto Rico as Successor of People of Puerto Rico

The Commonwealth of Puerto Rico shall be the successor of The People of Puerto Rico for all purposes, including without limitation the collection and payment of debts and liabilities in accordance with their terms.

Section 4 established that the new legal entity, styled "Commonwealth of Puerto Rico," would become, upon the constitution's adoption, the rightful successor to the legal entity, "People of Puerto Rico," as defined by Congress in the Foraker and Jones Acts, respectively.

The language included herein offered yet an additional layer of protection to those creditors already holding bonds issued by Puerto Rico. *See* 3 *Diario* 2168. Thus, the succeeding governments, organized under the new constitution, would be fully bound and liable to existing bondholders for debt issued prior to July 25, 1952.

Section 5
Citizen of the Commonwealth of Puerto Rico to Replace Term Citizen of Puerto Rico

When this Constitution goes into effect, the term "citizen of the Commonwealth of Puerto Rico" shall replace the term "citizen of Puerto Rico" as previously used.

Section 5 effected a change in style, not substance. Upon the constitution's entry into full force and effect, lawful residents domiciled in the island would no longer be styled "citizens of Puerto Rico" but rather "citizens of the Commonwealth of Puerto Rico." This cosmetic modification in no way altered the legal status of Puerto Ricans as citizens of the United States.

Section 6
Political Parties

Political parties shall continue to enjoy all rights recognized by the election law, provided that on the effective date of this Constitution they fulfill the minimum requirements for the registration of new parties contained in said law. Five years after this Constitution shall have taken effect the Legislative Assembly may change these requirements, but any law increasing them shall not go into effect until after the general election next following its enactment.

Section 6 put in place a rather novel mechanism for protecting minority parties. Registration requirements would remain unchanged until after July 25, 1957, and the incorporation, by legislative fiat, of additional restrictions was also frozen until after the 1960 election. In *Partido Renovación Puertorriqueña v. Estado Libre Asociado* (1984), the Puerto Rico Supreme Court infused (albeit temporarily) new life into this provision, announcing that Section 6 was the "genesis" of the "axiom of equality" which purportedly required that all local political parties be treated on an equal footing. In *Burgos v. Comisión Estatal de Elecciones* (2017), the court found that the so-called equality "axiom" has no constitutional basis and is now defunct.

Section 7
Laws Supplementing Transitory Provisions

The Legislative Assembly may enact the laws necessary to supplement and make effective these transitory provisions in order to assure the functioning of the government until the officers provided for by this Constitution are elected or appointed and qualify, and until this Constitution takes effect in all respects.

Section 7 endowed the legislature with authority to make all necessary and proper laws for the successful execution of all the transitory measures contemplated under Article IX. Arguably, both the pre-constitutional and the post-constitutional legislatures enjoyed this power even in the absence of this provision. In including this language here, the framers showed themselves overly cautious.

Section 8
Division of Department of Agriculture and Commerce

If the Legislative Assembly creates a Department of Commerce, the Department of Agriculture and Commerce shall thereafter be called the Department of Agriculture.

Section 8 revealed the framers' risk aversion. The inclusion of this provision was unnecessary due to the fact that the legislature, under both Article III's Section 16 and Article IV's Section 6, already enjoyed authority to "reorganize" and "consolidate" executive departments established under the constitution, such as the Puerto Rico Department of Agriculture and Commerce, and to "create" new ones altogether. Arguably, even in the absence of this provision, nothing stood in the way of the legislature's authority to rename and redefine the duties of the Department of Agriculture and Commerce, while establishing a new and independent Department of Commerce. This reorganization finally took place in July 1960, with the founding of the Department of Commerce following Governor Muñoz Marín's signature of P.R. Law No. 132 of July 19, 1960 (PR ST T.3, § 351).

Section 9
First and Second General Elections

The first election under the provisions of this Constitution shall be held on the date provided by law, but not later than six months after the effective date of this Constitution. The second general election under this Constitution shall be held in the month of November 1956 on a day provided by law.

Section 9 supplements Article VI's Section 4, which provides for the holding of elections every four years during the month of November. Both the 1952 and 1956 elections were held in compliance with the timetable provided herein.

Section 10
Effective Date of Constitution

This Constitution shall take effect when the Governor so proclaims, but not later than sixty days after its ratification by the Congress of the United States.

Section 10 must be read in tandem with Section 3 of U.S. Public Law No. 600, which had already established that the constitution would only become effective "upon approval by the Congress." Because the ratification timetable in Congress was out of the hands of the framers, the convention agreed on a formula whereby the constitution would become effective no later than sixty days *after* congressional ratification. The Puerto Rico Constitution was finally ratified on July 3, 1952, upon President Harry Truman's signing of U.S. Public Law 447. Only twenty-two days later, on July 25, Governor Muñoz Marín proclaimed the entry into full force and effect of the new constitution, and thereafter Puerto Rico began its journey along a new, uncharted path.

Table 1 Puerto Rico's Political Parties *circa* 1951–1952

Popular Democratic Party (*Partido Popular Democrático*)	Inaugurated on July 22, 1938, the Popular Democratic Party was Puerto Rico's majority party *circa* 1951–1952. By then it was in full control of the legislative and executive branches under the leadership of Governor Luis Muñoz Marín, who was elected governor in four successive general elections: 1948, 1952, 1956, and 1960.
Independence Party (*Partido Independentista Puertorriqueño*)	Founded by Gilberto Concepción de Gracia on October 20, 1946, from an ideological schism within the Popular Democratic Party, the Independence Party boycotted the 1951–1952 constitution-making exercise. The Independence Party did not nominate delegates to the Puerto Rico Constitutional Convention. In the general election held on November 4, 1952, the Independence Party came in second place after the Popular Democratic Party.
Statehood Party (*Partido Estadista Puertorriqueño*)	Established on July 4, 1948, under the leadership of Celestino Iriarte Miró, the Statehood Party was the successor to the old Progressive Republican Union. The short-lived Statehood Party was dissolved in 1952 only to be replaced by the Statehood Republican Party (*Partido Estadista Republicano*), which was the immediate precursor to the New Progressive Party (*Partido Nuevo Progresista*) founded on August 20, 1967.
Socialist Party (*Partido Socialista*)	Brought to life by the Spanish labor leader Santiago Iglesias Pantín on March 21, 1915, the Socialist Party favored statehood for Puerto Rico. Together with the then defunct Republican Union Party, it was in control of the legislature from 1932 until 1940.
Nationalist Party (*Partido Nacionalista*)	Founded on September 17, 1922, by José Coll y Cuchí and José S. Alegría, following an internal rupture within the Union Party, the Nationalist Party, like the Independence Party, boycotted the Puerto Rico Constitutional Convention, denouncing it as a futile colonial exercise. Radicalized under the leadership of Pedro Albizu Campos, the Nationalist Party refused to participate in electoral politics after the general election of 1932. By the time the convention was elected, Pedro Albizu Campos was in prison at *La Princesa* for violating the (unconstitutional) strictures of Puerto Rico's own Smith Act.[a]

[a] Refer to discussion under Article II's Section 4.

Table 2 Election of the Constitutional Convention August 27, 1951*

Registered Voters	781,914
Registered Voters Casting Their Ballot	439,745
Abstentions	342,169

Table 3 Constitutional Convention Delegates per Political Party*

Popular Democratic Party Delegates	70 (76%)
Statehood Party Delegates	15 (16%)
Socialist Party Delegates	7 (8%)
Total Number of Delegates	92 (100%)

*Source: *Proposiciones y Resoluciones de la Convención Constituyente de Puerto Rico* (San Juan: Academia Puertorriqueña de Jurisprudencia y Legislación, 1992), 682.

Table 4 Delegates to 1951–1952 Constitutional Convention Mentioned in Commentary

Delegate	Constituency	Role at the Convention / Public Office	Political Party Affiliation
Antonio Fernós Isern	At Large	President of the Convention / Resident Commissioner (1946–1964)	Popular Democratic Party
María Libertad Gómez	At Large	First Vice President of the Convention / Representative from the Arecibo District (1944–1956)	Popular Democratic Party
Víctor Gutiérrez Franqui	At Large	Second Vice President of the Convention / President of the Convention's Committee on Drafting and Style / Attorney General (1951–1952) / Senate Majority Leader (1948–1951; 1952–1956) / Senator At Large (1948–1951; 1952–1960)	Popular Democratic Party
Luis Muñoz Marín	At Large	President of the Committee on Preamble, Ordinances and Amendment Procedures / President of the Senate (1940–1948) / Governor of Puerto Rico (1948–1964)	Popular Democratic Party

Table 4 (Continued)

Delegate	Constituency	Role at the Convention Public Office	Political Party Affiliation
Ernesto Ramos Antonini	At Large	President of the Committee on the Judicial Branch Speaker of the House of Representatives (1946–1963)	Popular Democratic Party
Samuel R. Quiñones	At Large	President of the Committee on the Executive Branch President of the Senate (1948–1968)	Popular Democratic Party
Luis Negrón López	Mayagüez District	President of the Committee on the Legislative Branch Vice President and Majority Leader of the Senate Senator from the Mayagüez District (1940–1968)	Popular Democratic Party
Jaime Benítez Rexach	At Large	President of the Committee on the Bill of Rights Chancellor of the University of Puerto Rico (1942–1966) President of the University of Puerto Rico (1966–1970) Resident Commissioner (1972–1976)	Popular Democratic Party
Benjamín Ortiz Ortiz	At Large	President of the Committee on Calendar Majority Leader of the House of Representatives Representative At Large (1944–1952)	Popular Democratic Party
Cruz Ortiz Stella	Humacao District	President of the Committee on Rules Senator from the Humacao District (1944–1969)	Popular Democratic Party
Yldefonso Solá Morales	Guayama District	President of the Committee on Transitory and General Provisions Senator from the Guayama District (1948–1970)	Popular Democratic Party
José Trías Monge	At Large	Vice President of the Committee on Preamble, Ordinances and Amendment Procedures Committee on the Judicial Branch Attorney General (1952–1957) Chief Justice (1974–1985)	Popular Democratic Party

(*continued*)

Table 4 (Continued)

Delegate	Constituency	Role at the Convention / Public Office	Political Party Affiliation
Santiago Polanco Abreu	Aguadilla District	Vice President of the Committee on Transitory and General Provisions Representative from the District of Aguadilla (1948–1964) Speaker of the House of Representatives (1963–1964) Resident Commissioner (1964–1968)	Popular Democratic Party
Arcilio Alvarado Alvarado	San Juan District I	Representative from San Juan District (1948–1960) Representative At Large (1960–1968) Speaker of the House of Representatives (1964–1968)	Popular Democratic Party
Ramón Barreto Pérez	San Juan District I	Committee on Legislative Branch	Popular Democratic Party
Heraclio Rivera Colón	San Juan District II	Committee on Legislative Branch Senator from San Juan District (1948–1952) Senator from Bayamón District (1952–1964)	Popular Democratic Party
Lionel Fernández Méndez	Guayama District	Committee on Drafting and Style Senator from Guayama District (1948–1972)	Popular Democratic Party
Sigfrido Vélez González	Arecibo District	Committee on Calendar Representative from Arecibo District (1948–1968)	Popular Democratic Party
Luis Muñoz Rivera	San Juan District I	Committee on Publications and Disbursements Senator At Large (1960–1968)	Popular Democratic Party
Pablo Morales Otero	San Juan District II	Committee on the Executive Branch Representative At Large (1952–1968)	Popular Democratic Party
Francisco Paz Granela	At Large	Committee on the Bill of Rights	Popular Democratic Party
Virgilio Brunet Maldonado	At Large	Committee on Preamble, Ordinances and Amendment Procedures	Popular Democratic Party
Celestino Iriarte Miró	At Large	Committee on the Legislative Branch Minority Leader of the Senate (1928–1944; 1948–1952) Senator from San Juan District (1920–1944) Senator At Large (1948–1952)	Puerto Rico Statehood Party (*Partido Estadista Puertorriqueño*)

Table 4 (Continued)

Delegate	Constituency	Role at the Convention Public Office	Political Party Affiliation
Miguel Ángel García Méndez	Mayagüez District	Committee on the Judicial Branch Speaker of the House of Representatives (1932–1940) Senator At Large (1952–1968)	Puerto Rico Statehood Party (*Partido Estadista Puertorriqueño*)
Luis A. Ferré Aguayo	Ponce District	Committee on Preamble, Ordinances and Amendment Procedures Committee on Transitory and General Provisions Representative At Large (1952–1956) Governor of Puerto Rico (1968–1972) President of the Senate (1976–1980)	Puerto Rico Statehood Party (*Partido Estadista Puertorriqueño*)
Leopoldo Figueroa Carreras	At Large	Committee on the Bill of Rights Minority Leader of the House of Representatives Delegate from San Juan District House of Delegates (1914–1917) Representative from San Juan District (1932–1944) Representative At Large (1944–1968)	Puerto Rico Statehood Party (*Partido Estadista Puertorriqueño*)
Ramiro Colón Castaño	Ponce District	Committee on Preamble, Ordinances and Amendment Procedures Senator At Large (1956–1968)	Puerto Rico Statehood Party (*Partido Estadista Puertorriqueño*)
Héctor González Blanes	San Juan District I	Committee on Preamble, Ordinances and Amendment Procedures	Puerto Rico Statehood Party (*Partido Estadista Puertorriqueño*)
José Veray Hernández	Aguadilla District	Committee on Transitory and General Provisions	Puerto Rico Statehood Party (*Partido Estadista Puertorriqueño*)
José Gelpí Bosch	Mayagüez District	Committee on Rules Senator At Large (1954–1955)	Puerto Rico Statehood Party (*Partido Estadista Puertorriqueño*)

(*continued*)

Table 4 (Continued)

Delegate	Constituency	Role at the Convention Public Office	Political Party Affiliation
Lino Padrón Rivera	At Large	Committee on the Bill of Rights Committee on the Judicial Branch Committee on the Legislative Branch Vice President of the Senate (1940–1941) Minority Leader of the Senate Senator At Large (1936–1944)	Socialist Party
Antonio Reyes Delgado	At Large	Committee on the Bill of Rights Senator from Arecibo District (1932–1940)	Socialist Party
Jorge Font Saldaña	At Large	Committee on Preamble, Ordinances and Amendment Procedures	Popular Democratic Party
Ernesto Juan Fonfrías	San Juan District II	Committee on Preamble, Ordinances and Amendment Procedures	Popular Democratic Party
Ramón Mellado Parsons	San Juan District II	Committee on Preamble, Ordinances and Amendment Procedures	Popular Democratic Party
Jenaro Gautier Dapena	San Juan District I	Committee on Preamble, Ordinances and Amendment Procedures	Popular Democratic Party

Table 5 Puerto Rico Supreme Court Justices Mentioned in Commentary

Name	Nominated by	Position	Years on Court
Martín Travieso Nieva	President Franklin D. Roosevelt	Associate Justice Chief Justice	1936–1944 1944–1948
Roberto H. Todd, Jr.	President Franklin D. Roosevelt President Harry S. Truman	Associate Justice Chief Justice	1941–1951 1951–1952
Cecil Snyder	President Franklin D. Roosevelt Governor Luis Muñoz Marín	Associate Justice Chief Justice	1942–1952 1952–1957
Borinquen Marrero Ríos	President Harry S. Truman	Associate Justice	1947–1957
Luis Negrón Fernández	President Harry S. Truman Governor Luis Muñoz Marín	Associate Justice Chief Justice	1948–1957 1957–1972

Table 5 (Continued)

Name	Nominated by	Position	Years on Court
Raúl Serrano Geyls	Governor Luis Muñoz Marín	Associate Justice	1957–1962
Rafael Hernández Matos	Governor Luis Muñoz Marín	Associate Justice	1957–1972
Carlos Irizarry Yunqué	Governor Rafael Hernández Colón	Associate Justice	1973–1986
José Trías Monge	Governor Rafael Hernández Colón	Chief Justice	1974–1985
Antonio Negrón García	Governor Rafael Hernández Colón	Associate Justice	1974–2000
Víctor Pons Núñez	Governor Rafael Hernández Colón	Chief Justice	1985–1992
Miriam Naveira de Rodón	Governor Rafael Hernández Colón Governor Sila Calderón Serra	Associate Justice Chief Justice	1985–2003 2003–2004
Federico Hernández Denton	Governor Rafael Hernández Colón Governor Sila Calderón Serra	Associate Justice Chief Justice	1985–2004 2004–2014
Jaime Fuster Berlingeri	Governor Rafael Hernández Colón	Associate Justice	1992–2007
Baltasar Corrada del Río	Governor Pedro Rosselló González	Associate Justice	1995–2005
Efraín Rivera Pérez	Governor Pedro Rosselló González	Associate Justice	2000–2010
Anabelle Rodríguez Rodríguez	Governor Sila Calderón Serra	Associate Justice	2004–2020
Liana Fiol Matta	Governor Sila Calderón Serra	Associate Justice Chief Justice	2004–2014 2014–2016
Rafael Martínez Torres	Governor Luis Fortuño Burset	Associate Justice	2009 (present)
Erick Kolthoff Caraballo	Governor Luis Fortuño Burset	Associate Justice	2009 (present)
Luis Estrella Martínez	Governor Luis Fortuño Burset	Associate Justice	2011 (present)
Maite Oronoz Rodríguez	Governor Alejandro García Padilla	Associate Justice Chief Justice	2014–2016 2016 (present)
Ángel Colón Pérez	Governor Alejandro García Padilla	Associate Justice	2016 (present)

Table 6 Insular Cases Involving Puerto Rico

Case	Justice	Territory	Issue and Holding
De Lima v. Bidwell[a]	Henry Brown	Puerto Rico	Whether following the ratification of the Treaty of Paris, but before the enactment of the 1900 Foraker Act, Puerto Rico was a "foreign country" within the meaning of the 1897 Tariff Act. No. Puerto Rico was not a "foreign country" within the meaning of the 1897 Tariff Act.
Goetze and Crossman v. United States[b]	Henry Brown	Puerto Rico	Same question as above. Same answer as above.
Dooley (1) v. United States[c]	Henry Brown	Puerto Rico	Whether the tariffs imposed by President William McKinley, before and after the ratification of the Treaty of Paris, could be lawfully exacted from merchandise imported into Puerto Rico from New York even after the ratification of the above-referenced treaty. No. After the ratification of the peace treaty with the Spanish Kingdom, Puerto Rico was no longer a "foreign country" for tariff purposes, therefore President McKinley had no unilateral authority to impose tariffs on merchandise coming into Puerto Rico from New York unless Congress enacted legislation to that effect.
Huus v. New York & Porto Rico Steamship Company[d]	Henry Brown	Puerto Rico	Whether San Juan's port was a "U.S." or "foreign port" for purposes of New York's pilotage legislation. Yes. The San Juan port was a "U.S." port for pilotage purposes.
Dooley (2) v. United States[e]	Henry Brown	Puerto Rico	Whether Section 3 of the 1900 Foraker Act, which applied a duty on imports coming into Puerto Rico from American ports, ran afoul of the requirements of the U.S. Constitution's Tax Uniformity Clause. No. Puerto Rico, while belonging to the United States, was not a part of the Union for purposes of the Tax Uniformity Clause.
González v. Williams[f]	Melville Fuller	Puerto Rico	Whether Puerto Ricans were "aliens" for purposes of the United States' immigration legislation after Congress's enactment of the 1900 Foraker Act. No. While not U.S. citizens yet, Puerto Ricans were not "aliens" within the meaning of the federal immigration legislation. Puerto Ricans, who pursuant to Section 7 of the Foraker Act were now "citizens of Puerto Rico," enjoyed free access to the mainland while owing allegiance to the United States.

Table 6 (Continued)

Case	Justice	Territory	Issue and Holding
Kent v. People of Porto Rico[g]	Edward White	Puerto Rico	Whether the Fifth Amendment's protection against self-incrimination extended to defendant in Puerto Rico. No.
Kopel v. Bingham[h]	Melville Fuller	Puerto Rico	Whether the governor of Puerto Rico stands on an equal footing with the governors of the states and territories with respect to his (or her) authority to request the extradition of fugitives. Yes. Not because the Constitution (Art. IV, § 2) requires it, but rather because Congress has so established by statute.
Ochoa v. Hernández y Morales[i]	Mahlon Pitney	Puerto Rico	Whether the Fifth Amendment's Due Process Clause is applicable in Puerto Rico. Yes. The *Ochoa* Court intimates that the due process right is "fundamental" and is, thus, applicable to Puerto Rico.
Balzac v. People of Porto Rico[j]	William Taft	Puerto Rico	Whether the right to jury trial available under the Sixth Amendment is applicable to defendants in Puerto Rico. No. Even after Congress's enactment of the 1917 Jones Act, Puerto Rico remained an unincorporated territory and, thus, the Sixth Amendment's right to jury trial remained inapplicable.

[a] 182 U.S. 1 (1901). In *De Lima*, the litigation revolved around the importation of Puerto Rican sugar to the ports of New York before Congress's enactment of the 1900 Foraker Act.

[b] 182 U.S. 221 (1901). In *Goetze* and *Crossman*, the aegis of the dispute was the importation of goods from Puerto Rico and Hawaii into the ports of New York after the U.S. Senate's ratification of the 1899 Treaty of Paris and following the enactment by Congress of the 1898 Newlands Resolution annexing Hawaii.

[c] 182 U.S. 222 (1901). In *Dooley* (1), the litigation, different from *De Lima*, was triggered by the importation into Puerto Rico of goods sent from New York before the enactment by Congress of the 1900 Foraker Act.

[d] 182 U.S. 392 (1901). In *Huus*, the action leading to the litigation took place on or around June 25, 1900.

[e] 183 U.S. 151 (1901). In *Dooley* (2), the facts are almost identical to *Dooley* (1) with the caveat that the 1900 Foraker Act was then in full force and effect in Puerto Rico.

[f] 192 U.S. 1 (1904). Isabella González was an unmarried Puerto Rican woman, who resided in Puerto Rico and arrived in New York on August 24, 1902.

[g] 207 U.S. 113 (1907).

[h] 211 U.S. 468 (1909).

[i] 230 U.S. 139 (1913).

[j] 258 U.S. 298 (1922). This is the only Insular Case decided after Congress's enactment of the 1917 Jones Act and its conferral of U.S. citizenship to the people of Puerto Rico.

■ BIBLIOGRAPHICAL ESSAY

This bibliography provides the reader a basic catalogue of sources addressing some of the more salient aspects of Puerto Rico's constitutional law and history.

General Overview of Puerto Rican History

Published in 1788 by the Benedictine monk, Fray Íñigo Abbad y Lasierra, *Historia Geográfica, Civil y Natural de la Isla de San Juan Bautista de Puerto Rico* (annotated by José Julián Acosta y Calbo) (Madrid: Ediciones Doce Calles, 2002), is the first treatise on Puerto Rico's colonial history. Abbad's narrative begins in 1508, with the Spanish colonization at the hands of Juan Ponce de León and ends up in the eighteenth century. It, moreover, describes in detail Puerto Rico's ecosystem, lands, fauna, flora, and societal characteristics. In 1864 the Puerto Rican intellectual José Julián Acosta y Calbo annotated Abbad's work, significantly enriching its scope. Lidio Cruz Monclova's *Historia de Puerto Rico (Siglo XIX)*, 2nd ed., vols. 1–3 (Río Piedras: Editorial de la Universidad de Puerto Rico, 1958), is an indispensable tool for exploring the actions and omissions of the Spanish governors ruling Puerto Rico throughout the nineteenth century. Availing himself of numerous archival sources housed in Madrid's *Archivo Histórico Nacional*, Cruz Monclova successfully unearths the complex political jigsaw puzzle binding Puerto Rico to Spain all through the nineteenth century.

Other works that provide a general overview of Puerto Rican history include Reece B. Bothwell González, *Puerto Rico: Cien años de lucha política*, vols. 1–4 (Editorial de la Universidad de Puerto Rico, 1979); Salvador Brau, *La colonización de Puerto Rico* (San Juan: Heraldo Español, 1907); Adolfo de Hostos, *Historia de San Juan: ciudad murada* (San Juan: Instituto de Cultura Puertorriqueña, 1979); Eugenio Fernández Méndez, *Crónicas de Puerto Rico* (Río Piedras: Editorial de la Universidad de Puerto Rico, 1969); Gervasio Luis García, *Historia bajo sospecha* (San Juan: Publicaciones Gaviota, 2015); Juan Gualberto Gómez and Antonio Sendras y Burín, *La isla de Puerto Rico: Bosquejo histórico* (Madrid: Imprenta de José Gil y Navarro, 1891); Arturo Morales Carrión, *Puerto Rico: A Political and Cultural History* (New York: W.W. Norton & Company, Inc., 1983); Fernando Picó, *Historia general de Puerto Rico* (Río Piedras: Ediciones Huracán, 1986); Félix Ojeda Reyes, *El desterrado de París: Biografía del Doctor Ramón Emeterio Betances 1827–1898* (San Juan: Ediciones Puerto, 2001); Francisco A. Scarano, *Puerto Rico: cinco siglos de historia* 4 ed. (México: McGraw Hill, 2015); and Ada Suárez Díaz, *El antillano: Biografía del Doctor Ramón Emeterio*

218 ■ BIBLIOGRAPHICAL ESSAY

Betances 1827–1898 (San Juan: Centro de Estudios Avanzados de Puerto Rico y el Caribe, 1988). For an overview of Spain's colonization of the Americas, see Juan Bosch, *De Cristóbal Colón a Fidel Castro: El Caribe, frontera imperial*, 12ma edición (Santo Domingo: Alfa & Omega, 2005).

The Constitutional History of Puerto Rico

The most comprehensive study on Puerto Rico's constitutional history is José Trías Monge, *Historia constitucional de Puerto Rico*, vols. 1–5 (Río Piedras: Editorial de la Universidad de Puerto Rico, 1980–1994). Chief Justice Trías Monge's definitive work starts in the fifteenth century and takes the reader through the twists and turns of Puerto Rico's constitutional life up to the 1990s. The process leading to the 1951–1952 Constitutional Convention, together with the convention debates, are amply discussed in Volume 3. Other works on the constitutional history of Puerto Rico include: José Trías Monge, *El choque de dos culturas jurídicas en Puerto Rico* (Orford, NH: Equity Publishing Company, 1991); José Trías Monge, *Puerto Rico: The Trials of the Oldest Colony in the World* (New Haven: Yale University Press, 1997); José A. Alcaide, *Discursos de Ernesto Ramos Antonini* (San Juan: Cámara de Representantes, 1984); Fernando Bayrón Toro, *Elecciones y partidos políticos de Puerto Rico* (Mayagüez: Editorial Isla Inc., 1984); Carmelo Delgado Cintrón, *Imperialismo jurídico norteamericano en Puerto Rico (1898–2015)* (San Juan: Publicaciones Gaviota, 2015); Carmelo Delgado Cintrón, *Derecho y Colonialismo: La Trayectoria histórica del Derecho puertorriqueño* (Río Piedras: Editorial Edil Inc., 1988); Néstor Duprey Salgado (ed.), *Conversaciones en el bohío: Luis Muñoz Marín y Roberto Sánchez Vilella en sus propias palabras*, vols. 1–2 (Trujillo Alto: Fundación Luis Muñoz Marín, 2005); Luis Muñoz Marín, *Memorias 1940–1952* (San Germán: Editorial de la Universidad Interamericana de Puerto Rico, 1992); Bolívar Pagán, *Historia de los partidos políticos puertorriqueños 1898–1956*, vols. 1–2 (San Juan: Litografía Real Hermanos Inc., 1959); Néstor Rigual, *Incidencias parlamentarias*, vols. 1–2 (San Juan: Instituto de Cultura Puertorriqueña, 1972); Jorge Rodríguez Beruff (ed.), *Las memorias del Almirante William D. Leahy 1939–1940* (Trujillo Alto: Fundación Luis Muñoz Marín, 2012); Manuel Rodríguez Ramos, "Breve historia de los códigos puertorriqueños," *Revista Jurídica de la Universidad de Puerto Rico* 19 (1950): 233; Carmelo Rosario Natal, *La juventud de Luis Muñoz Marín: vida y pensamiento 1898–1932* (Río Piedras: Editorial Edil, 1989); and Tomás Sarramía, *Gobernadores de Puerto Rico* (San Juan: Publicaciones puertorriqueñas Inc., 1993).

The Constitutional Convention 1951–1952

Works on the constitutional convention include: *Diario de Sesiones de la Convención Constituyente de Puerto Rico*, vols. 1–4 (San Juan: Lexis-Nexis of Puerto Rico

Inc., 2003); *Proposiciones y Resoluciones de la Convención Constituyente de Puerto Rico* (San Juan: Academia Puertorriqueña de Jurisprudencia y Legislación, 1992), available online at https://www.academiajurisprudenciapr.org/propos iciones-y-resoluciones-de-la-convencion-constituyente/; Héctor Luis Acevedo (ed.), *La generación del 40 y la convención constituyente* (Hato Rey: Universidad Interamericana de Puerto Rico, 2003); Jorge M. Farinacci Fernós, *La constitución obrera de Puerto Rico* (Río Piedras: Ediciones Huracán, 2015); Antonio Fernós Isern, *Original Intent in the Constitution of Puerto Rico: Notes and Comments Submitted to the Congress of the United States* 2nd ed. (San Juan: LEXIS-NEXIS, 2002); Pedro Muñoz Amato (ed.), *La nueva constitución de Puerto Rico: Informes a la Convención Constituyente preparados por la Escuela de Administración Pública de la Facultad de Ciencias Sociales* (Río Piedras: Editorial de la Universidad de Puerto Rico, 1954); and Carlos Zapata Oliveras, *Luis Muñoz Marín, Estados Unidos y el establecimiento del Estado Libre Asociado de Puerto Rico 1946–1952* (Hato Rey: Universidad Interamericana, 2015). For the biography of María Libertad Gómez Garriga, who was the Convention's only female delegate and first vice president, see José Luis Colón (ed.), *María Libertad Gómez: mujer de convicción, líder de cambios* (San Juan: Cámara de Representantes & Universidad Interamericana, 2014).

Treatises on Puerto Rico's Constitutional Law

The foremost treatise on Puerto Rico's constitutional law is José Julián Álvarez González, *Derecho Constitucional de Puerto Rico* (Bogotá: Editorial Temis, 2010). Professor Álvarez González offers an illuminating rendition on most aspects of Puerto Rico's constitutional law, including the constitution's distribution of power among the three coequal branches of government. The Álvarez González treatise pays careful attention to the Puerto Rico Supreme Court's construction of the fundamental freedoms found in Article II's Bill of Rights. The interaction between the Puerto Rico Constitution and its federal counterpart is the subject of ample analysis. Another reference on Puerto Rican constitutional law is Raúl Serrano Geyls, *Derecho Constitucional de Estados Unidos y Puerto Rico* (Lillington, NC: Edwards Brothers, 2007).

Spanish Legal Tradition and History

Works on the Spanish legal tradition and history include: Manuel Torres Aguilar, *Manual de historia del Derecho* (Madrid: Tecnos, 2015); Federico Barrachina y Pastor, *Derecho foral español* (Castellón: J. Armengot e Hijos, 1911); Arnold Verduin, *Manual of Spanish Constitutions 1808–1931* (Michigan: University Lithoprinters, 1941); Raymond Carr, *Spain 1808–1939* (Oxford: Clarendon Press, 1975); and Jorge de Esteban, *Las constituciones de España* 2nd ed. (Madrid: Centro de Estudios Políticos y Constitucionales,

2000). For the historical background leading to the establishment of Puerto Rico's *Audiencia Territorial* and its structural design, see Gerardo Carlo Altieri, *Justicia y Gobierno: La Audiencia de Puerto Rico* (Sevilla: Consejo Superior de Investigaciones Científicas, 2007).

For a basic understanding of the geopolitical environment facing the Catholic Kings and the transformations undergone by Spain under their reign, see William H. Prescott, *History of the Reign of Ferdinand and Isabella* (New York: Heritage Press, 1962). For a complete analysis of the administrative structure of the Council of Indies and its interactions with the Spanish Crown, see Feliciano Barrios, *La gobernación de la monarquía española: consejos, juntas y secretarios de la administración de corte (1556–1700)* (Madrid: Centro de Estudios Políticos y Constitucionales, 2015). For an authoritative text on the origins of the Council of Castile and its subsequent role during the early days of Charles V's reign, see Salustiano De Dios, *El Consejo Real de Castilla (1385–1522)* (Madrid: Centro de Estudios Constitucionales, 1982). Other works on fifteenth-century Spain and the Council of Indies include: José María Ots y Capdequi, *Historia del Derecho español en América y del Derecho indiano* (Madrid: Aguilar, 1969); Ernst Schäfer, *El Consejo Real y Supremo de Indias*, 2 vols. (Sevilla: Carmona, 1935–1947); and Gerardo Carlo Altieri, *El sistema legal y los litigios de esclavos en Indias (Puerto Rico—Siglo XIX)* (San Juan: Ediciones Puerto, 2010).

Puerto Rico in the Context of the 1812 Cádiz Constitution

Regarding Puerto Rico in the context of the 1812 Cádiz Constitution, see for a detailed narrative of Ramón Power y Giralt's election as Puerto Rico's delegate, Aída R. Caro Costas (edited by María de los Ángeles Castro), *Ramón Power y Giralt: Diputado puertorriqueño a las Cortes Generales y Extraordinarias de España* (Río Piedras: Publicaciones Gaviota, 2012). For a biography of Bishop Juan Alejo Arizmendi, see Cayetano Coll y Toste, *Puertorriqueños ilustres* (Río Piedras: Editorial Cultural, 1978). For the role of the colonial delegates at the Cádiz Constituent Convention see, for instance, Rafael María de Labra, *Los presidentes americanos de las Cortes de Cádiz* (Cádiz: Manuel Álvarez, 1912). For a complete analysis of the measures implemented by Alejandro Ramírez during the 1811–1814 period, see, for instance, Luis González Vales, *Alejandro Ramírez y su tiempo* (Río Piedras: Editorial de la Universidad de Puerto Rico, 1978).

Puerto Rico's Autonomist Movement

José Gautier Dapena, *Baldorioty, Apóstol* (San Juan: Instituto de Cultura Puertorriqueña, 1970), covers Puerto Rico's Autonomist Movement. For the proceedings of the 1887 Ponce assembly where Baldorioty de Castro founded the Autonomist Party, see Pilar Barbosa, *De Baldorioty a Barbosa: Historia del Autonomismo Puertorriqueño 1887–1896* (San Juan: Instituto de Cultura

Puertorriqueña, 1957). For a detailed account of the meetings held in Madrid during this period between Puerto Rico's autonomist leadership and Spain's most prominent political actors, see, for instance, Pilar Barbosa de Rosario, *Historia del Pacto Sagastino a través de un epistolario inédito* (Río Piedras: Editorial de la Universidad de Puerto Rico, 1981). For a comparative analysis of the various European modalities of autonomy, see Rafael Cox Alomar, "The Ideological Decolonization of Puerto Rico's Autonomist Movement," in *Reconsidering the Insular Cases: The Past and Future of the American Empire* (Gerald L. Neuman and Tomiko Brown-Nagin eds.) (Cambridge: Harvard University Press, 2015), 129–166.

The Autonomic Charter of 1897

For a comparative analysis of the language of Article 32 of the 1897 Autonomic Charter vis-à-vis the textual structure of the Tenth Amendment and Section 9 of the 1950 Federal Relations Act, see, for instance, José Julián Álvarez González, "El viejo pacto: El elemento de bilateralidad en la Carta Autonómica de 1897," *Revista Jurídica de la Universidad de Puerto Rico* 67 (1998): 985.

American Imperialism

The idea of seizing Cuba was not foreign to the founding generation. Refer, for instance, to Benjamin Franklin's letter to his son William Franklin, dated August 28, 1767. William T. Franklin, *Memoirs of the Life and Writings of Benjamin Franklin* (London: Quarto Edition, 1817). Other sources on American imperialism include: W.H. Calcott, *The Caribbean Policy of the United States 1890–1920* (Baltimore: Johns Hopkins University Press, 1942); Perkins Dexter, *The United States and the Caribbean* (Cambridge: Harvard University Press, 1966); Walter LaFeber, *The New Empire: An Interpretation of American Expansion, 1860–1898* (Ithaca: Cornell University Press, 1963); Margaret Leech, *In the Days of McKinley* (New York: Harper & Brothers, 1959); Julius Pratt, *Expansionists of 1898* (Baltimore: Johns Hopkins University Press, 1936); Theodore Roosevelt, *The Rough Riders* (New York: Charles Scribner's Sons, 1899); and Theodore Roosevelt, Jr., *Colonial Polices of the United States* (New York: Doubleday, Doran & Company Inc., 1937).

The 1898 Spanish-American War and the Treaty of Paris

On the 1898 Spanish-American War and the Treaty of Paris, see Alfonso García Martínez (ed.), *El Libro Rojo: Tratado de París Documentos Presentados a las Cortes en la Legislatura de 1898 por el Ministro de Estado* (Río Piedras: Editorial de la Universidad de Puerto Rico, 1988); José López Baralt, *The Policy of the United States Towards Its Territories with Special Reference to Puerto Rico* (Río

222 ■ BIBLIOGRAPHICAL ESSAY

Piedras: Editorial de la Universidad de Puerto Rico, 1999); Fernando Picó, *1898: La guerra después de la guerra* (Río Piedras: Ediciones Huracán, 1998); and Carmelo Rosario Natal, *El 1898 puertorriqueño en la historiografía* (San Juan: Academia Puertorriqueña de la Historia, 1997).

The End of Spanish Rule in Puerto Rico, Cuba, and the Philippines at the Turn of the Nineteenth Century

For an indispensable study of Cuba's Ten Years War (1868–1878) and its antecedents, see, for instance, Ramiro Guerra, *Guerra de los 10 Años* (La Habana: Editorial de Ciencias Sociales, 1972); see also Manuel Moreno Fraginals, *Cuba/España España/Cuba: Historia Común* (Barcelona: Crítica, 1995); and Louis Pérez, *Cuba: Between Reform and Revolution* (New York: Oxford University Press, 1988). For a triangular view of Puerto Rico, Cuba, and the Philippines during this transformative period, see Consuelo Naranjo, Miguel Puig-Samper and Luis Miguel García Mora (eds.), *La nación soñada: Cuba, Puerto Rico y Filipinas ante el 98* (Madrid: Doce Calles, 1996). For the examination of the Cuban context, see Rafael Cox Alomar, "Cuba's Constitutional Moment," 23 *Texas Hispanic Journal of Law & Policy* 1 (Spring 2017). For an in-depth look at José Martí's political project, see his illuminating *Manifiesto de Montecristi* dated March 25, 1895, available in Raimundo Lazo (ed.), *José Martí: Sus Mejores Páginas* (México: Editorial Porrúa, S.A., 1992). For a detailed account of the Philippines's context, see Alicia Castellanos Escudier, *Filipinas: De la Insurrección a la Intervención de EE.UU. 1896–1898* (Madrid: Silex, 1998). For an in-depth analysis of the initial stages of the 1898–1899 Filipino-American War, see Benito J. Legarda, *The Hills of Sampaloc* (Makati City: The Bookmark, 2001).

The U.S. Military Government 1898–1900

Resources on the U.S. Military governance of Puerto Rico include: U.S. War Department, *General Orders and Circulars 1898–1900* (Washington, D.C.: Government Printing Office, 1900); Report of the Military Governor of Porto Rico on Civil Affairs (Washington, D.C.: Government Printing Office, 1902; Arcadio Díaz Quiñones, *Once tesis sobre un crimen de 1899* (San Juan: Luscinia, 2019); and María Eugenia Estades Font, *La presencia militar de Estados Unidos en Puerto Rico 1898–1918: Intereses estratégicos y dominación colonial* (Río Piedras: Ediciones Huracán, 1988).

The Fuller Court and the Insular Cases

For the origins of the fierce debate that raged in the pages of the *Harvard Law Review* following the conquest of Puerto Rico, Guam, and the Philippines in the aftermath of the 1898 Spanish American War, see Carman F. Randolph, "Constitutional Aspects of Annexation," *Harvard Law Review* 12 (1898–1899): 291; Christopher Columbus Langdell, "Status of Our New Territories," *Harvard Law Review* 12 (1898–1899): 365; Simeon E. Baldwin, "Constitutional Questions Incident to the Acquisition and Government by the United States of Island Territory," *Harvard Law Review* 12 (1898–1899): 393; and Abbott Lawrence Lowell, "Status of Our New Possessions a Third View," *Harvard Law Review* 13 (1899–1900): 155. For a detailed enumeration of the complete corpus of Insular Cases, see, for instance, Efrén Rivera Ramos, *The Legal Construction of Identity: The Judicial and Social Legacy of American Colonialism in Puerto Rico* (Washington, D.C.: American Psychological Association, 2001); and Juan R. Torruella, *The Supreme Court and Puerto Rico: The Doctrine of Separate and Unequal* (Río Piedras: Editorial de la Universidad de Puerto Rico, 1988). For a thoughtful analysis, see Christina Duffy Burnett, "A Convenient Constitution? Extraterritoriality After *Boumediene*," *Columbia Law Review* 109 (2009): 973; and Juan R. Torruella, "The Insular Cases: The Establishment of a Regime of Political Apartheid," *University of Pennsylvania Journal of International Law* 29 (2007): 283.

The Foraker and Jones Acts

On the Foraker Act, see José de Diego, *Obras Completas*, vol. 2 (San Juan: Instituto de Cultura Puertorriqueña, 1973), and Luis Muñoz Rivera, *Campañas Políticas*, vols. 1–3 (Madrid: Editorial Puerto Rico, 1925). For a detailed study of the legislative history leading to the Jones Act, see José Cabranes, *Citizenship and the American Empire* (New Haven: Yale University Press, 1979). José Julián Álvarez González, "The Empire Strikes Out: Congressional Ruminations on the Citizenship Status of Puerto Ricans," *Harvard Journal on Legislation* 27 (1990): 309.

Puerto Rico in the Post-1952 and Post-PROMESA Cycle

Sources addressing Puerto Rico in the post-1952 and post-PROMESA cycle include: Salvador Casellas, "Commonwealth Status and the Federal Courts," 80 *Revista Jurídica de la Universidad de Puerto Rico* (2011): 945; Adriel Cepeda and Neil C. Weare, "After Aurelius: What Future for the Insular Cases?," *Yale Law Journal Forum* 130 (2020): 284; Rafael Cox Alomar, *Fernós Isern y la Jornada Puertorriqueña ante la ONU de 1953*, in Héctor Luis Acevedo (ed.), *Dr. Antonio Fernós Isern: De Médico a Constituyente* (San Juan: Editorial de la Universidad Interamericana, 2014), 493–531; Gustavo A. Gelpí, *The Constitutional Evolution of Puerto Rico and Other U.S. Territories (1898–Present)* (Hato Rey: Universidad Interamericana, 2017); Rafael Hernández Colón, "The Evolution of Democratic Governance under the Territorial Clause of the U.S. Constitution," *Suffolk*

University Law Review 50 (2017): 587; Samuel Isaacharoff et al., "What Is Puerto Rico?," *Indiana Law Journal* 94 (Winter 2019): 1; Christina D. Ponsa-Kraus, "Political Wine in a Judicial Bottle: Justice Sotomayor's Surprising Concurrence in Aurelius," *Yale Law Journal Forum* 130 (2020): 101; Juan R. Torruella, "Why Puerto Rico Does Not Need Further Experimentation with Its Future: A Reply to the Notion of 'Territorial Federalism,'" *Harvard Law Review Forum 131* (2018): 65; and José Enrico Valenzuela Alvarado, "PROMESA's Stay in Civil Rights Cases: In Praxis View of Violations to Puerto Ricans' Constitutional Fundamental Rights," *Revista Jurídica de la Universidad Interamericana de Puerto Rico* 52 (2017): 411.

The Constitution and the COVID-19 Crisis

For a relevant analysis of the constitutional ramifications of the COVID-19 crisis, see Efrén Rivera Ramos, *Puerto Rico ante la Pandemia* in *Emergencia Sanitaria por el COVID-19: Derecho Constitucional Comparado* (Mexico: UNAM, 2020), 140–148.

Puerto Rico and the Non-Hispanic Caribbean

For Britain's withdrawal from the Anglophone Caribbean in the postwar period, refer to Rafael Cox Alomar, *Revisiting the Transatlantic Triangle: The Constitutional Decolonization of the Eastern Caribbean* (Miami: Ian Randle Press, 2009); and Arturo Morales Carrión, *Puerto Rico and the Non-Hispanic Caribbean: A Study in the Decline of Spanish Exclusivism* (Río Piedras: University of Puerto Rico Press, 1952).

The Preamble to the Puerto Rico Constitution
On the debate concerning the drafting of the preamble, see 2 *Diario* 1127–1154. Delegate Francisco Paz Granela's proposal to add the word "permanent" before "union with the United States of America" was defeated. For the statement of Delegate Héctor González Blanes supporting Paz Granela's amendment, 2 *Diario* 1153–1154. For the statement of Delegate Luis Muñoz Marín opposing it, 2 *Diario* 1128.

Article I: The Commonwealth

The Commonwealth of Puerto Rico
On the drafting of Article I's Section 1, refer to Chief Justice José Trías Monge's dissenting opinion in *Partido Socialista Puertorriqueño v. Romero Barceló* (1980). For the text of the first draft of Article I's Section 1, see 3 *Diario* 1909. For the revisions to the first draft, refer to the amendment proposed by Delegate Víctor Gutiérrez Franqui, 3 *Diario* 1910.

Article II: The Bill of Rights

Human Dignity

The concept of "human dignity," as a self-contained and independent legal construct, was foreign to the island's legal landscape prior to the inauguration of the 1952 Constitution.

On the international precedents considered by the delegates in drafting Article II's Section 1, refer to the statement made by Delegate Miguel Ángel García Méndez, 4 *Diario* 2487.

On a comparative analysis of the bill of rights found in the Puerto Rico Constitution, vis-à-vis the one found in the Jones Act, refer to statement proffered by Delegate Luis Muñoz Marín to the effect that the former one offered in many areas a more robust corpus of constitutional protections than the latter one. 2 *Diario* 1210.

Following the supreme court's decision in *Salvá Santiago v. Torres Padró* (2007), the legislature amended Articles 96 and 97 of the Puerto Rico Civil Code, introducing the "irretrievable breakdown of marriage" construct as an additional ground for divorce. See P.R. Law No. 192 of August 18, 2011 (PR ST T.31, § 321). Also see Article 425 of the 2020 Civil Code.

Suspect Classifications

Race or Color
The Spanish Crown introduced black slavery in Puerto Rico *circa* 1519, close to a decade after the commencement of the island's colonization at the hands of Juan Ponce de León in 1508. *See* Francisco Scarano, *Puerto Rico: Cinco siglos de historia* (Mexico: McGraw-Hill, 2015), 222–223; and Arturo Morales Carrión, *Puerto Rico: A Political and Cultural History* (New York: W.W. Norton & Company, Inc., 1983), 32. For an analysis of the legal framework of slavery in the island, see Gerardo Carlo Altieri, *El sistema legal y los litigios de esclavos en Indias (Puerto Rico—Siglo XIX)* (San Juan: Ediciones Puerto, 2010). With respect to the abolition movement in Puerto Rico, see Segundo Ruiz Belvis, José Julián Acosta, and Francisco Mariano Quiñones, *Proyecto para la abolición de la esclavitud en Puerto Rico* (San Juan: Instituto de Cultura Puertorriqueña, 1969).

During the Spanish colonial period, a showing of "purity of blood" or *limpieza de sangre* was often required in order to accede to public office or even to get married. See, for instance, Félix Ojeda Reyes, *El desterrado de París: Biografía del Doctor Ramón Emeterio Betances 1827–1898* (San Juan: Ediciones Puerto, 2001), 13–17.

For the supreme court's application of Puerto Rico's 1943 Civil Rights Act in the context of racial discrimination in private spaces, refer to *Pueblo v. Suazo* (1944) and *Muriel v. Suazo* (1951). These cases arouse out of the same factual transaction: plaintiffs were refused entrance at the *Esquife Club* in Santurce on account of their race.

Alienage

For a critique of *De Paz Lisk v. Aponte Roque* (1989) addressing its treatment of the applicable federal constitutional law, see José Julián Álvarez González, "Derecho Constitucional," *Revista Jurídica de la Universidad de Puerto Rico* 59 (1990): 247, 260–265.

Sex

Gender equality has transformed Puerto Rico's political landscape. From August 7, 2019 until January 2, 2021, the island's governor, chief justice, resident commissioner, attorney general, and mayors of San Juan and Ponce (among others) were all females. This is a far cry from the situation *circa* 1952 when only one female delegate (out of a total of ninety-two) sat at the convention. For the biography of María Libertad Gómez Garriga, who also served as the convention's first vice president, see José Luis Colón (ed.), *María Libertad Gómez: Mujer de Convicción, Líder de Cambios* (San Juan: Cámara de Representantes & Universidad Interamericana, 2014).

Birth

Since the inception of Spanish colonial rule, illegitimate children were subject to legal invisibility. Illegitimate children were further divided between "natural" (whose parents were unmarried at the time of birth) and "non-naturals" or "adulterine" (born out of an adulterous relationship). Pursuant to the Spanish Civil Code, the latter ones were legally precluded from establishing their paternity, let alone seeking their share of the parental estate. See, for instance, C.E. Mascareñas, "La Filiación en el Derecho Puertorriqueño," *Revista de Derecho Puertorriqueño* 1 (1961): 7. *Ocasio v. Díaz* (1963), in the words of Professor Efraín González Tejera, was Puerto Rico's *Brown v. Board of Education*. Efraín González Tejera, "Don Rafael Hernández Matos: Aportaciones al Derecho Puertorriqueño," *Revista Jurídica de la Universidad de Puerto Rico* 73 (2004): 1, 3. On the historical context leading to *Ocasio v. Díaz*, and the legal consequences flowing from it, see Jaime B. Fuster and Michel Godreau, "Ocasio v. Díaz," 33 *Revista Jurídica de la Universidad de Puerto Rico* (1964): 273–290.

Social Origin or Condition

The phrase "social origin or condition" was proposed by Delegate Lino Padrón Rivera. It was approved without debate. 2 *Diario* 1381. For a contemporaneous, yet unexhaustive, description of what the delegates understood by "social origin or condition," see Delegate Héctor González Blanes' statement at 3 *Diario* 2246.

Political or Religious Ideas

For the scope of this protection, see Delegate Santiago Polanco Abreu's statement, 3 *Diario* 2075. Also refer to 4 *Diario* 2562–2563.

The Right to Vote

From 1493 until the 1809 election of Ramón Power y Giralt to the *cortes* in Cádiz, no elections were held in Puerto Rico. The election of Power y Giralt, however, was conducted on the basis of a very selective and limited franchise pursuant to the dictates of a decree enacted by Cádiz's *Cortes*. Thereinafter, elections to the *Cortes* in Madrid, as well as to a discrete number of local posts, were conducted at irregular intervals marred by corruption, fraud, and illegality. By the time of the 1898 invasion, the 1890 Spanish electoral law (*ley electoral*) was in full force and effect in the island. See, for instance, Chief Justice José Trías Monge's detailed historical analysis in *Partido Socialista v. Romero Barceló* (1980). The first electoral process conducted under the American flag was a long-winded municipal election held between October 26, 1899, and February 5, 1900. The military government, under the control of General George Davis, severely limited the franchise for the so-called 100-day election (*la elección de los 100 días*). Universal male franchise, available for the last Spanish election held in the island (on March 27, 1898), was drastically reduced. Only tax-paying men or, in the alternative, literate men having resided in the island for the preceding two years were eligible to vote. The 1900 Foraker Act did not provide for universal male suffrage—unsurprisingly, in light of the fact that War Secretary Elihu Root opposed its extension to Puerto Rico. *Partido Socialista v. Romero Barceló* (1980). Pursuant to Section 35 of the Jones Act, Congress delegated to the local legislature authority to regulate the island's electoral franchise. The Jones Act granted the right to vote solely to men twenty-one years of age or older having American citizenship.

Contrary to Section 35 of the Jones Act, Article II's Section 2 and Article VI's Section 4 do not require American citizenship as a precondition for voting. The American citizenship requirement, established in Puerto Rico's electoral law, is purely statutory in nature. It is not constitutionally required. For a relevant discussion, see *Ramírez de Ferrer v. Mari Bras* (1997).

The right to vote was extended to Puerto Rican women who could read and write pursuant to local P.R. Law No. 27 of April 18, 1929, nine years after the ratification in the United States of the Nineteenth Amendment. The first female

228 ■ BIBLIOGRAPHICAL ESSAY

votes were cast in the 1932 election. Universal female suffrage in Puerto Rico came six years later with the enactment of P.R. Law No. 4 of March 23, 1935 (PR ST T.16, §§ 41–43). See Fernando Bayrón Toro, *Elecciones y Partidos Políticos de Puerto Rico* (Mayagüez: Editorial Isla Inc., 1984), 177.

By the time the constitutional convention met, the local electoral code required compulsory voting; failure to cast a ballot would forfeit an individual's right to vote in the next election. The enforcement of this requirement, however, was particularly erratic. The pre-1952 legislature often waived the disenfranchisement penalty. Refer to Delegate Jaime Benítez Rexach's statement in 2 *Diario* 1390–1391. Delegate Miguel Ángel García Méndez was in support of compulsory voting; refer to his statement in 2 *Diario* 1391–1392.

Freedom of Religion; Complete Separation of Church and State

The influence of the Madisonian concept of religious liberties was not lost on the Puerto Rican framers. See Chief Justice José Andréu García's opinion in *Mercado Quilichini v. Universidad Católica de Puerto Rico* (1997).

In his commentary of Fray Íñigo Abbad's work, José Julián Acosta y Calbo suggests that Bishop Alonso Manso did not arrive in 1511, but rather in 1513. Íñigo Abbad y Lasierra, *Historia Geográfica, Civil y Natural de la isla de San Juan Bautista de Puerto Rico* (Madrid: Doce Calles, 2002), 127.

The 1898 Treaty of Paris left intact the legal status of the Roman Catholic Apostolic Church with respect to its internal governance. Moreover, as the U.S. Supreme Court found in *Municipality of Ponce v. Roman Catholic Apostolic Church* (1908), the United States bound itself under Article VIII of the Treaty of Paris not to "impair the property or rights which by law belongs to the peaceful possession of property of all kinds, of [. . .] ecclesiastical [. . .] bodies [.]" Arguably, the scope of the Roman Catholic Apostolic Church's "juristic personality and legal status" in Puerto Rico is found in the 1851 and 1859 Concordats entered into by the Vatican and the Spanish Crown, in the 1888 Spanish Civil Code (made extensive to Puerto Rico in 1889), and in canon law.

Article II's Section 3 is not the only provision relating to religion in the Puerto Rico Constitution; refer to the Preamble ("placing our trust in Almighty God"), Article II's Section 1 (establishing that discrimination on the basis of religious ideas is a suspect classification); and the supporting clause found under Article II's Section 5. For a relevant discussion on the interplay among these constitutional provisions, see Efrén Rivera Ramos, "Religión y Derecho: Marco Jurídico," *Revista Jurídica de la Universidad de Puerto Rico* 84 (2015): 537, 539–540.

With respect to the applicability to Puerto Rico of the Religious Freedom Restoration Act (RFRA) note that in *Diócesis de Arecibo v. Secretario de Justicia* (2014), the Puerto Rico Supreme Court applied the *Church of the Lukumi* test without any reference to the standard found in RFRA. Yet four years earlier in *Lozada Tirado v. Testigos de Jehová* (2010), Chief Justice Federico Hernández

Denton had implied that despite its neutrality and general applicability, a governmental action unduly burdening an individual's free exercise rights could run afoul Article II's Section 3. See Efrén Rivera Ramos and Alexandra Sabater Baerga, "Derecho Constitucional," *Revista Jurídica de la Universidad de Puerto Rico* 85 (2016): 417, 424.

Freedom of Speech and Press; Peaceful Assembly; Petition for a Redress of Grievances

For a relevant overview of the tortuous path the expressive freedoms have traversed in Puerto Rico, see, for instance, Raúl Serrano Geyls, *Derecho Constitucional de Estados Unidos y Puerto Rico* (Lillington, NC: Edwards Brothers, 2007), 1274–1276.

For a relevant discussion on the constitutional protection of symbolic speech under Article II's Section 4, see *Rodríguez Orellana v. Comisión Estatal de Elecciones* (1993).

For a critique of the supreme court's characterization of the University of Puerto Rico as a limited public forum in *Universidad de Puerto Rico v. Laborde* (2010), see Efrén Rivera Ramos and Alexandra Verdiales Costa, "Derecho Constitucional," *Revista Jurídica de la Universidad de Puerto Rico* 81 (2012): 317, 334–335.

Public Education

During the Spanish colonial period there was no formal public-school system. The crown's approach to education was marred by utter neglect. Besides a handful of schools headed by various Catholic orders, such as the Franciscans and the Dominicans, as well as nonsectarian ones led by local teachers such as the illustrious Rafael Cordero (1790–1868), the island was bereft of schools up to the first half of the nineteenth century. By June 1898, Puerto Rico had 380 public schools for boys and 148 for girls. Children attending these schools were taught, among other subjects, Catholic ecclesiastical doctrine. Over 80 percent of the children were not enrolled in school. Equally disturbing, at no point under Spanish rule did Puerto Rico have a university, contrary to Cuba, where the University of Havana was founded as early as 1728. For the state of the education system in 1898, see, for instance, *Report on the Census of Porto Rico, 1899* (Washington, D.C.: Government Publishing Office, 1900), 74–75. See also Juan José Osuna, *A History of Education in Puerto Rico* (Río Piedras: Editorial de la Universidad de Puerto Rico, 1949), 103–122. The 1898 invasion brought with it the dismantling of the rudimentary (and theocentric) Spanish school system and the hurried and haphazard importation of an American educational model not suited to Puerto Rico's linguistic and cultural realities. The U.S. Department of War, with the support of Congress, soon weaponized the island's instruction

230 ■ BIBLIOGRAPHICAL ESSAY

system, using it as an ideological tool for "Americanizing" Puerto Rican children. From the time General Guy Henry signed U.S. General Order No. 12 of February 6, 1899, organizing the island's first Bureau of Education until the inauguration of the 1952 Constitution, the island's public school system was caught up in the crossfire of an intense ideological battle between those voices favoring the "Americanization" model and those opposing it. For an indispensable analysis of this phenomenon, see, for instance, Aida Negrón de Montilla, *Americanization in Puerto Rico and the Public-School System 1900–1930* (Río Piedras: Editorial Edil, Inc., 1970).

The precursor to the supporting clause found in Article II's Section 5 is Section 2 of the Jones Act, which established that no public money "shall ever be appropriated" for the use, benefit, or support of any educational entity not under the "absolute control" of the government of Puerto Rico. The Jones Act's explicit restriction mirrored both the language Congress had already incorporated to the 1916 Philippines Organic Act (39 Stat. 545 (1916)) (see Section K of the Philippines's Bill of Rights) and the texts of various state constitutions, such as the 1870 Illinois Constitution (Article VIII's Section 3), the 1875 Nebraska Constitution (Article VII's Section 11), and the 1950 Hawaii Constitution (Article IX's Section 1) (subsequently modified by Congress at the time Hawaii was admitted to the Union as a state in 1959).

On the description of the noneducational services the government can offer private schools without infringing the dictates of the supporting clause found in Article II's Section 5, refer to the statements proffered by Delegates Virgilio Brunet Maldonado and Antonio Reyes Delgado in 2 *Diario* 1480, 1487.

Freedom of Association

On the right not to associate, see *Rodríguez v. Estado Libre Asociado* (2019), where the supreme court, applying the rule announced in *Rivera Schatz v. Estado Libre Asociado* (2014), invalidated the statutory framework requiring auto mechanics' compulsory membership to the *Colegio de Técnicos y Mecánicos Automotrices de Puerto Rico*. For a commentary, see Efrén Rivera Ramos and Alexandra Sabater Baerga, "Derecho Constitucional," *Revista Jurídica de la Universidad de Puerto Rico* 85 (2016): 417, 429.

Death Penalty

For the death penalty cases heard by the Puerto Rico Supreme Court during the twentieth century, see *Ex Parte Acevedo* (1902); *Pueblo v. Nevárez* (1906); *Pueblo v. Rivera* (1905); *Pueblo v. Dones* (1905); *Pueblo v. Boria* (1907); *Pueblo v. Morales (Yaré Yaré)* (1906); *Pueblo v. Acosta* (1906); *Pueblo v. Flores* (1911); *Pueblo v. Rosado* (1911); *Pueblo v. Román* (1912); *Pueblo v. Améstico* (1912);

Pueblo v. Lasalle (1912); *Pueblo v. Izquierdo* (1917); *Pueblo v. Arrocho* (1924); *Pueblo v. Clemente* (1926); and *Pueblo v. Pascual Ramos* (1927).

For a narrative detailing Puerto Rico's death penalty cases from 1902 until 1927, see Jacobo Córdova Chirino, *Los que Murieron en la Horca* (México: Gráfica Panamericana, 1954).

For the framers' debate on whether to elevate to the constitution the abolition of the death penalty, see 2 *Diario* 1510–1512, 1520–1522.

Due Process

On how the Puerto Rico Supreme Court circumnavigated around the rule announced in *Lochner v. New York* (1905), see *Pueblo v. García & García* (1915). In *Taboada & Co. v. Rivera Martínez* (1937), the court discusses the timely undoing of the *Lochner* doctrine.

Procedural Due Process

For a nonexhaustive, yet comprehensive, list of the various liberty and property interests enjoying constitutional protection under the procedural due process guarantee found in Article II's Section 7, see José Julián Álvarez González, *Derecho Constitucional de Puerto Rico* (Bogotá: Editorial Temis, 2010), 606–608. In construing what constitutes a protected liberty or property interest for due process purposes, the Puerto Rico Supreme Court's dictates have, on occasion, proven problematic and somewhat arbitrary. While in *Hernández Colón, Romero Barceló v. Policía de Puerto Rico* (2009), the court found that former governors enjoy a constitutionally protected proprietary right over their publicly funded security detail, in *Domínguez Castro v. Estado Libre Asociado* (2010), that same court held that public servants enjoy no such proprietary right over their jobs.

Equal Protection

Since the early days, the issue of whether the constitutional source of equal protection emanated from the Fifth or Fourteenth Amendments remained unclear. In *Union Central Life Insurance Company v. Gromer* (1913) and in *Torruella v. Fernández* (1908), the Puerto Rico Supreme Court left the question unanswered. Six decades later, in *Examining Board of Engineers v. Flores de Otero* (1976), the federal Supreme Court, by voice of Justice Harry Blackmun, "declined to say whether it is the Fifth Amendment or the Fourteenth which provides the protection."

On the applicability of Article II's Section 7 to legal persons, refer to the statement proffered by Delegate Víctor Gutiérrez Franqui, 3 *Diario* 2296.

For the debate on whether disproportionate impact alone, in the absence of invidiousness, triggers an equal protection claim, refer to José Julián Álvarez

González, *Derecho Constitucional de Puerto Rico* (Bogotá: Editorial Temis, 2010), 903–906.

Contracts Clause

For an early treatment of the impairment of contracts protection, see *Quiñones v. Castelló* (1910) ("[T]he provision of the federal Constitution that precludes the impairment of contracts might not be applicable to Puerto Rico [...] In our Organic Act, which is our insular constitution, there is no provision prohibiting the enactment of laws that impair contracts.").

For an illuminating discussion arguing that the supreme court in *Trinidad Hernández v. Estado Libre Asociado* (2013) misapplied the contracts clause found in Article II's Section 7, see Efrén Rivera Ramos and Arturo Hernández González, "Derecho Constitucional," *Revista Jurídica de la Universidad de Puerto Rico* 83 (2014): 653, 676–678.

Right to Privacy

On the origin of the right to privacy found under Article II's Section 8, see *Indulac v. Central General de Trabajadores* (2021); and *Cortés Portalatín v. Hau Colón* (1975). Also refer to Proposition No. 11, submitted to the convention by Delegate Heraclio Rivera Colón on September 25, 1951, available at https://www.academiajurisprudenciapr.org/proposiciones-y-resoluciones-de-la-con vencion-constituyente/. See also José Trías Monge, *Historia Constitucional de Puerto Rico*, vol. 3, 189.

Searches and Seizures

On the historical trajectory of the protection against unreasonable searches and seizures during the Spanish colonial period, see Chief Justice José Trías Monge's observations in *Pueblo v. Dolce* (1976). Madrid had consistently refused to extend to the island the protection against unreasonable searches and seizures, except under the short-lived 1812 Cádiz Constitution and during the fleeting republican period (1873–1874).

On the basis of Article II's Section 10, refer to Delegate Jaime Benítez Rexach's statement: "[...] in this case, as previously, we have used the original source, which is the federal Constitution's Fourth Amendment [...]." 3 *Diario* 1568.

On the adoption by the supreme court of the "open fields" doctrine enunciated by its federal Supreme Court, see Ernesto Chiesa, "Los derechos de los acusados y la factura más ancha," *Revista Jurídica de la Universidad de Puerto Rico* 65 (1996): 83, 139–140.

Right to a Speedy Trial

The right to a speedy trial, as found in the Sixth Amendment, was nonexistent during the Spanish colonial period. Spain's 1872 *Ley de Enjuiciamiento Criminal*, extended to Puerto Rico by royal decree in 1888, did not contain an analogous provision. Upon acceding to the island's governorship in December 1898, General Guy Henry in his inaugural correspondence to President William McKinley referred to the need for speedy justice. For the historical trajectory of the right to a speedy trial in Puerto Rico, see, for instance, Gladys González Colón, "El derecho a juicio rápido en el Procedimiento Criminal," *Revista Jurídica de la Universidad de Puerto Rico* 48 (1979): 645, 647–648. Note that Congress granted the right to a speedy trial to the Philippines before extending it to Puerto Rico, see Section 5 of the 1902 Philippines Organic Act (32 Stat. 691 (1902)).

Right to a Public Trial

The concept of the public trial was not completely foreign to Puerto Rico. It had also been available (at least theoretically) under the 1872 Spanish *Ley de Enjuiciamiento Criminal* made extensive to Puerto Rico by royal decree in 1888. Refer to Justice Miriam Naveira de Rodón's opinion in *El Vocero de Puerto Rico v. Puerto Rico* (1992).

Right to Compulsory Process for Obtaining Witnesses in His or Her Favor

For the historical trajectory of the right to compulsory process for obtaining witnesses, see the opinion of Justice Carlos Irizarry Yunqué in *Pueblo v. Acosta Escobar* (1974).

Right to Jury Trial

For the historical evolution of the right to jury trial in Puerto Rico, see, for instance, the opinion of Justice Rafael Martínez Torres in *Pueblo v. Pablo Casellas Toro* (2017). Also see Carlos Noriega, "El Derecho a Juicio por Jurado en Puerto Rico," *Revista Jurídica de la Universidad Interamericana de Puerto Rico* 11 (1976): 15.

Habeas Corpus; Military Authority Subordinate

On the origins of the writ of habeas corpus in Puerto Rico, see Santos P. Amadeo, "El Hábeas Corpus en Puerto Rico," *Revista Jurídica de la Universidad de Puerto Rico* 17 (1947): 1.

On the debate at the convention with respect to Section 13, refer to the statement proffered by Delegate Samuel R. Quiñones ("in Puerto Rico the power

234 ■ BIBLIOGRAPHICAL ESSAY

to suspend the writ of habeas corpus, under our Constitution, shall exclusively reside in the legislative assembly."). 3 *Diario* 1863.

The command found under Article II's Section 13 requiring that courts entertain habeas petitions both speedily and free of costs was adopted at the urging of Delegate José Veray Hernández. 3 *Diario* 1605.

The inclusion of the language found under Article II's Section 13 establishing the subordination of military authority under civilian control was suggested by Delegate Antonio Reyes Delgado. 2 *Diario* 1385.

Employment and Imprisonment of Children

Legislative activity in the area of child labor antedates the constitution. The Foraker Act, unlike the Jones Act, had not provided for a charter of labor rights. This notwithstanding, local legislation regulating child labor goes as far back as 1913. See P.R. Law No. 42 of March 13, 1913. Three decades later, Puerto Rico's legislature enacted P.R. Law No. 230 of May 12, 1942 (PR ST T.29, § 431) regulating the employment of minors. This statute was still in full force and effect when the constitution was inaugurated in 1952. In the post-1952 period, the local legislature has remained particularly active in this field, amending the 1942 statute on various occasions. For a discussion on the legislature's power to regulate child labor pursuant to its powers under Article II's Section 19, see Attorney General José Fuentes Agostini's analysis in P.R. Op. § Just. 1997-10 (March 26, 1997).

Rights of Employees

On the right to a minimum wage, see, for instance, Jorge Farinacci Fernós, "El Derecho a un salario mínimo razonable," *Revista Estudios Críticos del Derecho* 14 (2018): 145.

Right to Strike, Picket, and Other Legal Concerted Activities

Puerto Rico's first legislation regulating strikes and pickets was enacted on March 1, 1902 (PR ST T. 29, § 41). See, for instance, David M. Helfeld, "La política laboral constitucional del 1952: Sus principios esenciales y los factores que la influenciaron," *Revista Jurídica de la Universidad de Puerto Rico* 72 (2003): 143, 160.

Article II's Section 19: Rights of the People and the Powers of Legislative Assembly

Article II's Section 19 must be distinguished from the Ninth Amendment of the federal Constitution. The Ninth Amendment is a byproduct of the United States' federal superstructure. Drafted by James Madison, its language was meant to guarantee that the pre-constitutional rights enjoyed by the people under the constitutions and laws of the several states did not disappear with the entry into force of the federal Constitution. Section 19's first clause, on the contrary, was not designed to address the complexities ingrained in a system of vertical federalism. Its sole purpose is to leave the door open to the prospective extension to the people of a corpus of unenumerated rights. See, for instance, Russell L. Caplan, "The History and Meaning of the Ninth Amendment," *Virginia Law Review* 69 (1983): 223, 253.

In construing the metes and bounds of the legislature's police powers under Article II's Section 19, the Puerto Rico Supreme Court has followed the blueprint articulated by the U.S. Supreme Court. See, for instance, Justice Erick Kolthoff's opinion in *Domínguez Castro v. Estado Libre Asociado* (2010) ("refers to the power of the legislature to prohibit or regulate certain activities, in order to safeguard the public peace, the morals, the health and the general welfare of the community.").

Article III: The Legislature

The Legislative Assembly

The island's first fleeting encounter with bicameralism coincided with the inauguration of the 1897 Autonomic Charter's dual legislature, made up of an elective house of representatives and an all appointed administrative council. (See Autonomic Charter's Article 4.)

At the convention there was no consensus on whether the legislature should be unicameral or bicameral in nature. Even within the Popular Democratic Party's own majority caucus there was no initial agreement on this issue. Refer to Governor Muñoz Marín's recollection in Néstor Duprey Salgado (ed.), *Conversaciones en el Bohío: Luis Muñoz Marín y Roberto Sánchez Vilella En Sus Propias Palabras* (Trujillo Alto: Fundación Luis Muñoz Marín, 2005), 169–170.

Pursuant to P.R. Law No. 447 of September 23, 2004 (PR ST T.16, § 971), a nonbinding referendum on whether the legislature should activate the constitutional amendment mechanism (found in Article VII's Section 1) for switching to a unicameral system was held on July 10, 2005. Only 22.6 percent of those registered to vote participated. Of those, 83.8 percent (464,010) voted in favor of the unicameral proposal. Following the referendum, the house of representatives refused to pass the concurrent resolution required for amending the constitution. In *Córdova v. Cámara de Representantes* (2007), the supreme court dismissed a mandamus petition demanding that the house of representatives comply with the will of the voters. For a look at the 2005 referendum, see Dennisse M. Dedos Ocasio, "Mandato del pueblo: Su realidad jurídica a través de la Ley del Referéndum sobre el Sistema Cameral de la Asamblea Legislativa," *Revista de Derecho Puertorriqueño* 47 (2008): 323.

The Number of Legislators

The constitution left unchanged the quadrennial electoral cycle found in Section 29 of the Jones Act. Notably, under Section 27 of the Foraker Act, the house of delegates was elected biannually. Thus, the modification effected by the Jones Act was adopted by the framers. Between 1917 and 1952, the island was divided in seven senatorial districts. This distribution remained unaltered until the inauguration of the 1952 Constitution. Refer to Section 26 of the Jones Act. From 1900 until 1917 the island was carved out into seven house districts, with each district electing five house delegates. Refer to Sections 28 and 29 of the Foraker Act. The Jones Act's Section 27 significantly altered this arrangement, dividing the island into thirty-five house districts, with each district electing one representative.

Senatorial and House Districts; Senators and Representatives at Large

In Puerto Rico, the concept of the at-large legislator came into existence with the enactment of the Jones Act. There had been no at-large legislators under the Foraker Act. On the legislator at large, see *Juan Manuel García Passalacqua v. Tribunal Electoral* (1976).

At the convention, the framers rejected the proposal put forward by the University of Puerto Rico's School of Public Administration, which called for the allocation of at-large seats solely on the basis of each party's proportion of the general election votes. Pedro Muñoz Amato (ed.), *La Nueva Constitución de Puerto Rico: Informes a la Convención Constituyente preparados por la Escuela de Administración Pública de la Facultad de Ciencias Sociales* (Río Piedras: Editorial de la Universidad de Puerto Rico, 1954), 264–266.

The convention, instead, kept the same arbitrary system existing prior to the constitution's inauguration. Under this method, which has survived to this day, each at-large candidate accumulates votes across the island's one hundred ten electoral precincts. Each political party determines the order in which the at large candidates appear on the ballot; whoever appears first on the ballot, on a given precinct, gets the straight vote cast under his or her political party's symbol, plus all split votes that might go his or her way. Despite the fact that under Article III's Sections 2 and 3 each political party can nominate up to eleven at-large candidates for each chamber, the majority parties (namely, the New Progressive Party and the Popular Democratic Party) have tended to nominate six, while the minority parties (namely, the Puerto Rico Independence Party, Movimiento Victoria Ciudadana, and Proyecto Dignidad) between one and two for each house. For an overview of this debate, see, for instance, Claudia Delbrey Ortiz, "La elección de la asamblea legislativa y la crisis de representatividad: Las bases legales de la partidocracia," *Revista Jurídica de la Universidad de Puerto Rico* 85 (2016). For a catalogue of concerns with the formula used for allocating at large seats, refer to the observations made by Virgilio Ramos González (member of three different Redistricting Boards under Article III's Section 4) in his 2002 and 2011 particular votes. *Determinación Final de la Junta de Revisión de Distritos Electorales Senatoriales y Representativos* (2011), 21–24, and *Determinación Final de la Junta de Revisión de Distritos Electorales Senatoriales y Representativos* (2002), 35–38.

Board to Revise Senatorial and Representative Districts

The framers' decision to vest in the chief justice the presidency of the redistricting board (see Article III's Section 4) still is the subject of debate. *Determinación Final de la Junta Constitucional de Revisión de Distritos Electorales Senatoriales y Representativos* (1991), 8–9.

On whether a lame duck governor (only days away from leaving office) has authority to nominate members to the redistricting board before the results of the federal census are certified, refer to the legal opinion rendered by Attorney General Anabelle Rodríguez on October 23, 2001, in *Determinación Final de la Junta Constitucional de Revisión de Distritos Electorales Senatoriales y Representativos* (2002), Appendix 1. Article III's Section 4 does not appear to place any limits on the governor's appointment power nor does it require that the two additional board members belong to any of the island's principal political parties. For an analysis of the constitutional standard governing the redistricting exercise, see Antonio García Padilla, "La Sección 4 del Artículo III de la Constitución del Estado Libre Asociado de Puerto Rico," *Revista Jurídica de la Universidad de Puerto Rico* 65 (1996): 489; and Federico Hernández Denton and Alfonso Martínez Piovanetti, "La Redistribución Electoral en Puerto Rico: Un Gran Acierto de Nuestro Ordenamiento Constitucional Democrático," *Revista Jurídica de la Universidad de Puerto Rico* 82 (2013): 13.

The Powers of Each House

Since 1952, the Puerto Rico Legislature has used the power of expulsion only occasionally. The senate expelled Nicolás Nogueras in 1996, while the house of representatives removed Iván Rodríguez Traverso and Ramón Rodríguez Ruiz in 2010 and 2018, respectively.

Privileges and Immunities of Senate and House Members

Legislative immunities were first introduced in Puerto Rico pursuant to local legislation enacted on February 21, 1902. (PR ST T.2, §§ 12 and 13).

238 ■ BIBLIOGRAPHICAL ESSAY

The Legislature's Daily Record, Investigative Power, and Anti-Rider Limitation

The first (unsuccessful) attempt at publishing a daily record was led by Speaker Manuel F. Rossy in 1903.

The publication of the daily record, moreover, does not preclude the legislature from informing the public of its proceedings and initiatives by using additional modes of mass communication. *Romero Barceló v. Hernández Agosto* (1984).

The outer limits of the legislature's investigative power are set by the bill of rights. For a recent manifestation of the legislature's oversight authority, refer to the various resolutions introduced in the house of representatives, at the height of the COVID-19 crisis, with the purpose of investigating the allegations of impropriety surrounding the Puerto Rico Health Department's purchase of rapid testing kits for around $40 million from companies with no experience in the medical supply industry. See R. de la C. 1745 (April 6, 2020).

For the scope of the anti-rider mandate found under Article III's Section 17, refer to Delegate Luis Negrón López's statement in 2 *Diario* 879. Also see *Herrero y Otros v. Estado Libre Asociado* (2010).

Joint Resolutions

The Jones Act's silence on the proper place of the joint resolution, vis-à-vis ordinary legislation, had led to the careless practice of indiscriminately legislating by bill or joint resolution, despite the fact that pursuant to Section 34, "[n]o law [could] be passed except by bill." See Delegate Luis Negrón López's statement attesting to the existence of this confusion in 2 *Diario* 858. This confusion was finally put to rest by the U.S. Court of Appeals for the First Circuit in *Sancho v. Valiente & Co.* (1937) (affirming Puerto Rico Supreme Court's decision that the local legislature could only impose a tax by passing a law not a joint resolution).

Passage of Bills; Approval by Governor

On the historical trajectory of the legislature's power to override the governor's veto, the following observations are pertinent: under Section 31 of the Foraker Act, the house of delegates and the executive council enjoyed authority to override the governor's veto. Congress took that power away with the enactment of the Jones Act. From then on, until the inauguration of the constitution, the island's legislature had no authority to go over the governor's veto. Under the Jones Act, if a bill was overridden by the legislature and the governor yet again disapproved it, it would only become law if signed or not vetoed by the president within ninety days from the time the governor transmitted the vetoed measure to the president. See Section 34 of the Jones Act. For the mechanics of the presidential veto, refer to *Parrilla v. Martín* (1948) (affirming the constitutionality of President Truman's veto of a bill declaring Spanish the official language of the island's public school system).

The legislature's first override of a gubernatorial veto took place in 2005 during the uneasy cohabitation of the Popular Democratic Party (then in control of the executive branch) and the New Progressive Party (then in control of the legislative branch). In 2016 and 2018, the legislature, controlled by the sitting governors' same political party, overrode their vetoes.

Line-Item Veto

It is safe to conclude that Congress, in enacting the Jones Act, vested in the governor the line-item veto in order to limit the political ascendancy of the island's fully elective legislature. Refer to Speaker José de Diego's vigorous opposition to the line-item veto in *José de Diego, Obras Completas*, vol. 2 (San Juan: Instituto de Cultura Puertorriqueña, 1973), 295. The archival record reveals that the line-item veto language found in the Jones Act came from Article IV's Section 12 of the 1876 Colorado Constitution, unsurprisingly, due to the fact that Colorado's Senator John Shafroth was the co-author of the Jones Act. José Trías Monge, *Historia Constitucional de Puerto Rico*, vol. 2, 100.

Impeachment Proceedings

On the scope of the impeachment mechanism, see Carlos Ramos González, "El proceso de residenciamiento," *Amicus: Revista de Política Pública y Legislación Universidad Interamericana de Puerto Rico* 2 (2019): 135.

At the convention, Delegate José Trías Monge argued that impeachment is a political process, in no way reviewable by a court of law. 3 *Diario* 1801. Delegate Víctor Gutiérrez Franqui shared Trías Monge's view; refer to his statement in 1 *Diario* 459. For a critique of the supreme court's apparent lack of self-restraint, and departure from *Nixon v. United States* (1993), see José Julián Álvarez González, *Derecho Constitucional de Puerto Rico* (Bogotá: Editorial Temis, 2010), 228–229.

Comptroller

On the nature of the comptroller's unique constitutional role, refer to Delegate Luis Negrón López's statement in 2 *Diario* 920. Also see Ileana Colón Carlo, "El ámbito de investigación del contralor de Puerto Rico," *Revista Jurídica de la Universidad Interamericana de Puerto Rico* 29 (1995): 743.

Pursuant to P.R. Law No. 9 of July 24, 1952 (PR ST T.2, §§ 72–73), the comptroller must be both a U.S. citizen and a bona fide resident of Puerto Rico, at least thirty years of age. The desirability of amending P.R. Law No. 9, for the purpose of requiring that no person other than a certified public accountant of ample technical expertise hold the office of comptroller, still is the subject of public debate.

Article IV: The Executive

The Governor

On the unitary nature of the executive branch, see, for instance, William Vázquez Irizarry, "El poder del gobernador de Puerto Rico y el uso de órdenes ejecutivas," *Revista Jurídica de la Universidad de Puerto Rico* 76 (2007): 951.

On the concept of the governor-arbitrator during the Jones Act period, see José Trías Monge, *Historia Constitucional de Puerto Rico*, vol. 3, 107. Also see William Vázquez Irizarry, "El poder del gobernador de Puerto Rico y el uso de órdenes ejecutivas," *Revista Jurídica de la Universidad de Puerto Rico* 76 (2007): 951, 980.

On the reorganization of the executive branch after Congress's enactment of the 1947 Elective Governor Act, see Marshall E. Dimock, Pedro Muñoz Amato, John D. Corcoran, Benjamín Ortiz Ortiz, and Roberto de Jesús, *La reorganización de la Rama Ejecutiva* (Río Piedras: Editorial de la Universidad de Puerto Rico, 1951).

Powers and Duties of Governor

For a look at the inherent powers debate, see José Julián Álvarez González, *Derecho Constitucional de Puerto Rico* (Bogotá: Editorial Temis, 2010), 256.

On the governor's power to make recess appointments, refer to Christian Cortés Feliciano, "Nombramientos de receso sucesivos: Despoje de la facultad de consejo y consentimiento del Senado," *Revista Jurídica de la Universidad de Puerto Rico* 86 (2017): 192.

Since the inauguration of the 1952 Constitution, no governor has declared the martial law. Interestingly, Governor Muñoz Marín did not declare the martial law in October 1950 during the nationalist uprising. Muñoz Marín, *Memorias 1940–1952* (San Germán: Editorial de la Universidad Interamericana de Puerto Rico, 1992), 239.

On the governor's pardon power, see José Julián Álvarez González, *Derecho Constitucional de Puerto Rico* (Bogotá: Editorial Temis, 2010), 239–240. Also see *Pueblo v. Albizu* (1955) and *Emanuelli v. Tribunal* (1953). Upon leaving office on January 2, 2021, Governor Wanda Vázquez granted clemency to thirty-one individuals.

Appointment of Secretaries

The Puerto Rico Constitution does not make an explicit distinction between principal and inferior officers. This omission has opened the door to potentially unconstitutional scenarios. For instance, in establishing the Puerto Rico Public-Private Partnership Authority and the Puerto Rico Fiscal Agency and Financial

Advisory Authority in 2009 and 2017, respectively, the legislature decided that the board directors of each of these instrumentalities would be appointed on the basis of a mechanism that bypasses the appointment and confirmation process required under Article IV's Section 4. While some of these board directors are appointed by the governor, others are designated by the legislative leadership and none of them goes to the senate for its advice and consent. On the constitutional infirmities of the above-referenced mechanisms, see, for instance, Aníbal Acevedo Vilá, *Separación de Poderes en Puerto Rico: Entre la teoría y la práctica* (San Juan: Ediciones Situm, 2018), 126–133.

On the role, duties, and challenges facing the governor's assistants, see Roberto Sánchez Vilella, *Función y Acción de la Rama Ejecutiva* (San Juan: Oficina del Gobernador, 1965).

Article V: The Judiciary

The Supreme Court

On the history of the supreme court, see Luis Rafael Rivera, *La Justicia en sus Manos: Historia del Tribunal Supremo de Puerto Rico* (San Juan: Ediciones Santillana Inc., 2007). Also refer to Carmelo Delgado Cintrón, *Derecho y Colonialismo: La Trayectoria Histórica del Derecho Puertorriqueño* (Río Piedras: Editorial Edil Inc., 1988); and José Trías Monge, *Sociedad, Derecho y Justicia* (Río Piedras: Editorial de la Universidad de Puerto Rico, 1986).

For the organization of Puerto Rico's *Audiencia Territorial* at the time of the 1898 invasion, see Articles 16–19 of the *Compilación de las disposiciones orgánicas de la administración de la justicia en las provincias y posesiones ultramarinas* (Madrid: M. Minuesa de los Ríos, Impresor, 1891). On the establishment of the *Audiencia Territorial*, see Gerardo Carlo Altieri, *Justicia y Gobierno: La Audiencia de Puerto Rico* (Sevilla: Consejo Superior de Investigaciones Científicas, 2007).

The shared history of the U.S. Court of Appeals for the First Circuit and Puerto Rico goes back to January 28, 1915, when President Woodrow Wilson signed legislation assigning Puerto Rico to the First Circuit. See 38 Stat. 803 (1915). Two years later, under Section 43 of the Jones Act, Congress provided for an appeal as of right to the First Circuit from the final decisions of the Puerto Rico Supreme Court. Interestingly, Congress treated the Puerto Rico Supreme Court with far less deference than its Filipino counterpart. Section 26 of the second Philippines Organic Act provided for direct recourse to the U.S. Supreme Court for the review of the final judgments and decrees of the Philippines Supreme Court.

For an illuminating commentary on the uneasy interaction between the Puerto Rican Supreme Court and the First Circuit during this period, see Stephen Breyer, "The Relationship between the Federal Courts and the Puerto Rico Legal System," *Revista Jurídica de la Universidad de Puerto Rico* 53

(1984): 307. For a detailed account of the process leading to the abrogation of the appeal as of right to the First Circuit from the final judgments of the Puerto Rico Supreme Court, refer to José Trías Monge, *Historia Constitucional de Puerto Rico*, vol. 4, 175–177. Also see U.S. Public Law 87-189 (August 30, 1961).

The Puerto Rico Supreme Court ceased to function as an European court of cassation pursuant to legislation enacted on March 12, 1903. See *Report of the Commission to Revise and Compile the Laws of Porto Rico*, H.R. Doc. No. 52, 57th Cong. 1st Sess. 10 (1901), 113. The supreme court would now exercise unencumbered authority to pass review over issues of both fact and law. Moreover, the format itself of the court's decisions was greatly transformed, as concurring and dissenting opinions would now be made available to the public.

The Eminent Domain Court was a special court established pursuant to P.R. Law No. 223 of May 15, 1948 (PR ST T.32, § 2914), under the aegis of the Puerto Rico District Court.

Unified Judicial System; Creation, Venue, and Organization of Courts

The drive toward a unified court system was deeply influenced by the 1947 New Jersey Constitution, the 1873 English Judicature Act, and, among other sources, the writings of Harvard Law School's Professor Roscoe Pound. See, for instance, Roscoe Pound, "Organization of Courts," *Journal of American Judicature Society* 11 (1927): 69.

On the unification of the court system, refer to the statement proffered by Delegate Víctor Gutiérrez Franqui on the floor of the convention: "This means that the jurisdiction of the supreme court is beyond the reach of the legislative assembly. It is, however, the court's competence that falls within its reach. [...] the legislative assembly will not be able to prevent cases from getting heard by the supreme court." 1 *Diario* 592 (Author's translation).

The convention's design of the island's judicial system still reflected the basic structural pyramid established by General George Davis in 1899 under U.S. General Order No. 118, whereby district courts coexisted with municipal courts, the latter ones being inferior in rank.

For a contemporaneous comparative critique of the 1950 Judiciary Act vis-à-vis the 1952 Judiciary Act, see Charles E. Clark and William Rogers, "The New Judiciary Act of Puerto Rico: A Definitive Court Reorganization," *Yale Law Journal* 61 (1952): 1147.

The Original Jurisdiction of Supreme Court

The writ of prohibition traces its origins back to English common law and was imported to the island by local legislation on March 10, 1904 (PR ST T.32, § 3461).

On the origins of the writ of prohibition in Puerto Rico, see, for instance, Domingo Toledo Álamo, "Autos inhibitorios en Puerto Rico," *Revista Jurídica de la Universidad de Puerto Rico* 15 (1946): 245.

The writ of quo warranto, enacted on March 1, 1902, preceded all other common law extraordinary remedies, except for the writ of habeas corpus. (PR ST T.32, § 339).

The writ of mandamus was established pursuant to local legislation on March 12, 1903. (PR ST T.32, § 3421).

The convention was persuaded by Harvard Law's Professor Henry Hart to limit the supreme court's original competence to habeas corpus petitions alone. 3 *Diario* 1653.

On the court's treatment of extraordinary writs, see Miguel Velázquez Rivera, "No ha lugar," *Revista Jurídica de la Universidad de Puerto Rico* 51 (1982): 453; and Aurea Rodríguez Hernández, "El Tribunal Supremo de Puerto Rico en el ejercicio de su jurisdicción original," *Revista Jurídica de la Universidad de Puerto Rico* 52 (1983): 897.

Rules of Evidence and of Civil and Criminal Procedure

On the court's rule-making authority, refer to Jeannette Ramos Buonomo, "La naturaleza del poder del Tribunal Supremo de Puerto Rico para adoptar reglas de Procedimiento Civil y Criminal y Reglas de Evidencia," *Revista Jurídica de la Universidad de Puerto Rico* 33 (1964): 391.

Chief Justice to Direct Administration and Appoint Administrative Director

On the chief justice's role as administrative head of the judiciary, refer to Delegate Ernesto Ramos Antonini's statement: ("[...] responsibility for the administration of the courts falls upon the chief justice [...].") 3 *Diario* 1667.

On the chief justice's constitutional authority to appoint the administrative director of the judiciary branch, see 1 *Diario* 616 and 3 *Diario* 1666.

The convention defined those administrative issues falling within the aegis of Article V's Section 7 rather expansively: compiling statistical data, rendering reports, leasing real estate, purchasing equipment, retaining professional services, granting vacations and licenses to employees, authorizing disbursement of funds, preparing budgets, assigning and transferring judges, and supervising the internal governance of the inferior tribunals, among others. This list is nonexhaustive, as the convention itself clearly emphasized. 4 *Diario* 2613 (Author's translation).

244 ■ BIBLIOGRAPHICAL ESSAY

Appointment of Judges, Officers, and Employees

During the Spanish period, the magistrates (*oidores*) of the *Audiencia Territorial* were royal appointees, recommended to the crown by the council of indies. Following the transfer of sovereignty in 1898, the justices of the newly established supreme court were appointed by the U.S. military governors. The Foraker Act put an end to this practice vesting in the president of the United States, with the advice and consent of the federal Senate, the power to appoint the justices of the Puerto Rico Supreme Court.

Under the Jones Act and Elective Governor Act the power to appoint the justices of the supreme court remained in the hands of the president. From 1947 until the constitution's inauguration in 1952, President Harry Truman appointed two chief justices (Ángel de Jesús and Roberto H. Todd, Jr.) and two associate justices (Borinquen Marrero and Luis Negrón Fernández). Justice Borinquen Marrero's appointment was made in March 1947, close to four months before the enactment of the Elective Governor Act.

Between 1900 and 1917, all district judges were appointed by the governor, with the advice and consent of the executive council, as required by Section 33 of the Foraker Act. Section 49 of the Jones Act went further, explicitly requiring the governor to appoint all inferior court judges (i.e., district judges, municipal judges, and judges of the peace) with the advice and consent of the newly established senate.

While not completely foreign to the concept of elected judges, both the Popular Democratic Party and Statehood Party delegations chose not to go down that path; tossing out the proposal put forward by the Socialist Party, which called for the election of the justices of the supreme court. See Proposition No. 94 (October 11, 1951), in *Proposiciones y Resoluciones de la Convención Constituyente de Puerto Rico*, 198, 200–201. Between 1904 and 1917, municipal judges across the island were elected by the voters. This experience, however, had proven highly unsatisfactory, due in no small measure to the pernicious effects of political patronage. See José Trías Monge, *El Sistema Judicial de Puerto Rico* (Río Piedras: Editorial de la Universidad de Puerto Rico, 1978), 64; and Carmelo Delgado Cintrón, *Derecho y Colonialismo*, 186–187.

Retirement of Judges

A retirement system for judges was first established in 1911 by local legislation. P.R. Law No. 71 of March 9, 1911 (PR ST T.32, § 1). During the Spanish colonial period, the judges' retirement benefits were governed by the same rules applicable to the Spanish civil service. See Article 160 of the 1891 *Compilación de las Disposiciones Orgánicas de la Administración de Justicia en las Provincias y Posesiones Ultramarinas*.

The judiciary's retirement system, as required by Article V's Section 10, was enacted into law in 1954. Refer to P.R. Law No. 12 of October 19, 1954 (PR ST

T.4, § 246). See José Julián Álvarez González, "La asamblea legislativa de Puerto Rico y las pensiones de los jueces del Tribunal Supremo: Reseña de un conflicto con la independencia judicial," *Revista Jurídica de la Universidad de Puerto Rico* 56 (1987): 265.

Under the Foraker and Jones Acts, presidential nominations to the Puerto Rico Supreme Court were implicitly considered lifetime appointments. Note that in the pre-1952 period, a handful of justices, such as Chief Justice José Conrado Hernández (72) and Associate Justice Adolph Wolf (71), served beyond their seventieth birthday. See Luis Rafael Rivera, *La justicia en sus manos: Historia del Tribunal Supremo de Puerto Rico* (San Juan: Ediciones Santillana, Inc., 2007) 39, 61.

Removal of Judges

On the removal of lower court judges, the framers paid heed to the Alabama, Louisiana, New Jersey, and Texas Constitutions. Antonio Fernós Isern, *Original Intent in the Constitution of Puerto Rico: Notes and Comments Submitted to the Congress of the United States* 2nd ed. (San Juan: LEXIS-NEXIS, 2002) 97. Also refer to Rules 12–20 of the Rules of Judicial Discipline (*Reglas de Disciplina Judicial*), available at https://www.poderjudicial.pr/Documentos/Supremo/Reglas/Reglas-Disciplina-Judicial.pdf. Note that inferior court judges can be removed from office on grounds of illegality, violation of ethical standards, gross negligence, manifest professional malpractice, and/or mental or physical unfitness to serve in the judiciary. See Rule 3 of the Rules of Judicial Discipline.

Political Activity by Judges

In drafting Article V's Section 12, the framers intended to prevent in future a repetition of the maneuver undertaken by Chief Justice Martín Travieso, who, while at the court, accepted the Statehood Party's nomination for governor and only left the court on August 31, 1948 (two months prior to the November 2, 1948, general election). Chief Justice Travieso lost the race at the hands of Luis Muñoz Marín, who went on to become Puerto Rico's first elected governor. For a biography of Chief Justice Travieso, see Luis Rafael Rivera, *La Justicia en sus manos: Historia del Tribunal Supremo de Puerto Rico* (San Juan: Ediciones Santillana Inc., 2007), 94. Also see José Trías Monge, *El Choque de Dos Culturas Jurídicas en Puerto Rico* (Orford, NH: Equity Publishing Company, 1991), 195–196.

Article VI: General Provisions

Municipalities

With the exceptions of Jayuya (1911), Guaynabo (1912), Guánica (1914), Villalba (1917), Cataño (1927), Canóvanas (1970), and Florida (1971), all

246 ■ BIBLIOGRAPHICAL ESSAY

other municipalities were in full legal existence by the time the Spanish Crown transferred its sovereignty over the island to the United States. Note that the town of Barros was renamed Orocovis in 1928 and that Río Piedras was annexed to San Juan following a popular referendum held in 1951. For a classical study of the conditions of the municipalities *circa* 1898, see Cayetano Coll y Toste, *Reseña del Estado Social, Económico e Industrial de la Isla de Puerto Rico Al Tomar Posesión de Ella los Estados Unidos* (San Juan: Imprenta de la Correspondencia, 1899). Also refer to the *Report of the Military Governor of Porto Rico on Civil Affairs* (Washington, D.C.: Government Printing Office, 1902), 37–39.

The 1898 invasion led to a significant regression in municipal affairs. Pursuant to Article 52 of the 1897 Autonomic Charter, which was in force and effect in Puerto Rico by the time General Nelson Miles disembarked in Guánica, the municipalities had been explicitly delegated full authority to articulate their own policies and regulations with respect to public instruction, highways by land, sea and rivers, public health, local budgets, and the appointment and removal of their respective officers. Under Article 62 of the 1897 Charter, the island's autonomic legislature had no legal authority to abrogate or nullify the powers entrusted to the municipalities under Article 52. Note that the mandate for municipal devolution, included in the 1897 Charter derived from Article 321 of the short-lived Cádiz Constitution of 1812. The immediate consequences of the 1898 invasion were the dismantling of the municipal autonomic regime and the importation to Puerto Rico's municipal affairs of the so-called Dillon Rule then in vogue in the United States—which viewed the municipality as a mere appendage or creature of the state—devoid of distinct legal personality. See, for instance, Alfonso Martínez Piovanetti, "Derecho Municipal de Puerto Rico: La Corte Hernández Denton y la distribución vertical de poderes gubernamentales," *Revista Jurídica de la Universidad de Puerto Rico* 83 (2014): 945.

Power of Taxation; Power to Contract Debts

On the taxing power of the municipalities before the inauguration of the constitution, see, for instance, Manuel Rodríguez Ramos, "En torno de la facultad impositiva de los municipios en Puerto Rico," *Revista Jurídica de la Universidad de Puerto Rico* 18 (1949): 207.

On the 1961 amendment to the debt ceiling formula found in Article VI's Section 2, see Carlos Ramos González, "Disposiciones sobre la deuda pública en la Constitución del Estado Libre Asociado de Puerto Rico: Breve reflexión histórica-constitucional," *Revista Jurídica de la Universidad de Puerto Rico* 85 (2016): 705.

Extraconstitutional debt refers to public debt issued by public corporations (and other public entities legally autonomous from the central government), which the Puerto Rico government is not constitutionally required to satisfy under Article VI's Section 2. For a definition of extraconstitutional debt, see, for instance, José Julián Álvarez González, *Derecho Constitucional*

(Bogotá: Editorial Temis, 2010), 246–247. Also see Luis Muñiz Argüelles, "El Banco Gubernamental de Fomento y la organización de la deuda pública puertorriqueña," *Revista Jurídica de la Universidad de Puerto Rico* 65 (1996): 661.

Rule of Taxation to Be Uniformed

The tax uniformity clause had first appeared under Section 9 of the first draft of the bill of rights submitted to the convention by Delegate Jaime Benítez Rexach on December 14, 1951. By the time the convention finalized the drafting of the constitution, the convention's committee on style had moved it to Article VI's Section 3. 4 *Diario* 2566.

On the tax uniformity requirement established under Section 2 of the Jones Act (which was analogous to the one the framers included in Article VI's Section 3), see *Mendoza v. Junta de Comisionados de San Juan* (1934) (nullifying a municipal tax imposed by the City of San Juan on all meat coming from the island's other municipalities as contrary to the Jones Act's tax uniformity requirement.)

Elections

In Puerto Rico it is statutorily (not constitutionally) required that general elections be held on the first Tuesday after the first Monday of November. Except for the 1899 municipal election and the 1917 general election (held immediately after Congress's enactment of the Jones Act), all general elections in Puerto Rico have coincided with the American presidential election.

Whether the legislature can change the election of the resident commissioner to a day other than the first Tuesday after the first Monday of November is an issue that has remained unexplored. Section 36 of the 1950 Federal Relations Act, contrary to Section 29 of the Jones Act, makes no mention to a specific election date for the resident commissioner. Yet it establishes that the resident commissioner's term expires on January 3, following the general election. It is not unreasonable to suggest that Congress purposefully chose not to specify a resident commissioner election date, leaving that issue to the local legislature alone. The proposition that the Uniform Election Date Act passed by Congress in 1875 (2 U.S.C. § 7) inadvertently trumps the Federal Relations Act's design and, hence, precludes Puerto Rico's legislature from changing the election date of the resident commissioner seems improbable.

Failure to Make Appropriations

The immediate catalyst behind Congress's enactment of the Olmsted Act (36 Stat. 11 (1909)) was the budgetary crisis of 1909 and the political branches' inability to agree on a budget. Because the Foraker Act had not provided a mechanism for addressing such a rupture, Congress amended it establishing that in

248 ■ BIBLIOGRAPHICAL ESSAY

case of an impasse the appropriations from the previous fiscal year would be automatically reassigned "for the support of the government." The blueprint of the Olmsted Act was found in both Section 54 of the 1900 Hawaii Organic Act (31 Stat. 141 (1900)) and Section 7 of the 1902 Philippines Organic Act (32 Stat. 691 (1902)).

Appropriations Not to Exceed Revenues

On the construction of Article VI's Section 7, from the vantage point of an economist, see Carlos Colón de Armas, "La Constitución de Puerto Rico y su requisito de un presupuesto balanceado," *Revista Jurídica de la Universidad de Puerto Rico* 85 (2016): 819.

Use of Public Property and Funds

For a critique of the supreme court's most recent construction of the "public purpose" requirement found under Article VI's Section 9, see the dissenting opinions authored by Justice Ángel Colón Pérez in *Aponte Rosario v. Presidente Comisión Estatal de Elecciones* (2020) and *Rosario Rodríguez v. Rosselló Nevares* (2021).

Land Holding by Corporations

On the catalysts leading to Congress's enactment of the 1900 Joint Resolution, close to three weeks after President William McKinley signed the Foraker Act, see Keith S. Rosenn, "Puerto Rican Land Reform: The History of an Instructive Experiment," *Yale Law Journal* (1963): 73.

Flag, Seal, and Anthem

Puerto Rico's flag was inspired in the Cuban emblem designed by Narciso López in 1851. For an accurate description of Narciso López's flag, see, for instance, Juan Bosch, *Cuba, la isla fascinante* (Santiago de Chile: Editorial Universitaria, S.A., 1955), 102. Puerto Rico's flag, like Cuba's, is rectangular in form, with five horizontal stripes and next to an "equilateral triangle with a five-point star." The only distinction is that Cuba's triangle is red, while its stripes are blue and white, and Puerto Rico's triangle is blue with red and white stripes. See P.R. Law No. 1 of July 24, 1952. Puerto Rico's flag was first displayed on December 22, 1895, in New York City's Chimney Corner Hall.

The flag stands as a symbol of the Puerto Rican nation. See José de Diego "Ultima Actio," in *Cantos de Rebeldía* (Barcelona: Casa Editorial Maucci, 1916), 193 ("Colgadme al pecho, después que muera, mi verde escudo en un relicario; cubridme todo con el sudario, con el sudario de tres colores de mi bandera."); and Ivonne Acosta, *La palabra como delito: Los discursos por los que condenaron a Pedro Albizu Campos* (Harrisonburg: Editorial Cultural, 1993), 155–163.

With respect to Puerto Rico's anthem, see P.R. Law No. 2 of July 24, 1952 ("La tierra de Borinquen donde he nacido yo, es un jardín florido de mágico primor. Un cielo siempre nítido le sirve de dosel y dan arrullos plácidos las olas a sus pies. Cuando a sus playas llegó Colón exclamó, lleno de admiración: ¡Oh! ¡Oh! ¡Oh! Esta es la linda tierra que busco yo; es Borinquen la hija, la hija del mar y el sol, del mar y el sol, del mar y el sol, del mar y el sol, del mar y el sol.").

With respect to Puerto Rico's coat of arms, see P.R. Law No. 7 of August 8, 1952 ("The coat of arms of the Commonwealth of Puerto Rico shall be 'a green shield' bearing a silver lamb resting upon a red book and bearing a flag with cross and banner, as shown in the device of Saint John, and having for border castles, lions, flags and crosses of Jerusalem, and having for a device an "F" and "Y" with its crowns and yoke and arrows, and a motto around it as follows: *Joannes est nomen ejus.*").

Under the first draft of Article VI's Section 15, future changes to the flag, coat of arms, or anthem would have required clearing the same steps necessary for amending the constitution under Article VII. At the convention, the framers agreed on the present formula. Refer to the statements proffered by Delegates Antonio Reyes Delgado and Yldefonso Solá Morales at 3 *Diario* 2098–2099. For the first draft of Article VI's Section 15, see 4 *Diario* 2615.

Oath of Public Officials and Employees

The expansion of the oath requirement came through an amendment introduced by Delegate Samuel R. Quiñones. See 3 *Diario* 2118.

Natural Resources; Historic or Artistic Sites; Penal Institutions; Delinquents

On the court's approach to environmental claims, see Luis E. Rodríguez Rivera, "No todo lo que brilla es oro: Apuntes sobre el desarrollo de la revisión judicial en la jurisprudencia ambiental a la luz de la constitucionalización de la política pública ambiental puertorriqueña," *Revista Jurídica de la Universidad de Puerto Rico* 72 (2003): 113 (2003); and Ernesto Chiesa, *Comentarios a la ponencia de la jueza Fiol Matta sobre el estándar de revisión judicial en casos ambientales, Revista Jurídica de la Universidad de Puerto Rico* 72 (2003), 93.

Article VII: Amendments to the Constitution

Proposal of Amendments

For a critique of the court's application of the "sole purpose" doctrine in *Berríos Martínez v. Gobernador* (1994), see José Julián Álvarez González and Ana Isabel García Saúl, "Derecho Constitucional," *Revista Jurídica de la Universidad de Puerto Rico* 65 (1996): 799.

The Constitutional Convention

A very pertinent distinction must be drawn between the constitutional convention contemplated under Article VII's Section 2 and the so-called status assembly. The second mechanism, which is eminently political in nature, is not bound by any of the procedural requirements established under Article VII. See Carlos Gorrín Peralta, "Autodeterminación del Pueblo de Puerto Rico mediante la Asamblea Constitucional de Status," *Revista Jurídica de la Universidad de Puerto Rico* 71 (2002): 809. The Obama administration's Task Force on Puerto Rico's Status identified the status assembly method as one of the various procedural vehicles available for disentangling the island's status conundrum. See *Report by the President's Task Force on Puerto Rico's Status* (March 2011).

On the constitutional convention mechanism, see, for instance, Jorge Farinacci Fernós, "Cómo cambiar nuestra ley suprema: Un análisis del Artículo VII de la Constitución de Puerto Rico," *AMICUS* 2 (September 2019).

For a catalogue of amendment proposals to the 1952 Constitution, see, for instance, Aníbal Acevedo Vilá, *Crisis en la agenda, Agenda para la crisis* (San Juan: Biblio Services, 2019).

Article IX: Transitory Provisions

Commonwealth of Puerto Rico Translates to Estado Libre Asociado

Pursuant to Resolution No. 22 (dated February 4, 1952), the constitutional convention established that the Spanish translation of "Commonwealth of Puerto Rico" would be "Estado Libre Asociado de Puerto Rico." For the English version of Resolution No. 22, see Antonio Fernós Isern, *Original Intent in the Constitution of Puerto Rico: Notes and Comments Submitted to the Congress of the United States* 2nd ed. (San Juan: LEXIS-NEXIS, 2002), 127–128.

■ LIST OF CASES

A

Acevedo Vilá v. Aponte Hernández, 168 D.P.R. 443 (2006) **129–30, 156–57**
Acevedo Vilá v. Meléndez, 164 D.P.R. 875 (2005) **143**
Administración de Terrenos de Puerto Rico v. Ponce Bayland Enterprises, 207 D.P.R. 586 (2021) **83**
Albino v. Municipality of Guayanilla, 925 F. Supp. 2d 186 (D. Puerto Rico 2013) **65**
Allgeyer v. Louisiana, 165 U.S. 578 (1897) **30n. 183–31**
Alvarado Pacheco v. Estado Libre Asociado de Puerto Rico, 188 D.P.R. 594 (2013) **150, 157**
Ambach v. Norwick, 441 U.S. 68 (1979) **62**
American Insurance Co. v. Canter, 26 U.S. 511 (1828) **30**
Ángel Febus Rodríguez v. Enrique Questell, 660 F. Supp. 2d 157 (D. Puerto Rico 2009) **65**
Aníbal Acevedo Vilá v. José Meléndez Ortiz, 164 D.P.R. 875 (2005) **56**
Aponte Martínez v. Lugo, 100 D.P.R. 282 (1971) **70**
Aponte Rosario v. Presidente Comisión Estatal de Elecciones, 205 D.P.R. 407 (2020) **53–54, 107, 177–78, 248**
Arbona v. Torres, 24 D.P.R. 450 (1916) **62–63**
Arizona v. Youngblood, 488 U.S. 51 (1988) **84**
Arroyo v. Rattan Specialties, Inc., 117 D.P.R. 35 (1986) **60–61**
Asociación de Academias y Colegios Cristianos de Puerto Rico v. Departamento de Educación, 135 D.P.R. 150 (1994) **73**
Asociación de Fotoperiodistas de Puerto Rico v. Thomas Rivera Schatz, 180 D.P.R. 920 (2011) **122**
Asociación de Maestros v. Departamento de Educación, 200 D.P.R. 974 (2018) **74**
Asociación de Maestros v. José Arsenio Torres, 137 D.P.R. 528 (1994) **74**
Asociación de Maestros v. Sistema de Retiro, 190 D.P.R. 854 (2014) **80**
Asociación de Periodistas v. González, 127 D.P.R. 704 (1991) **152**
Aurelius Investment, LLC v. Commonwealth of Puerto Rico, 915 F.3d 838 (1st Cir. 2019) **33**
Autoridad de Carreteras v. Adquisición de 8,554.741 Metros, 172 D.P.R. 278 (2007) **83**
A.D. Miranda, Inc. v. Secretario de Justicia, 83 D.P.R. 735 (1961) **103**

B

Báez Cancel v. Santos Rivera Pérez, 100 D.P.R. 982 (1972) **65**
Báez Galib v. Comisión Estatal de Elecciones, 152 D.P.R. 382 (2000) **53, 107, 177–78**
Baker v. Carr, 369 U.S. 186 (1962) **112, 132**
Baldwin v. New York, 399 U.S. 66 (1970) **93**
Balzac v. Puerto Rico, 258 U.S. 298 (1922) **31, 32–33, 32n. 203–33, 34, 77, 214**
Bearden v. Georgia, 461 U.S. 660 (1983) **97**
Belk Arce v. Martínez, 146 D.P.R. 215 (1998) **81–82**
Beltrán Cintrón v. Puerto Rico, 204 D.P.R. 89 (2020) **103**
Berríos Martínez v. Gobernador, 137 D.P.R. 195 (1994) **190–91, 249**
Betancourt v. Gobernador, 119 D.P.R. 435 (1987) **140–41**
Blockburger v. United States, 284 U.S. 299 (1932) **95**
Boumediene v. Bush, 553 U.S. 723 (2008) **45**

252 ■ LIST OF CASES

Boy Scouts of America v. Dale, 530 U.S. 640 (2000) **75**
Brandenburg v. Ohio, 395 U.S. 444 (1969) **75**
Brau v. Estado Libre Asociado, 190 D.P.R. 315, 353-354 (2014) **162–63**
Brown v. Board of Education, 347 U.S. 483 (1954) **62**
Brunet Justiniano v. Hernández Colón, 130 D.P.R. 248 (1992) **98–99**
Burdick v. Takushi, 504 U.S. 428 (1992) **67**
Burgos v. Comisión Estatal de Elecciones, 197 D.P.R. 914 (2017) **67, 107, 203**

C

Cabassa v. Rivera, 68 D.P.R. 706 (1948) **168**
Calero-Toledo v. Pearson Yacht Leasing Co., 416 U.S. 663 (1974) **38, 38n. 245**
Califano v. Torres, 435 U.S. 1 (1978) **38–39, 38n. 249–39, 45**
Castro v. Tiendas Pitusa, 159 D.P.R. 650 (2003) **81**
Chamberlain v. Delgado, 82 D.P.R. 6 (1960) **156–57**
Chicago, B. & Q. R.R. Co. v. Chicago, 166 U.S. 226 (1897) **82**
Church of the Lukumi Babalu Aye, Inc. v. City of Hialeah, 508 U.S. 520 (1993) **68–69**
Cirino González v. Administración de Corrección, 190 D.P.R. 14 (2014) **144**
Civil Rights Cases, 109 U.S. 3 (1883) **30–31, 30n. 183–31, 62**
Clinton v. New York, 524 U.S. 417 (1998) **130**
Colegio de Abogados v. Estado Libre Asociado, 181 D.P.R. 135 (2010) **56**
Collins v. Youngblood, 497 U.S. 37 (1990) **99**
Comisión Independiente de Ciudadanos v. Ética Gubernamental, 2004 WL 1609182
(May 20, 2004) **126**
Comisión para los Asuntos de la Mujer v. Secretario de Justicia, 109 D.P.R. 715 (1980) **63**
Compañía de Turismo v. Municipality of Vieques, 179 D.P.R. 578 (2010) **170**
Córdova v. Cámara de Representantes, 171 D.P.R. 789 (2007) **152, 191, 235**
Córdova & Simonpietri Insurance Agency v. Chase Manhattan Bank, 649 F. 2d 36
(1stCir. 1981) **37n. 235**
Cortés Portalatín v. Hau Colón, 103 D.P.R. 734 (1975) **81, 232**
Corujo Collazo v. Viera Martínez, 111 D.P.R. 552 (1981) **118–19**
Cosme v. Hogar Crea, et. al., 159 D.P.R. 1 (2003) **150**
Coss y la Universidad de Puerto Rico v. Comisión Estatal de Elecciones, 137 D.P.R. 877 (1995) **70–71**
Craig v. Boren, 429 U.S. 190 (1976) **63**
C.R.I.M v. Méndez Torres, 174 D.P.R. 216 (2008) **128**

D

Damián Marrero v. Municipio de Morovis, 115 D.P.R. 643 (1984) **66–67**
De Diego v. Cámara de Delegados, 5 D.P.R. 114 (1904) **119**
De Lima v. Bidwell, 182 U.S. 1 (1901) **214**
De Paz Lisk v. Aponte Roque, 124 D.P.R. 472 (1989) **62, 226**
Defendini Collazo v. Estado Libre Asociado, 134 D.P.R. 28 (1993) **72, 79**
Díaz Aponte v. Comunidad San José, Inc., 130 D.P.R. 782 (1992) **97**
Diaz Carrasquillo v. García Padilla, 191 D.P.R. 97 (2014) **123, 140**
Díaz Saldaña v. Acevedo Vilá, 168 D.P.R. 359 (2006) **130**
Dimas Zayas v. Levitt & Sons, 132 D.P.R. 101 (1992) **154–55**
Diócesis de Arecibo v. Secretario de Justicia, 191 D.P.R. 292 (2014) **68, 81, 82, 228–29**
Disidente Universal de Puerto Rico v. Departamento de Estado, 145 D.P.R. 689 (1998) **71**
Dobbs v. Jackson Women's Health Organization, 597 U.S. ____ (2022) **82**
Domínguez Castro v. Estado Libre Asociado, 178 D.P.R. 1 (2010) **168, 231, 235**

LIST OF CASES ■ 253

Dooley v. United States, 182 U.S. 222 (1901) **214**
Dooley v. United States II, 183 U.S. 151 (1901) **214**
Dorante v. Wrangler de Puerto Rico, 145 D.P.R. 408 (1998) **127**
Dorchy v. State of Kansas, 272 U.S. 306, 311 (1926) **105**
Dottin v. Rigo & Co., 22 D.P.R. 405 (1915) **62**
Downes v. Bidwell, 182 U.S. 244 (1901) **31, 31n. 185, 31n. 190, 31n. 192–32n. 197, 32n. 198, 32n. 200, 41**
Duncan v. Louisiana, 391 U.S. 145 (1968) **93**

E

El Vocero de Puerto Rico v. Puerto Rico, 131 D.P.R. 356 (1992) **90, 233**
El Vocero de Puerto Rico v. Puerto Rico, 508 U.S. 147 (1993) **90**
Elk v. Wilkins, 112 U.S. 94 (1884) **30n. 183–31**
Emanuelli v. Tribunal, 74 D.P.R. 541 (1953) **141, 240**
Estado Libre Asociado v. Aguayo, 80 D.P.R. 552 (1958) **83, 152**
Estado Libre Asociado v. Hermandad de Empleados, 104 D.P.R. 436 (1975) **70, 72**
Eva Prados Rodríguez v. Thomas Rivera Schatz, 2020 SJCV 05245 (Oct. 19, 2020) **71–72**
Examining Board of Engineers, Architects and Surveyors v. Flores de Otero, 426 U.S. 572 (1976) **38, 38n. 243, 231**
Ex Parte AAR, 187 D.P.R. 835 (2013) **61**
Ex Parte Acevedo, 1 D.P.R. 275 (1902) **230–31**
Ex Parte Andino Torres, 151 D.P.R. 794 (2000) **60–61**
Ex Parte Delgado Hernández, 165 D.P.R. 170 (2005) **61**
Ex Parte McCardle, 7 Wall. (74 U.S.) 506 (1869) **152**
Ex Parte Ponce Ayala, 179 D.P.R. 18 (2010) **96**
Ezratty v. Commonwealth of Puerto Rico, 648 F.2d 770 (1st Cir. 1981) **37n. 235**

F

Figueroa v. People of Puerto Rico, 232 F.2d 615 (1st Cir. 1956) **37n. 235, 40, 40n. 253**
Figueroa Ferrer v. Estado Libre Asociado, 107 D.P.R. 250 (1978) **59–60**
Financial Oversight and Management Board for Puerto Rico v. Aurelius Investment, LLC, 140 S. Ct. 1649 (2020) **42n. 269, 44–45, 44n. 276, 46**
First Federal Savings and Loan Association v. Ruiz de Jesús, 644 F.2d 910 (1st Cir. 1981) **37n. 235**
Foley v. Connelie, 435 U.S. 291 (1978) **62**
Fundación Surfrider Inc. v. ARPE, 178 D.P.R. 563 (2010) **187**
Fuster v. Busó, 102 D.P.R. 327 (1974) **116**

G

García v. Aljoma Lumber, 162 D.P.R. 572 (2004) **103–4**
García Martínez v. Gobernador, 109 D.P.R. 294 (1979) **162**
García Passalacqua v. Tribunal Electoral, 105 D.P.R. 49 (1976) **236**
Garib Bazaín v. Hospital Español Auxilio Mutuo de Puerto Rico, Inc., 204 D.P.R. 601 (2020) **64**
Gobierno de Puerto Rico v. Elizabeth Torres Rodríguez, 2022 SJCV 02578 (April 29, 2022) **152**
Goetze v. United States, 182 U.S. 221 (1901) **214**
González v. Alcalde de Utuado, 101 D.P.R. 47 (1973) **124**
González v. Williams, 192 U.S. 1 (1904) **29n. 178, 214**
González Vélez v. Tribunal Superior de Puerto Rico, 75 D.P.R. 585 (1953) **158**
Graham v. Richardson, 403 U.S. 365 (1971) **62**

254 ■ LIST OF CASES

Green Giant Co. v. Tribunal Superior, 104 D.P.R. 489 (1975) **104**
Guzmán v. Calderón, 164 D.P.R. 220 (2005) **140**

H

Hampton Development v. Estado Libre Asociado, 139 D.P.R. 877 (1996) **83**
Harris v. Rosario, 446 U.S. 651 (1980) **38–39, 38n. 248–39, 45, 45n. 287, 46n. 288**
Hernández Agosto v. López Nieves, 114 D.P.R. 601 (1983) **140–41**
Hernández Agosto v. Ortiz Montes, 115 D.P.R. 564 (1984) **120**
Hernández Agosto v. Romero Barceló, 112 D.P.R. 407 (1982) **144**
Hernández Colón, Romero Barceló v. Policía de Puerto Rico, 177 D.P.R. 121 (2009) **231**
Hernández Estrella v. Junta de Apelaciones del Sistema de Educación Pública,
    147 D.P.R. 840 (1999) **106**
Hernádez Gotay v. United States, 985 F.3d 71 (1ˢᵗ Cir. 2021) **46n. 289**
Hernández López v. Santana Ramos, 147 D.P.R. 116 (1998) **156–57**
Hernández Montañez v. Rosselló Nevares, 2018 WL 4903203 (Aug. 27, 2018) **144**
Hernández Torres v. Hernández Colón, 129 D.P.R. 824 (1992) **141, 173, 174–75**
Herrero y Otros v. Estado Libre Asociado, 179 D.P.R. 277 (2010) **172, 238**
Hester v. United States, 265 U.S. 57 (1924) **85**
Humphrey's Executor v. United States, 295 U.S. 602 (1935) **140**
Huus v. New York and Porto Rico Steamship Company, 182 U.S. 392 (1901) **214**
H.M.C.A. (P.R.), Inc. v. Contralor, 133 D.P.R. 945 (1993) **134**

I

Iglesias v. Secretaria de Corrección, 137 D.P.R. 479 (1994) **96**
Illinois v. Gates, 462 U.S. 213 (1983) **87**
*In re Aprobación de las Reglas para los procedimientos de investigaciones especiales
independientes de la Rama Judicial*, 184 D.P.R. 575 (2012) **160**
In re Designación del Secretario del Tribunal Supremo, 207 D.P.R. 949 (2021) **160**
In re Oliver, 333 U.S. 257 (1948) **89–90**
In re Pellot Córdova, 204 D.P.R. 814 (2020) **56**
In re Reglamento del Tribunal Supremo de Puerto Rico, 183 D.P.R. 386 (2011) **154–55**
In re Reglamento del Tribunal Supremo, 183 D.P.R. 386 (2011) **155**
In re Reglas para la creación y funcionamiento de la Unidad Especial de Jueces de Apelaciones,
    134 D.P.R. 670 (1993) **165**
In re Reinaldo Santiago Concepción, 189 D.P.R. 378 (2013) **163–64**
*In re Sesión Especial del Tribunal Supremo de Puerto Rico sobre el Proyecto de Reglas
de Procedimiento Criminal de 2018*, 201 D.P.R. 1053 (2019) **158**
*In re The Financial Oversight and Management Board for Puerto Rico as representative of the
    Commonwealth of Puerto Rico*, No. 17-BK 3283- LTS (D. Puerto Rico filed July 2,
    2019) **43n. 273, 163**
In re Zaida Hernández Torres, 167 D.P.R. 823 (2006) **165**
Indulac v. Central General de Trabajadores, 207 D.P.R. 279 (2021) **81–82, 232**
Irizarry Robles v. José Guillermo Rodriguez, 233 F. Supp. 3d 296 (D. Puerto Rico 2017) **65**

J

Jacobson v. Massachusetts, 197 U.S. 11 (1905) **53**
Junta de Relaciones del Trabajo v. Asociación de Servicios Médicos Hospitalarios de Yauco, 115D.P.R.
    360 (1984) **105–6**

K

Katz v. United States, 389 U.S. 347 (1967) **86**
Kilómetro O, Inc. v. Pesquera López, 207 D.P.R. 200 (2021) **71–72**
Korematsu v. United States, 323 U.S. 214 (1944) **30–31**

L

Landfill Technologies v. Municipio de Lares, 187 D.P.R. 794 (2013) **179**
Lemon v. Kurtzman, 403 U.S. 602 (1971) **68**
Lochner v. New York, 198 U.S. 45 (1905) **77, 231**
López v. Municipio de San Juan, 121 D.P.R. 75 (1988) **168**
López Vives v. Policía de Puerto Rico, 118 D.P.R. 219 (1987) **81–82**
Loughborough v. Blake, 18 U.S. 317 (1820) **30n. 180**
Lozada Sánchez v. Junta de Calidad Ambiental, 184 D.P.R. 898 (2012) **187**
Lozada Tirado v. Testigos de Jehová, 177 D.P.R. 893 (2010) **60–61, 228–29**
Lukoil Pan Americas v. Municipality of Guayanilla, 192 D.P.R. 879 (2015) **170**
Luther v. Borden, 48 U.S. 1 (1849) **193–94**
Lyng v. International Union, 485 U.S. 360 (1988) **105**

M

Malavé v. Oriental Bank & Trust, 167 D.P.R. 594 (2006) **104**
Malloy v. Hogan, 378 U.S. 1 (1964) **94**
Manny Suárez v. Comisión Estatal de Elecciones, 163 D.P.R. 541 (2004) **66, 116**
Mapp v. Ohio, 367 U.S. 643 (1961) **87**
Marimón v. Pelegrí, 1 D.P.R. 225 (1902) **155**
Marina Industrial, Inc. v. Brown Boveri Corporation, 114 D.P.R. 64 (1983) **78**
Marrero v. Municipio de Morovis, 115 D.P.R. 643 (1984) **177**
McConnell v. Palau, 161 D.P.R. 734 (2004) **78**
Meléndez, F.E.I., 135 D.P.R. 610 (1994) **94**
Mendoza v. Junta de Comisionados de San Juan, 47 D.P.R. 169 (1934) **247**
Mercado Quilichini v. Universidad Católica de Puerto Rico, 143 D.P.R. 610 (1997) **228**
Mercado Vega v. Universidad de Puerto Rico, 128 D.P.R. 273 (1991) **103**
Merle Feliciano v. Comisión Estatal de Elecciones, 2020 WL 5367111 (June 23, 2020) **114**
Michigan v. Long, 463 U.S. 1032 (1983) **75–76**
Miranda v. Secretario de Hacienda, 77 D.P.R. 171 (1954) **171**
Misión Industrial v. Junta de Planificación, 146 D.P.R. 64 (1998) **56, 152, 187–88**
Money's People Inc. v. López Julia, 202 D.P.R. 889 (2019) **80**
Mora v. Mejías, 206 F.2d 377 (1st Cir. 1953) **37n. 235, 77**
Morales Feliciano v. Romero Barceló, 497 F. Supp. 14 (D. P. R. 1979) **188**
Morales Morales v. Estado Libre Asociado, 126 D.P.R. 92 (1990) **105**
Morales y Benet v. Junta Local de Inscripciones, 33 D.P.R. 79 (1924) **62–63**
Municipality of Ponce v. Roman Catholic Apostolic Church, 210 U.S. 296 (1908) **228**
Municipios de Aguada y Aguadilla v. Junta de Calidad Ambiental, 190 D.P.R. 122 (2014) **187**
Municipio de Guaynabo v. Adquisición 180 D.P.R. 206 (2010) **83**
Municipio de Ponce v. Autoridad de Carreteras, 153 D.P.R. 1 (2000) **168**
Municipio de San Juan v. Junta de Calidad Ambiental, 152 D.P.R. 673 (2000) **187**
Muñiz v. Administrador del Deporte Hípico, 156 D.P.R. 18 (2002) **70**
Muratti v. Foote, 25 D.P.R. 568 (1917) **34**
Muriel v. Suazo, 72 D.P.R. 370 (1951) **225–26**
M'Culloch v. Maryland, 17 U.S. 316 (1819) **169–70**

256 ■ LIST OF CASES

N

NAACP v. Alabama, 357 U.S. 449 (1958) **75**
New York Times v. United States, 403 U.S. 713 (1971) **70**
Nieves Huertas v. García Padilla, et. al., 189 D.P.R. 611 (2013) **121, 139–40**
Nixon v. United States, 506 U.S. 224 (1993) **132, 239**
Nogueras v. Hernández Colón, 127 D.P.R. 405 (1990) **109, 120–21**
Nogueras v. Hernández Colón, 127 D.P.R. 638 (1991) **140–41**
Nogueras v. Rexach Benítez, 141 D.P.R. 470 (1996) **119, 131–32**
Noriega v. Gobernador, 122 D.P.R. 650 (1988) **72**
Noriega v. Gobernador II, 130 D.P.R. 919 (1992) **72**
Noriega v. Hernández Colón, 126 D.P.R. 42 (1990) **139, 141, 142**
Noriega v. Hernández Colón, 135 D.P.R. 406 (1994) **141**

O

Obergefell v. Hodges, 576 U.S. 644 (2015) **61**
Ocasio v. Díaz, 88 D.P.R. 676 (1963) **64, 226**
Ortiz v. Departamento de Hacienda, 120 D.P.R. 216 (1987) **103**
Ortiz v. Directora Administrativa de los Tribunales, 152 D.P.R. 161 (2000) **71–72**
Ortiz Angleró v. Barreto Pérez, 110 D.P.R. 84 (1980) **66**
Ortiz Cruz v. Junta Hípica, 101 D.P.R. 791 (1973) **103**

P

Pacheco Fraticelli v. Cintrón Antonsanti, 122 D.P.R. 229 (1988) **70–71**
Parrilla v. Martín, 68 D.P.R. 90 (1948) **238–39**
Partido Estadista Republicano v. Junta Constitucional, 90 D.P.R. 228 (1964) **112**
Partido Independentista Puertorriqueño v. Comisión Estatal de Elecciones,
 120 D.P.R. 580 (1988) **53, 107, 177**
Partido Independentista Puertorriqueño v. Estado Libre Asociado, 109 D.P.R. 403 (1980) **155, 177**
Partido Independentista Puertorriqueño v. Estado Libre Asociado, 109 D.P.R. 685 (1980) **155, 177**
Partido Independentista Puertorriqueño v. Estado Libre Asociado, 186 D.P.R. 1 (2012) **191**
Partido Nuevo Progresista v. De Castro Font, 172 D.P.R. 34 (2007) **75–76**
Partido Nuevo Progresista v. De Castro Font II, 172 D.P.R. 883 (2007) **66**
Partido Popular Democrático v. Gobernador, 139 D.P.R. 643 (1995) **176–77**
Partido Popular Democrático v. Gobernador II, 136 D.P.R. 916 (1994) **66–67**
Partido Renovación Puertorriqueña v. Estado Libre Asociado, 115 D.P.R. 631 (1984) **66, 203**
Partido Socialista Puertorriqueño v. Comisión Estatal de Elecciones, 110 D.P.R. 400 (1980) **66–67**
Partido Socialista Puertorriqueño v. Estado Libre Asociado, 107 D.P.R. 590 (1978) **53–54, 107, 177**
Partido Socialista Puertorriqueño v. Romero Barceló, 110 D.P.R. 248 (1980) **224, 227**
Partido Socialista Puertorriqueño v. Secretario de Hacienda, 110 D.P.R. 313 (1980) **66–67**
Penn Central Transportation v. New York City, 438 U.S. 104 (1978) **83**
Pierluisi y Bhatia v. Comisión Estatal de Elecciones, 204 D.P.R. 841 (2020) **66**
Plard Fagundo v. Tribunal Superior, 101 D.P.R. 444 (1973) **95**
Plaza de Descuentos v. Estado Libre Asociado, 178 D.P.R. 777 (2010) **83**
Plessy v. Ferguson, 163 U.S. 537 (1896) **30–31**
Posados v. Warner, Barnes & Co., 279 U.S. 340 (1929) **127**
Powell v. Alabama, 287 U.S. 45 (1932) **92**
Powell v. McCormack, 395 U.S. 486 (1969) **118**
Presidente de la Cámara v. Gobernador, 167 D.P.R. 149 (2006) **173–74**

LIST OF CASES ■ 257

Presidente del Senado, 148 D.P.R. 737 (1999) **123**
Printz v. United States, 521 U.S. 898 (1997) **43n. 272**
Pueblo v. Acevedo Escobar, 112 D.P.R. 770 (1982) **85**
Pueblo v. Acosta, 11 D.P.R. 249 (1906) **230–31**
Pueblo v. Acosta Escobar, 101 D.P.R. 886 (1974) **233**
Pueblo v. Agudo Olmeda, 168 D.P.R. 554 (2006) **93**
Pueblo v. Albizu, 77 D.P.R. 888 (1955) **141, 240**
Pueblo v. Aléstico, 18 D.P.R. 320 (1912) **230–31**
Pueblo v. Aponte Ruperto, 199 D.P.R. 538 (2018) **96**
Pueblo v. Arcelay Galán, 102 D.P.R. 409 (1974) **89**
Pueblo v. Arrillaga, 30 D.P.R. 940 (1922) **136**
Pueblo v. Arrocho, 33 D.P.R. 657 (1924) **230–31**
Pueblo v. Aspurúa, 61 D.P.R. 252 (1943) **94**
Pueblo v. Báez López, 189 D.P.R. 918 (2013) **85**
Pueblo v. Basilio Figueroa Pérez, 96 D.P.R. 6 (1968) **99**
Pueblo v. Boria, 12 D.P.R. 170 (1907) **230–31**
Pueblo v. Camacho Delgado, 175 D.P.R. 1 (2008) **89**
Pueblo v. Candelario Ayala, 166 D.P.R. 118 (2005) **99**
Pueblo v. Capriles, 58 D.P.R. 548 (1941) **87**
Pueblo v. Casellas Toro, 197 D.P.R. 1003 (2017) **233**
Pueblo v. Clemente, 35 D.P.R. 628 (1926) **230–31**
Pueblo v. Colón Rodríguez, 161 D.P.R. 254 (2004) **95–96**
Pueblo v. Daniel Cruz Rosario, 204 D.P.R. 1040 (2020) **91**
Pueblo v. Díaz Medina, 176 D.P.R. 601 (2009) **85**
Pueblo v. Dolce, 105 D.P.R. 422 (1976) **85, 232**
Pueblo v. Dones, 9 D.P.R. 469 (1905) **230–31**
Pueblo v. Duarte, 109 D.P.R. 596 (1980) **82**
Pueblo v. Fernández Rodríguez, 188 D.P.R. 165 (2013) **87–88**
Pueblo v. Ferreira Morales, 147 D.P.R. 238 (1998) **85**
Pueblo v. Flores, 17 D.P.R. 178 (1911) **230–31**
Pueblo v. García & García, 22 D.P.R. 817 (1915) **231**
Pueblo v. González Colón, 110 D.P.R. 812 (1981) **94**
Pueblo v. Izquierdo, 25 D.P.R. 382 (1917) **230–31**
Pueblo v. Lasalle, 18 D.P.R. 421 (1912) **230–31**
Pueblo v. Lausell Hernández, 121 D.P.R. 823 (1988) **91**
Pueblo v. Lebrón, 108 D.P.R. 324 (1979) **85**
Pueblo v. Malavé González, 120 D.P.R. 470 (1988) **85**
Pueblo v. Martínez Torres, 120 D.P.R. 496 (1988) **87**
Pueblo v. Morales (Yaré Yaré), 11 D.P.R. 306 (1906) **230–31**
Pueblo v. Muñoz, Colón y Ocasio, 131 D.P.R. 965 (1992) **87**
Pueblo v. Negrón Rivera, 183 D.P.R. 271 (2011) **98–99**
Pueblo v. Nelson Daniel Centeno 2021 T.S.P.R. 133 **93–94**
Pueblo v. Nevárez, 10 D.P.R. 94 (1906) **230–31**
Pueblo v. Nieves Vives, 188 D.P.R. 1, 19 (2013) **94**
Pueblo v. Ortiz Alvarado, 135 D.P.R. 41 (1994) **87**
Pueblo v. Ortiz Couvertier, 132 D.P.R. 883 (1993) **92**
Pueblo v. Ortiz Martínez, 116 D.P.R. 139 (1985) **85**
Pueblo v. Pascual Ramos, 36 D.P.R. 321 (1927) **230–31**
Pueblo v. Pepín Cortés, 173 D.P.R. 968 (2008) **90**
Pueblo v. Pérez Méndez, 83 D.P.R. 228 (1961) **98–99**
Pueblo v. Pérez Santos, 195 D.P.R. 262 (2016) **91**

258 ■ LIST OF CASES

Pueblo v. Riscard, 95 D.P.R. 405 (1967) **85**
Pueblo v. Rivera, 9 D.P.R. 505 (1905) **230–31**
Pueblo v. Rivera Cintrón, 185 D.P.R. 484 (2012) **95**
Pueblo v. Rivera Collazo, 122 D.P.R. 408 (1988) **85**
Pueblo v. Rivera Morales, 133 D.P.R. 444 (1993) **63**
Pueblo v. Rivera Robles, 121 D.P.R. 858 (1988) **63**
Pueblo v. Rivera Tirado, 117 D.P.R. 419 (1986) **89**
Pueblo v. Rodríguez López, 155 D.P.R. 894 (2001) **90–91**
Pueblo v. Rodríguez Rodríguez, 128 D.P.R. 438 (1991) **85**
Pueblo v. Román, 5 D.P.R. 8 (1903) **91**
Pueblo v. Román, 18 D.P.R. 219 (1912) **230–31**
Pueblo v. Rosado, 17 D.P.R. 44 (1911) **230–31**
Pueblo v. Santiago, 176 D.P.R. 133 (2009) **93**
Pueblo v. Santiago Cruz, 205 D.P.R. 7 (2020) **91, 92**
Pueblo v. Santiago Feliciano, 139 D.P.R. 361 (1995) **86**
Pueblo v. Santiago Lugo, 134 D.P.R. 623 (1993) **94**
Pueblo v. Santos Santos, 189 D.P.R. 361 (2013) **95**
Pueblo v. Soto Soto, 168 D.P.R. 46 (2006) **86**
Pueblo v. Suazo, 63 D.P.R. 905 (1944) **225–26**
Pueblo v. Torres Rivera, 204 D.P.R. 288 (2020) **93–94**
Pueblo v. Vélez Bonilla, 189 D.P.R. 705 (2013) **84**
Pueblo v. Vélez Rodríguez, 186 D.P.R. 621 (2012) **90**
Pueblo v. Wilfredo Suárez Alers, 167 D.P.R. 850 (2006) **102**
Pueblo de Puerto Rico v. Terry Terrol, 106 D.P.R. 588 (1977) **155**
Puerto Rico v. Coca Cola, 115 D.P.R. 197 (1984) **84, 85**
Puerto Rico v. Franklin California Tax Free Trust, 136 S. Ct. 1938 *also at* 579 U.S. 115 (2016) **41–42, 41n. 261, 41n. 265, 46, 176**
Puerto Rico v. Sánchez Valle, 136 S. Ct. 1863 *also at* 579 U.S. 59 (2016) **40–41, 46, 95, 186**
Puerto Rico Telephone Co. v. Martínez, 114 D.P.R. 328 (1983) **86**
Puerto Rico Telephone Company v. Ramón Rivera Marrero, 114 D.P.R. 360 (1983) **134**

Q

Quiñones v. Castelló, 16 D.P.R. 493 (1910) **232**

R

Ramírez de Ferrer v. Mari Brás, 144 D.P.R. 141 (1997) **53, 66, 227**
Ramos v. Louisiana, 140 S. Ct. 1390 (2020) **93–94**
Ramos Acevedo v. Tribunal Superior, 133 D.P.R. 599 (1993) **98**
RDT Const. Corp. v. Contralor I, 141 D.P.R. 424 (1996) **82, 134**
Reynolds v. Sims, 377 U.S. 533 (1964) **112**
Rivera Padilla v. OAT, 189 D.P.R. 315 (2013) **103**
Rivera Rodriguez & Co. v. Stowell Taylor, 133 D.P.R. 881 (1993) **78**
Rivera Santiago v. Secretario de Hacienda, 119 D.P.R. 265 (1987) **78**
Rivera Schatz v. Estado Libre Asociado, 191 D.P.R. 791 (2014) **75–76, 157, 230**
Rodríguez v. Estado Libre Asociado, 202 D.P.R. 428 (2019) **230**
Rodríguez v. Popular Democratic Party, 457 U.S. 1 (1982) **38, 38n. 241, 118**
Rodríguez v. Secretario de Hacienda, 135 D.P.R. 219 (1994) **170**
Rodríguez Orellana v. Comisión Estatal de Elecciones, 134 D.P.R. 612 (1993) **229**

Rodríguez Pagán v. Departamento de Servicios Sociales, 132 D.P.R. 617 (1993) **79**
Rodríguez Quintana v. Rivera Estrada, 192 D.P.R. 832 (2015) **172**
Roman Catholic Archdiocese of San Juan v. Acevedo Feliciano, 140 S. Ct. 696 (2020) **69**
Romero Barceló v. Hernández Agosto, 115 D.P.R. 368 (1984) **122–23, 238**
Rosario v. Toyota, 166 D.P.R. 1 (2005) **64**
Rosario Rodríguez v. Rosselló Nevares, 207 D.P.R. 795 (2021) **67, 248**
R.C.A. v. Gobierno de la Capital, 91 D.P.R. 416 (1964) **170**

S

Salas Soler v. Secretario de Agricultura, 102 D.P.R. 716 (1974) **187**
Salvá Santiago v. Torres Padró, 171 D.P.R. 332 (2007) **61, 225**
Sánchez v. González, 78 D.P.R. 849 (1955) **96**
Sánchez Rodríguez v. López Jiménez, 116 D.P.R. 392 (1985) **155**
Sánchez Vilella y Colón Martínez v. Estado Libre Asociado, 134 D.P.R. 445 (1993) **67**
Sancho v. Valiente & Co., 93 F.2d 327 (1st Cir. 1937) **238**
Santa Aponte v. Hernández, 105 D.P.R. 750 (1977) **118–19**
Santana v. Gobernadora, 165 D.P.R. 28 (2005) **136–37, 139, 140**
Santiago v. Nogueras, 214 U.S. 260 (1909) **27**
Schilb v. Kuebel, 404 U.S. 357 (1971) **96**
Senado de Puerto Rico v. Gobierno de Puerto Rico, 203 D.P.R. 62 (2019) **147**
Senado de Puerto Rico v. Tribunal Supremo de Puerto Rico, 2021 TSPR 141 **56–57**
Serè v. Pitot, 10 U.S. 332 (1810) **30n. 180**
Siaca v. Bahía Beach Resort, 194 D.P.R. 559 (2016) **81–82**
Silva v. Hernández Agosto, 118 D.P.R. 45 (1986) **123, 127**
Soto v. Secretario de Justicia, 112 D.P.R. 477 (1982) **71–72**
Strickland v. Washington, 466 U.S. 668 (1984) **92**
Suárez Cáceres v. Comisión Estatal de Elecciones, 176 D.P.R. 31 (2009) **67**
Suárez Martínez v. Tugwell, 67 D.P.R. 180 (1947) **152**

T

Taboada & Co. v. Rivera Martínez, 51 D.P.R. 253 (1937) **231**
Terry v. Ohio, 392 U.S. 1 (1968) **85**
Timbs v. Indiana, 139 S.Ct. 682 (2019) **96**
Toll v. Adorno Medina, 130 D.P.R. 352 (1992) **87–88**
Tonos Florenzán v. Bernazard, 111 D.P.R. 546 (1981) **113, 118–19**
Torres Marrero v. Alcaldesa de Ponce, 199 D.P.R. 493 (2017) **83**
Torres Montalvo v. Gobernador, 194 D.P.R. 760 (2016) **157**
Torruella v. Fernández, 14 D.P.R. 609 (1908) **231**
Trinidad Hernández v. Estado Libre Asociado, 188 D.P.R. 828 (2013) **80, 152, 232**
Tugwell v. Corte de Distrito de San Juan, 64 D.P.R. 220 (1944)

U

Unidad Nacional de Trabajadores de la Salud v. Soler Zapata, 133 D.P.R. 153 (1993) **71**
Union Central Life Insurance Company v. Gromer, 19 D.P.R. 900 (1913) **231**
United States v. Acosta Martínez, 106 F. Supp. 2d 311 (D. Puerto Rico 2000) **76–77**
United States v. E.C. Knight, 156 U.S. 1 (1895) **30n. 183–31**
United States v. López Andino, 831 F.2d 1164 (1st Cir. 1987) **37n. 235, 95**

260 ■ LIST OF CASES

United States v. Lovett, 328 U.S. 303 (1946) **99**
United States v. Quiñones, 758 F.2d 40 (1985) **86**
United States v. Robinson, 414 U.S. 218 (1973) **85**
United States v. Vaello Madero, 596 U.S. _____ (2022) **45–46, 45n. 286, 45n. 287**
United States v. Vaello-Madero, 956 F.3d 12 (1st Cir. 2020) **45n. 286**
Universidad de Puerto Rico v. Laborde, 180 D.P.R. 253 (2010) **71, 106, 229**
U.T.I.E.R. v. Junta de Relaciones del Trabajo de Puerto Rico, 99 D.P.R. 512 (1970) **105**

V

Viajes Lesana, Inc. v. Saavedra, 115 D.P.R. 703 (1984) **97**
Vigoreaux Lorenzana v. Quizno's, 173 D.P.R. 254 (2008) **82**

W

Wackenhut Corp. v. Rodríguez Aponte, 100 D.P.R. 518 (1972) **62**
Waller v. Georgia, 467 U.S. 39 (1984) **90**
Washington v. Davis, 426 U.S. 229 (1976) **79**
Washington v. Texas, 388 U.S. 14 (1967) **91**
Weber Carrillo v. Estado Libre Asociado, 190 D.P.R. 688 (2014) **60–61, 82**
Weeks v. United States, 232 U.S. 383 (1914) **87**

Y

Youngstown v. Sawyer, 343 U.S. 579 (1952) **142**

Z

Zachry International v. Tribunal Superior, 104 D.P.R. 267 (1975) **63, 103**
Zequeira v. Universidad de Puerto Rico, 76 D.P.R. 338 (1954) **134**

■ LIST OF U.S. TREATIES AND STATUTES

1898 Treaty of Paris 30 Stat. 1754 (1898) **26, 26n. 142, 32–33, 37, 57, 61, 68, 98, 214, 221–22, 228**

1900 Foraker Act 31 Stat. 77 (1900) **27, 28–29, 31, 34, 35n. 224, 36, 52, 57, 61, 65, 70, 79–80, 93, 100, 105, 111–12, 113, 114, 115–16, 117, 118, 119–20, 122–23, 125, 128, 129–30, 133, 137, 139, 141, 143–44, 146, 147, 152, 155, 157–58, 159, 160, 163, 167–68, 169–70, 173, 180, 181, 183–84, 185–86, 201–2, 214, 223, 227, 234, 236, 238–39, 244, 245, 247–48**

1917 Jones Act 39 Stat. 951 (1917) **33–34, 35, 35n. 224, 36, 52, 57, 59–60, 61, 65, 68, 70, 75, 77, 78, 79–80, 81, 82, 84, 86–87, 88–90, 91, 92, 93, 94, 95–96, 97, 98–99, 100, 101, 102, 105, 111–12, 113, 114, 115–17, 118, 119–20, 122–23, 124, 125, 126–27, 128, 129–30, 133, 137, 139, 141, 143–45, 146, 147, 152, 155, 156, 157–58, 159, 160, 163, 167–68, 169–70, 171, 172, 173, 174, 175, 176, 178, 180, 181, 183–84, 185–86, 201–2, 214, 223, 225, 227, 230, 234, 236, 238–39, 240, 241, 244, 245, 247**

1947 Elective Governor Act 61 Stat. 770 (1947) **34–35, 129, 131, 136, 137, 138, 146–47, 160, 240, 244**

1950 Public Law No. 600 64 Stat. 319 (1950) **35–36, 35n. 225–36–35n. 226–36, 37, 37n. 235, 37n. 238, 44, 47, 55–56, 100, 156, 191–92, 193–94, 204–5**

1952 Public Law No. 82-447 66 Stat. 327 (1952) **35–36, 35n. 229–36, 47, 191–92, 194**

2016 Puerto Rico Oversight, Management and Economic Stability Act 130 Stat. 549 (2016) **41–44, 44n. 277, 47, 55–56, 80, 83–84, 106, 131, 143, 162–63, 181**

■ INDEX

For the benefit of digital users, indexed terms that span two pages (e.g., 52–53) may, on occasion, appear on only one of those pages.

Note: Tables are indicated by *t* following the page number

abolition of slavery, 16–17
absolutist powers *(poderes omnímodos)*, 10
Acevedo Vilá, Aníbal, 129
accounting authority of comptroller, 133
accusations, right to be informed of, 90–91
Acevedo Vilá v. Aponte Hernández, 129–30, 156–57
Acevedo Vilá v. Meléndez, 143
Acosta y Calbo, José Julián, 16–17
A.D. Miranda, Inc. v. Secretario de Justicia, 103
Adams Onís Treaty (1819), 26, 32–33
additional minority party legislators, selection of, 114–16
ad honorem positions, 125
adjournment clause, Legislature, 122
Administración de Terrenos de Puerto Rico v. Ponce Bayland Enterprises, 83
Alaska Cession Treaty (1867), 26, 32–33
Alfonso X, King, 4
Alfonso XII, King, 18–19
alienage as suspect class, 62, 226
Alito, Samuel, 69
Álvarez González, José Julián, 219
Ambach v. Norwick, 62
amendments to constitution. *See also* Puerto Rico Constitution Amendments; U.S. Constitutional amendments
constitutional bibliographical essay, 249–50
Constitutional Convention to propose amendments, 192–93, 250
Legislative Assembly proposal of, 189–92, 249
limitations to amendment mechanism, 193–94
American citizenship, 29, 53
American Declaration of the Rights and Duties of Man, 75, 81
American imperialism, 221

Anglophone (British) Caribbean, 224–50
anthem, matters of law, 182–83, 248–49
Aponte Martínez v. Lugo, 70
Aponte Rosario v. Presidente Comisión Estatal de Elecciones, 53–54, 107, 177–78
Appellate Court, 152
appellate jurisdiction, 150–51
appointment of judges, 160–61, 244
appointment of secretaries, 143, 240–41
Appointments Clause, 44–45
appropriations
failure to make, 172–74, 247–48
not to exceed revenue, 174–75, 248
Arbona v. Torres, 62–63
Arecibo, Senatorial and Representative Districts, 197
Arizmendi, Juan Alejo, Bishop, 8
Arizona v. Youngblood, 84
arrest warrants, 86–87
Arroyo v. Rattan Specialties, Inc., 60–61
Arthur, Chester Alan, 30–31
artistic sites conservation and development, 186–87
Asociación de Academias y Colegios Cristianos de Puerto Rico v. Departamento de Educación, 73
Asociación de Fotoperiodistas de Puerto Rico v. Thomas Rivera Schatz, 122
Asociación de Maestros v. Departamento de Educación, 74
Asociación de Maestros v. José Arsenio Torres, 74
Asociación de Maestros v. Sistema de Retiro, 80
assembly, freedom of, 69–72, 229
association, freedom of, 17, 75–76, 230
at-large legislators, 236–37
auditing authority of comptroller, 133
authority of comptroller, 133–34

263

264 ■ INDEX

Autonomic Charter (1897), 22, 23–25, 28, 135–36, 189–90, 221, 235, 246
autonomist movement, 20–22, 220–21
Autoridad de Carreteras v. Adquisición de 8,554.741 Metros, 83
ayuntamientos (municipalities), 10

Báez Cancel v. Santos Rivera Pérez, 65
Báez Galib v. Comisión Estatal de Elecciones, 53, 107, 177–78
bail, right to, 95–96
bails and fines, prohibition against excess of, 96–97
Baker v. Carr, 112
Baldorioty de Castro, Román, 20–22
Baldwin v. New York, 93
Balzac v. Puerto Rico, 32–33, 34
bankruptcy crisis (2015-2016), 39, 168
Barreto Pérez, Ramón, 76
Bayamon, Senatorial and Representative Districts, 196–97
Belk Arce v. Martínez, 81–82
Beltrán Cintrón v. Puerto Rico, 103
Benítez Rexach, Jaime, 60, 65–66, 98, 110, 137, 186, 232
Berríos Martínez v. Gobernador, 190–91
Betances, Ramón Emeterio, 182
Betancourt v. Gobernador, 140–41
bicameral model of Legislature, 24, 109–10, 235
Bill of Rights, Puerto Rico Constitution. *See* Puerto Rico Constitution Bill of Rights
bills of attainder, 99
black codes, 16
Blackmun, Harry, 38
Bonaparte, Napoleon, Emperor, 7
Borbón, Carlos María Isidro de, 11
Borbón y Dos Sicilias, María Cristina de, Queen Regent, 10–11, 13, 14–15
Boumediene v. Bush, 45
Bracetti, Mariana, 182
Brandenburg v. Ohio, 75
Brau v. Estado Libre Asociado, 162–63
Brennan, William, 38, 161
Breyer, Stephen, 40–41
British North America Act, 21
British Privy Council, 4–6
Brown, Henry, 31–32, 41
Brunet Maldonado, Virgilio, 52–53

Brunet Justiniano v. Hernández Colón, 98–99
Burdick v. Takushi, 67
Burger, Warren, 38, 68
Burgos v. Comisión Estatal de Elecciones, 67, 107

Cabassa v. Rivera, 168
Cádiz Constitution, 6–11, 69–70, 220, 232
Calero-Toledo v. Pearson Yacht Leasing Co., 38
Califano v. Torres, 38–39, 45
Cánovas del Castillo, Antonio, 19
Carlist Wars, 10, 11
Carolina, Senatorial and Representative Districts, 199
Castilian Council (*Real y Supremo Consejo de Castilla*), 4–6
Castilian legal tradition, 4–6
Castro v. Tiendas Pitusa, 81
Catholicism, 67–69
censorship, governmental, 14
Cerón, Juan, 6
Chamberlain v. Delgado, 156–57
Charles IV, King, 7
Charles V, Emperor, 4–6
Chicago, B. & Q. R.R. Co. v. Chicago, 82
child employment and imprisonment, prohibition of, 101–2, 234
church and state, separation of, 67–69, 228–29
Church of the Lukumi Babalu Aye, Inc. v. City of Hialeah, 68–69
Cirino González v. Administración de Corrección, 144
Civil Code (1902), 82
civil law system, 4
civil rights, 61, 97–98, 99–107
Civil Rights Cases (1883), 62
Cleveland, Grover, 30–31
Clinton v. New York, 130
Code of Conduct for Puerto Rico Judges (*Cánones de Ética Judicial*), 165
Code of Criminal Procedure (1902), 88–90, 92, 94, 95
Código de Enjuiciamiento Criminal, 87
collective bargaining rights, 104
collective political rights, 39
Collins v. Youngblood, 99
Colón Castaño, Ramiro, 52–53
Colón Pérez, Ángel, 64
colonial *anciene régime*, under Ferdinand VII, 9–11

colonial assimilation, (Cádiz *Cortes Constituyentes*), 7
colonialism under U.S., 33
Colonial Laws Validity Act (British colonial statute) (1865), 28
colonial legislation, 4–6
Columbus, Christopher, 3
Comisión para los Asuntos de la Mujer v. Secretario de Justicia, 63
commander-in-chief of the militia, 141
Commonwealth of Puerto Rico, 55–56, 202–3, 224, 250
Compañía de Turismo v. Municipality of Vieques, 170
Compensation Clause, 179
comptroller appointment, 132–34, 239
compulsory process for obtaining witnesses, right to, 91, 233–34
compulsory voting, debate at the Constitutional Convention, 228
condescending biases, gender as suspect class, 62–63
Consejo de Regencia, (Cádiz *Cortes Constituyentes*), 7
conservation clause of Article VI, Section 19, 187–88
Constitution (1837), 13–14
Constitution (1845), 14–17
Constitution (1869), 17–18
Constitution (1876), 19–20, 21–22
constitutional amendments. *See* amendments to constitution; Puerto Rico Constitution Amendments; U.S. Constitutional amendments
constitutional bibliographical essay
amendments to the constitution, 249–50
American imperialism, 221
Anglophone (British) Caribbean, 224–50
Autonomic Charter (1897), 221, 235
autonomist movement, 220–21
Bill of Rights, 225–34
Cádiz Constitution, 220, 232
COVID-19 pandemic, 224
end of Spanish rule, 222
Executive branch powers, 240–41
Foraker Act (1900), 223
Fuller Court, 222–23
general overview, 217–18
general provisions of constitution, 245–49

Insular Cases, 30–33, 214*t*, 222–23
Jones Act (1917), 223, 230
judicial power, 241–45
Legislative Assembly powers, 234–39
preamble to constitution, 224
PROMESA, 223–24
Spanish American War (1898), 221–22
Spanish legal tradition and history, 219–20
transitory provisions of constitution, 250
treatise on Puerto Rico's constitutional law, 219
Treaty of Paris (1898), 221–22
U.S. Military governance of Puerto Rico, 222
Constitutional Convention
bibliographical works on, 218–19
delegates mentioned in commentary, 208*t*
delegates per political party, 208*t*
election of, 208*t*
revisions to constitution by, 192–93, 250
constitutional history
Autonomic Charter (1897), 22, 23–25, 28
autonomist movement, 20–22
bibliographical essay, 218
Cádiz Constitution, 6–11
colonial *anciene régime*, under Ferdinand VII, 9–11
Constitution (1837), 13–14
Constitution (1845), 14–17
Constitution (1869), 17–18
Constitution (1876), 19–20, 21–22
continued challenges, 46–48
Council of Indies, 3–6, 12
Elective Governor Act (1947), 34–35
Foraker Act (1900), 27, 28–29, 34
Jones Act (1917), 33–34
ominous decade (Spanish *década ominosa* 1823-1833), 10–11
PROMESA and, 41–46
Puerto Rico v. Sánchez Valle, 40–42
Spanish American War (1898), 25–26
Spanish Royal Statute of 1834, 11–13
U.S. military rule, 27–28
U.S. Public Law 600 (1950), 35–37, 44, 47
U.S. Supreme Court and, 30–33
continuance of judicial officers, 202

266 ■ INDEX

contracts clause, 75–76, 79–80, 232
Cordero, Rafael, 229–30
Córdova v. Cámara de Representantes, 152, 191
corporate landholding, 181–82, 248
Corpus Iuris Civilis (Justinian, Emperor), 4
Corrada del Río, Baltasar, 53
Cortés, Hernán, 4–6
Corujo Collazo v. Viera Martínez, 118–19
Coss y la Universidad de Puerto Rico v. Comisión Estatal de Elecciones, 70–71
Council of Castile (Real y Supremo Consejo de Castilla), 4–6
Council of Indies (Real y Supremo Consejo de las Indias), 3–6, 12
counsel, right to, 92
coup d'états (Spain 1843 & 1868), 14–15, 17
Court of Eminent Domain, 149–50
Court of First Instance, 152
court of last resort, 152–54
COVID-19 pandemic
constitutional bibliographical essay, 224
emergency legislation, 43–44, 46, 107
governor's powers during, 142–43
municipal restructuring after, 168
rapid testing kits and, 238
use of face masks, 91
video conferencing of preliminary hearings, 92
Craig v. Boren, 63
criminal actions, 185–86
C.R.I.M v. Méndez Torres, 128
cruel and unusual punishments, protection from, 98–99
Cuba libre, 26
Cuban Revolutionary Party (1892), 182
daily record of legislative proceedings, 238
Damián Marrero v. Municipio de Morovis, 66–67

Davis, George, 100, 242
death penalty, 75–77, 230–31
debt, prohibition of imprisonment for, 97
debt contracting, power of, 168–70, 246–47
debt priority ranking, 175
decisions of judiciary, 154–55
decolonization, 47
Defendini Collazo v. Estado Libre Asociado, 72, 79

De Paz Lisk v. Aponte Roque, 62
Derecho Constitucional de Puerto Rico (Álvarez González), 219
derecho indiano, 4–6
Díaz Aponte v. Comunidad San José, Inc., 97
Diaz Carrasquillo v. García Padilla, 123, 140
Díaz Saldaña v. Acevedo Vilá, 130
Dillon Rule, 246
Diócesis de Arecibo v. Secretario de Justicia, 68, 81, 82
Disidente Universal de Puerto Rico v. Departamento de Estado, 71
Dobbs v. Jackson Women Health's Organization, 82
Domínguez Castro v. Estado Libre Asociado, 168, 235
Dorante v. Wrangler de Puerto Rico, 127
Dottin v. Rigo & Co., 61
Double Jeopardy Clause (U.S. Constitution), 40–41
double jeopardy, protection from, 95
Downes v. Bidwell, 31, 41
Due Process Clause (U.S. Constitution), 77, 88–90, 96
due process of law, 75–76, 77–78, 231
Duncan v. Louisiana, 93

ecclesiastical affairs, Council of Indies, 4–6
effective date of constitution, 204–5
Eighth Amendment (U.S. Constitution), 98–99
Eisenhower, Dwight, 161
elections, general, 171–72, 204, 247
Elective Governor Act (1947), 34–35, 129, 131, 135–36, 137, 138, 146, 160, 244
Electoral Code, 56–57
Electoral College, 177
electoral franchise, 65–67
electoral zones, 199–200
El Plan de Ponce manifesto (1886), 21
El Vocero de Puerto Rico v. Puerto Rico, 90
emergency removal of governmental seat, 184–85
employees, rights of, 102–4, 234
employment of children, prohibition of, 101–2, 234
English Boundary Commission, 112
English Judicature Act (1873), 242
environmental clause of Article VI, Section 19, 187

Equal Protection Clause (U.S. Constitution), 62, 79
equal protection provision, 78–79, 231–32
Espartero, Baldomero, 14–15
espionage by Spanish colonial authorities, 18
Establishment Clause (U.S. Constitution), 68, 74
Estado Libre Asociado, 36
Estado Libre Asociado v. Aguayo, 83
Estado Libre Asociado v. Hermandad de Empleados, 72
estamento de los procuradores (Spanish Royal Statute of 1834), 12–13
Estrella Martínez, Luis, 64
Eva Prados Rodríguez v. Thomas Rivera Schatz, 71–72
Examining Board of Engineers, Architects and Surveyors v. Flores de Otero, 38
exclusionary rule, fruit of the poisonous tree, 87–88
executive departments, governor's cabinet, 143–45
executive power. *See* governor's/gubernatorial branch; Puerto Rico Constitution Executive Power
exemption of property from attachment, 80–84
existing officers, continuance, 201–2
Ex Parte AAR, 61
Ex Parte Andino Torres, 60–61
expenditure-to-income ratio, balanced budget requirement, 174–75
ex post facto laws, prohibition of, 99
extra compensation for services of public officers and contractors, prohibition of, 178
extrajudicial arrests, 14

Federal Bankruptcy Code, 41
Federal Death Penalty Act, 76–77
Federal Relations Act (1950), 36, 47, 183–84, 194
Ferdinand VII, King, 6, 10–11
Fernández Juncos, Manuel, 183
Fernández Méndez, Lionel, 164
Fernós Isern, Antonio, 37, 110, 172
Ferré Aguayo, Luis A., 52–53, 137
Fifth Amendment (U.S. Constitution), 62–63, 77, 79, 94, 95
Figueroa Ferrer v. Estado Libre Asociado, 59–60

Figueroa v. People of Puerto Rico, 40
Figueroa Carreras, Leopoldo, 76, 119, 126–27, 176, 184–85
Filipino Constitutional Convention (1934), 150
Financial Oversight and Management Board, 42–44
Financial Oversight and Management Board for Puerto Rico v. Aurelius Investment, LLC, 44–45
First Amendment (U.S. Constitution), 68, 70, 72, 74
fiscal year appropriations, 172–74, 247–48
flag, matters of law, 182–83, 248–49
Foley v. Connelie, 62
Fonfrías, Ernesto Juan, 52–53
Font Saldaña, Jorge, 52–53
Foraker Act (1900)
    appointment of judges, 160
    constitutional bibliographical essay, 223
    constitutional history and, 27, 28–29, 34
    contracts clause, 79–80
    fiscal year appropriations, 173
    franchises, rights, privileges, 181
    judicial review and, 155
    municipalities organization, 167–68
    oath of public officials and employees, 183–84
    passage of bills with approval by governor, 129–30
    Preamble and, 52
    regular legislative sessions, 119–20
    removal of judges, 163
    retirement of judges, 245
    succession to the governorship, 146
    terms of legislative office, 117
Fourteenth Amendment (U.S. Constitution), 62–63, 77, 79, 88–90, 96
Fourth Amendment (U.S. Constitution), 86
franchises, rights, privileges, 180–81
freedom of assembly, 69–72, 229
freedom of association, 17, 75–76, 230
freedom of press, 16, 17, 69–72, 229
freedom of religion, 17, 67–69, 228–29
freedom of speech, 17, 69–72, 229
Free Exercise Clause (U.S. Constitution), 68, 69
Friedrich, Carl, 167–68
Fuller Court, 30–31, 222–23
Fuster v. Busó, 116

268 ■ INDEX

García v. Aljoma Lumber, 103–4
García Méndez, Miguel Ángel, 65–66, 76, 162, 173
García Padilla, Alejandro, 129
Garib Bazaín v. Hospital Español Auxilio Mutuo de Puerto Rico, Inc., 64
Gautier Dapena, Jenaro, 52–53
Gelpí Bosch, José, 76, 137, 168, 175–76
gender equality, 62–63, 226
general elections, 171–72, 204, 247
general provisions to constitution. *See also* Puerto Rico Constitution General Provisions
corporate landholding, 181–82, 248
debt contracting and taxation, power of, 168–70, 246–47
emergency removal of governmental seat, 184–85
extra compensation for services, 178
fiscal year appropriations, 172–74, 247–48
flag, anthem, seal, matters of law, 182–83, 248–49
franchises, rights, privileges, 180–81
general elections, 171–72, 247
judicial power over criminal actions, 185–86
municipalities organization, 167–68, 245–46
natural resource conservation and development, 186–88, 249
oath of public officials and employees, 183–84, 249
promulgation of laws, 172
public property and funds use, 176–78, 248
residence of governor, 180
revenue appropriations, 174–75, 248
revenue disbursements, 175–76
rule of taxation, 170–71, 247
salaries of officials, 178–80
geographic area, Puerto Rico Constitution, 57
gifts from foreign sovereigns, 100–1
Gladstone, William, 21
Gobierno de Puerto Rico v. Elizabeth Torres Rodríguez, 152
Gómez, María Libertad, 110
González v. Alcalde de Utuado, 124
governmental censorship, 14

governmental form, Puerto Rico Constitution, 56–57
governmental negligence, 84
governor's/gubernatorial branch. *See also* Puerto Rico Constitution Executive Power
appointment of secretaries, 143, 240–41
as commander-in-chief of the militia, 141
constitutional bibliographical essay, 240–41
executive departments and, 143–45
executive power of, 135–37
issue of succession by Legislative Assembly, 145–47
passage of bills with approval by, 128–30, 238–39
powers and duties, 138–43, 240
power to call Legislative Assembly, 139
qualifications, 138
removal of governor, 147–48
residence of governor, 180
salaries of officials, 178–80
term limits, 137
vacancy in office of, 145
Grito de Lares, 182
Guadalupe Hidalgo Treaty (1848), 26, 32–33
Guayama, Senatorial and Representative Districts, 198
Gutiérrez Franqui, Víctor, 55–56, 105, 175, 176, 242
Guzmán v. Calderón, 140

habeas corpus, 100, 155–57, 233–34
Habsburgo y Lorena, María Cristina de, Queen Regent, 22
Hampton Development v. Estado Libre Asociado, 83
Harlan, John, 30–31
Harlan, John Marshall, 75
Harrison, Benjamin, 30–31
Harris v. Rosario, 38–39, 45
Hart, Henry, 243
Hawaiian Organic Act (1900), 29
Hay, John, 25
Hays, Rutherford, 30–31
Hearst, William Randolph, 25
Henry, Guy, 159, 229–30, 233
Hernández Agosto v. López Nieves, 140–41

Hernández Agosto v. Ortiz Montes, 120
Hernández Agosto v. Romero Barceló, 144
Hernández Denton, Federico, 122, 128, 142, 162–63
Hernández Estrella v. Junta de Apelaciones del Sistema de Educación Pública, 106
Hernández López v. Santana Ramos, 156–57
Hernández Montañez v. Rosselló Nevares, 144
Herrero y Otros v. Estado Libre Asociado, 172
Hester v. United States, 85
historical sites conservation and development, 186–87
H.M.C.A. (P.R.), Inc. v. Contralor, 134
Holmes, Oliver Wendell, 85
Humacao, Senatorial and Representative Districts, 198–99
human dignity, inviolability of, 59–61
human rights, 51, 59, 72–73
Humphrey's Executor v. United States, 140
Hurricane Fiona (2022), 43–44, 107, 168
Hurricane María (2017), 43–44, 107, 168

Iglesias Pantín, Santiago, 117
illegitimacy, as suspect class, 63–64, 226
Illinois v. Gates, 87
immunities of legislators, 122–23, 237
impeachment proceedings, 4–6, 131–32, 239
imprisonment for debt, prohibition of, 97
imprisonment of children, prohibition of, 101–2, 234
incarceration prior to trial, 96
Indulac v. Central General de Trabajadores, 81–82
innocence, right to be presumed, 93
In re Zaida Hernández Torres, 165
Insular Cases, 30–33, 214*t*, 222–23
intendencia, 9
involuntary servitude, prohibition of, 97–98
Iriarte Miró, Celestino, 137, 165
Irish Home Rule Bill (1886), 21

Jackson, Robert, 142
Jacobson v. Massachusetts, 53
joint resolutions, 128, 238
Jones, William, 33
Jones Act (1917)
appointment of judges, 160, 244
catalogue of individual rights, 88–89
constitutional bibliographical essay, 223
constitutional history and, 33–34
contracts clause, 79–80

criminal actions, 186
debt priority ranking, 175
double jeopardy and, 95
franchises, rights, privileges, 181
governmental expenditure, 174
judicial review and, 155
legislative proceedings and, 126–27
municipalities organization, 167–68
number of legislative members and, 111
oath of public officials and employees, 183–84
passage of bills with approval by governor, 129–30
Preamble and, 52
public education and, 230
regular legislative sessions, 119–20
removal of judges, 163
retirement of judges, 245
succession to the governorship, 146
José De Diego v. Cámara de Delegados, 119
judges, appointment of, 160–61
Judicial Council (*Consejo Judicial*), 159
judicial power. *See also* Puerto Rico Constitution Judicial Power; Puerto Rico Supreme Court
appointment of judges, 160–61, 244
in changed or abolished court, 165
chief justice as administrative chief, 159
constitutional bibliographical essay, 241–45
continuance of judicial officers, 202
court of last resort, 152–54
functions in changed or abolished court, 165
habeas corpus, 100, 155–57
over criminal actions, 185–86
political activity of judges, 164–65, 245
qualification of justices, 161–62
removal of judges, 163–64, 245
retirement of judges, 162–63, 244–45
rules for the administration of the courts, 159–60, 243
rules of evidence and of civil and criminal procedure, 157–59, 243
sessions and decisions, 154–55
of Supreme Court, 149–51, 212*t*
unified judicial system, 151–52, 242
Junta de Información (1867), 16–17
Junta de Relaciones del Trabajo v. Asociación de Servicios Médicos Hospitalarios de Yauco, 105–6

270 ■ INDEX

jury trial, right to, 93–94, 233
just compensation for private property,
    82–84
Justinian, Emperor, 4

Katz v. United States, 86
Kennedy, Anthony, 45
Kilómetro O, Inc. v. Pesquera López, 71–72
Kolthoff, Erick, 235

labor rights, 104–6
la Diputación Provincial (island-wide
    legislative body), 10
La Granja de San Ildefonso (Segovia) revolt,
    12–13
Landfill Technologies v. Municipio de Lares, 179
landholding corporations, 181–82, 248
laws
    continuance of, 201
    ex post facto laws, 99
    promulgation of, 172
    special laws (leyes especiales), 15–16, 19
    vagrancy laws, 16
Legislative Assembly. See also Puerto Rico
    Constitution Legislative Assembly
    adjournment clause, 122
    amendments to constitution, 189–92, 249
    at-large legislators, 236–37
    bicameral model of, 24, 109–10, 235
    comptroller appointment, 132–34, 239
    constitutional bibliographical essay,
        234–39
    Constitutional Convention revisions,
        192–93
    daily record of, 238
    emergency removal of governmental
        seat, 184–85
    franchises, rights, privileges, 180–81
    governor's power to call, 139
    immunities of, 122–23, 237
    impeachment proceedings, 4–6, 131–32,
        239
    issue of governor's succession, 145–47
    issue of gubernatorial succession,
        145–47
    joint resolutions, 128, 238
    line-item veto, 130–31, 239
    meeting place of, 122
    member privileges and immunities,
        122–23

member qualifications, 113
municipalities organization, 167–68
number of members, 236
open sessions in, 121
other offices, incompatibilities clause ,
    123–25
passage of bills with approval by
    governor, 128–30, 238–39
powers of, 106–7, 109–10, 118–19,
    234–35
power to change executive departments,
    125–26
privileges of, 122–23, 237
proceedings of, 126–27
proposal of amendments, 189–92, 249
quorum in, 121
Representative Districts, 111–13,
    195–200, 236–37
retirement of judges, 162–63
salaries of officials, 178–80
Senatorial Districts, 111–13, 195–200,
    236–37
unicameral model of, 109–10, 235
Lemon v. Kurtzman, 68
Ley de Expropiación Forzosa, Law (1879),
    82
liberal construction of rights, 106–7
liberty, right to, 75–76
life, right to, 75–76
limitations to amendments, 193–94
line-item veto, 130–31, 239
Lochner v. New York, 77
López v. Municipio de San Juan, 168
Louisiana Purchase Treaty (1803), 32–33
Louis XVIII, King, 10, 11
Lozada Tirado v. Testigos de Jehová, 60–61
Lukoil Pan Americas v. Municipality of
    Guayanilla, 170
Lyng v. International Union, 105

Madison, James, 59–60, 234–35
Magruder, Calvert, 40
Mahan, Alfred T., 25
Malavé v. Oriental Bank & Trust, 104
Manifest Destiny, 25
Mapp v. Ohio, 87
Marina Industrial, Inc. v. Brown Boveri
    Corporation, 78
Marshall, John, 30, 169–70
Martí, José, 182

Martínez de la Rosa, Francisco, 11
Martínez Torres, Rafael, 155
Mayaguez, Senatorial and Representative
    Districts, 197–98
McConnell v. Palau, 78
McKinley, William, 27, 30–31, 233
meeting place of Legislative Assembly, 122
Mellado Parsons, Ramón, 52–53
*Merle Feliciano v. Comisión Estatal de
    Elecciones,* 114
Michigan v. Long, 75–76
Miles, Nelson, 27, 30, 34
military authority as subordinate to civil
    authority, 100, 233–34
minority parties, rights of, 114–16
minority parties representation, 114–16
*Misión Industrial de Puerto Rico, Inc. v. Junta
    de Planificación,* 152, 187
monarchical absolutism, under Spanish
    rule, 9
Morales Morales v. Estado Libre Asociado,
    105
*Morales y Benet v. Junta Local de
    Inscripciones,* 62–63
Mora v. Mejías, 77
municipalities organization, 167–68,
    245–46
Municipio de Guaynabo v. Adquisición, 83
Muñiz v. Administrador del Deporte Hípico,
    70
Muñoz Marín, Luis, 35, 52–53, 110,
    136–37, 204–5
Muñoz Rivera, Luis, 179

NAACP v. Alabama, 75
Narváez, Ramón María, 14–15
National Historic Preservation Act (1966),
    187–88
natural resource conservation and
    development, 186–88, 249
Negrón Fernández, Luis, 155
Negrón García, Antonio, 118–19, 132, 155
Negrón López, Luis, 115–16, 117, 178–79,
    238
New Jersey Constitution (1947), 242
New Progressive Party, (*Partido Nuevo
    Progresista*) 129
New York Times v. United States, 70
Nieves Huertas v. García Padilla, 121,
    139–40

Ninth Amendment (U.S. Constitution),
    234–35
Nogueras v. Hernández Colón, 109, 120–21,
    140–41
Nogueras v. Rexach Benítez, 119, 131–32
Noriega v. Hernández Colón, 142
Northwest Ordinance (1787), 26, 36
number of members, Legislature, 110–11

oath of public officials and employees,
    183–84, 249
Obama, Barack, 44
Obergefell v. Hodges, 61
Ocasio v. Díaz, 64
O'Daly, Demetrio, 9–10, 12
offices/officers
    continuance of existing, 201–2
    continuance of judicial officers, 202
    incompatibility of members, 123–25
    oath of public officials and employees,
        183–84, 249
    permanent vacancy of governor, 145
    public officer, 179
    temporary vacancy of governor, 145
    terms of office, 116–18, 137
    vacancy in gubernatorial office, 145
    vacancy in legislative office, 116–18
ominous decade (Spanish *década ominosa*
    1823-1833), 10–11
open sessions in Legislative Assembly, 121
Oregon Treaty (1846), 26, 32–33
Oronoz Rodríguez, Maite, 64
Ortiz Angleró v. Barreto Pérez, 66
Ortiz Cruz v. Junta Hípica, 103
Ortiz v. Departamento de Hacienda, 103
Ortiz Stella, Cruz, 117
other offices incompatibility of legislative
    members, 123–25

Pacheco Fraticelli v. Cintrón Antonsanti, 70–71
Padrón Rivera, Lino, 126–27
pardons, governor's power over, 141
Partido Autonomista Puertorriqueño, 21
*Partido Estadista Republicano v. Junta
    Constitucional,* 112
*Partido Independentista Puertorriqueño v.
    Comisión Estatal de Elecciones,* 53,
    107, 177
*Partido Independentista Puertorriqueño v.
    Estado Libre Asociado,* 177, 191

272 ■ INDEX

Partido Liberal Conservador, 18
Partido Liberal Reformista, 18
Partido Nuevo Progresista v. De Castro Font, 75–76
Partido Nuevo Progresista v. De Castro Font II, 66
Partido Popular Democrático v. Gobernador, 176–77
Partido Popular Democrático v. Gobernador II, 66–67
Partido Renovación Puertorriqueña v. Estado Libre Asociado, 66, 203
Partido Socialista Puertorriqueño v. Comisión Estatal de Elecciones, 66–67
Partido Socialista Puertorriqueño v. Estado Libre Asociado, 53–54, 107, 177
Partido Socialista Puertorriqueño v. Secretario de Hacienda, 66–67
passage of bills with approval by governor, 128–30, 238–39
Paz Granela, Francisco, 102
penal rehabilitation clause of Article VI, Section 19, 188
Penn Central Transportation v. New York City, 83
permanent vacancy in office of governor, 145
personhood, protection of, 60–61
petitioning for redress of grievances, 69–72, 229
Philadelphia Convention (1787), 52–53, 75, 136
Philippines Organic Act (1902), 79–80
Philippines Organic Act (1916), 33, 130
Pierluisi y Bhatia v. Comisión Estatal de Elecciones, 66
Pierluisi Urrutia, Pedro, 142, 147
Pizarro, Francisco, 4–6
Plard Fagundo v. Tribunal Superior, 95
Plaza de Descuentos v. Estado Libre Asociado, 83
plenary powers of Congress under Territorial Clause, 55–56
Polanco Abreu, Santiago, 187–88
political activity of judges, 164–65, 245
political classifications, 65–76, 227
political parties, 203, 207t, 208t
political rights of minority parties, 114–16
Ponce, Senatorial and Representative Districts, 198
Ponce de León, Juan, 6, 135

Pons Núñez, Víctor, 112
Popular Democratic Party, (*Partido Popular Democrático*) 52, 53, 55–56, 110, 129, 136–37, 146
Posados v. Warner, Barnes & Co., 127
post-auditing authority of comptroller, 133–34
Powell, Lewis, 90
Powell v. McCormack, 118
power to change executive departments, 125–26
Power y Giralt, Ramón, 8, 9–10, 12
Preamble, Puerto Rico Constitution, 51–54, 224
Presidente de la Cámara, 173–74
Presidente del Senado, 123
press, freedom of, 16, 17, 69–72, 229
printing press offenses, 15–16
prisoners, suspension of civil rights, 99–107
privacy, right to, 60–61, 81–82, 134, 232
private property, just compensation for taking of, 82–84
privileges of Legislative Assembly members, 122–23, 237
probable cause and warrants, 86–87
prohibition against excessive bails and fines, 96–97
prohibition of imprisonment for debt, 97
PROMESA. *See* Puerto Rico Oversight, Management, and Economic Stability Act (PROMESA)
promulgation of laws, 172
pronunciamiento, 9, 12–13
protection against abusive attacks, 80–82
protection from cruel and unusual punishments, 98–99
provisional government, 17
public education, right to, 72–74, 229–30
public officer (*funcionario*), 179
public policy debates, 141
public property and funds use, 176–78, 248
public trial, right to, 89–90, 233
Pueblo v. Acevedo Escobar, 85
Pueblo v. Agudo Olmeda, 93
Pueblo v. Aponte Ruperto, 96
Pueblo v. Aspurúa, 94
Pueblo v. Báez López, 85
Pueblo v. Basilio Figueroa Pérez, 99
Pueblo v. Camacho Delgado, 89
Pueblo v. Candelario Ayala, 99

Pueblo v. Capriles, 87
Pueblo v. Casellas Toro, 233
Pueblo v. Colón Rodríguez, 95–96
Pueblo v. Daniel Cruz Rosario, 91
Pueblo v. Díaz Medina, 85
Pueblo v. Dolce, 85, 232
Pueblo v. Duarte, 82
Pueblo v. Fernández Rodríguez, 87–88
Pueblo v. Ferreira Morales, 85
Pueblo v. González Colón, 94
Pueblo v. Lausell Hernández, 91
Pueblo v. Lebrón, 85
Pueblo v. Malavé González, 85
Pueblo v. Martínez Torres, 87
Pueblo v. Muñoz, Colón y Ocasio, 87
Pueblo v. Negrón Rivera, 98–99
Pueblo v. Nelson Daniel Centeno, 93–94
Pueblo v. Ortiz Alvarado, 87
Pueblo v. Ortiz Martínez, 85
Pueblo v. Pérez Méndez, 98–99
Pueblo v. Pérez Santos, 91
Pueblo v. Rivera Robles, 63
Pueblo v. Rivera Tirado, 89
Pueblo v. Rodríguez López, 90–91
Pueblo v. Santiago, 93
Pueblo v. Santiago Cruz, 91, 92
Pueblo v. Santiago Feliciano, 86
Pueblo v. Santiago Lugo, 94
Pueblo v. Santos Santos, 95
Pueblo v. Soto Soto, 86
Pueblo v. Torres Rivera, 93–94
Pueblo v. Vélez Bonilla, 84
Pueblo v. Vélez Rodríguez, 90
Pueblo v. Wilfredo Suárez Alers, 102
Puerto Rican Federal Relations Act, 24
Puerto Rico Bar Association (*Colegio de Abogados y Abogadas de Puerto Rico*), 75–76
Puerto Rico Broadcasting Corporation, 140
Puerto Rico Constitution
   Article I, Section 1, 55–56, 224
   Article I, Section 2, 56–57
   Article I, Section 3, 57
   Article I, Section 4, 57
   Preamble, 51–54, 224
Puerto Rico Constitution Amendments
   Article VII, Section 1, 189–92
   Article VII, Section 2, 192–93
   Article VII, Section 3, 193–94
Puerto Rico Constitution Bill of Rights

Article II, Section 1, 59–65, 225
Article II, Section 2, 65–67
Article II, Section 3, 67–69
Article II, Section 4, 69–72
Article II, Section 5, 72–74
Article II, Section 6, 75–76
Article II, Section 7, 76–80
Article II, Section 8, 80–82
Article II, Section 9, 82–84
Article II, Section 10, 84–88
Article II, Section 11, 88–97
Article II, Section 12, 97–99
Article II, Section 13, 100
Article II, Section 14, 100–1
Article II, Section 15, 101–2
Article II, Section 16, 102–4
Article II, Section 17, 104
Article II, Section 18, 104–6
Article II, Section 19, 106–7
Puerto Rico Constitution Executive Power
   Article IV, Section 1, 135–37
   Article IV, Section 2, 137
   Article IV, Section 3, 138
   Article IV, Section 4, 138–43
   Article IV, Section 5, 143
   Article IV, Section 6, 143–45
   Article IV, Section 7, 145
   Article IV, Section 8, 145
   Article IV, Section 9, 145–47
   Article IV, Section 10, 147–48
Puerto Rico Constitution General Provisions
   Article VI, Section 1, 167–68
   Article VI, Section 2, 168–70
   Article VI, Section 3, 170–71
   Article VI, Section 4, 171–72
   Article VI, Section 5, 172
   Article VI, Section 6, 172–74
   Article VI, Section 7, 174–75
   Article VI, Section 8, 175–76
   Article VI, Section 9, 176–78
   Article VI, Section 10, 178
   Article VI, Section 11, 178–80
   Article VI, Section 12, 180
   Article VI, Section 13, 180–81
   Article VI, Section 14, 181–82
   Article VI, Section 15, 182–83
   Article VI, Section 16, 183–84
   Article VI, Section 17, 184–85
   Article VI, Section 18, 185–86
   Article VI, Section 19, 186–88

274 ■ INDEX

Puerto Rico Constitution Judicial Power
  Article V, Section 1, 149–51
  Article V, Section 2, 151–52
  Article V, Section 3, 152–54
  Article V, Section 4, 154–55
  Article V, Section 5, 155–57
  Article V, Section 6, 157–59
  Article V, Section 7, 159–60
  Article V, Section 8, 160–61
  Article V, Section 9, 161–62
  Article V, Section 10, 162–63
  Article V, Section 11, 163–64
  Article V, Section 12, 164–65
  Article V, Section 13, 165
Puerto Rico Constitution Legislative
    Assembly
  Article III, Section 1, 109–10
  Article III, Section 2, 110–11
  Article III, Section 4, 111–13
  Article III, Section 5, 113
  Article III, Section 6, 113–14
  Article III, Section 7, 114–16
  Article III, Section 8, 116–18
  Article III, Section 9, 118–19
  Article III, Section 10, 119–21
  Article III, Section 11, 121
  Article III, Section 12, 121
  Article III, Section 13, 122
  Article III, Section 14, 122–23
  Article III, Section 15, 123–25
  Article III, Section 16, 125–26
  Article III, Section 17, 126–27
  Article III, Section 18, 128
  Article III, Section 19, 128–30
  Article III, Section 20, 130–31
  Article III, Section 21, 131–32
  Article III, Section 22, 132–34
Puerto Rico Constitution Senatorial and
    Representative Districts
  Article VIII, Section 1, 195–200
Puerto Rico Constitution Transitory
    Provisions
  Article IX, Section 1, 201
  Article IX, Section 2, 201–2
  Article IX, Section 3, 202
  Article IX, Section 4, 202
  Article IX, Section 5, 203
  Article IX, Section 6, 203
  Article IX, Section 7, 203–4
  Article IX, Section 8, 204

  Article IX, Section 9, 204
  Article IX, Section 10, 204–5
Puerto Rico Corporation Debt
    Enforcement and Recovery Act
    (2014), 175–76
Puerto Rico Corrections and Rehabilitation
    Department, 188
Puerto Rico Department of Agriculture and
    Commerce, 204
Puerto Rico Department of Health, 71
Puerto Rico Department of Natural
    Resources, 187
Puerto Rico Election Commission, 56–57,
    116
Puerto Rico Oversight, Management, and
    Economic Stability Act (PROMESA)
  constitutional bibliographical essay,
    223–24
  contracts clause and, 80
  debt restructuring process, 47
  franchises, rights, privileges, 181
  governor's constitutional role and,
    142–43
  impact of, 42–46
  just compensation claims, 83
  labor rights and, 106
  line-item veto, 131
  passing of, 41–42
  plenary powers of Congress and, 55–56
  retirement of judges, 162–63
Puerto Rico's Constitutional Convention,
    73
Puerto Rico Supreme Court
  appointment of justices, 160–61, 244
  composition of court, 152–54, 212t
  contracts clause, 75–76, 79–80, 232
  as court of last resort, 152–54
  due process of law, 75–76, 77–78, 231
  equal protection clause, 78–79, 231–32
  habeas corpus, 100, 155–57
  judicial functions in changed or
    abolished court, 165
  original jurisdiction of, 242–43
  political activity of judges, 164–65, 245
  power of, 149–51, 241–42
  qualification of justices, 161–62
  removal of judges, 163–64, 245
  retirement of judges, 162–63, 244–45
  role of, 56–57
  chief justice as administrative chief, 159

rules for the administration of the courts, 159–60, 243
rules of evidence and of civil and criminal procedure, 157–59, 243
sessions and decisions, 154–55
unified judicial system, 151–52, 242
Puerto Rico v. Coca Cola, 84
Puerto Rico v. Franklin California Tax-Free Trust, 41–42
Puerto Rico Judiciary Act (1950), 150, 163, 165
Puerto Rico Judiciary Act (2003), 152
Puerto Rico v. Sánchez Valle, 40–42, 95, 186
Puerto Rico Telephone Company v. Martínez, 86

qualification of justices, 161–62
Quiñones, Francisco Mariano, 16–17
Quiñones, José María, 9–10, 12
Quiñones, Samuel R., 110, 137, 233–34
Quiñones-Varela bill (1823), 10
quorum in Legislative Assembly, 121

racial discrimination, race as suspect class, 62
racial equality, 61–62, 225–26
Ramírez, Alejandro (*intendencia*), 8
Ramírez de Ferrer v. Mari Brás, 53, 66
Ramos Acevedo v. Tribunal Superior, 98
Ramos Antonini, Ernesto, 52–53, 110, 153
Ramos González, Virgilio, 112
Ramos v. Louisiana, 93–94
R.C.A. v. Gobierno de la Capital, 170
RDT Const. Corp. v. Contralor I, 82, 134
Real Cédula de Gracias (1815), 12, 16
Real y Supremo Consejo de las Indias. See Council of Indies
reasonable belief (*motivos fundados*), 87
redistricting board, authority, 111–13
redress of grievances, petitioning for, 69–72, 229
regular legislative sessions, 119–21
religious classifications, 65–76, 227
religious freedom, 17, 67–69, 228–29
Religious Freedom Restoration Act (RFRA), 68–69, 228–29
removal of governor, 147–48
removal of judges, 163–64, 245
Representative Districts, 111–13, 195–200, 236–37
republican period (1873), 17

residence in district prior to election, 113–14
residence of governor, 180
retirement of judges, 162–63, 244–45
revenue appropriations, 174–75, 248
revenue disbursements, 175–76
Reyes Delgado, Antonio, 52–53, 101
Reynolds v. Sims, 112
Riego, Rafael del, 9
rights of employees, 102–4, 234
rights of minority parties, 114–16
right to bail, 95–96
right to be informed of accusations, 90–91
right to be presumed innocent, 93
right to compulsory process for obtaining witnesses, 91, 233–34
right to confront witnesses, 91
right to counsel, 92
right to jury trial, 93–94, 233
right to liberty, 75–76
right to life, 75–76
right to not bear witness against self, 94
right to organize and bargain collectively, 104
right to privacy, 60–61, 81–82, 134, 232
right to public education, 72–74, 229–30
right to public trial, 89–90, 233
right to speedy trial, 88–89, 233
right to strike and picket, 104–6, 234
right to vote. *See* universal suffrage
Rivera Padilla v. OAT, 103
Rivera Pérez, Efraín, 53
Rivera Rodríguez & Co. v. Stowell Taylor, 78
Rivera Santiago v. Secretario de Hacienda, 78
Rivera Schatz v. Estado Libre Asociado, 75–76
Rodríguez, Anabelle, 122, 155, 173–74
Rodríguez Pagán v. Departamento de Servicios Sociales, 79
Rodríguez v. Popular Democratic Party, 38, 118
Rodríguez v. Secretario de Hacienda, 170
Roman Catholic Archdiocese of San Juan v. Acevedo Feliciano, 69
Romero Barceló v. Hernández Agosto, 123
Romero Barceló, Carlos, 144
Rosario Rodríguez v. Roselló Nevares, 67
Rosario v. Toyota, 64
Roselló González, Pedro, 154
Roselló Nevares, Ricardo, 46, 129, 147, 148

276 ■ INDEX

Ruiz Belvis, Segundo, 16–17
rule of taxation, uniformity requirement, 170–71
rules for the administration of the courts, 159–60, 243
Rules of Criminal Procedure, 63, 92, 96–97
rules of evidence and of civil and criminal procedure, 157–59, 243
Rutledge, John, 161

Sagasta, Práxedes Mateo, 19
salaries of officials, 178–80
Salas Soler v. Secretario de Agricultura, 187
Salic law, 10–11
Salvá Santiago v. Torres Padró, 61
Sánchez v. González, 96
Sánchez Vilella y Colón Martínez v. Estado Libre Asociado, 67
San Juan
    Electoral Zones, 199–200
    seat of government, 57
    Senatorial and Representative Districts, 195–96
Santa Aponte v. Hernández, 118–19
Santana v. Gobernadora, 136–37, 140
Sanz, José Laureano, 18
Schilb v. Kuebel, 96
seal, matters of law, 182–83, 248–49
searches and seizures, 84–86, 232
search warrants, 86–87
seat of government, Puerto Rico Constitution, 57
secretaries (cabinet members) appointment, 143, 240–41
self-incrimination, protection from, 94
Senado v. Tribunal Supremo, 56–57
Senatorial Districts, 111–13, 195–200, 236–37
separation of church and state, 67–69, 228–29
Serrano, Francisco, 17
sessions of judiciary, 154–55
sexenio revolucionario, (Spain 1868-1874), 17
sexist stereotypes, gender discrimination, 62–63
sexual abuse claims, 82
Siaca v. Bahía Beach Resort, 81–82
Siete Partidas (Alfonso X), 4
Silva v. Hernández, 127
Silva v. Hernández Agosto, 123

Situado Mexicano, 6
Sixth Amendment (U.S. Constitution), 89–90
slave economy, 6
slavery and involuntary servitude, prohibition of, 97–98
Socialist Party, 52
social origin or condition, suspect class, 64–65, 226–27
Solá Morales, Yldefonso, 188
Sotomayor, Cristobal de, 6
Sotomayor, Sonia, 40–41
Soto v. Secretario de Justicia, 71–72
Spanish American War (1898), 25–26, 97, 221–22
Spanish Constitution (1869), 68
Spanish Constitution (1876), 24, 68
Spanish Council of Ministers, 16, 23, 24
Spanish Criminal Code, 20–21
Spanish Crown, 3–4, 52
Spanish legal tradition and history, 219–20
Spanish Royal Statute (1834), 11–13
Spanish Supreme Court, 20–21
special laws *(leyes especiales)*, 15–16, 19
special (extraordinary) legislative sessions, 119–21
speech, freedom of, 17, 69–72, 229
speedy trial, right to, 88–89, 233
Statehood Party, 52, 53
strike and picket, right to, 104–6, 234
Suárez Cáceres v. Comisión Estatal de Elecciones, 67
Suárez Martínez v. Tugwell, 152
Suárez v. Comisión Estatal de Elecciones, 116
succession to the governorship, 145–47
suffrage. *See* universal suffrage
Supplemental Security Income (SSI), 45
suspect classes
    alienage as, 62, 226
    gender equality, 62–63, 226
    illegitimacy, 63–64, 226
    political or religious ideas, 65–76, 227
    in Puerto Rico Constitution, 61–76
    race or color equality, 61–62, 225–26
    social origin or condition, 64–65, 226–27

Taft, William, 32–33, 34
taxation
    power of, 168–70, 246–47
    rule of, 170–71, 247

INDEX ■ 277

tax court, 149–50
tax reform, 12
Tax Uniformity Clause, 28, 31
temporary vacancy in office of governor, 145
Tenth Amendment (U.S. Constitution), 24
terms of office
  executive, 137
  gubernatorial, 137
  legislative, 116–18
Territorial Clause (U.S. Constitution), 32–33, 37–38, 42–43, 45
Territory Fiscal Plan, 42–43
Terry v. Ohio, 85
Thirteenth Amendment (U.S. Constitution), 98
Thomas, Clarence, 69
Timbs v. Indiana, 96
titles of nobility, 100–1
Toll v. Adorno Medina, 87–88
Tonos Florenzán v. Bernazard, 118–19
Torres Marrero v. Alcaldesa de Ponce, 83
Torre y Pando, Miguel de la, 10
trade liberalization, 12
transitory provisions of constitution.
     See also Puerto Rico Constitution
     Transitory Provisions
  civil and criminal liabilities, 201
  Commonwealth of Puerto Rico in, 55–56, 202–3, 250
  continuance of existing officers, 201–2
  continuance of judicial officers, 202
  effective date of constitution, 204–5
  general elections, 204
  laws supplementing, 203–4
  political parties, 203, 207t, 208t
  Puerto Rico Department of Agriculture
    and Commerce, 204
travaux préparatoires, 154
treatise on Puerto Rico's constitutional
  law, 219
Treaty of Basel, 150–51
Treaty of Paris (1898), 26, 32–33, 61, 98, 221–22
Trías Monge, José, 52–53, 59–60, 86, 151, 155, 187, 232
*Trinidad Hernández v. Estado Libre Asociado
  de Puerto Rico*, 80, 152
Truman, Harry, 34–35, 204–5, 244
Twenty-Second Amendment (U.S. Constitution), 137

unanimity requirement, jury verdicts, 93
unicameral model of Legislature, 109–10, 235
*Unidad Nacional de Trabajadores de la Salud
  v. Soler Zapata*, 71
unified judicial system, 151–52, 242
United States (U.S.). *See also* U.S.
  Constitutional amendments
  colonialism under, 33
  Elective Governor Act (1947), 34–35
  Foraker Act (1900), 27, 28–29, 34
  Insular Cases, 30–33, 214t, 222–23
  Jones Act (1917), 33–34
  military interventions by, 33
  military rule of, 27–28
  Spanish American War (1898), 25–26
  U.S. Constitution, 24, 163–64, 181, 194
United States v. Lovett, 99
United States v. Quiñones, 86
United States v. Robinson, 85
United States v. Vaello Madero, 45–46
Universal Declaration of Human Rights
  (1948), 46–47, 55, 59, 63–64, 65–66, 73, 75, 76, 81, 102, 105,
universal suffrage, 65–67, 227–28
Universidad de Puerto Rico v. Laborde, 71, 106
University of Puerto Rico's School of Public
  Administration, 150, 153, 154, 156
unreasonable searches and seizures,
  protection from, 84–86
U.S. Constitution, 24, 41, 163–64, 181, 194
U.S. Constitutional amendments
  Eighth Amendment, 98–99
  Fifth Amendment, 62–63, 77, 79, 94, 95
  First Amendment, 68, 70, 72, 74
  Fourteenth Amendment, 62–63, 77, 79, 88–90, 96
  Fourth Amendment, 86
  Ninth Amendment, 234–35
  Sixth Amendment, 89–90
  Tenth Amendment, 24
  Thirteenth Amendment, 98
  Twenty-Second Amendment, 137
U.S. House of Representatives, 35
U.S. Military Government, 222
U.S. Provisional Court, 29
U.S. Public Law 447 (1952), 24, 35–36, 194, 204–5
U.S. Public Law 600 (1950), 24, 35–37, 44, 47, 56, 156, 194, 204–5

278 ■ INDEX

U.S. Senate's Committee on Territories and Insular Affairs, 146
U.S. Supreme Court, 30–33, 40–42, 161, 176
U.S. v. Acosta Martínez, 76–77
U.S. War Department, 33
USS Maine, 22
U.T.I.E.R. v. Junta de Relaciones del Trabajo de Puerto Rico, 105

vacancies in office of governor, 145
vacancies of legislative seats (district and at-large), 116–18
vagrancy laws, 16
Varela y Morales, Félix, 9–10
Vázquez, Wanda, 142–43
Vélez González, Sigfrido, 178–79
Veray Hernández, José, 137
Viajes Lesana, Inc. v. Saavedra, 97

Vigoreaux Lorenzana v. Quizno's, 82
voting rights. *See* universal suffrage

Wackenhut Corp. v. Rodríguez Aponte, 62
Waller v. Georgia, 90
Warren, Earl, 161
Washington v. Davis, 79
Weber Carrillo v. Estado Libre Asociado, 60–61, 82
Weeks v. United States, 87
White, Edward, 32–33
Wilson, Woodrow, 33
wiretapping protection, 86
witnesses, right to confront, 91
Wood, Leonard, 27

Zachry International v. Tribunal Superior, 63, 103
Zequeira v. Universidad de Puerto Rico, 134

■ ABOUT THE AUTHOR

RAFAEL COX ALOMAR is a professor of law at the David A. Clarke School of Law of the University of the District of Columbia in Washington, D.C., and has been a Visiting Professor of Law at Harvard Law School (Winter 2022). He is the author of *Revisiting the Transatlantic Triangle: The Constitutional Decolonization of the Eastern Caribbean* (2009). Professor Cox Alomar received a BA *magna cum laude* from Cornell University; a DPhil in history from the University of Oxford (Trinity College), where he was a Marshall Scholar; and a JD from Harvard Law School.